FAMILY CORNERS

Their Children Within

Joan T. Petrosine

ISBN 978-1-64569-427-4 (paperback)
ISBN 978-1-64569-429-8 (hardcover)
ISBN 978-1-64569-428-1 (digital)

Christian Faith Publishing, Inc.
832 Park Avenue
Meadville, PA 16335
www.christianfaithpublishing.com

Printed in the United States of America

To the men in my life who made being a woman the grandest of adventures and to Mom for opening the doors.

The lives of two Italian families migrating to America around 1900 are seen through their choices in living life to impact a third generation descendent with a problem all her own. The families sharing this world's wonders and dangers are led to mistakes, failures, and successes that aid a confused young woman on a search for self, where faith and evil glide through everyday. All are presented fictionally but reflect the struggles good and bad that life brings.

Since the families were large the story has been kept that way.

Don't get lost in all the relatives, stay with the happenings and enjoy the fun created, as they find their way in life. Though fictional the faith, love and settings are real.

Contents

The corners of life continue for *Family Corners: Their Children Within* through a second volume

Acknowledgments

My first thank you is to my ancestors for their courage in seeking the United States; Gaetano Petrosino, Raffaele Scarapico, Frank Manfredi and Teresa Penzo. Of course, my parents Joseph and Marian Petrosine are thanked for always being there and my brother Joseph too. I must include the many cousins for sharing what information they could. I also thank cousin Tom Velotti, a retired NYPD officer and PBA V.P. for the police specifics. I must also thank them for their criticisms which forced me to try harder while allowing my fictional twisting. I was lucky to have several readers; my mom(gone at 100), cousins and Bernadette Berkery. And finally my computer Guru Joanna Petrosine, a new sister. All this help was needed and appreciated to get Family Corners written and published including the help of Christian Faith's Erica and editing staff.

Parents in Wonder

The autumn season just north of New York City has long filled the area to bursting with trees in beautiful hues of colors no earthly artist can rival. It is a time when human sighs of appreciation mix with a subtle dread of winter's impending cold.

It was no different on a very typical middle class street in Yonkers, New York, in the year 1960 until the sun decided to hide behind the gray clouds of storm.

From the front window of her family's home, Jean Prezzemoli was waiting for Bill Perry already dressed to meet the change in weather. As she watched the afternoon turn grizzly, she felt a prickly of shiver that began an emotional chain reaction that was all-too familiar.

As the bright yellows and bronze of autumn fall prey to the pervasive storm clouds, her turmoil deepened. The graying landscape seemed to collude with a mind-stabbing confusion to deny an escape from a surging panic. As her terror grew, she became more determined to do what had to be done.

Her silent prayer was, "Please, God, let this be over," joined all the pleas gone before that found no understandable answers."

Her comfortable, in control stance, so well suited to her athletic presence, so very misleading in social encounters had succumbed to being at home. Something rare, her guard being down had revealed her agonizing to her parents. While waiting, her thoughts were interrupted with sensing that her parents, Joe and Marian Prezzemoli, had picked up her mood and her upset deepened.

It's happening with Marian and Joe being home meant Jean had taken a wrong turn into a very short dead end street.

The truth of what was happening was something she couldn't share with them. For a moment, she shut her eyes to waste an imaginative wish to elude their concerned presence. Unfortunately, the heat of the small, pleasant living room wretched a stuttering breath from her pitching lungs to choke her imagery with reality. The last of her patience tore away from her like a piece of paper in a violent wind.

She turned abruptly from her vigil's station to pace between the small kitchen and the living room. The adult in her was torn between the guilt of her child within not telling them and the healthy habit this family had in sharing problems.

In a quick step over, Spot, the family mutt their eyes met. Whatever made Spot family disarmed her, so she spoke to him.

Whispering, she said, "Don't look at me that way. I know I should tell them, but I can't. I need an explanation Mom and Dad can accept, and I need it now. You know, I've got to be careful what I say to them because of what it could do to Dad."

Barely time for her words, her long legs took her through the too-tiny kitchen and back in mere seconds. Now Spot was sitting head up next to Marian as though he wanted to hear every word said. Jean crossed the living room threshold knowing what to expect.

She was right.

Joe and Marian Prezzemoli never tolerated the muffle of spectators in bouts with day-to-day living. To them, caring about someone demanded trying to help. In this instance, they understood that to reach inside of Jean called for diligence in doing because they would have to do battle with her cursed independence.

Such traits of strength in women were not particularly admired in 1960 but claimed high honors in the Prezzemoli home. Watching Jean's current dilemma, her prolonged silence had them both worried and prepared to challenge for in spite of their pride in their oldest, they both felt they had failed in teaching her to seek and accept help. It was a human function of life Jean still had to come to understand, but only about herself for that parental pride also acknowledged her willingness to care and help others.

Marian and Joe, anticipating her return, took only a split second to convey one of those silent signals all good parents develop through years of fending off their children's ploys. They rose as one and stood in Jean's path.

In spite of the distress, Jean smiled and thought, *God, they're always in sync.*

With feeling her father's hand on her shoulder and her mother's hand in hers, she welcomed the familiar warmth, but "it" happened just the same. She stiffened almost unnoticeably. It was just another sad taste of her battle's many flavors. One she was yet to realize had cursed Joe with years of guilt. Surrounded by their love, her mind pounded away at her like a hydraulic bit boring into the ground.

How can I tell Mom and Dad the truth when I don't know the truth and I hate myself for it? If I try to explain, I'll only make things worse. I don't know why I'm scared. Even if I could tell them, Dad's knowing would bring him another stroke. Dear God, what do I do?

Hearing the concern in her father Joe's voice—"Honey, is this something we can help you with? Is Bill giving you a hard time?"—ended the thinking. The worried tone demanded attention.

His danger turned her mind agile and powered her tongue. "I wish you could, Dad, but I'm the only one who can do this." In a soft, firm alto, she said, "Bill wants more than I can give."

Joe's face flushed, making his fingers tighten on Jean's shoulder, while Marian's calm reflected her usual patience allowing her to hear Jean out.

When Jean said, "Bill wants to marry me," Joe's grip eased, and his patience joined Marian's in practicing the art of listening as Jean continued.

"I just don't feel that way about Bill. He's such a good guy, and I feel worse because he's going to hurt more than most. I have to do it now. It wouldn't be fair to wait any longer."

Marian and Joe nodded with the comprehension gained from Jean's sharing many parts of her single life. Both had recognized Bill's love long before Jean sensed it. This very thing always seemed strange to Joe and Marian since Jean could read people with a generous insight at times mysterious in its awareness. They knew Bill was fun and Jean enjoyed his company and bright mind.

Marian quickly studied Joe as she often did these days and found her own feelings for Bill's position mirrored in his warm brown eyes as he nodded in understanding. It saddened them both that Bill had joined the list of wishful consorts gone before him. To date, only Bill had stood a chance with her.

Marian—all mother again—said, "Honey, we know he'll hurt more, but you're doing the right thing. Bill's a good man, and telling him won't change that. Everyone hurts when things don't work out."

"I know, but it doesn't make it any easier. He deserves better." *At least better than me.* The silent battle was still going on.

Jean's spoken words, a blatant bypassing of basic truth for hurting Bill, forced her to step away from accepting the moment's nesting so freely given only to stop at the window, to turn and say, "Thank you for trying."

Again, on vigil, she realized, *Oh, God, I wanted it to work with Bill. I wanted it to be different.*

But underneath, she knew that couldn't be. She was still the same person she was when she met Bill, and that made her wrong for him for anyone, even herself. That terrified her, but she remained unrelenting in purpose. As her gaze returned to the window, she saw Bill's gray Chevy take the corner and park in front of the house. Her body temperature rose like an express elevator, and the human urge to run away jerked through her like an electric current gone amok, one in danger of blowing all her mental fuses.

As Bill's lean, lithe six-foot-four frame rose from the car, his humorous habit of running fingers through a barely there blonde crew cut brought her a mental quirk that leapfrogged to dancing with him and getting that kooky crick in her neck for looking up from her five foot eight and a gentle smile touched her lips only to be interrupted with, *Oh, Bill, you are dear to me, and you're so fond of Mom and Dad.*

The panic returned and triggered, *Oh, Jesus, you don't need the added hurt of realizing Mom and Dad know I'm sending you away. God, how stupid can I be.*

She whirled, buttoned her jacket against the October chill, and pushed her athletically trim body through the front door as though she was Road Runner with Wile E. Coyote snapping at her heels.

As Bill reached for his hair, his fine Irish eyes lacked the fun-loving glint usually found in their azure blue. With a jaw set grimly in his now pale features, he instinctively approached the gate to go in for her, a must, but his mind was elsewhere wrestling with their last conversation. As he reached for the gate, he saw her quick exit from the house and realized he was in big trouble. *Oh, shit.*

Joe watched their leaving and chose to avoid an impotent silence and said, "Marian, do you think she's all right?"

"Yes, she'll handle it."

"It's too bad Bill isn't tough enough to hang in there. I like him."

"I do too. So does she."

Joe saw Marian's reaction to Jean flick across her features as though something didn't fit.

He asked, "What?"

"I worry that's she's not telling us everything. I don't know if it's an advantage to be her parents. Do you think our knowing she's different prevents us from helping?"

"You mean special."

She smiled her accord, and he said, "Maybe it's more that we understand her too stubborn streak, and I wish we could change that. Oh Joe, I think it's going to take an unusual man to understand Jean. When she finds him, it'll probably be one battle after another unless she comes to understand herself by then."

"I hope that's all it is because with the right guy, they'll work that out. Only, there may not be enough good guys out there for her to find one. Look how many she's sent away. Our times have robbed many a young woman of the right man."

"Doesn't that have more to do with your being her father than history? She only dates men she truly enjoys and they read more into it. Take my word for it, she'll find the right guy. I did."

Twenty-six years of marriage favored Joe with enjoying Marian's ability to read him. More important was the fact she always touched the parts of his mind and heart that needed their love and it's directing.

His hand moved tenderly across Marian's cheek, as she said, "You don't still worry about the strange things that happen to her, do you?"

"Not really. We've both learned that for all the danger they bring, something else keeps her safe. Somebody upstairs is really on her side. It's the physical danger she places herself in that really gets to me. But even that's not the problem. It's just that I want her happy and she's not. I can't help it. I have to do something about it."

"I know. Only we won't know that answer until she tells us. Perhaps not marrying worries her. Most twenty-five-year-olds are married and have families. But I doubt it. Maybe being ill for three years robbed her of too much time. There's so much she wants to do." Her voice became sterner. "Maybe it's more."

Marian paused and brusquely said, "But she doesn't want our help."

Joe expected her poignant reaction whenever they discussed Jean's self-determined and frustrating isolation. He hated seeing her troubled by having done the right thing. It was Marian who deliberately taught Jean the value of independence and finding it now housed roots never intended diluted Marian's accomplishment with guilt. Joe understood his own desire to protect his family, but the most important person to him, his wife, had fought his protection and in attaining adulthood so did Jean. Both endlessly and it frustrated him that they were usually right. But the exceptions and his love demanded he try.

Automatically, Joe intercepted Marian's troubled reaction. "Then she's not all right? No one can go through life without help, and that's something she decided herself. We didn't teach her that. There's always something we can do, we just haven't found it yet, but we will. Remember how many times the doing of nothing was the right thing to do?" Taking a deep breath, he added, "Mar, I don't care if she never gets married. I just want her happy?"

Rushed feelings began to take their toll on his troubled body, and Marian's concern for Jean disappeared into Joe's need.

"Joe, she knows that, and you did all you could." She slipped her arms around him. "Hon, you can't worry like this." She was all wife again. "It's not good for you." She stroked his temple where his vain popped and said, "Jean has to make her own mistakes. She's managed some tough corners already, but it will always hurt to watch her take them. Joe, she's going to be all right, I know it. She left childhood behind a long time ago."

"But she makes me angry when she refuses to let us do anything for her. Even when she was sick, she wouldn't."

Fatigue intruded on Joe's posture, and Marian changed her tack.

"Is it really so bad? The power of the Prezzemoli women is in their strong will and honest affections." A teasing smile lit her round, pretty, freckled features as she said, "It certainly hasn't been hard to live with me!"

Joe's boisterous laughter filled the room, as he stepped willingly into his love's trap. Marian snuggled up and then pulled away their fingers lingering as she said, "Come on, hon, I'll make a pot of coffee and we'll be here when she gets home."

As Joe's foxy lady drifted away, his laughter took him to other plains of loving. *Mar, at forty-six, you look more thirty to my forty-nine. God, how did I manage to keep you? When I think about you're determination to find your own way, I realize how much alike you and Jean are, and yet you're so different—you're worlds apart. I'm one lucky man. If our Joey finds a woman just half of what you are, he could be a happy man.*

He joined her effort to lighten the parental load. "Our hellions are certainly different. With a twenty-five-year-old and twenty-year-old at home, it's never dull. Joey doesn't behave anything like Jean, so we don't have to worry about him taking help. He'll take any assist that isn't nailed down, offered or not."

The cheery sound of his words told Marian the tension was gone. Thoughts about Joey usually did that, and he added, "What

I'd like to know is how our number one and only son turned into a ladies' man. I am excluding those Manfredi good looks you gave him."

Marian laughed and said, "Oh, Joe, he made that choice all by himself, and we don't seem to be able to change it."

"Hey, I know it's something he has to deal with by himself, but I am his father—I have to try to get through to him."

"Yes, and you've set the best possible example. Besides, we know he'll never hurt a woman physically but emotionally—he just doesn't get it. My biggest fear is he never will. Still he's only twenty, he has time, and we'll both keep trying."

Joe started to take a look out the window but dismissed the idea and headed for the kitchen table with Spot following and sitting right at his feet. "Hon, you're right about rough corners. We've sure turned our share but so did our parents. I know we're partially a result of what they did, but then we learned to make our own way. I think we've given our two the space they need, don't you?"

"Uh-huh, and we've let them chose their own paths, but there was never enough money to do more."

Joe started to ask something but felt Spot rubbing his skinny, still muscular leg, so he said, "Spot wants something too," as his fingers dropped to scratch Spot's ear.

With the coffee on, Marian got some liverwurst for Spot, some homemade cake, and said, "Joe, remember Pop's mistakes? How easy they were to see, and how good he was at the same time. I wonder if he could have changed? And I wonder about the mistakes we've made but don't recognize." She threw a hunk of liverwurst into the air and smiled as Spot leaped up and caught it like a talented right fielder.

Joe said, "Great catch, Spot," and continued with, "Mar, we learned to change directions, but I don't know about your pop or my mom? They had fewer choices. We've made mistakes, but we learned about hidden fears and how hard it is to find them. Look how long it took to find ours. We were lucky."

"Lucky, yes, but we worked very hard at it." After placing the goodies on the table, Marian joined two of her men in waiting for Jean. In the warmth of their kitchen, they would easily pass the time as they always could, but this choice in how would be with a visit to the past.

These caring parents were not the only ones concerned about Jean and others in the family.

In a place where spirits dwell—a place called by many names, by many peoples, where time has no meaning—a spirit called the archer wearing a small quiver filled with shafts of light walked among the endless watchers to instruct a particular watcher in relative ways for the Prezzemoli troubling. But he is only one in this universe of vigilance where little can be done until decisions based in free will are made by those humans in trouble.

Still other spirits in a darker place, in a similar mode of time and numbers but of opposite intention, shadowed this family, as they do all humans, daring anything to prime a detour.

Gino, Tess, and Raffaele

Marian and Joe's journey into the past begins in 1896 with fourteen-year-old Gino Manfredi trying to wave reassuring goodbyes from aboard an ocean going vessel as it began its voyage to that land of magnetic expectations and wonders called the United States of America. Drawn to it, as is metal to a magnet, the trip had become a necessity to the living of a good life to millions of struggling humans.

As the warm rising sun awakened to find the ship leaving a harbor, it touched the teal blue waters off Italy's western landfall creating an uncountable burst of sparkles across the quiet waves, more suited to a greeting than a farewell.

The craggy hills above the Italian waters seemed to cry out to the thousands aboard the ship, "Stay," but no one could hear above the frantic calls to those waving goodbye to those leaving.

Gino took no heed of the beautiful wheat hued sunrise as it touched the mountain peaks, except to unconsciously be grateful for easing the strain to see Madre Manfredi and Antonio, a younger Fratello, as they became specks in the distance. Aware their farewells were filled with tears, he smiled under his wide brimmed Homburg heedless of its hitting the stem of the Mandolin slung across his back while he gripped his only suitcase tightly between his legs.

When he could no longer see his family, he turned to look at the expanding sea before him, tipping his hat so he could see against the sun's glare. With every degree of his turn, his heart began to race in pace with his excitement. It was better than the first glass of truly fine wine he made.

In that same instant, his mind switched plains and bumped into the sadness of remembering his padre.

His father's recent death left him the man of the family at a time when the Italian economy drove the departure of thousands of desperate or adventurous Italians more powerfully than the engines of the ship vibrating beneath Gino's feet.

He leaned against the railing and remembered kneeling next to his father's bedside, very much the younger image of the man in bed, and listened to the dreams and advice of the padre he loved who expected him to carry on from where he left off. The greatest of padre's concerns was for madre—her care and her already bitter reaction to his dying too soon. The bitterness, so much a part of her growing up, was deeply engrained except in loving him. Padre, unseeing of the toll her bitterness could take from the two young sons he was leaving behind, passed on the duty of her care as a trust only one must fulfill. Honor demanded it of Gino, the eldest of his two sons.

"Gino, you are my oldest, and I have taught you all I that I know." Pride glowed from the dying man as he said, "You will do well out in the world. But as my oldest"—he took a struggling breath—"you must take care of your madre. It will be difficult at times, and you must help Antonio too, but both must be done, and it is yours alone to do. It is the way of the world and of a caring man. I need your promise and your word of honor that you will not dishonor this obligation. Please, son, give me your hand on this."

Gino watched Padre's laborious effort to speak and leaned in close to Padre's ear, put his hand over Padre's, and said, "Hush, you must rest. You have trained me well, in many arts, for which I thank you. You have my word, I will take care of Madre always and in all things, and I will help Antonio." Their eyes met one last time as Gino watched the older man's eyes flutter and heard the rattle-loving children hate. Gino put his head down and cried for the last time as a boy, as the mantle of head of the Manfredi family descended upon him.

Gino stared at the roughening sea and once again sought to reassure Padre.

Papa, I will find work in the United States as we planned, I will open a barbershop then send for Madre and Antonio. I will not forget my promise to care for Madre and help Antonio. Going to America alone is the first step. Soon, I will send for the others. Before the Holy Father, I promise to honor Madre—always.

At fourteen, a promise to honor went very, very deep.

Below Gino, the sea roughened sending a salt spray up to touch him like many intimate fingertips wanting to muss his hair causing him to instinctively move away, for a barber must always show his trade to those around him. His Padre fastidiously skilled him in the arts of tonsorial presentation, Italian culinary and their welcome companions; wines and liquors distilled from their pure alcohol also suitable for medicinal needs. His father's hand often trembled when he touched his oldest with the realization Gino must go to America alone, that he would not live to join him, such was their fain.

Here was the wealth Gino would take to the sea with him to master his quest and improve everyday life for the Manfredi family in America. Such skills linked Gino with an era long ago when a warring family called Borgia, rudely kicked Gino's prince of an ancestor out of his northern Faenza principality to learn about life by earning it.

What passed down to Gino, however young, was a measure of life that valued human worth on a stringent yardstick called respect. Too soon the man of the family, he could not foresee the part of his deathbed vow to his father that would menace both his honor and the adult he was determined to be.

He was distracted from his too serious thoughts by an aged gentleman. Immediately, Gino gave the older man his complete attention, as respect demanded for the elderly.

The man assuming Gino was German greeted him in a lengthy salutation that revealed much loneliness. The elder had on a frayed but clean jacket, and Gino smiled for understanding most of what he had said and extended his hand speaking in his best-schooled Italian in hopes the old man would understand. The man stammered through an apology for the assumption and quickly switched to Italian. In moments, Gino laughed and realized he was enjoying the company much as he had the many talks during Padre's illness. The two spent time together talking about an uncertain future before seeking their bunks below.

Many new acquaintances were deceived by Gino's appearance. For his heritage favored the long gone Germanic blood of that princely ancestor. He was very fair with a flawless milk-white complexion molded in soft but not quite handsome features, while his hair was coiffed in straight, fine meticulously cut blonde hair. A companioning five-foot-four height and an almost-stocky figure compounded the illusion.

As days passed, Gino's mental gnawing of loneliness vanished into the sea of people aboard the ship, mindful of a whale that he had seen disappear below the surface of the open sea from a great leap. Gino's mind fed on his love of people and enjoyed mental meals of sharing, particularly when joining other homespun musicians in bringing a pleasant distraction to the squeezed in travelers. Afterward, he would share their hopes and his own for the homes they sought. The sounds of destinations rang in his mind like the perfect notes of a Mandolin and fascinated him as he listened. Places where Indians roamed like Arizona, Oregon, Wyoming, and Colorado enthralled him and forged a promise within him of a different type.

I will travel my new country. There is so much to see.

The shipboard immigrants were answering the call to fill America's need for skilled workers. Gino enjoyed discussing the varied talents of other passengers like a mason, carpenter, vintner, ironworker or farmer and how they would help America grow. These were the kind of people whose hair he would cut, and he enjoyed all he could learn from them.

Gino, the barber, housed a mid-school education and an essential phrases of basic English. Most formidable was his belief in himself for he had been taught well. He often finished the sharing with others with, "God has furnished me with the talent, but the rest is up to me. Come visit me, I will cut your hair and offer you a fine wine or liquor of your choice. All I need is the chance." He knew he was not alone.

In that land of spirits, Gino's watcher said to the vigilant archer, "Can we"—he paused without embarrassment to say—"I'm still asking questions of Gino's world." The archer touched the watcher with his knowing aura and said, "You learn well."

"This Gino does not appear to need help, but I've learned that demons are there and he could lose his way and I must wait.

"As said, you learn quickly. Be watchful."

One bright morning, New York City came into view, and Gino held his breath as he gazed up at Miss Liberty amid a harbor of unending activity. To him, she was a welcoming La Commara (godmother) stationed next to Ellis Island determined to shelter arriving immigrants as they rushed to disembark.

With the time to leave the ship nearing, Gino ran below, grabbed his gear, and joined the horde below deck as it slowly moved to a landfall pier. Suddenly, he slowed even more and deliberately raised a heel, brought it down on the foot of the man behind him, quickly turned to find a man a head taller than he, and spoke sincerely, "Oh, signore, 'Scusatemi,'" and thought, *Now, signora, now!*

A struggling teenage mother grabbed the opportunity to join those in the gangway. There was a baby nestled in a sling across her bust while managing several bundles almost as big as she, yet finding a way to smile and say, "We are in America!"

Amazed at her feat, Gino and the man behind gasped simultaneously laughed and said, "Dio Mio," and rushed behind her as excited as she.

When Gino felt the land under his feet for the first time in weeks, he wobbled slightly on his sea legs. A few firmer steps later, he entered Ellis Island's Great Hall, named for its size. He didn't hear the sound of the hollow echo of the hard wood stairs beneath his feet heralding the generations to come.

An insatiable curiosity had him eyeballing everything from the ceiling stories above, to the balconied tiers between the stories that allowed viewing the crowded floor on which he stood. At least until immigration officials hung a number around his neck and deloused him. His fastidious nature shivered through the violation, but he understood the need.

Next was the wait between squared off metal railings with nothing to sit on except an occasional backless bench. He was in a square on the edge quite near the group of doctors examining people to clear them physically for entry. From there, he craned his neck to view the high-bordered walkway wondering what the people up there did. As the waiting bore down on him, he turned his attention to the people around him. There was no one near that he knew, so he tried to play with the youngest of a family of five in the next square but could not make the child laugh. Not good with children, it didn't surprise him. When the Army physician called for them, he watched as the doctor found the unsmiling child had an ailment forcing the family to decide between reaching for the dream without her or returning to Europe.

Gino felt the surge in the anger born aboard ship when thinking about how shippers deliberately used them and became rich.

What if America insists that shipping companies guarantee the return of the disappointed? It doesn't help the family or the bambino. The ship owners already have their money, and it doesn't affect their profits.

Gino would never know the decision the family made or realize he had tears on his cheek because hunger took him from the travail. He was moved along with 2,999 others to a very large dining room.

His eyes popped at the scene, and he beamed with appreciation for the tables wore immaculate cloths upon which laid perfect place settings.

"Eh, bella. Bene Fortuna."

As was his way, he sat like a vertical steel beam yet, without stress, ate slowly with proper elegance, as carefully as he'd shear a head of hair. To eat was an art that brought him pure pleasure.

The meal, designed to revitalize the hope of the immigrants, did its job well.

Once again, Gino returned to the grand hall, answered all the questions put to him, passed his physical, and—in a few hours— crossed the Hudson River aboard a Myers Ferry where he bent his head in respect to the huge lady who watched over his ride. He left the dock to find the grime and stench of New York City exhilarating. There was no one to meet him unless you count those who would prey on the innocent, unwary traveler.

A gruff man approached him. "Eh wio, welcome to the Big Apple. I'll take ya to a place to live." The greasy-looking man put his strong hand over Gino's to take the bag.

Gino took one look, pulled away, and said, "No, signore. Non sono stupidita."

Gino felt honored when the man raised a closed fist to the crook of his arm, for he had judged the man correctly and greeted the crass Italian gesture with an appropriate frown and quietly tipped his hat. Only minutes later, he asked a workingman for directions and began his search noting the greasy man had already found another mark.

Though he faltered through questions, punctuated with the pounding of an excited heart, he found Little Italy and a place to house his personal treasures: two new fashionable suits, accessories, plus his barber frocks and tools, including those that belonged to his padre.

Padre, Antonio will use your tools when he comes.

The next morning, he went to a local bank converted his extra lire to dollars and opened a small account after visiting with the bankers to establish his first business contact. He was sure he had enough to hold him until working and his mandolin would keep him company until he joined some clubs and made new friends.

Now was the time to take the next step of his plan. *I will find work as a cook. But I will work for no man—as a barber—I will be my own, what is the American word? Eh, yes, it is* boss. *I will be my own boss, open my own shop, and bring Madre Mia and Antonio here.*

He took two precious days to familiarize himself with restaurants where his talents could command more. Once he found the

Arturo restaurant both clean and full of smells both familiar and tempting, he respectfully approached the owner, Arturo himself, and said in his practiced English, "Senor, I will cook for you today without pay, as long as I am allowed to cook in my own way. In this way, you can judge my work and hire me knowing what you are paying for."

Arturo tasted every dish leaving the kitchen and, by evening, told Gino, "Eh, you've done well," and then said, "You will be called Gene, and I'll put you on the payroll as a full time assistant cook but only for the specialties you did today."

They agreed on his pay and shook hands. Then Gino rushed to the nearest church to light a candle in thanks, and then he wrote to Madre and Antonio.

As the days passed, his intellect refused the trap of comfort solely among his own, he soon became comfortable with English and did much to lose his accent. Successful business called for opening many doors, so Gino took great care to become fluent knowing it oiled the hinges of those doors.

Without offense, he accepted Arturo's well-meant lesson and became Gene to all.

New York's hustle and bustle of overlapping cultures matured and nourished his human force to push his way to becoming another firm strand in the strengthening of a common cord. A cord made strong by the magnificent mix of immigrants that secured the United States in a potential seldom found in history despite intruding rotten strands.

Though too serious, Gene quickly won a mutual liking from business contacts as well as friends. His ability to enjoy people came easily to this polite industrious young man. The people he met added to his everyday pleasure. His personal drive made plans happen, and when Arturo offered to finance his first barbershop, Gene formally responded, "Ah, senor, I appreciate all you teach me, but my shop is mine alone to make happen." Arturo now "Art smiled" for he had known the answer before he made the offer.

To make it happen, Gene pressed to make contacts in other nationalities, without the obvious prejudice that so many immigrants brought with them and Italians were no different. Nor was Gene. His quick genuine smile wrapped in respect cooled many a hostile look. That harsh yardstick, respect, served him well when he crossed those barriers dodging the cruel and dangerous actions that deprived people of greater success while managing to stay clear of involvement in illegal activities so much a part of the land he left behind only to find the criminal leagues so troubling in Italy had crossed the sea just as he had and said to Art, "I had hoped we as Italians would not bring our evil with us."

Art explained sarcastically, "Eh, like that were possible." Art went on about the workings of Little Italy helping Gene to recognize a safe niche and avoid errors too easily trapping the honest. The darker side of Italy was deeply entrenched in New York, and his life there would one day touch on it in a way he would never anticipate.

Gene, infatuated with New York City culturally, physically craved all the new things the fast-growing economy allowed him to share and learn from. In short time, it was truly his home.

Gene called out daily, "Art, I am taking lunch." It had become his habit to head for the alley entrance and take off his cook's apron before passing through the door donning his barber frock to spend his lunchtime at his real profession. A glance down the alley beside the restaurant often brought smiles. Any passerby might see a man or boy sitting on an empty wooden barrel in front of his barber. Dressed in that meticulous white frock with every hair in place, Gene placed a viewing mirror on a ledge in the brick wall of the building next door and then toweled and sheeted his client to barber him. Either might be talking to neighbors in windows overhead.

It was an honest start, and Gene only took what people could afford knowing they would tell others.

One day, his boss came to the door. "Hey, Gene! Didn't I hire you as a cook?" He was smiling as he said it, but Mrs. McDuffy, ensconced in her second floor window, took his words as a challenge.

"Artie, leave Gene be. He's the best cook you got. Besides, you ne'er looked so good 'til he started takin' care a yer hair and yer oogly face."

Art's upward glance changed from a scowl to, "Thank you, Mrs. McDuffy. I do look good, don't I?" He smiled again, rubbed his chin, waved, and left.

Gene raised his clipping shears in a salute to Mrs. McDuffy.

"Don't yee try to fool me, Bucko. Church going though you be, Gene, I'll still not let a Latin boy like yee near me darlin's."

Gene took no offense so sure was he that the remark was correct for all nationalities and said, "Your ragazze (girls) are lucky having a madre like you."

It was time to go. He slowly took the towel and sheet from his client's shoulders, brushed his neck with powder, and graciously took the few pennies the Greek had. What the man did have were well-established and hardworking friends. Only after cleaning and storing his tools did Gene rush. He owed Art a full day's work.

The day came when Arturo heard Gene say, "I have rented a shop on the border of Little Italy and China Town. I must leave your employ, and I hope you will remain my favored customer."

"Favorite customer, Gene—favorite." Art's correction and smile mixed sadness with his pride in a young friend. Gene's English errors were now rare, and the mentor grabbed the younger man's hand and watched him leave knowing he would be fine.

Blessed with New World's kind embrace while avoiding its horrors, time would pass quickly for Gene.

The year Gene left Italy, a fourteen-year-old in Sorrento stood before her padre with her hand in Gaetano Prezzemolo's. Her father had refused to receive them in the traditional way, so the young couple went to his factory office unannounced and quietly stated their intention to marry. They no longer sought permission.

Anger filled the office like the aroma of a rotting carcass. The wealthy man's face turned ugly in delivering abuse. His fist crashed upon a desk in a demand for servile capitulation.

"Raffaele, you will not marry this—this cafone (boor), this contadino (peasant)! Do so and I will disown you. You will cease to exist as my daughter. I will leave you nothing. Do you hear me, Raffaele? Nothing!"

The iron man's trump card fell wastefully, but the abuse was not unheeded. Gaetano stepped forward, his anger taking command. Raffaele placed her other hand on him. He turned toward her, felt her mood, and stepped back. The hurts of her father no longer meant anything to her. She was fine and in possession of a clear conscience.

Raffaele stood as erect as she could, met her father's glare, waited one second more, and then—with a shake of her head—turned in wordless acceptance to meet this corner in life on its own terms. The brave young woman truly understood her father. The filial outrage meant nothing. The harsh words had little to do with love and everything to do with dominance, and seeing he had nothing more to say, they walked out of her father's life for all time, though a part of her would never stop caring. Fortunately, hope did not live in that part of her mind.

Only then did Gaetano take his first human breath since the moment they entered the office and brought Raffaele's hand tightly to his body. Her father's words to her had enraged him, but now he was more worried about doing right by her. He held the door for her as they left the factory, stepped into the sunlight, and pulled her close. Gaetano spoke softly, for Raffaele had heard enough harsh words to last many lifetimes.

"Cara Mia, I want you for our lifetime, but again, I beg you to realize that being poor is cruel."

In a worn but immaculately clean old hand-me-down dress cinched to perfection, she, Raffaele, relaxed in his arms. The features of her strongly attractive face softened with a smile that met his troubled look as she answered with the truth.

"Gaetano, my father would marry me to anyone for the sake of business. I have never had anything truly mine until you. It wouldn't matter to him, if the man beat me." She felt his grip around her tighten, smiled, and continued, "I was not a son." Her eyes filled with tears that did not fall. "I am fit only to work in his shoe factory and clean his floors and toilet. I am not even fit to cook his meals." She paused. "But you already know this. The Blessed Mother will watch over us. Gaetano, if I hadn't found you, I'd have lived a love-less life. You will find work, if not as a musician at whatever you can, and I will find houses to clean, for it is what I do better than anyone."

"Si Cara Mia, I know you speak the truth, and I also know your poppa made a big mistake for your strength comes in part from working in his miserable factory. As you grew, that strength mixed with your own to make you stronger than he and now he knows that too."

There was much Gaetano did not say because it would change nothing. Not blinded by love, he saw the future all too clearly. The land his father farmed could not support another family, and they would have to make decisions to change that. Still being in love, he knew they must marry.

The sensation of Raffaele's fingers on Gaetano's face made everything better, but the confidence was hers. Fear for her gripped him, like a finger caught in a slamming door. Such faith belonged to others. What Gaetano believed in was Raffaele.

Only after playing with a band at a party her poppa had given did he notice her. He realized she had not been at the party but was there to do the cleaning and was shocked to find she was the factory owner's daughter. He was moved by the rest of what his friend told him, so he cased his instrument and walked over to introduce himself offering to help. In short time, he knew where his future lay.

He soon learned of the long hours spent in her father's factory without special privilege or education.

Why would a father school a strong, healthy, hardworking daughter when she can replace a peasant he would have to pay? Working the same long hours as the townspeople, she received only room and board. This Italian Cinderella cleaned and washed for her stepmother, two stepbrothers, and the man who sired her. Her stepmother did only the cooking, and to her, Raffaele was but the maid.

Gaetano and Raffaele were married in Gaetano's hometown and began a vain struggle against the barren soil. At the signing of their marriage certificate, no one noticed the misspelling in Raffaele's signature. Without education, she was proud she had learned to write her name—a spelling that would follow her to her grave, not that anyone loving her would care a hoot.

She was welcomed to Gaetano's home with open arms, and though the parsley their name Prezzemolo stood for would no longer grow in the used up land and the monies Gaetano made as a musician barely fed them, they found in each other a warmth unmatched by the fire in their hearth.

Raffaele's enlivening spirit and devout cleanliness brought an affectionate spark into the lonely senior Prezzemolo's home. But the lands slow death brought hopelessness exceeded only by the hurt of Mary, their first child's death. Her going devoured the old man's will to live, and he was soon buried next to Mary.

Raffaele was quickly pregnant again. A son Luigi joined them, and then he had a sister. This Mary was healthy and honored the Blessed Mother and her dead child. Raffaele believed the Blessed Mother had kept her safe in her years of cruelty, and she prayed to her in hopes of keeping her always near. Raffaele loved and trusted the Mother of the Baby Christ, and her guidance showed in how she lived.

Until 1906, Gaetano read Raffaele the letters from cousins in the United States full of tales about family members making good in New York's fish market and on New York's busy docks. The words fed their imagination, and they sold the land for enough to sail around another of life's corners. They arrived in the States after a longer, harder trip than Gene's.

The Prezzemolos walked down the Myers Ferry gangplank with Louis riding Gaetano's shoulder and Mary in a sling across Raffaele's bust. Louis was the first to see the cousins waving happily at seeing them. Raffaele thanked the Blessed Mother for a safe arrival and held on tightly to young Mary. The cousins found them an apartment in a tree-laden town called Yonkers on an avenue called Vineyard on a section of town called The Hill.

Raffaele looked around, smiled, and said, "Gaetano, we're home."

"Si, Cara Mia, si."

Gaetano was soon working on dangerous docks, and the family knew their first security. Soon, a daughter Margaret joined the family, and in 1911, another son, Guisseppe, howled his way into life in a new land bringing them favor. Luigi and Giuseppe were soon Anglicized to Louis and Joseph.

At twenty-one, Gene had sidestepped the evil around him without offense and had brought Madre and Antonio to New York where they shared a railroad type apartment in a good apartment house in Little Italy. All were supported well by the now four-chair barbershop located on Mulberry Street where the Italian area meets China Town.

He found his mother more difficult than he remembered and as troublesome as his father warned. Gene tried hard to help Antonio overcome the sadness he had acquired in the years he and Madre had been together without him and was grateful to his fratello for carrying the burden. But it was now his, and he handled her demands as his father expected giving Antonio respite and accepting the situation for his honor bound promise demanded being responsible for her. To him, it meant among other things, meeting her daily requests to meet her self-determined needs.

Meanwhile, he took pride in being sought after on days men choose to marry. Like a priest or a doctor of his time, he answered the call of the groom no matter the time or day.

It was an aptitude that kept him one of the best informed men in the neighborhood. Men loved to talk and share when in a barber's chair.

He had earned his public reputation because he sent a groom to his bride looking his best. His special hot towel facial brought clients back for more. At twenty-one, a full business and a widely varied social life companied his promise detouring any time to think of a wife and family, and he was untroubled by that. His self-image was held close by his commitment to the poor he saw every day in the world around him. His shop often held items like lemons or vegetables the poor could not afford but these always found their way to them.

He took great satisfaction in keeping his promises, especially the one he made to himself about the poor. His shop often held items they could not afford, but he gifted a family or client as thank-you for their patronage. All was given freely when pride permitted.

Until now, only one promise eluded him. One he made to himself. Now a man of confidence, he held no fear for his future or his soul when turning one of life's corners.

"It's time, Antonio."

"For what, Gene?"

"To see America!"

"Yes, it is. Go, you've worked for years to get us here. It is time."

Antonio took his place at the shop, and Gene kept the promise to himself. To cover Madre's requests, several storekeepers had their delivery boys stop by each day allowing Antonio to remain at work and free to care for the greater workload. Arturo's Restaurant had a guest each evening treated with great deference. Family friends and available gentlemen of the neighborhood would often keep the still lovely-looking woman company at dinner yet would never leave with her. When Antonio finished for the day, he would see her safely home.

All this arranged, the well-known barber packed the same suitcase he'd arrived at Ellis Island with and left to travel America. He returned many months later to proudly hang a picture of himself with an Indian chief on his shop wall. The tales of America and Red men would entertain customers for a long time. He decided he would continue to travel. There was no reason he could see that would change that decision. Now he planned to see the world.

In the Prezzemolo household, young Giuseppe was now called Joe by his older siblings. At two, he was a toddler well on his way to being spoiled by his older siblings when death cruelly took Gaetano in a dock accident.

After the funeral, the cousins left Raffaele and the children to deal with the sadness. Raffaele tucked the children in, spent time with each of her crying girls, and then went to the boys who shared a bed in a small bedroom. Struggling with watching her sadness, Louis gave her a hug and turned to seek refuge in feigned sleep. He could not watch as his mother stood over two year old Joseph to wipe a tear from a chubby cheek and take it to her lips. Eyes red with grief, she leaned against the nearby wall for support. Fierce hugs and sharing the children's tears did nothing for her desperation. Gaetano's savings would not last long leaving her little but prayer to fight off life's demons.

Joseph gulped a tear in his sleep as his mother prayed.

"Holy Mother, how can Giuseppe understand not seeing that loving man again when even I cannot. He waited for Gaetano tonight. I could only let him cry himself to sleep. I know in time he will stop looking, but, dear Mother, how will I? Who will hold me? I've known love for such a short time?" After kissing Joseph, she crossed herself and went to bed, pleading, "Mother of God, give me strength. I need more houses to clean."

The New World's embrace on Raffaele was a strangle hold, and without Gaetano, it was worse than the old world she left behind.

Meanwhile, the fortunes of the Manfredi family continued as strongly as before. Over the years, Gene had learned the need for and the fun in, laughing with his customers and business contacts. The teasing was often reminiscent of a friendly Bocce game particularly about the pictures of Gene's travels west.

"Gene, that ten gallon hat is almost as big as you are." Officer Denaher, a regular, could not resist the tease.

But Gene—without missing a clip—said, "Eh, Wio, I do not have your big Irish ears to hold up such a capello," his fingers lifting his scissors to point at the top of Denaher's head.

Denaher looked into the polished clean mirror laughing and pressed his ears to his head.

Though Gene's accent was gone, he mixed the languages in a sentence like the vegetables in one of his soups.

Officer Denaher was particularly fond of teasing the barber because he flushed when humored.

Gene's serious nature also found release in enjoying anything new but still geared everything to that yardstick called respect and often deprived himself of good moments for its tight reign. In his free time, he sought out anything new in New York's ever-changing scene.

In 1904, he joined the first subway ride from city hall to 96th street on the Interboro Subway. He insisted on trying all the nuances and arts making New York so special and talking of what he saw and heard. Frequently, he enjoyed the pleasure of eating in the many ethnic restaurants adorning his city.

Visits to the wholesale markets to make contacts or to buy goods and clothes were profitable and filled many every day needs. Many trips procured the items to make use of his vintner skills to produce a pure alcohol used and appreciated for it medicinal qualities, which he sold to many ethnic buyers including several Chinese shopkeepers.

As America's growing surrounded him and made itself part of his hometown, he looked forward to becoming a citizen in fact as well as in heart.

The Manfredi family fared well on the shop's income, and he lived his life based on what he had been taught and seen and reached for anything new and seemingly exciting to everyday doings.

Where there was no food, Gene would discreetly help including an effort to ensure a family's honor and need were carefully balanced.

At almost twenty-three, Gene contracted an illness the doctor's did not understand. He slipped into an unconscious state to rant about scissors and promises. Madre Manfredi cried at finding his blonde hair in chunks on his wet pillow. After weeks in bed, he began to recover, and though completely bald, his head showed signs of new growth.

One morning, before going to the shop, Antonio shaved Gene as he checked his much thinner image in a hand mirror.

Antonio asked, "Whatta you think?"

"Eh, I'm still delirious. Eh, Wio, my hair is coming in black, like a melanzana (eggplant) like yours Antonio."

Just then Madre passed his room and wailed, "You are no longer your father's son. I hate it." Madre was not one to smile a lot, and humor did not amuse her, so Gene respectfully remained quiet until she passed but smiled at a now glum Antonio who said, "She's never happy," then quickly avoided Gene's chastising look by concentrating on Gene's sideburns.

Though younger, Antonio was wiser in understanding what Madre was about, but he lacked the instincts to avoid her affecting his disposition. While understanding his brother's promise, he was grateful it had not been his to make. Still living with Madre left Antonio bitter, and he had all but given up trying to make Gene understand his promise had been wrong.

With Madre gone, Antonio teased, "Gene, you thinka the gentle ladies likea you better this way?"

"Who knows what a Donna will think, but they'll enjoy hearing the story. They like my stories." He affectionately tapped Antonio and said, "Little brother, we look more like Gemini now than ever."

Gene knew his brother's feelings about Madre, but for Gene, there was no exception to what he believed he had to do.

Of the women in Gene's life, Madre knew little first because he was discreet, and because Gene did not want to deal with her constant criticism of any woman, he gave his time too. So he chose his lady friends carefully and usually squired them away from Little Italy. Gene attended mass regularly with Madre and Antonio, but typical of the time, he lived in the symmetry of believing with his needs as a man.

In the weeks it took to recuperate, he took in fresh air by sitting on the front stoop of the apartment house. The hustle of the neighborhood and familiar faces passing by entertained him.

Mr. Chu, walking to his restaurant, often asked what Gene wanted for lunch and later sent his son to deliver it. Mr. Loo delivered Gene's personal laundry and sat on the stoop with hands precisely folded and talked no more or no less than five minutes first to socialize and to ask about his son's next order for Gene's pure alcohol for use in his chemistry shop. After he left, Gene watched Mrs. Quattro, displaying, just out of the oven, bakery goods in her street side window. She looked up and waved as she always did and smiled as he waved back wondering if he would enjoy a bun.

Other neighbors chatted with him from windows as the goats and chickens roamed the area's small yards amid the horse drawn wagons that filled the busy streets.

After a bit, the beat policeman, Officer Danaher, tapped his cap with a nightstick and said, "Gene, I'll be in for a haircut as soon as you're back."

"Antonio will cut it for you."

"Oh, be Jesus. The lad cuts a great head, but he's no sense of humor. I'll be waitin' for yee."

Denaher's head wheeled at the sound of young people not in school. "Blast 'em, those hooligans are at it again. I can hear Mrs. Lucci yelling for her apples. I best be goin'."

Gene was still smiling when Willy, the street's hawking newsboy, ran up the stairs. "How ye be feelin', Mr. Manfredi?"

Gene mimicked the lad's brogue, "Better, Willy, Mi Boyo, better."

Willy giggled as he handed Gene his daily paper. An Irish brogue from Gene's softer palate was mighty ridiculous to the boy.

Willy's thank-you for the tip went unheard because an unexpected distraction called Tessa Pento had Gene's complete attention.

Everyone in the neighborhood knew and called her Tess. They also knew her love for people, particularly children because she passed through the neighborhood regularly caring for those less fortunate.

Gene watched Tess lift a happy youngster that ran to her and found his masculine appreciation was rising in surprise. The last time he'd noticed her, she'd been more the child, but suddenly, he found himself thinking, *She's beautiful!*

He was grateful for the newspaper in his lap for his white complexion flushed brightly, as he hardened beneath it. A deep breath sheltered the surprise and recognition of how womanhood had touched her. *She has become very desirable, and yet she has a caring soul. She's proven herself unspoiled. How can one so young be such a caring and giving human? I see her going from home to home when people need help. There is no one that does not respect her and yet.* He turned his mind from a darker thought, *Ah, her poppa,* to enjoy her firm, curving body graced by a sensuous bustline that remained high in carriage despite her bindings. Her walk though proud was full of ease and the enjoyment for what she was doing. Gene whistled in a breath to put himself in order while he savored the classic beauty in her angular Roman features, brightly flared with freckles beneath a marvelous head of hair. Short hair, dipping in thick waves of blue black, glistened under the sunlight as her head moved. Perhaps, that was only the barber-taking note, but he wanted to run his fingers through those waves.

At thirteen, Tess was unmarried, an age when many were already mothers. Tess wanted that more than life itself.

She was much older than her years due the effects of her years being ill, constantly under the parents' watchful eyes that kept her among adults learning probably too soon about values of adults and applying those she believed in to how she lived her life rather than adopting the examples of her immediate though loving home. Early on, her pattern of respect had gone deep, but she learned how to stand up for the things she needed to make her life the way she wanted it. Of course, it helped that she had a father who adored his only daughter. A family of her own with scores of children was her heart's desire, and because of illness and life in general, she suspected she might not live the longest of lives. What was missing to help her make wise choices for herself was not having the range of emotions to know her limitations. Perhaps the gentle handling of three older brothers and two younger ones deprived her of the lessons of childhood rivalry that quite often is the cement that can hold an inner self to its other complicated parts when challenged by disrupting emotion.

Tess sensed Gene's watching but chose not to acknowledge it beyond a shy smile. In the last year, the admiration of men was something she had become used to, and she enjoyed it without encouraging it for knowing it would upset her parents.

It never occurred to her to challenge a man's harmless admiration because being Poppa's daughter offered unusual safety and she instinctively used that freedom to grace the neighborhood. Though born in Italy, she arrived here shortly after her birth and never thought of herself as anything but American. She was educated here and had in caring accepted the social boundaries set by loving parents. What she knew of Gene crossed her mind as she nuzzled the youngster.

Lots of lady friends walk with Mr. Manfredi. He's unmarried. We've seen him at church. Momma says he's an honest, hardworking man with many friends but that his momma is an unpleasant woman. That seems too bad. Perhaps, that's why he hasn't married. Momma also said he's been a fine addition to the neighborhood, is well respected, and Poppa says he's done many kind things. Of course, I shouldn't know any of that, but Momma and Poppa had no idea I was in the hall and heard he had offered much to people in need. Poppa also praised his barber skills saying he makes men proud of their skin, and Momma says Manfredi's own skin makes him look so much younger that many a woman has asked his help. He obviously has chosen not to marry. Blessed Mother, why can men can do that while I am not allowed to just seek someone to love and marry. I will probably have to wait for someone to come to Poppa. I know Poppa loves me and wants to protect me, but he doesn't understand how much I want children and with Momma so ill. Oh, Poppa, what will happen to me when Momma is gone and my brothers marry? The thought saddened her. *I am well now, and I want Momma to see my children, her grandchildren.*

Tess lost her train of thought as the youngster told her of the new ball he had and she promised to play with him saying, "I want little boys just like you."

Tess, though young, understood that being Poppa's daughter had disadvantages. For no one had yet approached her father for her, and his being stringent about the old ways of courtship left her feeling it might never happen. Life as it is was what she accepted as a woman of her time. It did little to allay the distress found when meeting school friends already mothers or waiting on a child's coming.

Years of being ill had taught Tess the compassion she showered on the poor and forced her to leave childhood behind very quickly. But those same years had made Poppa Pento more and more protective. In an effort to distract an ailing daughter, Momma Pento encouraged her to act upon her feelings for the sick.

Tess gently put the child down and walked him back to his mother promising herself to talk to Poppa again about her hopes for the future, so Mr. Manfredi was not given another thought on that day.

The morning Gene returned to work, Officer Danaher was the first one in his chair. It was good to be back, but it was different. His illness had blitzed him with a new lesson.

Thoughts of Tess sauntered in between each customer, and he put the lesson into a decision-making thought: *The city's no place to raise a family.* When he found his mind groping with a growing lust for the future the man he had become demanded action.

Weeks later, he'd become aware of a new habit. He was looking out of the shop window to see if Tess might be passing his barber pole. It was worse than an itch. Only in church would his eyes find Tess where he could only nod a polite but warm hello. When that earned him a hello, he wished the accompanying smile were not the same as given to other male churchgoers.

Finally, he turned the next corner in life's opportunities.

Perhaps, Signorina Tess is still free due to Poppa Pento's influential and questionable ties.

Perhaps, no man dares knock upon Signore Pento's door. If that's the case, I will do it. At least I have a chance and will be especially careful so that people will not misunderstand my approaching Pento. Tess is a gem in a questionable fortress.

Gene and most of Little Italy's neighborhood knew about the chauffeured, shining cars that frequented the Pento's. The why all supposed about, but no one really knew or dared not say.

Some of Officer Danaher's unsubstantiated remarks about Pento's possible business ties and Madre's mean-spirited ones placed a cautious fence around any thoughts and actions Gene planned.

Whatever Pento's business, it did not take place in the neighborhood.

As an Italian, Gene understood the troubling implications, for the Mafia is a reality, but he was not frightened by the prospect and relied on his reputation and skills where honor would clear the way. And so his thoughts sought his chances.

I am a self-made man, and Senor Pento will honor that if I approach him with the traditional respect due a father. His reputation assures that. But still I must be careful. There can be no other ties to his world.

I am sure I can refuse any compromise and not jeopardize my own position in the community. I will seek Papa Bear. He chuckled to himself. *I will ask permission to court Tess. Until I have his decision, I will tell no one, especially not Madre. I can only hope Tess will not think me too old. My God, I'm not. I am only twenty-three.*

Pento, about forty in age, stood six feet tall with a head of wavy, salt-and-peppered black hair. This strong, broad-shouldered, handsome man dressed impressively in crisp white suits, whatever the time of year. One could envision Pento on a southern plantation. This mysterious man's physical strength was earned through the hard work and disciplines found on New York's ever busy docks, though his trade like Gene's was barbering. On the docks he soon found himself in touch with and in league with unexpected opportunities.

One afternoon, Pento was not surprised to hear Tess asking to talk to him, and the tone of her voice told him what to expect.

Poppa Pento came from around his desk, thinking, *When did we, fools, decide that a female child is a woman at thirteen. Eh, we are out of our minds.*

Pento accepted Tess's kiss with a happy heart but troubled mind while listening to all she had to say again.

"Poppa, I know I've been repeating everything I've said to you before, but it means so much to me. I want to give Momma and you grandchildren while there's still time for Momma to enjoy them. Please." Her hand rested on his forearm as they sat on a settee.

"Oh, Tess, your momma and I know you should not marry just to have children. Why this rush. You have been truly well such a short time?"

"Oh, Poppa, I know marriage is more than that. I'm no longer a child, and it is right for me, truly. I seek a good man, one who cares for me and people, someone who will love our children the way you love me. That is what I want."

"Hmmm. Your momma and your uncle Murph argue for you, and I have not agreed with them." He stopped, took a breath, and said, "But I am wondering if I should relent."

Poppa kissed her cheek, saying, "I do not believe this right for you." Words failed him, and the room seemed to close around him like an airtight closet. He needed time to think more about it, but business demanded he clear the house for an important meeting.

His tone changed from father to all business. "Tess, we will discuss this again, but right now, I want you to take the other children to Aunt Rose until I send for you. I am expecting visitors."

"Of course, Poppa, but—"

"Hush, Tessa, I think I understand, but we must talk about the kind of men so I can consider it further. This is not an easy thing." He met her troubled hazel eyes so like his own. "We will have dinner with Momma upstairs later."

"Poppa, after I take the boys to Aunt Rose, may I go see Fr. Fratella to see who needs help and to discuss our conversation with him."

"Hmmm. Must you use him against me too?" It was said in jest and with a warm smile.

Tess kissed him again. He watched her leave and found himself feeling saddened more than he had at any other time in his life except for his wife's illness.

In minutes, the Pento children were gone, and soon, the shiny black limousines arrived. Poppa was a man his family knew little about, but he made them all feel safe and loved while being silent about knowing he could be very dangerous.

Gene properly arranged for the needed meetings. He left them knowing they reeked of a father's reluctance to introduce him to Tess. But the caring father, in an attempt to help his daughter find happiness, acknowledged Tess wanted to marry and have a large family. Pento could refuse her nothing, but Pento made himself very clear.

"My daughter will make up her own mind. I will speak for neither you nor the young doctor asking to court our Tess. Why you should both appear at the same time is beyond me?"

Gene's surprise showed, but he remained silent knowing Pento was not finished with him.

"Manfredi, understand that she is our gift from God. Harming her is an affront to all her mother and I believe in. If you were to harm her, I would deal with you personally."

Pento came around from his desk and stood towering over Gene who met his stern gaze with a fully aware and piercing calm and listening while intently viewing the first mountain he must climb to find his way home. Pento continued with, "Any man hurting Tessa would not live to regret it." He paused for a second and added, "Since my wife's illness prevents her taking your measure, I will be twice as careful. In my eyes, no man is fit to be Tessa's husband."

Gene accepted the threat wondering what man would be fool enough to physically hurt Tess knowing Pento would kill him but believing he could never hurt any woman, he felt no danger.

Pento returned to his desk and said, "Gene, you may walk with her on Sunday afternoon while another walks with her on Saturday. Whether she will walk with you again is entirely up to her."

Though not bothered by the threat, accepted it would be deserved if he brought her any harm and knew the mountain would create a landslide that would damn his river of life.

Still he felt hammered by his reactions to finding he was not alone in the quest and that the doctor was to walk with her first.

It troubled him, so he spoke to Officer Danaher saying only that he was curious about him and wondered if the many brothers were testing a sister's suitors. Liking the boys, he'd be ready for their neighborhood antics.

A few days later, Danaher said, "Gene, there's nothing on the bucko officially, but he is well known in Sicilian League circles as a handsome lad who worked hard to become a doctor. I asked a detective friend Joseph Petrosino about the lad. Petrosino is our finest source on the league. What he said is he's proving to be his own man and the lass could do lots worse. Tis glad I was to hear that, for Tessa is a rare jewel."

"Si, you are right."

Gene thanked his friend, and when Danaher got to the door, he stopped to add, "Gene, tis also said he has a way with the ladies." Danaher's knowing glance told him, Danaher knew he had visited Pento and was wishing him luck. The Irishman laughed and Gene flushed.

As the door closed, Gene took a moment before opening the shop to think. *Signore Pento meant every word he said, so it's between the handsome beau and me. A doctor may prove the greater attraction for a kindhearted woman, but with luck, the intelligente uno can win. If he favors the ladies, then it's an even battle. I believe it is important to know what she wants. If he is truly a man of medicine, it would explain why he spoke for Tess who loves so many. In that case, he and I are thinking alike.*

Gene suddenly wanted to hurry the next step while dreading what first must be done.

Day after tomorrow, I will walk with Tess for the first time. It's time to tell Madre.

He realized that the beau's Sicilian connections held no threat but would add considerable fuel to familial doubts, for Madre hated Pento's black-hand contacts and his hidden activities while fiercely believing the worst. Her experience as a child made her privy to much Mafia evil, never forgotten it deeply made her much that she is.

It's fortunate Pento is not going to make the decision for Tess. But I'll never know the why of that. I hoped my reputation would favor me. I am truly grateful that Tess is sent away when the limousines come.

Madre screamed, "Gene, you cannot. You dishonor us. He is working for the devil. I forbid it."

"Madre, this is a man's business that you can say nothing about." Gene waited for that to take effect, for Madre knew well how the Italian world worked.

Silence and a chilling stare were her only answer. Gene continued firmly.

"I will never dishonor us. I have kept my word of honor in every sense, and it is time I marry and have a family. But nothing is decided, for there are two of us seeking Tess's hand, and Senor Pento is refusing to make the decision for her. The other walks with her tomorrow, and I walk with her on Sunday."

Madre stood, turned, and left the room and refused to speak to him except to make the demands she felt due her knowing Gene would fulfill them. At the doorway, she said, "Figlio mia, familia ignominia, stabbato figlia mia! It oozed in bitterness."

Gene felt wasted while Antonio shrugged his shoulders, wished Gene luck, and said, "Madre will never forgive you. Not only because of Pento but because Tess is beautiful and well liked. Still it is a fine choice, brother."

Gene nodded and said, "Madre will change her mind once she has grandchildren." Gene did not notice how Antonio flinched.

Antonio put his hand on Gene's shoulder and said a serious "Good night, fratello" and left remembering the mistakes he'd made that Madre had yet to forgive. *I still hear about them, and I hate it.* He flushed with the realization of the true meaning behind his thought.

In that unknown place, Madre's saddened watcher did nothing for free will was the only way, while her dark watcher smiled and moved closer for her hatred welcomed his cruel whisperings.

Sunday came and many more that allowed Tess to walk the neighborhood with her beaus, doing much her way.

Gene walked proudly beside her on Sunday afternoons, though Tess was two inches taller. His working on Saturday left him little time to watch for her and his competition.

His fashionable air honed by a caring approach earned Tess's friendship as it had with the ladies of the neighborhood. Meanwhile, the other young man, handsome and wiser in the romantic finesse that pleasures and tempts a woman, found much to give Tess that she enjoyed while sharing many topics.

Gene spent time valuing her opinions and discussing many new thoughts with her and expanded it to include many new facilities and cultural progress New York had to offer.

Though Tess enjoyed the discussions, the doing of it seemed unimportant when there were serious things she intended in her life style.

Gene felt secure that he would win the lady's choice. Gene never learned in his hardworking youth or in the wide talents his father had instilled of those all-important inner workings of a female so essential to the sustaining of a fine marriage. It was definitely not the strong point of the men of his time, and his intense insistence on respect before all things threatened much he had to understand and appreciate to truly be happy.

Still their time together as friends allowed an area of honesty that brought much still missing seem possible, in facing the difficulties presented by the parents they had.

Gene realized and enjoyed her clear thinking and the way she faced reality. Any presents he gave her were small treasures while the younger man sent the more romantic flowers and other feminine pleasures.

One Saturday, Tess openly worried about a new family in the neighborhood and said, "Someone should help."

The tall, handsome beau commented genuinely, "Tess, if I am your husband and you wish to help someone, you will be free to do so. And I will see that you have the means to."

The very next day, on a walk with Gene, she exclaimed, "Oh, Gene, those poor children. Fr. Fratella says they are going hungry. They look like they haven't eaten in weeks. How can people see this and not help? Someone must."

"Tess, no one can take care of the whole world." There was no missing the fury that lit her beautiful hazel eyes, as he added, "There are just too many who really don't care about the poor, only about what they themselves can have."

The soft quality to Gene's statement without any personal response to reassure her confused Tess, so it irked her, and she came back with, "Gene, people have to try. That's why God put us here." Tess raised herself as high above him as she could and added, "I will always choose to take care of those who touch my small part of the world. How can people bring new life into the world without caring for those already here?"

"I agree, I don't understand that either, Tess." He was nodding seriously but hid a smile and a distraction in tipping his hat to two pretty neighbors who lived in his apartment house. In acknowledging them both, he received warm smiles in return.

When Gene turned to Tess, her strong look of disappointment could not be missed, and Gene didn't know whether to smile or say something. It was now his turn to be confused.

Il che. Is it my words about helping or my tipping my hat to a pretty woman?

Neither said anything to clarify the moment, and when he took Tess home, he bid her a gentle good night, only to leave her very troubled. When he asked her to see him next Sunday, her answer was full of hesitation. As he walked toward home, he stopped under a tree, sat on its bench, and thought his way to what he could do to reach Tess. In moments, he realized his answer to Tess's question had been less than complete, and he headed for Murphy's Grocery Store even though it was out of his way.

If this doesn't work—but Tess is a smart lady. My mistake is we should have done it together, but it's too late for that. Murphy is a good friend of Senor Pento, and we met at a social club, so he'll probably remember me. Tess told me that Murphy and her Poppa grew up together, that they worked the docks together and maintained a strong relationship in spite of choosing separate paths, and that she was very fond of the Irishman. He's familia. She also said her brother, the first of her five, is named Murph and was the Irishman's godchild. The decision sent troubling thoughts scampering through his mind but decided that Tess's desire for children and a home of her own would be more than enough to ensure her happiness. *What else could a woman truly want?*

In an age where women's role seemed clearly defined, it somehow didn't seem necessary to him to consult with the woman most affected by the decision.

The grocery door's bell rang out announcing Gene arrival. Mr. Murphy looked up and said, "Hello, Manfredi. My missus tells me you and Tess are taking longer walks. Does that mean it's going to cost me a wedding present?" The question lacked any definable emotion for or against Gene's quest, so he hesitated to answer, thinking, *I'm being slow.*

He rushed to answer, "I'm not the only man she walks with, Mr. Murphy."

Murphy's face gnarled.

Gene felt a little better knowing Murphy didn't like the other beau or at least his affiliations. *Now if only you'll support my idea.*

Gene said, "Mr. Murphy, I've come to request a favor." Then he rushed to explain because Murphy gave him a glare that clearly meant he mistrusted favors. He leaped into the explanation of what he wanted to avoid any misunderstanding.

Murphy said, "Give me a few minutes to take care of some customers while I think about it."

Gene stepped out of the way wishing the customer well as he did.

Murphy took care of four customers but also took in Gene's manner and attitude. Gene rightly began to think, *Jesus, he's making me wait deliberately. I don't know if that's good or bad. My hands are sweating.*

Finally, Murphy called his son out from the back stockroom and told him to take over for a few minutes. The young man was startled at seeing Gene there but smiled at him. Gene quickly and softly greeted him with a simple "Hello, Kenny" while noting that Murphy was walking away and immediately followed him to the only clutter in the tidy store, a group of unopened fresh vegetables. Murphy turned to face Gene and sat on a case of cabbages to say, "All right, Gene. I understand why you want to do this, and because I see no hurt in it to Tess, I'll keep your secret. But I warn you as I'm sure her father has. She's special don't hurt her."

Gene swallowed hard, discussed the best of what was needed, and followed the Irishman to the counter to take care of the favor.

The next day, Murphy looked up and smiled at a frequent visitor who rarely came on Monday's because she normally accompanied her mother to the doctor on Monday's.

"Tess, what are you doing here today? Is your momma all right?"

"Not really, Uncle Murphy. The doctor will be coming to her from now on."

"I'm sorry, child. What do you need?"

"Just an answer to a question."

Murphy came around the counter to stand close to her, as she said, "I stopped by to offer some help to that nice Rizzo family to see what they needed. Fr. Fratella told me how ill the mother is, but he wasn't sure what they needed most. I was on my way to see her to find out exactly what she needed, and then I planned on coming to you as usual. Only I met Kenny coming down the stairs after delivering a large bushel of food to them. Who sent it?"

Kenny heard his name mentioned and popped up from behind a counter where he was repairing a damaged shelf and said, "Hi, Tess," and ducked right back down for catching his father's go away glare.

Murphy answered the question brusquely, "Sorry, Tess, I can't tell you that."

"Or won't?" said softly, it was still a challenge.

"Tess, you know me better than that. I've given my word."

"I'm sorry, Uncle Murphy. I just want to be sure I pick the right man?"

"You assume too much. You apparently think it was one of your beaus?"

"Because I hoped they would." Tess wanted to do battle, but her love for the man called Murphy demanded respect.

Murphy busied himself hoping to escape Tess's compelling look but decided the truth was the best defense.

"I'm sorry, girl. I cannot discuss this."

"Uncle Murphy, you wouldn't want me to marry someone who doesn't understand kindness because it's a part of himself, would you?" She leaned against the counter while he filled a bag of beans never taking her eyes off his face.

The caring grocer began to understand, regretted his promise, and wondered what the chances were Tess would be there the few seconds it took his son Kenny to deliver the basket of food.

Holy saints, why have you laid such a trap for me?

He wanted to crawl into the bag to hide from her snaring cat-like-hazel eyes and—suddenly understanding—said, "You put the lads to a test, didn't you, girl?"

Their eyes met as Tess flushed and said, "Yes."

"Tis a smart girl you are, but I still can't break my word."

Murphy hated her upset, so he tried to make her laugh.

"Besides, chose the wrong man, and I'll just have him shot. Then you can marry the right one."

Tess smiled without mirth and flexed to serious again. "Choosing is so hard." Tears filled her eyes, but she refused their shedding.

"Take your time, Tess." Murphy reached out touching her shoulder reassuringly. "Your poppa hasn't chosen them for you. They came to him. You are the one who wishes to marry. Your father won't allow anyone or anything to pressure you. As your godfather, I am doing the same. You don't have to take either boyo. Wait, there will be others." The last was emphatic.

She shook her head and said, "Time passes so quickly. You're sure you won't tell me." She told no one that she feared her illness would come back and deprive her of a future in the way it deprived her of years of doing. It was a fear rushing her to have the babies she longed for.

"Holy saints! Tess, I can't. I regret it, but I can't." Murphy's flush of anger hurt them both.

"Oh, Uncle Murphy, I know so little about choosing a man. Dreams are not like this."

Her lingering sigh revealed such confusion Murphy needed to find a way to help her. As Tess withdrew, she said, "I'm sorry, Uncle Murph, I shouldn't have asked. I'll see you at dinner Sunday."

Tess's resigned acceptance of his words galled Murphy. As the bell announced her exit, he called out, "Tess, the next time you walk with Manfredi, tell him something for me."

Tess stopped.

"Tell him, I'm going to let him cut my hair this week. I think I need a change."

Tess was befuddled for a moment. Murphy's hair had obviously been recently cut.

The moment allowed the message to filter into their conversation and become realization. *He'd never go to to him for a haircut... unless...* She blew him a kiss and gave him a beautiful smile that made her hazel eyes gleam with delight. The big Irishman blushed as she left, and Kenny was finally able to get off his knees, giving his father an impish smile of approval.

Murphy eyed his son and laughingly said, "Back to work, you Irish bumpkin."

Angry voices heard from the Manfredi apartment were rare. Today, only Italian was being spoken.

Madre chose now to break her silence with rants about Tess in hope of pulling the strings she used to control Gene as a boy to control the man he had become.

"You cannot marry the daughter of a Sicilian gangster."

"Madre! Tess is innocent of whatever her father does, and we don't know what he does. You have been unfair to her from the day we began walking out." Gene was fighting a rare anger.

"Are you blind?" Madre spit.

"Mother of God, you think I dishonor us. I will never ask favors of Signore Pento. There has been no favor in my asking to walk with Tess. Besides, Tess has not decided." Gene could do nothing about the fact that his mother was expecting him to spend much of his life catering to her, for believing he must do just that.

Madre was relentless, and while she raged, Gene lost himself in thought. *Padre, if I allow this, I will honor you, but if Tess accepts me, then I will be dishonoring her.* Being distracted and without having an answer, he sadly returned to listening to Madre's bruising drone.

"This Tessa, she is not stupido. She will choose you. But marry this girl, and I will never enter your house."

Gene, full of turbulence, walked away. The disrespect galled him, and he stopped. A father's words burned him to the spot. "Promise me you will honor your mother. She has loved me well. Promise me."

All the feelings of childhood and that deathbed vow returned to grip his mind like a tree full grown between two giant boulders preventing his pulling the roots for transplant. It never occurred to him that the vow was wrong or revisable.

Without turning around, Gene leaned into the wall and said, "Madre, should Tess accept me and if you do not come to our home, which will not be here, then I will come to yours, as will your grand-children. But Tess will not. And, Madre, the dishonor will be yours, if you do not respect our marriage on the day we marry, if we marry?"

His promise, to care for her no matter what, had allowed Madre to maneuver some of Gene's strings even after he reached manhood. As a man committed to both marrying and Madre, he sought to forge a bond between the man he was and the child within. Though an honorable man, he was yet to realize the vow knotting him to Padre was so tight even Richard's great sword would not cut it.

So he decided. "Padre, I will always keep my promise, but if Tess says yes, I will put Madre in a place of her own and see her every day, and she will never enter our home."

Madre advised both sons she wished to be escorted to more social club events. Apparently, Madre had plans of her own.

Being deprived of Gene's full attention, she wanted another full-time male in her life. That, she had to work at finding.

Elsewhere, a watcher learned more, but there was no answer to free will's determinate, and Gene's decision was made. He could do nothing to help while her dark watcher smiled at Madre's direction. He had he high hopes for her future deeds.

Before much else could happen, Tess's mother died, and the sadness took the Pento family into a period of solitude. Both suit-ors attended all services, and Gene watched Tess more intently than before, more beautiful than before. Seeing her in black made it a color he never wanted to see again and he feared her changing her mind about seeking a family of her own for being needed at home. That didn't happen. Aunt Rose came to help and would stay until some change occurred.

Pento, in keeping with his wife's wishes, kept the mourning period short and sent both beaus notes letting them know they could call upon Tess again.

Madre had been right. Tess chose Gene, but before Gene could officially pop the question, he must again seek Poppa Pento's permission and explain his position with Madre first to Tess then to her father but only after he seriously forewarned Tess.

On their next walk, Gene chose a small but lovely neighborhood park with the laughter of children so loved by Tess. It was a pleasant place to discuss his hope for marrying her while needing to discuss Madre's bitter approach to it.

Tess listened saying nothing and quietly waited for him to finish. He finished with, "That is what my father asked of me and what I must do as a man."

"Gene, we've talked of our parents and who and what they are as friends do, but now it's very different."

"Si Cara Mia, it is." Gene sat up straighter to listen.

The personal endearment from Gene for the first time sounded right to her, but she was worried because there could be deserved criticism of his madre's hatred. "I don't know if your mother is wrong about my father's business, but I have never seen him do anything wrong. None of us know about the men in the cars. I don't want to know, though his opinions in politics and about people are," she hesitated, "very powerful. All I know is I love him dearly and he would do anything for any of his children and that will include his grandchildren. As long as I don't know about the cars, I will never allow that part of his life to touch my children just as Poppa has never let it touch any of us. I also know that what your mother asks of you is wrong. And if she dislikes me, how can we hope to be happy."

Gene was shaken by her capacity to express herself. "Tess, I cannot break my vow."

"I understand that. In a husband, I wouldn't want a man who didn't keep his word. My poppa would never break his word."

"True, Tess, very true."

"Oh Gene, I don't understand much about your mother. I know you know the difference between right and wrong. I guess it frightens me for I have done nothing to hurt her. I just can't grasp why she would hate me so."

Jesus, she thinks like a woman twice her age. The thought was full of pride in someone he desired. The feeling saturated his answer.

"I don't either. Obviously, we don't know much about our parents, but I want you for my wife, and I can promise you that Madre will not enter our home, not ever. But I must ask you to understand my taking our children to see her, if you can see your way to doing that I will do everything in my power to make you a good husband and make life as easy for you as possible. Please take time to think this over before I ask you officially to accept my proposal. I must also tell your father. I was wrong not telling him initially about Madre."

Gene was puzzled by her silence marked by a subdued expression, only to realize she was watching the children nearby and waited.

Finally, she turned, and this time, it was the sad smile he'd seen so often since her mother's death and longed to hold her. Instead, he listened with trepidation to, "Gene, he will not be surprised. The decision is mine, so do not speak to Poppa of this. I will think more about it, but if I decide we should marry, I will explain to Poppa that I insisted on doing it this way."

"Tess, it only right that I tell him. It is a matter of respect."

"Only what I want will make a difference, so whatever you say will not help. I will tell him that you wanted to and that I insisted you not. Besides, it's not necessary. Both Poppa and I know of your mother's hatred. She's left no doubt about it in speaking to neighbors and friends, even Fr. Fratella. You know how parish people share information. Secrets are easily passed along."

Gene nodded in acceptance and said in a husky voice, "Would you have married the doctor?"

Tess's head inclined in decision, took another glance at the children, turned to look him in the eye, and said, "No."

There was a tone in that simple word that told Gene the subject was closed.

Gene's head dropped for a moment, and he said, "Thank you, Tess. You make me very proud."

He took her hand, and they returned to her home.

Now Gene and Tess walked on both Saturday and Sunday and her other beau was seen with another lovely lady.

After many troubling moments, Gene finally asked Tess to marry him. And Tess—so young and still in the grip of sadness surrounding her mother's death, wanting to believe in Gene, his feelings for her and above all wanting a family—said, "Yes."

Gene spoke to Signore Pento and received his still reluctant blessing, and the date was set.

By then, it was late in the evening, and the stores were closed, but Gene rushed to the home of a jeweler friend. "Kurt, please, just put on your pants and hurry. Please, I have to buy a proper ring. Tessa and I are getting married."

Kurt laughed all the way to the store and teased Gene mercilessly. It was worth the trip to see his too serious friend beg.

Gene quickly ensconced Madre in a fine nearby apartment and apologized to Antonio for leaving him alone with Madre. Madre made new friends at social club activities her sons escorted her to, and since she was still a woman who could quicken a pulse, the Manfredi men had hopes she might change.

While it raised Gene's hopes for Madre finding happiness, Antonio understood Madre and wished his brother could see their mother's selfishness more clearly.

At fifteen, Tess became a bride, and at twenty-five, Gene became a husband.

At the wedding reception, Papa Pento raised his glass to Madre Manfredi with gracious politeness enhancing his charming personality while further alienating Madre Manfredi.

Madre inclined her head and smiled but had no intention of surrendering a son without a fight and callously acknowledged losing this moment to a devil but knew the wedding was not the right time to win a challenge.

Malcontent, she intended to reclaim her son, and she had the tenacity to try one day at a time.

Tess had told her father about Gene's vow before they married and knew Gene would keep his word that Madre would neither live nor visit with Tess and Gene.

Poppa initially respected Gene's vow, and on the day of the wedding, Pento tried to please Gene's mother with problem-free attentions to further family relations but found her foul disposition too unpleasant to bend and wondering what dark force of past Mafia doings had birthed her hatred souring her life and now deepening his own capacity for vehemence because it threatened Tess.

In short time, Madre's over-the-top tirades would reach Pento only to fuel his ever watchful caring for Tess. He too was a man who kept his promises.

Gene and Tess agreed New York was not the place to raise children and chose to move to the country where Gene opened a barbershop in that city called Yonkers. Their move joined the slow exodus from New York to Yonkers and points north. Poppa was waiting for Manfredi to buy a home and planned on moving north to live somewhere near Tess.

To start, Gene found a perfect location and leased a shop in Petersen's Hotel on an Avenue called Nepperhan and an apartment for them but a block away at the foot of a popular area known as The Hill.

Yonkers in 1905 was a growing, lively community lined with trees with centers of business and nationalities spread across its hills and valleys that ran to the Hudson on the west, the Bronx River on the east, and the Bronx borough on the south while the northern border was giving birth to many small towns and their county seat.

The area was homed in an expanse of wilderness where you could collect wild berries and mushrooms, stop for a drink of water at a natural spring coursing from the fertile earth, and catch a bounty of sea life in the rivers and streams within its borders. The people drawn to this area were a collection of many different plants that would bear the fruit of many nationalities.

Petersen's, the center for community activities frequented by the influential people of the city, was located at the foot of that stand of nature called The Hill directly across from one of the city's largest commercial enterprises, Alexander Smith's Carpet Shop, along the Saw Mill River. Gene's hotel barbershop was an excellent location. The carpet-manufacturing firm filled four city blocks and employed hundreds. The other large industrial sights—Otis Elevator and The Sugar Factory, both were beside the Hudson River where the New York Central Rail Road bordered the river's enhancing his decision on location for its access to New York City.

The Hill that towered above Petersen's had three ascending streets where it flattened at top for a quarter of a mile before dropping sharply to the western beaches of the Hudson River opposite the marvelous Palisades on the New Jersey side. Atop The Hill sat Broadway running from the city's northern line to its southern border and continuing into New York City. The steep riverside of The Hill homed large estates of the rich who kept houses in the country on the leveling out shoreline of the Hudson River. It was an ideal way to escape the heat of New York City during the summer. Even in 1905, the shoreline at the river's edge was becoming a granite-like garden widening its shore line. The river border was being sought for building estates, the abundance of river food and its natural path for commercial traffic. Both sides of the hill included sets of stairs appearing on the inclines permitting pedestrians an easier traverse up The Hill's steep inclines between work and home.

The Hill was the beginning of the chain that became the Catskills and Adirondacks connecting the length of New York State to Canada.

In times past Yonkers was a bountiful, well-cared-for home of the American Red Man; for oh, so long before the white man came. Nepperhan Avenue was named for the Nappeckamak Indians, while the city itself took its name from an early Dutch settler, all whom had used the Saw Mill River to paddle to the Hudson River in seeking adventures or in the doing of everyday chores.

Tess, a bride without culinary skills, found laughter and creativity in Gene's range of tutelage. The five Pento men bravely dared her cuisine, relished, and came back for more while the couple nested themselves in seeking a family.

Their growing to know each other was unmarred initially because Madre kept her promise never to enter their home but quickly followed them to Yonkers, with Gene's encouragement, and found an apartment on the hill, and Gene continued to fulfill his vow daily.

Madre had succeeded in planting a destructive kernel in the garden of life Tess and Gene planned to cultivate. It was a damaged seed that would prove able to grow and spread its taint even beyond their own generation.

In time, Gene found an odd but large house on the east side of The Hill that brought Tess joy for the many rooms she intended to fill with children. She was carrying their first child as they visited the house in its unfinished state hoping it would become home. Sadly this child was not to be.

This house they would call home, had two apartments, with three stories of rooms above a ground-level cellar that had originally been a stable for horses. The only remnants of which were large hooks hanging from the ceiling beams. The building was constructed right into the stone of The Hill. They planned to fill the lower seven-room, two-floor apartment with children and rent the top floor with its indoor toilet. The house was plumbed for heat, had a full bathroom in their apartment and an unusual toilet off the kitchen downstairs. Gene was especially interested in the cellar for storage that would help Tess as their family grew and allow him to store much that would earn or save them money.

The sound of children reached them as they viewed the bathroom on the second floor. They went to the window, and as Tess looked up the hill at the children playing on the street above, she imagined what their children would look like and the house was suddenly home and said, "Oh, Gene, our babes will have many playmates. This will do fine."

"Good. Then I'll have a set of stairs built up to Orchard Street with a fence so the children have a yard and you can easily get there." Her pleased smile made Gene feel proud, so he offered her his hand as they took the corner to home.

The streets on the eastern side began atop with High Street, housed mostly by Irish, the street below, Vineyard Avenue sheltered Italians, a bathhouse, a fire company, a neighborhood store/house, and spring of fresh drinkable water. Just below was Orchard Street where they would live and be the first Italians there, right at the top of the arcing street. It was here that, many of Gene's customers lived; on the down-sides of Orchard street. One side Irish the other side Polish. Soon the factory workers would be living in tenements being built by the owners of the factory complete with heat and indoor plumbing. Of course, there were those who would call them Wops and other fighting words. Naturally the Manfredi brood, once here would loudly use the battle cry words, Mick and Pollack.

It was a time when nationalities felt threatened by the closeness of another heritage. Some prideful and argumentative of what they left behind and insisting offspring stayed within their own in all things. Once in the house Tess greeted every day with just being herself. She soon had the neighborhood children as her friends just as she had in New York. One day she hooked up a hose, ran it to the front yard to offer the children a safe play area, a treat in the summer heat and found a way for the many youngsters lacking indoor facilities to have a shower. Through the children most hostile neighbors came to see Tess through their eyes while their husbands came home with knowledge of the generous barber. Gene and Tess grew into this new world honoring the decision that nationalities did not matter at the shop or at home. For now; business and friendships were to be measured on the yardstick of respect. At least, not until their children choose to marry. Then they too would marry Italians, and though Gene and Tess had no desire for the old country, it was an imperfect beginning to the meaning of being American.

As in every generation, their children would challenge the arrangement in many ways as the young were always intended to do, hopefully for the better.

Petersen's Hotel, directly across from the Alexander Smith Carpet Factory, offered Gene the ideal because he could trade his services as bartender, vintner, and cook between acquiring heads to shear and cheeks to shave in a room with a private entrance right next to the entrance to the three-story hotel. His clients could pass from his shop right into the hotel's gathering place with its beautiful wooden bar and restaurant. The location also gave Gene usable lessons in the politics of the area and showed him where and how he could quickly move into an arena called success. He was smack-dab in the middle of the city's growing social and political scene.

One evening, as he cleaned off the excess head of a cold beer he asked his customer, "Mr. Mahoney, you're a plant manager. How many people are now employed at the factory?"

"Better than a thousand, Gene. Kinda offers yee a goodly business once the folk know yer here."

He answered with a smile, "I think you're right, sir." And he added the thought, *If I wisely select the social clubs to join, it will not be long before it all becomes as it should be. I must remember to bring Tess the basil she needs.*

In the political machine dominated by the city's large Irish community, he found those he could admire and some he could not, but he played the game of life in a way to serve his business and family well.

In short time he found himself fishing in the Hudson with influential people of means while his toes tingled with cold. At riverside, they landed large sturgeon, sea bass, perch, and flounder, along with eels and crabs. The river's bounty seemed endless. On one occasion, Gene was having a hapless day when the tug on his fishing pole nearly pulled him off the rocks he stood on. It was a cold day, and a factory employee said, "Bring it in, Gene." Someone else yelled, "Hey, Wio, you've got a big one. Pull!"

Gene hauled and found it taking time and muscle he didn't know he had. When the fish broke the surface, he yelled, "Oh, Mio, it's an enormous sturgeon." With help, he pulled it ashore. When it measured thirty-six inches long, weighing sixteen pounds, the masculine bragging began as newfound friends congratulated the stocky barber who soon told his chair captives the story in a way that made them laugh.

Someone called for a picture of the magnificent seafarer's sacrifice surrounded by Gene and others. The picture—fish, fisherman, and hecklers—would soon hang alongside the transplanted photo of the Indian chief in Gene's shop.

Later that month, while serving a round of drinks to the favored table of local politicians, Gene heard, "Hey, Gene boyo, when you're finished, come on over—we want to talk to you."

Gene was mystified but smiled, looked forward to it, and found himself pleasantly surprised at their suggestion.

After rushing home, he said to Tess, "And they'd like me to run for alderman. They feel the growing Italian community needs representation. I need to know how you feel about it."

Tess said, "Gene, it's flattering, but wouldn't we owe favors, like those owed to the Sicilian League?"

"Si, politics are very much that way, but it's not necessarily a bad thing."

"I know. But you have to decide, just remember we promised never to allow ourselves to become involved like that."

He hesitated to show his enthusiasm, leaned back in his chair, and remembered the dangers, and looking into Tess's troubled hazel eyes, he found himself quickly taking the corner to decision.

"Tess, we don't have to do this, but I must give them an answer, and since business at the shop has grown so quickly, I really don't need to work at the hotel anymore. I'll tell them no, but I'll stay at Petersen's a while longer to keep their friendships because it is good for business, I enjoy their favor, and I like them. Besides, I can recommend a friend who will jump at the opportunity."

Tess's eyes filled with the light of relief, and Gene felt as a man should in his own home. He led Tess to bed and turned out the light. Later, before the welcome sleep of a satisfied man, he thought, *A beautiful wife who is honest and smart too. You've done well, Manfredi, very well.* He slept without knowing that he had just planted a seed in his own garden.

Gene's people sense nurtured trade, and he soon left the hotel to tend his shop just a block away but on Nepperhan Avenue opposite one of the factory entrances.

Antonio was now married and opening a smaller shop of his own further south on Nepperhan next to a new drugstore called Jacobs Pharmacy at the cross street of Ashburton Avenue.

When the Manfredi family moved to Yonkers Madre was shortly after moved there too. Madre insisted on an apartment within blocks of Gene's shop. The lady managed to find a beau and was soon married seemingly without a change in life style. By the time the couple had found their home Madre had manipulated her familiar foothold into Gene's and Tess's lives with nail grabbing intent. She never entered their home but still reached for and won a daily doing from Gene's vow.

Poppa Pento lonely without Tess and his wife packed his boys and moved to Yonkers to be near her. Nearer than Madre for sensing Madre's plan he found a home on Vineyard Avenue on The Hill just above the Manfredi house loved being close to Tess and visited frequently. Knowing Madre's hatred Pento enjoyed rubbing salt in her enmity's wound. Madre, stopped by her own vehement words, would never be able to visit Gene and Tess. Perhaps Pento found a way to smite the Philistine.

The limousines still came, as did many newfound lady friends to cook and please this tempting man whose flourishing head of hair would soon be pure white.

One night, Poppa Pento, his oldest son Murph, and his youngest Arthur joined Gene to savor Tess's homemade pasta soaked in a rich meat sauce. It was now obvious she would surpass much Gene taught her. After the compliments, they began to tease about the baby growing in her womb.

Poppa said, "It could be a girl, Gene."

"That's all right, Poppa, as long as she is Bella like her momma."

Tess grinned as Gene continued with, "But I don't know, boys run in both families." His finger pointed at Murph and Arthur who looked up long enough to smile and take a breath between mouthfuls.

Murph took time to say, "I like the idea of having a niece. I plan on spoiling the hell out of her."

The word *hell* at the dinner table brought a punishing look from both Poppa and Gene.

Murph ducked them both. "I'm sorry, Tess. I'm just excited about the baby." Arthur, a confused young man, laughed at his brother's goof.

Tess missed the apology as a cramp, suddenly worse, took her away. In less than a breath, she went deadly pale and terrified every male at the table. She grabbed the table for support and blood stained her housedress. The dishes careened off the table, as the tablecloth followed her to the kitchen floor where everything seemed to crash atop her. The men rushed to help.

As Gene touched her, he heard her say his name before she slid into unconsciousness. Gene screamed, "Arthur; get the midwife. Merciful God in heaven—run!"

Poppa Pento reached for his daughter torturously, calling, "Tess, Tess!"

Murph stepped between the terrified father and husband, picked Tess up with the care in handling a fragile doll, and rushed her through the kitchen and dining room heading for the stairwell up to a bedroom. The narrow stairwell would not allow them through. Murph, unmindful of the blood staining his clothes, took a deep breath, lifted Tess's weight, turned side ward, and took flight.

A wordless husband and father put her to bed amid the blood flow while Murph paced. In agonizing minutes, Arthur returned with a midwife who chased them all from the room, and in a short time, a boy—they would name Tony—arrived, but he was too small to survive.

Finally allowed in the room, the men carefully sat on the bed. Father and son-in-law shivering with the experience waited for Tess to wake while a room away the midwife carefully cleaned the too small child and readied a son, a grandson for burial.

When Tess opened her eyes, she merely said, "Gene?" That one word told him what she was asking.

"Oh, Tess! He was beautiful, but he was not big enough."

She sighed and her hazel eyes loosed the salt of grieving. Gene took her hand and said, "Cara Mia, don't cry, please. We'll try again." Nodding weakly in a chilling cave of sadness, she fell asleep.

Gene didn't know what to say to a worried father and missed the mark with, "I have to tell Madre. You'll stay?"

"Where else would I be?" The vacillating anger of his fury was aimed at Gene's destination and an unseeing man who would not let go.

Gene escaped into wondering, *What can I get Tess to make her smile, perhaps…*carefully put Tess's hand aside, backed out of the room, went to his son, cried for a moment, and left.

Tess woke almost as soon as Gene's hand left hers. Poppa heard the street door close and, letting out a long sigh, said, "He's gone to tell her?" She clearly understood who he meant.

Their eyes held as a father and daughter should, and Tess said, "Poppa, she'll never come to us even when she's a grandmother. Gene doesn't understand her or why this won't change her. Imagine, she's remarried and pregnant but still insists on a box of Uneeda Biscuits from Gene every day." Her fatigue slowed her speech. "He doesn't see what she really is. It's so unfair. Oh, Poppa, I'm so tired." She fell asleep again, this time deeply and with healing.

Poppa had the thoughts of a father who could never ignore his daughter's pain.

My poor Tessa. At first, I thought it was truly because of me, but daughter, it's not. I can't say this to you, but if the bitch weren't his mother, I would put an end to the hatred. Since you are a child of God and you believe in all that you do, if I did anything wrong to change it, you would catch me in a lie as you always do, and I would lose you. I will not lose you over the likes of her.

Pento watched Tess's struggle and brushed the thought away, along with the wet curls from her forehead. Then he bowed his head.

The mystery of Pento's life style would mystify and entwine the next generation but would never be explained.

Madre Manfredi said little. Silent spews of venom after taking in the news went unseen by an upset, saddened Gene.

Madre's dark eyes were downcast as Gene paced. *I knew that daughter of the devil could not give Gino a bambino.* She patted her swollen belly housing a growing child. *Even I can give a man a boy.*

As Gene prepared to leave, she said, "Gene, non ya forget my biscotto Uneeda."

"Have I ever forgotten?" The words crumbled like a stale cracker, and though he expected them, he could still not see what there was to see.

Madre ignored his question knowing he would return the next day, biscuits in hand.

Gene escaped into the wondering of what he could get Tess to make her smile, perhaps something she can share with the children on The Hill who she loves to watch and play with. Gene dispersed his own sadness over the maze of mind that held no answers to the real problem.

Tess and Gene, so much a part of a time that lacked knowledge; they next lost a set of twin babes and another boy. It was beginning to look like Madre was right but then came their first bambina a girl named Angie and two years later a son, Tony. Followed in two years by Beth all as healthy as they come.

Gene and Tess had begun the unending lessons of parents, as they continued to expand their world in a home open to all.

The Families

Woodrow Wilson declared neutrality for the USA as World War I took a strangle hold on Europe. It was the day after when Gene had gone into New York to shop longing to visit Mexico and unable to convince Tess to join him because the revolution there had yet to be resolved. That and the rumbles of war in Europe made him decide to stay put at least for a while.

He entered the house to find seven-year-old Angie and five-year-old Tony in the midst of some efforts by Tess to help them learn to cook while young Beth, little more than a year old, slept in a nearby bassinette. Tess was obviously tired for she was just sitting and watching what appeared to Gene, as sheer home spun chaos. Angie looked up at him, misread his scowl, and quickly looked away but respectfully said hello and continued to pound away at some macaroni dough while Tony kept throwing more flour on the pile "to help" make the macaroni. Tess struggled to her feet again to greet him and his scowl yet cautioning him to, "Remember how little they are. They need to do things that help them grow. It will make life easier for us all."

Understanding the thinking Gene tried to gain Angie's favor always feeling she was angry at him, by telling her he'd bought her a beautiful hat she could wear to church. "Want to try it on."

"No, Poppa, I have to finish the macaroni because Mommy is so tired."

Gene scowled again looked at Tess harder and said, "Cara Mia, is it more than being tired?"

"No, Gene, but little Beth eats more than either of them did, and it does tire me. Dinner is ready, but I want all the children to

71

learn to enjoy their chores, but they must also learn to help each other." She laughed and added, "They are enjoying this one."

Gene's scowl deepened as his fastidious nature warred with her knowing about children more than him.

Later, they talked and he marveled at how much "my Angie" now looked like Tess.

There was little time to ponder on it because this night, as they prepared for bed, Tess said, "Oh, Gene, I'm so happy and so tired because I am pregnant again. I just wasn't sure until today. My dream of having many children is coming true. Thank you."

"Cara mia, it's my place to thank you." Gene lifted her hand and kissed it warmly.

The days rushed by, and on September 28, 1914, Gene cradled the latest Manfredi arrival in the crook of his arm, kissed his newest girl, handed her to Tess for a feeding, and called out, "Angie, Tony, Beth come meet your new sister Marian." They rushed in, pulling young Beth along and climbed on the bed to be nearer Momma, kissed Tess, and begged to hold the little chub called Marian. Each got their turn holding Marian including Beth who struggled just to get her arms around her while, an anxious Gene stood poised to quickly grab if needed.

While Tess rested, Gene found himself again in the kitchen just like on Sundays seeing to meals for their hungry, growing brood with Angie right at his side doing much Tess had already taught her and filling the kitchen with the chatter and laughter. He was proud of his oldest but spent little time with her while spending more with Tony as his father had with him.

There was much a boy must learn to become a man, and it was a man's responsibility to do this and a woman's to train the girls.

He found himself wondering how Marian, the only one so far with Tess's gleaming hazel eyes, would grow to fit into the busy scene of their more than large enough kitchen.

Holy saints, our's was a slow start, but now the children come quickly. Thank you.

There was little time to ponder such things and he gave little thought to the arrivals of his new sisters except to smile at his children being able to grow-up with their aunts, Madre's girls— Oops, no boys.

As the Kaiser's war tramped across Europe's continent, it suddenly struck, like lighting, to leap across the Atlantic Ocean with the sinking of the Lusitania.

One day, Gene saw Babe Marian sit erect and said, "Tess, its time I take Marian to Cooper's Studio on Ashburton Avenue for a formal portrait."

He watched Tess smile as she remembered the likenesses of Angie, Beth, and Tony he had made. Her smile assured Gene's doing the same with all their children.

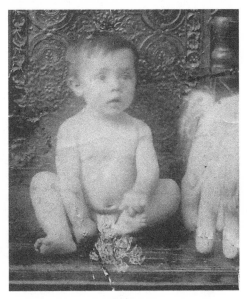

Baby

At the studio, Marian sat up straight with a tingling curiosity about for all around her and seemed to sense the importance and formality of the camera, as Cooper and Gene urged the reaction they wanted. Marian went erect in the high backed, antiqued Spanish chair and glossed being nude with a sulky and almost sexy expression very much at home in a robust child. Perhaps the mood was set by the beautiful red rose discreetly placed between her legs, or perhaps the child was foretelling the woman she was destined to become.

The same years for Raffaele Prezzemolo, were very different. She thought little of the Kaiser's war, for knowing the hell of a private one. Poverty was the all-consuming enemy. Her only weapons to meet its tearing onslaught were washing clothes, cleaning houses, and prayer. Her view from a genuine perch of goodness was in a time when many women struggled just to survive and when many still didn't recognize their true worth in a world that narrowed their everyday to unending toil.

As she stood at the coal-burning stove and made the children a cup of tea from leaves two weeks old, she choked on a sob. Gaetano's savings were gone, the children were too thin, she could no longer breastfeed young Guisseppe, and all the hard work—hers and Louis's—could barely sustain them.

Thirteen-year-old Louis wanted to help. "Mom, let me quit school. I can make a good day's pay. I can do it."

"No. You no make enough for our needs. Your poppa, he right. Here you must have school. I will find another way. I will find another way." The words coming from a troubled and spiraling mind were filled with determination.

A sad Louis said, "Okay, Mom," He watched her drift away, realizing she was repeating herself and his expression changed. He had other reasons for wanting to leave school. Nature had awakened his need to be a man on his own terms.

Raffaele made a cruel decision.

It was time. Joseph, almost three, wept as Mary and Margaret prepared to leave for the Westchester County home for children. It was a safe haven on a top a hill opposite Nepperhan Avenue nestled above the loneliness of the cemetery. Here, overlooking the carpet shop, it perched directly opposite The Hill nesting the Manfredi family.

Young Joseph could not understand why those he loved went away, yet he felt the happening as he had with Gaetano's death. He again buried his unfathomable emotions somewhere in his young growing mind.

As he watched Louis clench his fists, Young Joe instinctively moved closer to Raffaele. He watched as Mary and Margaret wept climbing into the horse cart taking them away from him. He grabbed Raffaele's leg and looked up into her face. As her hand came to rest on his head, he saw her drawn features as white as granite, staring after her girls until she could no longer see them.

He didn't understand, but it made him cry, and his grip became as desperate as his mother's.

With the girls gone, time weighed more heavily on Raffaele than the bundles of washes she cleaned in the same moments. Her faith and prayers made strength possible but did little to appease the struggle. Cousins gave what they could. Chicken feet and stale bread were the gifts that filled their bellies. Others found cleaning jobs for her.

The knowledge her girls were safe, well fed, and schooled rubbed Raffaele raw with failure. *Oh, sweet, Jesus, I have failed so miserably. All I can do is keep trying. At least my girls are safe. I thank your Blessed Mother for what they have, but this cannot go on. We are a family.*

As Joseph followed her from room to room, not letting her out of his sight, she wondered what went through his young mind. She thrived on his quick smile whenever she turned to look at him.

Blessed Mother, why is it that when I look at my youngest, I want to smile in spite of everything. Oh, Gaetano, how he grows.

As time passed without his sisters, a lonely Joseph cried and begged until Raffaele allowed him to follow Louis around the streets while lighting the city's gas lamps. Louis was glad for the company and often said, "Hey, little brother, just think you'll soon be big enough to help too." As it started getting darker, Young Joe always grabbed hold of Louis's back pocket. Louis turned and looked into Young Joe's smile. He could see Joe wasn't afraid of the dark but refused to let go of the pocket, and his fatigue would mellow. Young Joe replaced some of Louis's sadness with adulation for his older brother. It reached deep inside his older brother, making the lifting of the long rod easier. As Louis lit the next lamp thinking how tired his arms had been, he said, "Hey, Joe, be careful you don't pull my pants down, but hang on tight. Lil brother, you got somethin' the rest of us don't n' I like it."

A couple of blocks away, Raffaele left her washtub to meet them knowing Young Joe would now be tired and to allow Louis the freedom to quickly finish and get home.

Though tired and lonely, Raffaele could not deprive the boys of her strong, loving influence and shared whatever time she could with them. Once home, Young Joe usually went to sleep, begging to be awoken when Louis came home and then she would leave her washtub to sit with them over an inadequate supper and bless them when they went to bed. Young Joe usually fell asleep at the table. They took turns carrying him to bed, and then Raffaele would tuck them both in. Her strong calloused hand stroked their tired faces with affection as she bent and kissed them good night.

Raffaele rushed toward every Sunday for seeing her girls was a spring day no matter the season.

"Come, ragazzos. Today, we see Mary and Margaret. And when we are able to get them home, I will do all I can to make it up to them."

For too many months, no matter the weather, they walked down The Hill, took the small bridge at the icehouse to cross the Saw Mill River, and climbed through the cemetery to the next hilltop to spend the whole day with the growing, changing girls. After long months of listening to the chatter, the heart-sore mother realized she was missing the most important time in Mary and Margaret's growing. The girls shared their bountiful lunch with their brothers while Raffaele took very little and made another decision. Later, her hands again in wash water, she told a cousin of the decision and went over it in her mind again and again.

Blessed Mother, I must marry someone who brings home a good wage but only if I can bring the girls home. Tomorrow, I will speak to all the cousins, but first, Guisseppe must start school tomorrow in clean clothes. Eh, he is so excited.

In a few days, the cousins began a search.

An excited five-year-old Joe entered School #9. The school sat squarely on the south plateau at the top of The Hill.

On the first day of school, Raffaele walked Joe there, before going on to clean a house. Joseph lingered only a moment to watch her leave and then joined others waiting to go in, mindful of her last words to honor his teachers. He was so excited he was almost dancing while chatting with all those near him. It never occurred to him to be upset for not having any shoes simply because he didn't have any.

He liked his teacher's smile and had no idea that his teacher sending him to the principal's office was bad. He just did what he was told, and he was determined to be a good boy.

Joe sat on the wooden bench swinging his feet back and forth and smiled at anyone passing by while his mind flew to the wonders fed by imagination and realities of being in school. Everything seemed possible, then he heard the principal kindly say, "Hello, Joseph, please come in." The door closed behind him. Today, he would learn a lifelong lesson.

The devastation in Europe, after almost two years of war, called for conscripting more American troops and local Dough Boys left for camp from the station in the heart of Yonkers called Getty Square at the southwest end of The Hill.

Marian's Family

Joe's Family

The people of Yonkers and other nearby towns lined Getty Square to see them off. The Manfredi brood waved the Stars and Stripes and looked closely as they filed by. Angie, Beth, and Tony called out the names of marching friends. Poppa Pento held Tess's arm while they too, canvassed the marchers.

Poppa let go, yelling, "Tess, there he is. There's Murph."

Tess's tears tainted her raised voice calling out her endangered brother's name. Shifting Marian to his shoulder, Gene waved, as the children screeched, "Uncle Murph, Uncle Murph." Murph was now a man in uniform and a new bridegroom. At the train, he blew kisses at his nieces and nephews while holding a young wife's trembling hand. The family's national sense of danger had become personal.

One night, after the gas lamps were lit for the night, Raffaele greeted her son Louis with hot tea, stale bread, and a declaration in mind that included Young Joseph who always came to sit at the table with them. Tonight, she encouraged Young Joe to remain silent until she explained.

"Mr. LaQuido, the hod carrier and I will marry, and your sisters Mary and Margaret will come home. Mr. LaQuido is a good man, a kind man and will be your father, and you will respect him as your father." Raffaele understood Louis's worried look, but they had talked of what was needed, and she knew he would accept whatever it meant to him for the good of the family, and since he had shared his wish to see the world, it had helped her make the decision and perhaps help her oldest to find his way to manhood.

The joy of the girls soon coming to a home where food and kindness would be plentiful made it a good time, but it wasn't perfect.

The marriage was a simple one at Mount Carmel and LaQuido as quiet, gentle, and hardworking as in the telling, brought home a good wage by helping to make Yonkers grow. Though kind, he intended to be the man of the house and Louis knowing that took his chance to enlist in the army. Raffaele's heart broke once more, for she had hoped for other decisions. Yonkers would soon be adding Louis's name to the city's honor roll on a page just like Murph Pento's.

The day Louis was to board the train for camp, Joseph pleaded, "Mommy, don't let Louis go."

Louis said, "Mom can't stop me, Joe. It's what I want." Louis bent, hugged Young Joe, and left.

Joseph, sensing but not understanding, saw Raffaele's eyes fill with tears that matched his own and shivered in their mutual vulnerability. Raffaele saw the sadness in Joseph's moist eyes as he took a fist full of her dress in his hand and hugged her. Quietly, she said, "Guisseppe, walk Louis to the station."

Joe flew out the door and down the stairs running as fast as he could to grab his brother's hand. Louis, the fifteen-year-old big brother and the youngster Joseph walked to the train talking of everything. While they waited at the station, Louis squatted and said, "Joe, it's up to you to take care of Mom and the girls. Mr. LaQuido is a good man, but he's not blood. Promise me you'll do this. Ya see, after the war, I won't be coming back. I wanna see the world, so it's up to you."

The child nodded as a massive iron engine slipped by creating a strange world of steam around them on the station platform blurring the scene and causing just enough wind for Joe to feel himself sway. Louis hugged Joseph again and disappeared into the railway car. Joseph stayed until the train was out of sight.

His walk home, powered by tears, left dirty tracks down his face. Joe tried so hard to understand everything but couldn't, and yet some things were very clear to his young mind. He pulled a hand out of his pocket, wiped a snotty nose on his clean but frayed sleeve, and had a scary thought. *Why do they leave me?*

The troubled youngster made a promise to himself to work harder at being liked to bury the cruel pain called loneliness, only it reminded him of Raffaele's sadness. He stopped, looked up the long hill home, thought about Raffaele again, deliberately shoved his hand into his pockets, and took the first fierce step toward manhood placing a lifelong value on the women in his life.

I gotta take care of Momma and the girls.

Raffaele, Mary, Margaret, and Joe liked Mr. LaQuido for his kind and simple needs made their days and a marriage bed, an easier adjustment than expected. Young Joseph found his stepfather a quiet but attentive man. Mr. LaQuido touched his loneliness and Joseph began to deeply care for his stepfather.

Two years brought Raffaele a peace of sorts and two children, Bart and Louise, while Mr La Quido, worked too hard in the worst of weather and contracted pneumonia.

Joseph, his stomach in knots, watched the wasted efforts of the physician from the bedroom doorway. His journey to manhood would not know the treasure of a good man's guidance. To Joseph, it was another person leaving him. Young Joseph buried his hurt in a dark corner of his mind.

Raffaele once again found herself in the war with poverty, and this time, it would be seven-year-old young Joseph who would walk and light the streets of Yonkers. By doing so, Joseph began to know his town intimately and shared conversations with many towns-people.

The nationalities and races along his route came to know a young boy who struggled with a pole too big for him but got the job done and, as time passed, grew ever thin but strong.

Time passed and one night, a now streetwise Joseph was lighting a lamp at a trolley stop on Nepperhan and Ashburton and couldn't help but hear Mr. Jacobs', the pharmacist, complaint to a friend.

"Hank, my business grows so fast I need another delivery boy after school."

His friend smiled and said, "This is a complaint?"

Joseph spoke up, "Excuse me, Mr. Jacobs."

"Yes, Joseph?"

"Sir, I can do that for you. I know where all the streets are, and I know my numbers."

The two men laughed, but the young pharmacist saw something that made him take another look at the respectful smiling, tenacious boy called Joe that his son Victor went to school with and knew him as part of the neighborhood. The longer look somehow convinced Jacobs he wasn't too young to do the job.

"I'm not sure about that, Joseph, but come to my shop after school tomorrow. And you make sure you tell your momma where you'll be. I'll let you try. You can work until dark, okay?"

He said, "Gee willikers, Mr. Jacobs, thanks a lot," and took off to run to the next light dragging his pole. He was in a hurry to tell Raffaele.

"Mom, Mr. Jacobs is nice. I'm gonna do a good job." His sister Mary checked him to see if there were any cuts that needed tending just as she did every night before kissing him good night just as Mom and Margaret did. The younger children were always a sleep by the time Joseph finished lighting the lights.

In a few short weeks, Joe was doing both jobs, and Jacobs enjoyed dickering over the salary he would pay the young man who seemed to have a natural talent for business. The boy always seemed to be running.

One night, Joe was leaving the pharmacy when Mr. Jacobs stopped him. His young son Vinny was beside him learning about the stock. Jacobs smiled as he watched Joe's bushy eyebrows scrunch up over his dark eyes and said, "Joe, how come you're so fast when you make a delivery?"

Joseph blushed and said, "I run, Mr. Jacobs. I love to run. Is that okay?"

Jacobs ruffled his hair and told him, "It's more than okay, and Vinny tells me you're so fast that I should give you a raise, and I agree. I'm going to give you two cents more for every delivery you make. Okay?"

"Wow" was all Young Joe could say. Young Vinny hid his smile for recognizing his father's tight fisted approach to money, waiver in his buddy's favor.

Time was passing quickly for the Prezzemolo and Manfredi families.

In the fifth grade, Joe Prezzemolo and Tony Manfredi were in the same class and shared a love of sports. One day, a transfer student arrived, and the boys exchanged curious glances when he walked in. He was an Irish bucko, whose dark blonde hair pointed in as many directions as the bristles of a worn-out hairbrush. A minor crisis with a class nuisance denied the boy his due in a friendly welcome. Joe and Tony felt the new boy's discomfort, turned, and smiled at him. Joe Prez shook his head at the troublemaker's foolishness but had to laugh at his choice of song. He sang it all the way to the cloak room, "Horsy keep your tail up, horsy keep your tail up." They shared a laugh not realizing they would one day laugh at it again as grown men.

The teacher put the new boy between Joe and Tony and a life-long friendship began. The teacher returned to the lesson, The American Indian League of Nations, so Joe immediately gave her his attention. Indians, were a subject Joe loved to hear about.

The Irish lad John Glynn became Chippy, and Joe Prezzemolo became JP, Justice of the Peace Prezzemolo. Tony was always Tony. After school, the three boys joined others in a quick game of stickball in the schoolyard. Joe left after the third inning to head for Jacobs, as did Tony heading for his father's barbershop. They both turned when Chippy called their names.

"I found an old crab net. Let's go to the river early tomorrow and share the catch. Bring anything we can use for bait."

Early the next morning, they stretched out on a large boulder along the riverbank, and the ten-year-olds took turns pulling in the net and putting the crabs in a pillowcases each of them swiped from home put them into the wire nets and left them in the water, well protected to pick up after school. As Joe cast with either hand, Chippy called out, "Hey, JP, are you righty or lefty, I can't tell?"

"A lefty, but I can go either way. I wasn't allowed to write lefty, so when I was in kindergarten, they made me change."

That night, they took home eight live hard-shelled crabs a piece.

By now, that left-handedness was no longer a problem.

Joe never mentioned the confusion it caused; he just smiled for being glad to please someone he liked. His answer when learning was always "Yes, ma'am," and by the time he was in third grade, he could do anything with both hands. And being ambidextrous served him well.

The Prezzemolo family's struggle to survive continued when a pregnant teenage Mary left home to marry a strikingly handsome young male, she idolized, and placed herself in an atmosphere worse than hunger.

Raffaele pleaded, "Cara Mia, please stay home. Do not rush this marriage. Give yourself time to grow. We will raise the child as one of us." The plea did as much as a droplet in a fast-running river. Raffaele watched the handsome young man, looked at her pregnant daughter, and what she—the mother—saw, terrified her for there was only malevolence in his eyes.

Months later, with the child due momentarily, Raffaele found Mary crumpled in pain from a beating. Fury surrendered to Mary's immediate need followed by Mary's decision to stay with her personal cur. That decision raked Raffaele's flesh as cruelly as a three-pronged gardener's tool. Unable to change it, Raffaele left Mary to her choice, feeling she had failed as a mother. The joy of a granddaughter named Anna arriving did nothing to ease the torment.

With no other friend to talk to, Raffaele's prayers took a companion's place. *Holy Mother of God, have I cursed Mary with my bad luck? Have I given her the worst of me? If it were not for Guisseppe, there would be so little. Margaret helps now, but he makes us laugh, and I thank you for him. But I fear telling him of Mary, he loves her so.*

Raffaele found answering Joseph's what-happened-to-Mary questions difficult but felt he was old enough to understand. She immediately regretted the telling because his fist crashed upon her breadboard. The passion of his blow showed an unthinking capacity for anger for those he loved. Only her restraining hands on his shoulders prevented him from foolishly seeking Mary's tormenter.

Though he obeyed her, he walked away with a carriage she'd never seen before, and it frightened her. His silence made Raffaele realize there was a cold part of Joe's mind she could not touch and mindful of what she'd seen in Mary's beast.

Such thoughts about Joe quickly disappeared into that magic about him that made her smile. *Ah, Guiseppe, you grow into your place as the man of the family more every day. Blessed Mother, thank you for such a good son.*

What she saw in him every day was a person who chose laughter, love of people and learning as the roads to new and different paths to follow. And taking those roads with him allowed the family and Raffaele to laugh in spite of the hardships.

The world and time, seem to conspire to make things happen so quickly, neither Gene or Tess fully sensed that the day-to-day activities were pulling them further and further from their deeper purpose to each other. That they were now, more vulnerable to themselves.

After Marian's arrival in 1914, the Manfredi ranks grew every two years with JJ (Joseph John) and Millie. As they continued to grow, the children were caring for each other in ladder formation to help Tess, something both Tess and Gene fostered.

Next came Salvatore. Two-year-old Millie was unable say his name and called him Sossy. He found himself stuck with it while young. His family and friends liked it but so did he. Sossy became and easy going hellion who you could not help but laugh at. He would be stuck with the name until adulthood, because his pals liked it.

Unfortunately, Tess's dream of children had a price.

By the 1920's Tess was troubled by a recurring illness that Poppa Pento recognized as what had threatened her dramatically as a child.

The doctor's still did not know what it was, and each coming and going offered no ease, getting worse little by little taking its toll on Tess and all their relationships.

In the mean time, Angie their oldest began pulling a heavier end of the workload, soon joined by Beth and Marian. Angie was already looking forward to when she was old enough to earn her own money and other unspoken wishes. Being the first of many brings the danger of responsibilities unfairly weighted and fiercely judgmental of parent's positions.

Though the illness derailed much of the energy Tess shared with her ever-growing world of children, the situation turned her more and more mother and less lover for nothing changed where Madre was concerned. The many gifts Gene had tempted her with, no longer, did anything more than bring some help to the children she loved beyond her own. While slowly shredding the understanding of the man she married.

At the same time, Gene using a man's view of healing, spent freely. Initially the time and intrusion in the daily lives was eased by their time together as family but then the children were pulled into the problem; one or two at a time as they became old enough to share the weekend visits to Madre. The children became targets and Gene would not grasp the problem and rarely dealt with its effects. Especially on the children. He felt it was their duty to do for Madre. While many Italians had set aside the kissing of an elder's ring, Gene insisted upon it. Gene's Americanization was falling prey to its demand. Madre's further insistence on duties from Gene's children besieged them, each in turn.

Family gatherings so enjoyed in their earliest years eroded as more time went to Madre and away from Tess and her need was growing.

Still as time passed, Tess and gene continued to grace their years by looking after those beyond their immediate family. Both admired the other's efforts. It was truly a better part of them both.

The passing of time brought a better life for the Manfredi brood materially but slowly brought the family an uphill journey on a vessel losing power whose crew would tire under its sea anchor of respect.

By now, the Eighteenth Amendment of 1917 enforcing prohibition had given organized crime the time to seriously endanger the growing United States of America. The same time period was very different for the growing children in the Prezzemolo and Manfredi families, both were growing as quickly as the wild flowers on the face of The Hill.

Gene prospered during prohibition. His cellars bounty was joined by a larger illegal still, that saw no police action due to his increased production going to more Pharmacies and filling the needs of known ill citizens. It was tip-toeing but beneficial.

Jacobs Pharmacy often had Joe Prezzemolo delivering to the Manfredi home. And Jacobs need to have a facial had him saying, "It's to please my Mrs. Gene." And Gene's serious approach allowed it in front of other male clients, while at the drugstore the teasing of a son and friend about his bright and shiny face made all convulse with young laughter and Mrs. Jacobs proud of her shining dinner date.

Madre's new family were growing right along with her grandchildren.

The first to fall victim to Madre's debasing efforts were Angie and Tony when they reached the age of seven and five. Poor Angie was the first to taste her lethal venom.

Angie and Tony, even Beth and Marian, would return to Tess after visiting Nonna and ask questions. "Momma, why does Grandmother dislike us?"; "Momma, why does Grandma say mean things about you and Nonno Pento?"

She wanted to say, "Ask your poppa." But that left the children vulnerable, so she used the truth.

"Your grandmother hates me, not you, and she hates me because of Grandpa. Madre is just not a nice person, but she is your grandmother, so behave and be respectful. Your father would be very upset with you if you do otherwise."

That seemed to quiet the immediate question in their minds but did little else and the children immediately took sides. Madre's venom would never find a home within any of Gene's children while Gene moved through time oblivious to the problem's answer.

Gene's circumstance allowed his return to traveling after the war, but Tess still preferred to tend her brood, though her body's slow weakening left her little choice. During the 1920s, Gene traveled as far as Russia, but the trips became shorter because home always called him back. Though frustrated by Tess not joining him, he insisted she join him at social club functions that allowed the ladies of members to attend. Not feeling well for long periods of time, the efforts were beyond Tess's sense of comfort, and neither would enjoy themselves. Sadly, a confused Gene nursed his bad luck and his smiles lessened and bitterness touched them. Still Gene continued his gifts.

A street away, the Prezzemolo's struggle had taken another harsh corner.

Young Mary's situation reeked of vile contempt when Mary's husband kicked her in the womb housing their second child.

This distorted era did not deal with a cur abusing his wife, not even when that abuse created an ugly lump the size of a football on Mary's side where she'd been kicked.

Raffaele feared for the unborn child's well-being, but the arrival of a beautiful, healthy son called Freddy did nothing to change the brutality of his father.

One beating included both children, and the hurt to young Freddy caused an infection and the loss of a rib, while his sister Anna was a mass of black and blue. Still Mary would not leave him, saying, "Momma, he's my husband."

Raffaele stood between thirteen-year-old Joseph and the door; his eyes filled with hatred and only using all her strength prevented his leaving the house to do his brother-in-law some form of harm.

Not until Mary's personal beast sired a child with another did Mary scream, "No more!"

Though possible to legally divorce the louse and she did, the unfair times meant Mary would not receive a penny for Anna and Freddy's care, so Mary and the children came home to Raffaele. The family forsook all pride and took public assistance while Young Joseph and Raffaele showered the young ones with love to replace a sire's loathing.

Joe enjoyed a younger brother and sister, but having a toddler and a baby in the house truly made him smile. He would crawl on his knees after coming through the door to play with Freddy putting Anna on his back when she came running to him for a hug and kiss. He teased them mercilessly but never hurting them for possessing an instinct that kept them safe. He was developing a need to father in the same way a need to mother can touch a growing girl, and he was determined to be their protector. He hoped and reached for the same for with his step brother Bart and sister but they quietly sought their own counsel. When Joe could not make them laugh he turned to those he could.

When Joe came in late after work, Raffaele would be waiting despite the early hours she had to keep. They would share a cup of tea while Joe did his homework. Between filling composition book pages, they talked of many things. Joe might look up and find Freddy or Anna standing in the doorway. He would smile, and they would crawl into his lap where they would fall asleep again. He'd carry them to bed and kiss them good night. Some of Joe's early morning and evening hours were spent at part-time jobs because he determinedly hung on to his successes at school where academics and sports filled his own need to build a better future.

Joe loved to run and trained for track meets by running from one place to another, as he always had. He instinctively knew working the hills added speed to his stride. He'd even found a way to get paid for running in the city's annual schoolboys race around town and did the same thing in the Yonkers Marathon as he got older. And there was part of him that ran just for the release it offered the human mind.

The day-to-day efforts of the women in his life made Joe admire their capacity for loving, especially in loving him. He tucked that feeling into affectionate and oft time humorous doings to tease and endear Mary's youngsters. The ties grew stronger day by day while his brother and sister, seeing what the world offered, turned inward and perhaps wanting.

The Prezzemolo girls were proud of Joe, and with what the ladies and Joe earned, they dropped public assistance before Joe entered high school where his skill and love of sports would bring them all pleasure. Still the best they could afford were crowded cold-water apartments with toilets on the porches. It was the famous "bachouse."

When Joe and Tony Manfredi entered high school, both were after-school athletes who enjoyed the competition but did not compete. Their sports were very different both in skill and ambitions.

Early one morning, Poppa Pento arrived flustered and concerned. "Tess, the children must not go to school today. The sun is going to darken, and evil will run the streets. Keep them home."

Gene walked into the kitchen and surprised Poppa by not being dressed for work.

"Tess, look, even Gene has enough sense to stay home today."

Tess and Gene tried not to laugh.

Tess said, "Poppa, it's only an eclipse of the sun."

Gene smiled broadly and said, "Poppa, I'm staying home so I can watch the eclipse, but keeping the little ones home is a good idea. Tess, they should see it too."

"Gene, you're pazzo," said Poppa Pento as he struggled for breath.

Tess hid her laughter behind a smile. "Poppa, believe me, there's no danger. We'll watch with the children, and you'll understand it better."

The only thing that ran amok was the excitement of the children. Gene had them running back and forth with buckets full of water to fill the large basins he had placed on the porch angled to catch the sun. The children spilled almost as much as went into the larger pan because of their laughter. Angie and Beth, who normally could talk Pento into anything, took turns trying to get him to join them on the porch, but Poppa refused to leave the safety of the kitchen.

The children, on their knees, huddled around the basins with their eyes glued to the water's reflection. They "ewed" and "ah'd" as the moon took its walk across the sun and turned the world backward. Tony boldly tried to sneak a peek only to receive a whack from Gene while Beth's rising to the awesome darkening was merely held in place. Meanwhile, he squeezed Marian with his legs for laughing at their being caught. She had slipped between them to claim the space she needed to see the wondrous reflection. Gene had finally learned to smile at their antics as long as respect was not lost.

After the sun made it's miraculous return, Poppa Pento began to relax and join in the busy household.

The porch screen door squeaked time and time again as other youngsters home from school came to join in the informal party at the Manfredi home.

Tess laughed as the youngsters piled into the dining room, calling them each by name.

"There's plenty of room, don't hurt each other. You'll all be able to hear."

Right behind came some of their parents with food or musical instruments for use later on. Others would appear unannounced as they came home from work.

The food many brought to add to the family stores made it an international feast. Sometimes, it was Perogi filled with cheese, potato, sauerkraut, or even prune filling that reminded Tess of the ravioli she filled with cheese. Others might bring Irish Soda bread or cooked cabbage to eat.

Such parties occurred often with Gene walking the hill and entering the house ready to eat only to find children galore. He would hand Angie his jacket and tie, accept her dutiful kiss, and nod at Tony who would scramble over the legs of others to return in minutes and hand Gene his mandolin. Meanwhile, he'd greet Tess with a kiss and then join the adults on the porch to wait to listen to *Burns and Allan* or *The Eddie Cantor Show* and enjoy the laughter they brought.

Their radio, the only one on Orchard Street for quite some time, was turned up high, so even neighbors in the next building could hear as they sat at their windows just beyond the two-and-a-half-foot alleyway separating the two buildings. Tess made sure the poorest were there, though they brought nothing. Gene welcomed them all and was happy to share whatever was needed from their cellar because he could easily afford it and it was in keeping with a promise he could keep without quilt about the poor he'd made aboard ship on his voyage to the states. It felt wonderful keeping a promise to himself so unlike the grasp of the vow to his padre. The dining room table always seemed to overflow with good food.

After the broadcast, Gene retrieved his mandolin from the porch as the signal to the other musicians to play. Just about then, more parents came to seemingly claim an offspring only to stay for the music and fun. At such gatherings Marian began to join the musicians by playing the piano moved next to the open porch window. The musicians laughed at her mistakes, and she quickly improved, and it never disturbed those dancing on the porch and living room with the table pushed back against a wall.

It was taking Gene a long time to learn about children's emotional needs, but he was improving. Still he could not meet Tess at her level and made mistake after mistake with his growing brood.

Angie, now in her teens, was seen by Gene as beautiful as Tess but found himself unable to reach her for she always seemed angry with him.

Gene did not see or understand the impact of Angie catching most of Madre's bile for being the firstborn and for so resembling

Tess. Angie bore up under words like, "What can one expect from those whose mother and grandfather are children of the devil." Angie buried the hatred deep within herself right beside her love for Tess. Only it was a living thing that needed direction, and the child in her unable to understand aimed it at Gene no matter how Tess tried to help her understand.

Whenever Tess tied to reach Angie on the subject, Angie's face would seem to freeze over. Tess knew she was listening, but words seemed to hit a hidden wall only to break up and mean nothing to Angie. Angie would smile after the gentle lecture and kiss Tess sweetly before leaving her to ponder the whys.

Tess was left only with her prayers for thought. *Dear Mother of God, forgive me. I have shared too much with Angie about Gene's vow to his father. Her knowing had hurt her so. We never meant that to bring such torment to us all. My body is telling me I'll no longer have the strength to give them to help them grow.* The tears could not be held any longer, so she put her head on a pillow to rest, thinking, *If I'm going to die, please show them the way.* And then sleep took her.

Angie's childhood love for Tess took in everything, but in growing, all of Tess's hurt became Gene's fault for not putting a stop to the hurting.

Of the girls, only Angie and Marian would stand their ground with Madre along with barrel-voiced Tony. All took the abuse in quiet to appear respectful, but the family trait to ball their fists making their knuckles whiten gave away their anger, and Nonna enjoyed the reaction.

While Angie struggled with darker reactions, Tony learned to ignore Madre and favored Tess with more attention. The younger Marian watched, learned, and found an understanding more complete than her older siblings. Her youth gave her time to find a way to use her love for Tess and Gene while channeling her animosity when dealing with Madre personally. While sad about Gene's doing nothing to change it. Marian learned by watching Angie's pain when chastised by Gene turn more and more ugly. She watched her become her own enemy. Marian sadly watched Angie's growing hatred while she instinctively found a way to handle Madre's demands.

The first time Madre used words to cut into Marian, Angie, and Tony were outside Madre's bedroom listening and ready to take the bile for their younger sibling. Hearing the usual fault finding tirade about Tess and Poppa Pento ending, they stepped across the threshold only to be stopped when a smiling Marian answered Madre's usual, spawn of the devil speech with, "I knew you would tell me that, Nonna. I guess you want me to clean your toilet today."

"Si. And you will make it shine."

"Of course, I will. Isn't it good that Momma taught me how to clean so much better than my aunts?"

"What!" The word was spit through Madre's lips, as Marian added, "Gosh, Nonna isn't that why you wanted to ask me to do it?"

Marian's innocent, questioning smile showed no sign of warring guile or disrespect, and though Madre squinted and looked for the telltale tight fists closed against her sides, they weren't there. Marian's hands hung patiently beside her, and Madre had the sudden realization that she wouldn't be able to hurt Tess through Marian, but Madre tried, like the devil herself.

Tony and Angie left in awe of a younger sister's finesse marveling at what this sister, being tough, and smart enough to do, what they could not.

Early on, the open bond the girls had with Tess meant she heard all Madre's remarks but only until her illness prevented her bearing up under the strain. Tony, by virtue of being a male, escaped personal abuse by Madre, but loving his sisters left him ornery for not being able to put a stop to it and not finding a way to approach Pop with it. Finally, age brought the children the realization of how much they hurt Tess by bringing Madre's words home with them.

Madre was used to compliance, and the children's animosity never bothered her. She enjoyed their predicament, while Gene continued to believe a man must honor a boy's vow no matter the hurt. The changes and their insidious effects on Tess and their relationship made him more aware that his keeping his word had robbed them of being truly happy. He wanted to take advantage of all that was possible in life, but as time went on, he began dealing on his growing bitterness, his, began to rob them all of much a family needed and he tried to deal with it.

At home, in all other matters, the Manfredi children were allowed an opinion as long as they presented it respectfully and did what Tess and Gene said they must.

A time came when Madre's husband had to move his family to Rockaway Beach. Madre used her hold on Gene to keep him visiting. She was not about to surrender her twisted pleasure.

About that time Gene and the family celebrated his becoming a citizen of the United States of America. The noise accompanied with cheers filled the house and what a great excuse for a party. Tess and the girls led the parade around the living room and JJ waved the flag with gusto. It brought Gene a small wakening to ease the stress of Tess's usual request about the demands for respect as seen from his old country views and he pulled her aside of a few moments.

Apparently, he had discussed some acts of respect with distinguished friends and had made decisions.

Cara Mia, he said, "I am telling the children they will no longer kiss anyone's ring as a mark of respect, not mine, not momma's. You and Poppa are right it is too old country." The hug and kiss Tess preferred as respects' expression were spontaneous his and he held her for the moment wishing, *Ah Tess, if only you understood a man as well. A man must do what a man must do.* "I know you hate the children and my being away each weekend. And added, I also told Madre that they are Americans and its old country. And that I will continue to come each weekend but only one of our children will accompany me each time."

Dear God let this help at least a little for I must keep my word. But oh, how I miss our joy together.

Tess's simple, "Thank you Gene," made him feel good but the deeper part of him knew, that she knew he could not do what needed doing.

In that quiet somewhere, Gene's watcher smiled sadly knowing it was far from enough.

The first time a child did not kiss Madre's ring, she stormed to her room where she spit and decided to make the time the child spent with her harder. The touch of each kiss on her cheek infuriated her. Now there was more for the children to do. As usual, she continued to couple that with vicious comments about Tess and Grandpa Pento only after Gene and her husband left the house to do manly things.

By now the children each in turn did what was expected and closed their minds to Madre's hatred.

Gene still thrived on anything new about town, and when his brother joined a minstrel group, he came home all excited and told the children, "After supper, we are all going to see Uncle Antonio in a minstrel show at Proctor's theater."

The entire brood marched into the magnificent theater, and though the older girls had been there before for other performances, it was Marian's first visit. She missed nothing from the thick patterned rug on the floor to the grand chandeliers high above in the domed gold gilded ceiling. She saw the box seats on either side with the stage with bright brass railings facing forward wondering who was lucky enough to sit there just as they all sank into plush seats right up front. She immediately craned her neck to see the balcony sticking out of the back wall behind and above them. She suddenly wanted to run up one of the long curved staircases on the left and right side of the back wall that brought hundreds of people to where they could see the show for less money. Suddenly, the show started, and she was thrilled to be so close and when Angie said, "Look, Marian," her gaze followed Angie's pointing finger and recognized Uncle Antonio under the black face. So she giggled, laughed, and applauded as loud as she could and laughed even harder when she recognized another uncle only this one a Pento dancing in front of the singers. Marian loved being with Angie.

When parks had outdoor social affairs, Gene took the children, for it was always a fun event to attend. Though Yonkers was now a big city, these happenings created new experiences they could all enjoy while thriving on the small town atmosphere each neighborhood brought to its smaller area.

One day, after school at the Manfredi house, all the children were home when the crash of the porch door interrupted the chatty, busy atmosphere of the kitchen. Tess's youngest brother Art, now a troubled young adult, came running into the room terrified. His panting and emotional upset galloped through the children who instinctively went to where Tess stood and huddled closely.

He blurted, "Tess, hide me. I've killed a man, and the police are chasing me."

Tess's eyes went wide with terror, and she could feel the children begin to shake. A man they knew more as an equal than an uncle became something fearful.

Tess, the mother, railed, "How could you come here? You've frightened the children."

"Where could I go, Tess, please." His tears touched the sister in Tess while right and wrong clawed at the part of her protecting her young.

Frantic, the sister choked out, "Go to the cellar. I won't tell."

In minutes, the police surrounded the house, and a well-known police sergeant, gun drawn, entered the house. When he saw the children, the officer holstered the weapon, met Tess's troubled eyes, and said, "Mrs. Manfredi, we know Art is here. We followed him. We have to search the house. Stay here with the children." He could see Tony and JJ were not there, stopped, and asked, "Mrs. Manfredi, are Tony and JJ safe?"

The sergeant, a family man from The Hill, normally called her Tess. He and his family had often joined the fun on the Manfredi porch. His formal approach helped him avoid asking Tess anything that would compromise her.

"Yes, Officer Mike, the boys are safe. I sent them to get Gene. They left just moments before you arrived."

The sergeant nodded and gave orders to cover all exits and proceed with a quiet, careful search from top to bottom. Gene came through the door with the boys leading the way just as the Sergeant Mike returned to the kitchen and passed the crying girls. Sergeant Mike nodded for Gene to join his family as he and his team headed into the cellar knowing Art was hiding there. They descended the steps from the kitchen while others entered the backyard door into the cellar simultaneously.

Art was squeezed between the wall of The Hill and Gene's still until he heard Sergeant Mike say, "Art, we know you're here. Don't make us hurt you in your sister's house. Your nieces are crying for fear we'll hurt you. Come out with your hands up, and you won't get hurt."

Art had no heart for a fight. He stood and said, "I'm here. I won't cause any trouble," and went meekly, his head down to avoid seeing a terrified sister, crying nieces, or the boys who always loved to play with him. The search party took him out through the cellar door.

As they passed the kitchen window going up to the street, Tess heard their muffled voices and whispered to Gene, "Maybe if Momma had lived?"

Gene pulled Tess and the children closer and thought, *Maybe if Poppa had chosen a different path.*

Art was sent to jail for a long time.

Except for the usual harmless childhood diseases, bumps, and bruises, the Manfredi brood thrived until Marian needed a mastoid operation.

That year, Gene heard Tess say, "Oh, Gene, she's so weak. And the doctor said she needs glasses because they had to scrape an eye nerve to remove the mastoid. He wants her to have the hops of a finely brewed beer to regain her strength so she can get back to school. I know you can get it for her regardless of prohibition."

"Tess, take her for the glasses tomorrow, and I will see she has the beer every day. I promise I will come home for lunch and take her to Fagan's speak easy. She will get better, I know it."

Gene decided on Fagan's because he knew his beer was an excellent product.

The older girls sat talking to Marian before leaving for work and teased her about the beer. After they left, Tess told Marian, who began to fidget and twitter, to dress nicely for the occasion. Tess was having a hard time fixing Marian's straight hair and felt badly Marian didn't get waves like her own but Gene's very straight locks.

"Momma, we have to hurry, or I won't be ready when Poppa gets here."

"Little one, Poppa has to change first." The fact Tess was enjoying her anxiety perplexed Marian. Tess tried to get Marian's attention.

"Marian, listen to me." When that didn't work, Tess placed her large hands on Marian's freckled cheeks to make her sparkling hazel eyes meet her own while thinking, *She's so excited. I wonder if she realizes she's the only one whose eyes are like mine. I wish the glasses weren't necessary. People will not get to enjoy her lovely eyes.* Tess smiled at how pretty she looked and then spoke firmly, "Remember, you are a young lady, and make Poppa proud."

Gene's voice called out, "Tess, is Marian ready?"

Marian nodded, and *poof,* she was gone. Tess's hands were still in the air.

Tess watched from the window as they slowly climbed the stairs to Orchard Street passed the front-yard windows. Gene had handed Marian a sprig of peppermint, as they passed the large batch growing opposite the kitchen windows.

Watching brought new thoughts to Tess about Marian. *Blessed Mother, this one is different. She thrives on the unusual, she's bright, and she's tough enough to make her way with the other children. Even the older ones can't bully her. Tony and Angie tell me she actually stands up to Madre and she does it without offending Gene. I guess that's why I rely on her most. She's the one most willing to take care of the others, and she's good at whatever she does. Please let her be well, there's so much ahead of her. So much I could never do she will do, I know it. So different from my dear, dear Angie who is determined to do the opposite of what we ask. I'd expect that from one of the boys, but she seems so unhappy. Even I can't explain it in a way I can understand so that I can help her. Have I failed her? Ah, well, I have much to do.*

The differences in Marian would warm Tess most on the days when her strength waned. Marian was as tortured by Tess's illness as the older children but was focused on doing whatever she could to help. Tess reached to Marian for the strength she needed to replace her own; sure that Marian had more than she herself ever had.

The time would come when she'd she would tell Gene, "If the worst happens, ask Marian to take care of the younger ones. She's best for them. She will love them hard and well."

"Si, Cara Mia, si." His words would stumble over the fear she could be right.

As Gene and Marian walked down Orchard Street toward the Speakeasy, they past Mrs. Mike's store then the open lot that allowed them to look down the side of the hill to Mr. Polchak sitting in the backyard of his house above Nepperhan Avenue. He was leaning over a shoe tree repairing a child's beat up pair of shoes. Polchak was a small man with huge hands looking more the blacksmith than the shoemaker who spent his lunch hours eating and fixing shoes for the poor children without charge. To the children who watched him repair their shoes, he seemed a diminutive elf going about the making of magical gifts, though the gifts were only pairs of their shoes repaired again and again.

Gene called out, "Mr. Polchak, cum a sta."

Polchak raised the shoe in salute to Gene and said, "Fine, Gene, fine. Ah, Marian, you look pretty today."

Marian beamed and said, "Thank you, Mr. Polchak. Poppa and I are going out to lunch."

Ivan laughed the happy laugh of an affable, contented man and said, "How nice. Have a good time and feel well soon."

Gene was proud to have Polchak as a customer, and it pleasured him to take extra care to make the less-than-handsome neighbor look his very best. Polchak was one of the many people that made The Hill a good place to live.

The warm sunlight and the gleam of a daughter's pride popped Marian's many freckles and softened her illness' sallow complexion.

Gene didn't miss the change, and the sunlight caught in her hazel eyes reminded him of the first time Tess caught his eye followed by the guilt of not making life all it should be for the mother of his bambinos.

The local speakeasy was located where Orchard met Vineyard in an odd-shaped building that rested in line with the corners of the two streets with its widening into a triangle as it headed up and down the streets to became an oddity readily accepted by the neighborhood. Once there, Marian's efforts to appear the adult both amused and honored Gene.

This daughter of mine has the natural warmth of her mother, and though she resembles Angie and Beth, she is more me with her round face, and I've cursed her with my straight locks. I must be watchful she is tiring.

Just then, the owner came over and said, "Gene, I see you brought Marian."

"Si. Marian, this is Mr. Fagan who makes the finest beer in the area and it will make you well again."

Marian looked up at Fagan's ruddy face and said, "Mr. Fagan, is your beer as good as my poppa's wine. I like that very much."

"Wee one that is a fine question, and yes, it is, though I not be sure you'll be liking it."

Marian's brow wrinkled, and then she grinned. "I promise you I will, Mr. Fagan, because I liked what my brothers let me taste the last time they brought some home for Poppa." Marian was thrilled with having time with Pop.

For once he was hers alone, and that made it special. She watched everything he did, everything he said and would, over the time it took to get well, learn much about the Gene that made him less stern and taught her how to reach the man he was while accepting his imperfections and became more the lady for the experience. It was an advantage none of her siblings would attain.

Marian filed the information for future use along with the recipes Tess was teaching her for cooking pork.

Whenever they came home after lunch, she shared speakeasy secrets with Tess but couldn't wait for Millie and JJ to get home and blather as a child would full of giggles, laughter, and playful secrets. But she didn't share everything. Much she saved just for herself. Later after a healing sleep, she told Beth, Tony, and Angie about the trip. Though Angie was pleasured by Marian's telling she found no pleasure in the hearing. Her own feelings for Gene were already different, harshly determined and Marian saw it in Angie's expression.

As Marian began to slip into sleep's REMS, she thought, *Pop was so handsome, and he looked nicer than anybody there, and everyone liked him. And he dressed special. Just to take me and Momma let me wear my good clothes.* The last thought as sleep claimed was about Angie's expression, *Angie is always mad at Pop?*

At other times and as growing changed her views, she remembered how people admired Gene for the kindness he showed the neighborhood and how lady friends came over to talk to her and make her comfortable. Rather than lauding Poppa's other attentions to her siblings, she kept them for her private world. In doing so, she found that hidden world girls have for their fathers. The diamond horseshoe stickpin Gene wore in his silk tie for every dress-up occasion came to be a fond and personal item in her growing mind. She liked the way the five matching stones glistened in the colored bar lights. The memory would ring personal bells for all her years to come.

Time passed, and their father daughter bond deepened, and Marian grew well again. On their last lunch together, Marian said to Mr. Fagan, "Sir, I know I can't come anymore because I'm all well now, but I enjoyed coming, and I do like your beer. Thank you."

This she did on her own for she had already told Gene, "Poppa, I like your wine more than Mr. Fagan's beer but beer is so much better with roast pork."

"Si. You are a fine cook to understand that. That's exactly why I send your brothers for it when we have Momma's delicious pork. And I know we'll do it when you make the pork. Filame, I know that because you help Momma so well."

Marian liked what Poppa said except that she didn't like his referring to Tess as Momma, *She's our momma.* She said nothing but counseled her memories with, *When I'm a mommy, I won't let my husband call me Momma.*

A strong child again, Marian rejoined her siblings in doing for their growing family and once again visiting Madre.

All The Hill's children nurtured on its earthen streets shared them with the warbled touting of street vendors and their wagons or pushcarts. There were vegetables, fish, meat, and house goods pulled up the hill by strong horses. But as the years passed, the horse-drawn vehicles slowly began to change to the horses of a motorized kind on bubbling tarred streets that allowed the young and old to pop tar bubbles appearing in the black surface caused to sizzle by the hot summer sun where the Manfredi kids shoved and pushed for the honor of the biggest bubble to burst.

Tess recognized the hard labor of deliveries to her cellar and kitchen and always had something for the smut-covered coal man, the garbage man, the mailman, and the milkman whose clanging bottles announced his very early arrival, sometimes with frigid bottles that popped paper lids with inches of frozen milk.

To bring the large Manfredi brood the fine things Gene could afford, the deliverymen had to navigate two steep flights of stairs to reach the kitchen level and three to reach the cellar. Tess appreciated the effort even more when remembering lugging the children up the same stairs.

Tess often climbed them to join neighborhood mothers vying for a vendor's best price or to talk about their young. When the mothers moved on, there often appeared an equal number of puddles disappearing into the soil.

The Hill had become that field of growing children that Tess had envisioned when Gene found the house. They were like the wildflowers on the hillside tilting down to the factory. Tess loved and reached for them all even when it proved wise for her own to take short-cuts home on The Hill because they were "wops." It didn't bother her. Hearing the what for's told her they were just being mischievous and that her Tony or JJ often shared or started the rhubarbs. Too often their being mischievous was lead by Tony and JJ and their attempts to hide that meant their bruises were well deserved. Anything more and Gene took the boys aside and a whack with a razor strap ended their ideas.

As they grew, the same encounters finally turned social. The people of the ethnic areas reached out in varied social outings and wiped away many childhood misconceptions. Yet there were those who were just mean or dangerous and to be feared, like those who set burning crosses above the cemetery on the slopes east of The Hill. Many a night, Gene and Tess had watched the fiery crosses burn knowing the children could see them from the upstairs windows. The hatred of the Ku Klux Klan present even in the north was something they tried to explain to the children but really couldn't and only served to enforce the belief that marriage among their own, Italians, by their children was best for them.

Tess made sure each of the girls learned the household arts as soon as they were able. She found Angie very good at them, Bella disinterested but knowledgeable, and then it was Marian's turn to learn. In the kitchen, Tess realized Marian would surpass even Gene as could Angie if she decided to do so. Millie would be the last to learn and, though excellent, was the least inclined to harbor with the family as she grew.

Early on, Tess had each at the stove. In Marian's case, she often stood behind her with her hands on Marian's shoulders guiding her moves.

Tess said, "You really enjoy cooking, don't you?"

Marian looked up over her shoulder and said, "Uh-huh. We all have so much fun getting together that I want to have big parties like you do."

Marian lifted a spoon to Tess who tasted the sauce.

"Wonderful, honey. Poppa will be amazed." Tess rubbed a spot of sauce off Marian's freckled cheek and thought, *How strange. Angie looks more like me every day yet is so different. Marian looks very much like Gene except for my eyes and freckles, but she's more like me in other ways. Angie and Marian are very alike in skills and emotional strength, while Beth is softer while very much at home in the kitchen. None of my babes are really alike, and yet people recognize them as family wherever they are, and they are as beautiful as I knew they'd be. How different each of them are. Our plans for them seem very—I lack a word for it.*

As the girls grew to beautiful young women, the young men of the hill were quick to respond.

Angie, Tony, and Beth were heading for adulthood at lightning speed with Marian right behind them.

At home, Marian and Angie were quite alike, but while Marian was basically outward, Angie turned most things inward and smiled less and less. Both were very responsive when challenged and capable of dire reactions, but Angie was in some ways too like Madre. Her fierce emotions were turned inward aimed at getting even without forgiving, while Marian would meet and openly confront the wrong doing. Win or lose she fought for her due and got on with life. She shied from what she saw growing in Angie and chose the new challenges life allowed and gradually found the magic in smiles. She somehow found the way to handle the embarrassment or punishment for her wrongful attempts.

The growing years for Raffael's children were different. Young Joe's growing took on more and more importance. With deliberate effort, he lifted them above the trodden emotions of survival so swamping to the poor with laughter and hard work.

The first time Joseph brought his new Irish friend Chippy home with him; was typical. Joe brought his new Irish friend Chippy home, kissed his ladies and struck a serious pose. Having caught Raffaele, Mary, and Margaret's attention, he spoke very slowly and seriously.

"This is Chippy Glynn. He's Irish and he looks down on us Italians."

A stunned Chippy wheeled on Joe, the women threw Chippy a disapproving look, Joe burst into a wide grin and added, "Chippy lives on the street above us. He looks down on us from up there." His comic timing had been perfect.

Chippy threw a friendly punch, and the girls burst into laughter and then embarrassed Chippy with the casual gesture of a kiss for greeting a friend. Raffaele, unable to catch all of Joe's quick fire joking, needed an explanation in dialect, so Joe explained. Finally understanding, her lilting laughter drained the stress lines from her features, and Joe smiled.

Chippy and Joe left to play baseball in the park opposite the carpet factory on Nepperhan. On the sidelines, Angie and Beth were watching the game. Tony had introduced Angie and Beth to the sport, and Angie took it to heart. She became an avid Yankee fan as did Tony until he found golf. Angie, far more committed, read about and listened to every game she could while able to bespeak the roster like an old-timer.

Young Joe enjoyed baseball, but basketball and running were his first loves. Joe was up, and he hit a double, the runner from second slid into third. Chippy as second baseman pointed out the rhubarb happening at third. Joe shook his head at Chippy and trotted over to third base, saying, "Hey, you two. The older guys are gonna call for the field in a minute, so let's play ball." He put his arm around the teammate called out and said, "Remind me to tell the joke I heard about two girls," and playfully pushed him away from the baseline and headed back to second base where Chippy whispered, "Hey Joe, I got a new nickname for you—JP for Justice of the Peace."

"Chip, don't hang that moniker on me. It's awful." A pitch connected to a bat, and Joe was away to third laughing at Chippy's suggestion and heard, "Okay, Joe, but that's what you'll be to me."

When not working the friends often went to the river to swim… Chippy went no further than fifty feet to swim while Joe and Tony joined the older boys in a swim to New Jersey. They usually swam right back and then they'd meet Chippy and head home for supper or work.

An excited Gene returned from a trip to the World's Fair in Chicago with a wonder of the times as a gift for Tess.

"Cara Mia, I have brought you a wonderful present."

Tess eyed the steel monster, as though it intended to squash and bounce her around in its wide belly.

"But, Gene, I don't do the wash now."

"Tess, you won't even know you're doing it. I promise."

She knew Gene believed what he said because he was always insisted on ways to make the work of a large family easier for her. So she tried.

Day after day, Tess shook her beautiful head of hair and said terrible things to the new present. It was slow, it took her from more important chores, and the children hated the added chores. The holy saints heard continuously, "Take this demon away." The harangue was short-lived because the steel clunker could not survive the workload of ten and quickly found a corner in which to hide, broken. A mischievous smiling Tess thanked the saints, and Gene sheepishly reminded her to call the laundryman.

Gene could only wonder about feelings between Tess and the children. More than just Momma, Tess was their friend especially to the girls who shared secrets Gene would never know. But he did hear what Tess felt she could share with him, and she protected them from his too-strict attitude.

Both allowed the children an opinion but refused abusive responses, and each child in turn either knew or heard, "There's a bottomless suitcase in that closet. Speak to your mother or me like that again, and you'll pack it and go." A barber strap occasionally found use, but no hand was ever raised between adults, and the only arguing was about Gene's time spent with Madre. And as the years became the past, her ability to accept it disappeared. As Tess weakened, Gene's vow became a bitter drain on her endurance and her ability to explain Gene's choices to their confused children.

Like Gene's silencing an erring child while she could not. Silence disturbed Tess's sense of being with her brood, so it was unfit for rearing the young, and she sought other ways to punish those who committed a boo-boo.

When the child asked about the silencing, she told them, "You did wrong, and you must accept your punishment. I don't agree with your poppa about not talking to you. But you know he can't stay mad for very long, so behave."

While Tess would never silence a child, silencing Gene did not bother her a bit. After a visit to Madre and the usual argument, leaving her more and more unhappy, the quiet was all the children heard. Sadly, Tess's withdrawal denied the family of its usual intimacy.

Gene hated the silence. Instead, he quickly sought something special like a case of large, perfect apples and telling his brood, "Don't touch. These are for Momma's other children."

Most times, Tess would melt because he tried and laughter would return. One day Gene's visit to Madre delayed his coming home and when he finally arrived the world between them imploded.

Tess had been ill and though recovering her strength was no longer a thing to marvel at. Gene had taken two of the youngest to Madre with him and Tess wanted them home. Upon their return Gene found Tess exhausted, in the kitchen trying to keep their meal from drying out. Harsh words were spoken. The children gathered in the dining room hearing the impassioned words grow to needless cruelty; on both sides. Gene paced the few feet in front of Tess while the children listened sensing supper would not be happening.

Tony said, "I think it's time we told Pop why we don't want to go to Nonna's at all, maybe he'd understand." The children came to no decision, as fright took its toll in paralyzing fear. Except for Angie. She could not stand it, and wishing she wasn't the oldest, she headed for the kitchen without a clear idea of what to say but needed to see it stop.

The argument was going nowhere, and with a face puffed with anger and red with rage. Gene's words tore from him. "I will not renounce my vow for anyone. She is my mother. Not for anyone!"

Tess, cut him off with eyes ablaze, her words a snarl said, "There's a name for a man who puts wanting their mother before their own. You are a—"

Gene's palm struck Tess's face. The harsh offensive blow was a surprise to them both. Worse, Gene turned away from the horror to see Angie standing in the doorway with a look of hatred so strong, it overwhelmed him with shame that made him run. Tess stunned by the blow fought her way through the shock, with eyes as dull as the garbled confusion of her mind, forced her to relive her own words and returning her sanity. She turned to say something only to freeze; seeing only Angie's reaction.

Gene had run passed Angie, head down and left the house, while Tess floundered between go after him or deal with Angie.

Tess chose Angie's reaction.

Angie belligerently said, "Mom, Pop, he hit you."

Tess silenced her with a raised hand and said, "Angie, your father did not mean to do that. I said something horrible to him."

The other children having watched Gene's leaving heard both the slap and Angie's words. All became silent victims of a castle's usually protecting walls crashing dangerously around them without a place to run for safety.

Tony stepped beside Angie and said, "Mom, Angie's right. Pop always told us there's no excuse for a man to hit a woman."

Angie screamed, "I hate him. I'll always hate him." As Gene passed the kitchen window, the words hit him with the force of a hammer making him fall up the stairs as he ran away from home.

In those worlds apart, the watchers of both domains saw and heard. The dark one smiled for Angie willingly opened her mind to root her words in the deep canyons of the mind that light almost never awakens.

While in the domain of light, the archer placed a calming presence over the family watcher for the advantage now belonged to the dark side until each of the family made their own decision.

Young Marian quieted the crying children and went to Angie and placed a hand on her arm hoping to quiet her, but Angie shivered under her touch, and Marian instinctively knew nothing could be done now.

Tess's tried but her explanations to Angie did no good. The blow went too deep with too many emotions not understood. When Tess followed Angie into the dining room and felt the anguish of the other children, she found herself without the words to help, knowing only she needed to find Gene or their family would cease to exist. Knowing it couldn't be put right without him, she said, "I want all of you to go to Poppa Pento's. I will join you there after I find your father." Coping with the anger in Angie's and Tony's expressions, outdone only by the fear she saw in the younger children, she added, "Go and go now." It was an order. Tess left thinking, *He won't be with his mother, but where would he go. I'll try the shop first and then his brother.*

After exhausting hours of searching fruitlessly, she went to Poppa Pento's to collect the children only to be told her five brothers were on a vengeful search.

The look on her father's face told Tess too much about the danger Gene was in. A devastated Tess told the children to go home, saying, "I'll see you at home in a little while." Once they were safely away, she confronted her father, "Poppa, I did not intend you knowing Gene hit me, or maybe I did, I don't know. But if my brothers hurt Gene because you sent them after him, in my eyes, you become like his mother. You will no longer be my father."

Pento stared. There was a wall between them, one he was seeing for the first time. It was a wall he could not breach, but because he could not live without Tess's love, he took a step backward.

"Daughter, I love you and what a father can give, I will give. Gene will not be harmed." *Thank God I told the familia to bring him to me for that.*

Tess said, "Thank you, Poppa." Her wall of fatigue suddenly worsened, and Tess, thinking his silence had dismissed her, turned to leave reaching to the wall for support.

"Tess. Are you all right, you're so pale." His hand already holding her arm in case.

She grabbed a much-needed breath. Then very slowly, she answered, "Yes, Poppa? I'm just very tired."

His hand moved to hers, saying, "All right, we will not harm him, but I will never speak to him again."

She stared for a moment and took her hand away, and when she spoke, her voice cracked.

"It is sad, Poppa, that my mother-in-law will never enter my home or speak to us, and now my father will never speak to my husband. How can a family be happy if they cannot forgive? Gene didn't want to hit me. I love you, Poppa, but Gene is my husband. We have a family to raise. That must come first. Do what you must. Either way, you are always welcome in our home."

Tess got as far as the new flight of stairs that traversed The Hill and took people from High Street, to Vineyard Avenue, to Orchard Street, to Nepperhan Avenue. About halfway down, she grabbed the banister because her legs wouldn't hold her, so she sat on the nearest step. Too strong to pass out but too weak to go on, she waited for the spell to pass and noticed how swollen her legs were. Here was the real danger to all that she loved. Its malevolence threatened to take her away from her children. She felt as though the candle lit, for each child sent to her to share her world could go out one by one.

Dear Jesus, what is happening to us? To me? Please, there's so much I want to do. I'm so unhappy, and I'm not ready to leave.

A child's voice pulled her from the threatening darkness.

"Hello, Mrs. Manfredi."

Pretty Connie with the dark olive skin of her Greek heritage, a friend of Marian's, sat beside her and said, "Can I sit wit ya."

"Of course." Tess reached out and put her arm around Connie in greeting. It was hard to smile.

Connie had wanted to talk a blue streak about school and how Marian was her best friend having sought Tess to ask if Marian could come to her birthday party but instinctively knew Tess was ill and didn't know what to do.

Tess said, "Oh, Connie, I need your help. I am not feeling well."

"I'll go get my mommy."

"No little one just run and get my children to come for me. Please."

The youngster did as asked, and minutes later, Tony and Angie arrived and all but carried Tess home, while Marian and Beth took over in the kitchen and kept the younger children occupied.

Three days later, a bearded, putrid Gene walked up The Hill looking more the street bum than the meticulous man the town knew. He had lived as dirty as he felt. Hitting Tess tortured him while a daughter's glare fouled the measure of himself as a man. But it changed nothing. The child within held him too tightly. He had no honorable place to go except to his family, and for the first time in his life, the thought of his mother's death offered a peace he would never know because the thought shamed him.

He found Tess alone standing at the stove. The children were due home from school shortly. With tears on his face, he softly said, "Cara Mia, forgive me." He was speaking to her back for she could not face him, as he said, "There is no excuse for hitting you." He gagged on the last words.

The mirror above the stove showed her what he looked like, and she refused to let him see the tears in her eyes as she quietly answered.

"Gene, the children will be home soon. You don't want them to see you looking like that. I tried to talk to Angie and Poppa Pento too, but it didn't help. Poppa will not do anything to you, but he will never speak to you again, and I don't know what to do about Angie. Maybe time will help." She turned slightly. "It's a sad thing that we have allowed our parents to bring us to this."

Gene shook his head in agreement and went to clean up. There was now a weight between them that neither was strong enough to move.

Poppa kept his word. He visited often knowing Gene continued to visit Madre. The younger children accompanied him while an unforgiving Angie refused, as did Beth and Tony.

Gene allowed it. How could he punish them for disrespect when his own deed was worse? He missed the laughter most, and worse, Tess's smiles were getting fewer and fewer. Now he faced the creeping dread of facing life without her and bitterness set in that he could not avoid. His own smiles were far fewer.

For a while, Marian continued to go to Madre for the sake of the younger children, though she was reaching an age that she'd brook no nonsense from the older woman, and the time soon came when she told Gene she would no longer go and the younger children needed to be home with Tess.

That time came when the doctor didn't know what to tell them about Tess's bloating, now a constant companion and forcing Tess to spend more and more time in bed. The children were needed at home. Gene saw the differences in Marian that made her the strongest of his children and recognized her many influences on those around her.

Both Prezzemolo and Manfredi families forged ahead companioned by the growth of America and the wondrous inventions that made the growth rate of the United States phenomenal.

As Joe grew, he took on better paying part-time jobs and continued with Jacobs but as a counter man and passing the deliveries on to a younger boy. With his sister Margaret working and Mary working part-time, the quality of family life improved while his growing capacity to make others laugh had become the balm they all enjoyed. Meanwhile, growing and the passing of time continued.

Joe, now in high school, touched the end of the YMCA's pool, shook the water from his eyes, and beamed a perfect, long-toothed smile at the cheers. It was his freshman year in Commerce High School, and he had just beat upperclassmen from other schools and set a city record at a swim meet. Joe felt himself hauled from the water and lifted high over the heads of teammates. Though laughing loud and proud, he still heard a familiar voice say, "Let me help." When they threw him back into the water, he did a half nelson that he turned into a belly whopper before "kerplunking" into the water and spraying all those standing near.

He came up laughing only to be pushed below the surface by friendly hands. Chippy had dived in fully clothed to grab Joe in playful camaraderie.

"Chip, I knew I heard you."

"Couldn't let the Justice of the Peace have all the fun now could I?" Joe laughed as he coughed up water, put his arm around his friend as they climbed out of the pool, and headed for the locker room.

Chip joined the celebration at the Italian club in someone else's clothes, and they discussed their futures. While Joe went to Commerce High School, Chipper went to Gorton High so they had scarce time together.

"Joe, I've decided to become a politician after college."

"Cheez Chip, an honest politician and an honest banker? It's a great idea. After you graduate, I'll be sure people vote for you, and you can put all your money in my bank."

Chip turned serious. "Jesus, Joe, I wish you could go to college too."

"Hey, Chip, I am going. It's just going to take me a lot longer, that's all."

"I know, one course at a time, but it's not fair. Look, if I can help in any way, you'll tell me, won't you? And forget that independent crap that you can't take help. Promise me? Okay?"

"Only if you promise the same thing." They shook on it with a grip solid with good feeling.

Joe was determined to pursue a degree no matter how long it took but remained determined to do it alone.

In 1928, Tony Manfredi stood to join his Commerce High School classmates in assembly, cheering the state basketball champs as they took the stage and Joe Prezzemolo in particular. He and Joe were great school chums, and Joe was one of the team's star forwards. He watched Joe take the stairs two at a time among the class heroes. Tony shifted his golf trophy to make as much noise as possible, having enjoyed Joe's wild cheers for him just minutes before.

After the team received medals in the shape of basketballs and the din of pride subsided, the principal made a request.

"Joseph Prezzemolo, please remain on stage. Mrs. Morrissey and Mr. McClennan have something for you."

Joe enjoyed the jostling of caring of state champ teammates as they left the stage. Without fluster, Joe enjoyed the attention of top math honors and placing second in the state typing contest. He had typed 117 words a minute with two errors on the latest clunker of the twenties.

High School

After the assembly, the celebration moved to Jacobs' drugstore where Joe joined them. Mr. Jacobs' son Vic was swamped with the orders, so Joe grabbed a bar towel, put on his apron, bumped Vic over, and started filling orders.

Vic looked at Joe as though he'd been given a trophy of his own. "Thanks a lot, Joe."

Tony Manfredi reached across the soda fountain and took Joe's hand. "Congratulations, Joe, I see the basketball hero found a way to escape the admiring ladies."

"Hey, Tony, well done. Love that trophy, let me see it." Joe admired it and used his bar towel to exaggerate his polishing effort.

Tony laughed and said, "Give it back, Prezzy, you've enough trophies of your own."

Joe finished up a root beer float and a black-and-white soda with bulging scoops of ice cream and set them on serving dishes to catch the seltzer and milk as it ran over the top of the tall glasses.

Joe teased Tony about the girls giving him the eye and adding, "It's a good thing your brother JJ isn't here. He may be younger, but the girls flock to him."

"Yeah, I hate being ignored." Tony laughed, revealing the pride of an older brother in a younger brothers growing capacity.

Tony had the rugged good looks of the Pento family while JJ had a quality neither of the young men understood or faulted that had the ladies of many ages panting. JJ was more a Manfredi. Joe too had come into his own with the ladies but was still growing into his long, gentler features graced by a classic Roman nose.

Graduation was just weeks away, and the fifteen-year-old young men already had jobs. As the crowd settled down to enjoy their sodas, the two young men talked of more serious things. Graduation from Commerce High, a two-year high school attended mornings was just weeks away. Joe would work as a full-time teller at the next to largest commercial bank in the area and had signed up for his first college course at night at NYU. He had plans for making things better, so he planned on keeping his part-time job at Jacobs. Tony would join Pop at the barbershop, though it wasn't what he wanted to do.

Joe asked, "Hey, Tony, how'd you make out with talking to your pop about going Pro."

"I can't budge him. He refuses to allow it. But when I'm twenty-one, I'll be able to make my own decision."

"Work at it, Tony. I'm sure you can convince him." *Cripes, maybe I shouldn't say that I don't know anything about fathers, but jeez, Tony's too good not to try.*

"I doubt it, Joe. He just doesn't understand." Joe told him to keep trying and to keep playing in hope Mr. Manfredi would change his outlook. While they talked about the problems of growing up, Joe mentioned he and his family needed to find a new place to live.

"We hate leaving, but Mr. Costa needs the apartment for this daughter. She's getting married."

A Corner Threatened

The 1920s for Yonkers was proving a boon, as Westchester earned a national reputation for real growth.

By 1927, Joe Prezzemolo had a couple of years as a teller in the local bank and proved he was one strong blade of that growth. His willingness and capacity proved him an asset in the country's thriving field of life. Joe was now enjoying his employers' and clients' respect for him while they enjoyed his unending ability to accumulate appropriate jokes that made them laugh.

He was growing in understanding the intrinsic financial world as quickly as it was changing, and some of it frightened him for the good of all. He was becoming a knowledgeable young man who read the papers faithfully, earnestly applying what he learned both at work and during his one course a semester in downtown colleges. This year, he was attending Columbia University. He knew he was still too young to know it all, so he carefully used his sharpening instincts about people in ways that aided his need to help others. Even at this young age, townsfolk were reaching for him both in and outside the bank for advice because he cared.

The twenties had also turned infamous as a time of gangsters, highly successful in the wide scope of American possibilities.

In 1929, when the business heart of the United States had a serious stroke, Joe thanked God that locally, his world remained intact. Newspapers in the days following the market's collapse bore headlines about Richard E. Byrd's journey to the pole stirring national pride, alongside President Hoover's reassuring messages about the state of the economy being able to withstand the effects of the depression, while reading on the same page descriptions of suicides after financial loss, factory wage cuts, and the plight of thirty states affected by closing of their banks.

Joe's stomach would ache after reading about all the horrors.

When the crash first hit the papers, the bank officials confirmed that the bank where Joe worked, First National Bank and Trust, would merge with another and that it was secure from the losses that other banks were closing from. In fact, they were about to merge with the largest commercial bank in the area and would be called simply, "First National Bank," with assets of $50,000,000.

Joe believed every word.

A local follow-up story told that the bank would one day move into the twelve-story building in Getty Square at 20 South Broadway. Joe smiled remembering watching the building's progress during his morning runs and felt safe.

The next couple of years that brought him to 1932 were terrible for the general population, and he began to understand the situation around him more clearly.

Joe was just one of many people realizing the use of credit had become a far-reaching, destructive development in America's decisions. Credit was an infatuating tool used as a means to broaden worlds both for the rich and the working poor that was as dangerous as a gangster's gun unless used wisely. Joe wasn't comfortable with its directions. He was glad to hear about the government's move to strongly regulate the banks, but he continued to believe in the safety of the bank he worked for and believing, "At least we're in capable hands."

Because of his family's crushing financial past, he saw everything through the eyes of those who had little or nothing. He recognized a bank's capacity to use credit for everyone's betterment if used wisely. Any threat to that safety reached deep into his hungry childhood. The more he learned, the more he wanted to help the have-nots to find and work for balance with those that have. This desire went so deep that the bank had become the second home of his heart; his family would always be the first.

Now it was early March 1933, and the almost twenty-two-year-old Joe left the house as he did most mornings before the sun rose.

Today his watcher, in the land of the spirits, sat back wondering what unusual turn Joe's mind would take to make the running less lonely. He smiled, as Joe stretched his long, lean body at the spoke fence above the front yard where he lived, heard him wish the darkness away, and yearned for the glow of morning as he began a training run for another Yonkers marathon.

The darkness on his long handsome features produced somber shadows far too serious, too alone for the man wearing them.

Joe's run begins at the peak of Orchard Street and down The Hill past dark company tenements to reach the Nepperhan Avenue valley that floors the carpet industry and in moments leaves Pop Manfredi's shop behind.

Garbled streetlight on the factory's dirty windows encourages his imagination to run with him. By this time, he's running past Jacobs' drugstore where a left turn takes him passed the Terrace Movie Theater and the Ice House to cross the small bridge over the Saw Mill River as it ambles on to the heart of town where it will disappear under the buildings of Getty Square's Main Street to feed the Hudson River.

Some of Joe's route this morning would follow the same path.

Joe, hating the isolation of practice running, opened his mouth a little as he took the incline beside the cemetery and conjured up the company of the Indians who cared for the area in earlier times and used the Saw Mill River to reach the Hudson to fish or to go inland to hunt. He mentally joined an expedition.

A nearby, natural spring usually meant grabbing a drink, but the damp morning curbed Joe's need.

Imagination transformed trees into early American spirits that filled him with mischievous wonder. Mentally, he enjoyed being a woodsman, clothed in buckskins, toting a long rifle and making friends with the Nappeckamak Indians. His childhood love of American history was still with him as an adult, and as time allowed, he enjoyed reading and learning.

A shortcut took him to the new Tibbetts Brook Park not yet fully developed over the 161 acres it covered. He quickened the pace in readiness for one sweep around what had been Peekman Lake where the gray pale light of the setting moon brings him back to thoughts of canoe rides with Marian or maybe a walk in the moonlight.

While his mind wandered, his body zigzagged through the trees tunnel like shadows, where lunar darts tumbled through to touch the ground before him and turned into the hazel like gems he sees in Marian Manfredi's eyes.

He crossed a small bridge at the south end of the now Tibbetts Brook Lake north of McLean Avenue not far from where Yonkers meets that borough called the Bronx and began his return route. In moments, he hurdled its meandering brook, backtracked his run to the cemetery, and headed down the hill. This time, he took a drink at the spring and then turned left into the Ukrainian/Russian sector of town, nicknamed the Hollow to pass two churches topped by gold onion domes heralding the faiths only to be taunted by the scent of baking Bobka that rousts his stomach with a whirlwind called hunger.

Mr. Pojer, one of the bank's depositors, had opened a bakery on Walnut Street, and he must pass it to get to the aqueduct that hovers above the Nepperhan Valley. Once there, he continues his run that now cuts back into The Hill before he descends through the area where the Negro predominates. He waves at Toby a high school classmate returning home from work.

"See you at the marathon, Joe." They both laughed knowing that was hard to do since Joe ran covered with local advertiser's placards.

Just yards beyond is Glen Park where all thought ceases, and he tore into a grueling mile where his heels all but kick his butt. As he rounded the city's largest track and athletic field, he passed the tennis courts at the local brewery where the Prezzemolo and Manfredi families play tennis, or ice-skate, or watch free movies. His mind could not help but remember how often he put his rear to the ice with the laughter of the younger children enjoying his folly even though he was grabbing for gulps of oxygen to feed his speed.

Wet and dripping with sweat, he slowed and left by following the route the brewery pipes use to deliver beer to the river for transport.

Joe blessed himself before the Eucharist of St. Casimir's church and wished the sun were out to bounce off the unusual, yellow-orange brick structure. Minutes later, cutting through the open-air market called Chicken Island, just setting up for the day's business, he turned into New Main Street and headed for Getty Square past the Zion Congregation location and the butcher store where his best friend Nick works to arrive at Getty Square.

He stopped in the middle of the Square on an island where trolleys make their pickups for locations all over the city. The island held a fountain where he took a long satisfying drink and rested for a moment appreciating his growing town and the fact his job was helping it to grow. Then he's off again.

Here he passed St. John's Episcopal Church, a Yonkers landmark since 1752 when colonial settlers built it. It stood in contrast to the one across Broadway. Its partial steel frame constructed the building the new First National Bank and Trust would move into after completion. A right turn on Hudson Street took him past the YMCA where he swam competitively. Here an old friend sneaked up behind him to create a friendly competitor; his shadow passed him and, as always, won their race to the river where he walked past the trolley barn to the Main Street pier on the Hudson River. He stopped.

With a deep relaxing breath, he turned to take in the lush trees, and the sense of country they bring to the stone plants of human design growing between and around them only to disappear where the New York Central Railroad bed allowed an unhampered view of the river.

He walked the pier past numerous fishermen hoping to catch their breakfast to where he could watch the now gray-orange river as it coursed beneath the rough, upright Jersey Palisades. As though by magic, sunrays touched them and created a godlike gift of Golden Castles to enhance the days of the people lucky enough to share them. Beneath the castles were manned canoes from the river front club, in an early workout reminiscent of tribal birch bark vessels coming down the river beneath the castles in an era when God shared this land with wiser people.

An unheralded memory reminded him of a time when he was frail and hungry.

I remember when the Palisades looked like a loaf of bread cut with a rough knife. I was so hungry. Thank God it's only a memory.

Joe belched. The healthy burp burst into a quick chuckle for picturing Raffaele's rebuff and said, "Sorry, Mom."

A glance down river took in the view of the unfinished span built to bridge the river between New York and New Jersey to be named after George Washington, a bridge that seems to be whispering, "Dive in, son, the water's fine." The river air caused a slight chill from dripping sweat. He was tempted to answer the call, but there wasn't time. Nudged on by a gnawing thirst, he licked his lips free of drying salt and began a stride to take him home setting a gentle pace as the chatting seagulls bid him bye. The train station was left behind as he crossed Larkin Plaza where he grabbed a handful of water at its fountain near another colonial landmark, Phillipse Manor, and then he picked up his pace at the base of The Hill.

The rising sun forced him to squint as its companionable heat crept up his churning muscles. After the dampness, the warming felt good, as he lengthened his stride. His long, sinewy muscles flow dramatically through the amazing complex structure of a fit man, with a graceful balance, more from swimming than running that took him up the steep grades of the west side of The Hill without harsh effort.

Here the incline of The Hill begins. It takes him home past the State Armory to its eastward climb past St. John's Hospital and Yonkers General Hospital where a left turn takes another incline to pass a tucked in park where gentlemen walk with ladies just before cresting The Hill where Whalen's Funeral Home sits in a converted Victorian house a block away from School Nine.

Here his expressions change into a wide-toothy smile that transformed the stressed features of an earnest runner into the pleasant, handsome young man the town knew. He was the one who ran mornings and called people respectfully by name as they wash down the sidewalks in front of their stores.

A turn into Lake Avenue neared the end of his run. He softly took in large gulps of air to bolster the particles of humanity that fed his love for life. His pace changed to lazy because he chose to socialize as an answer to aloneness. A hello to one of Marian Manfredi's Pento uncles opening his barbershop and the sweaty baker taking a break outside the Busy Baker. In moments Joe tapped old man Dorley on the shoulder as he passed behind him. Mr. Dorley was deaf, but Joe enjoyed his laughter because he's now jogging backward so he could wave to the old man. In short time, Joe left the junction of Lake Avenue and High Streets behind to descend The Hill on the east side.

After a quick drink of spring water on Vineyard Avenue, near the apple trees once a part of an early American orchard, he ran past the homes of cousins, friends, and Grandpa Pento to where he waves at firemen buddies washing down the fire truck. They shared their building with The Hill's only bath house. It's here he meets the local milk man, a cousin, as he turns the corner to Ashburton Avenue.

His cousin holds out a bottle of milk that Joe grabbed like the ring on a carousel and said, "Tell your folks I said hello." In seconds, he took a left on Orchard Street and sprinted the incline to where he went down the steps to home at the Manfredi House.

At breakfast, Joe enjoyed a portion of fresh bread and tea while younger siblings shared the milk that he marked down to remember to pay for weekly. Mary had married a Mr. Chelloti and moved to the Bronx taking Freddy and Anna and soon presented him a new nephew Thomas. Joe mirrored the loneliness their leaving brought to his mother and sister, and he promised he'd find a way to visit them often. Margaret, about to leave for work, stuck her head in to say, "Morning. If I'm lucky, I'll be going out with Harry tonight."

Joe winked, made a funny face at the kids, and suggestively said, "Oh, oh, oh!" Margaret winked at the kids and stuck her tongue at Joe and left him laughing. He remembered Harry so nervous he almost choked when he asked permission to marry Margaret. Harry was away on a building painting project, and because she was pregnant, she was staying with them until he returned. Raffaele had welcomed his proposal openly while Joe had wanted to give him a hard time but couldn't. He was pleased as punch when Margaret asked him to walk her down the aisle.

Washed and dressed, Joe looked very smart and dapper. At five foot seven and a half, Joe's lean, even-cocky walk gave his bartered for clothes the right places to fit, and he enjoyed the female attention it had brought him.

After a quick stop, he walked to work, chatted with retail customers, helped stack apples on an outside grocery stand, and stuck his head into the chicken market on Ashburton to say hello to cousins.

A block further on, he entered the First National Bank and Trust across from a single friends family butcher shop to trade jokes with their Negro guard Henry before entering his teller's cage.

After four years with the First National Bank and Trust, Joe earned sixteen dollars a week. His cage was a doorway to a world of communication and a future helping people make American dreams a reality that wiped away many childhood longings. He was living his dream even though he still held down his part-time job as soda jerk and clerk at Jacobs' Drugstore and took on personal accounting jobs for client's who needed help and willingly bartered their services for his.

Joe's schedule of one college course at a time did not diminish his determination to earn a financial degree.

Besides, he was in love and getting married next year to Marian Manfredi, and he lacked the words to describe how good he felt when he saw the pride in her eyes when speaking of him. He just knew he was happy, but that was this morning.

At the end of the day, an unexpected meeting of all bank employees changed his lovely day to an exhausting unending hill only he could run.

He trudged home, a piece of rubble in the crushing depression. He felt shriveled and angry. *They said this couldn't happen. They said the Reconstruction Finance Corporation would put the banks back on their feet. Why aren't we part of it? Why are we closing? They said our bank was sound. They don't know what the hell they're doing.*

The ramifications chewed at his self-worth until he cried out, "Jesus, Joseph, and Mary, we can't get married. I have nothing." Misery closed in on him like a lion on a downed Wildebeest.

Joe's concern for taking Marian from an affluent surrounding to a cold water flat became puny compared to losing his job.

This morning, he lived in the greatest country in the world, and though it was in deep trouble, he was luckier than most. He'd found Marian and longed to start a family. All that gave the future a magnetic draw, but that was this morning.

Dark, tortured whisperings transported him to a bitter winter night. To being seven years old and lighting streetlamps with a stick so long, he could barely hold it to the gas jet. Raffaele had lined his frayed jacket with newspapers so he wouldn't freeze, but the winter cold never left his feet. Any shoes he had on had been someone else's and were always too big. How alone he felt, but the shoes suddenly took his mind to another memory.

Mrs. Hailey, the principal of School Nine, looked up from her desk and saw Joseph Prezzemolo sitting at the end of bench usually reserved for in-trouble kids and went to the door. She knew it was his first day, and when she looked into those excited deep-set brown eyes in a too-thin face with drawn cheeks, she fell in love again. She didn't need the note he handed her that told her why he was there. Joe's smile was so trusting, so big her heart swelled with giving again. For a moment, his clothes held her attention. *They're so threadbare but as clean as any I've ever seen, but the poor thing has no shoes. Dear God, why do so many children have to do without?*

She watched his toes rub together like lovers discovering each other. Afraid her silence would frighten him, she quickly introduced herself. "Hello, Joseph Prezzemolo. I'm Mrs. Bailey, the school principal. Come into my office, I'd like to talk to you." She led him to a chair and pulled her own next to him and said, "Joseph, you cannot be in school without shoes on because it could make you sick." Mrs. Bailey saw his eyes cloud with disappointment and rushed to say, "I want you to come with me. You can't go back to your class until you have a pair of shoes, so let's go get you a pair." Then she took his hand, enjoyed the warmth of his now adoring expression, and marched him to the nearest shoe store where she and the owner had an understanding. There she bought Joseph a pair of brand new shoes, large enough for him to grow into; these were his alone. Up until now, the only shoes he had ever worn were those thrown away by other people.

The moment's recall softened his fury with the kindness of another. *I remember polishing those shoes every night with spit and smut from the fire on Mom's cooking stove. Mom used to smile at how hard I worked to get them shining.*

The good feeling disappeared into, *Oh, God, hasn't Mom suffered enough. Now I gotta tell her I've lost my job! Why, Dear God, why?*

With Marian only moments away, he rebounded to what Pop Manfredi might say.

Joe treasured the deference a banker's position offered a man, but he needed Gene's respect more. Worse was the worry losing his job might destroy Pop Manfredi's affections.

Loving Gene, as one does a father, he wanted its equal with his own children, but his next thought leaped to Marian.

Oh, Jesus! Will Marian wait for me? There are others who want her as much as I do.

Just before their graduation from high school, Tony Manfredi approached his father Gene about Joe Prezzemolo's family needing a place to live. "And the upstairs apartment is empty right now. I thought maybe—well he's a friend."

Gene studied his usually gruff son for a moment and said, "All right, Tony, I'll speak to Momma."

Gene told Tess what he knew of the family, and after she remembered Joe, they spoke to Tony. Between the three of them, they figured out what the Prezzemolo's could afford, and the next day, Tony sent Joe to Pop.

So the Prezzemolo's moved into the upstairs apartment. Joe knew Tess because he delivered to her from the drugstore but he had seen her more often laughing and playing with neighborhood children. In good weather, she was frequently in the upper yard with her water hose doing a dance with a bar of soap, as both sent the dirt rushing off the neighborhood little ones and laughing at their antics. He knew Pop Manfredi from the barbershop and working at Jacobs and playing with Tony and his siblings on the side of The Hill.

The day they moved in Joe took the first opportunity to show his admiration for the beautiful lady of the house who recently gave birth to Carmella Grace.

Joe hurried down the back porches. To make a good impression, he wore his business suit and an easy smile.

Marian opened the door covered with flecks of flour much of which had settled on her face, brushed a hair from her round freckled face, and wiped a pair of floured hands on the towel tied at her waist. The impromptu apron gave her twelve-year-old changing body, something the straight waist style of the day normally denied. Though curious about Joe and aware of Tony's high regard for Joe, she was determined to make up her own mind about the new tenants, including him.

"Hi, Marian. I'm here to pay my respects to your mother."

Marian liked his confident toothy smile and the smarts to call quickly, but she sensed a discomfort in him and decided not to be her usual straightforward, challenging self. She had learned to do so pleasantly, and though wrong in her reasoning, her instinct had been right on. She had no way of knowing Joe was squeamish rather than shy. Ill people made Joe very uncomfortable, and Tony had told him Tess wasn't really well.

"Momma is expecting you, Joe, and she enjoys company. Just go up the stairs and turn right. She's in the second room with my sisters Angie and Beth. They just got home from work."

"Thank you, Marian." He thought, *Tony's right, she's a good kid,* while taking the stairs two at a time. As he passed into the upstairs living room, he saw a large bedroom off to the left with three twin beds next to the door going out to the porch. There he saw the reason for Marian's powdered look. There were more homemade macaroni and more Cavatelli that he'd seen on the dining room table downstairs. Here they were strewn across a white sheet on a bed waiting to dry.

No wonder Marian looked like a powdered ghost. They sure eat well in this house. His stomach automatically did a wishful flip.

His attention was caught by the ladies giggling and beginning a sentence with, "And then he—"

Joe had sisters. *Sounds just like Mary and Margaret when they're discussing men.* As he entered Mrs. Manfredi's room, he saw Carmella Grace propped on the pillow beside her.

Both Angie and Beth were beauties. Angie had the edge for looking so like Tess, and since both had many beaus, Joe understood there was much to discuss.

Just then, Tess raised her shadowed face to where the late afternoon sunlight filled her hazel eyes mirroring him as she spoke.

"Joseph Prezzemolo, come in. How fine you look. I'm so happy you and your family will be living upstairs." Her hand waved him to the bed, and that too tight feeling in his gut disappeared. Joe nodded at the girls.

The sunlight softened Tess's freckles, and he realized Marian was the only daughter who had them. He quickly moved to claim a place on the bed, saying, "Thanks, Mrs. Manfredi. Dare I ask who the lucky guy is you ladies are discussing?"

A laughing Tess began, "Joe, how did you know," and stopped. All heads went to the doorway as Raffaele and Gene entered through the hallway door and joined the group on the bed. Joe's warm feeling of welcome slipped into laughter as he leaped up to offer his mother a seat. Gene called out to Marian, kissed Tess, and the girls kissed

Gene, and Carmella Grace started wailing for dinner just as Marian herded JJ, Sossy, and Millie into the room.

Without missing a beat, Tess covered her bust with a diaper and gave Carmella a nipple and friendship between the two families began strong and deep as Joe said, "Looks like Baby Grace knows it's time for supper already—smart girl."

Tess gave him the nicest heavy lidded smile he'd ever seen, and he was glad he remembered Tony had told him about Gene wanting to call their latest child Carmella and Tess wanting to call her Grace. Joe was the only one who called her Grace, and Gene enjoyed the playful scene as much as anyone.

That Sunday, Tess insisted on returning to her morning doings having asked the Prezzemolos to join them for breakfast before going to St. Joseph's, a dominantly Irish parish, to attend mass. She joins Gene at the stove making pancakes for all with eggs and sausage, fruit, milk, homemade jellies, and cakes to fill the many different appetites around the table. Only after the meal reached the table did Tess and Gene join the pleasant gathering with their children responding to any further needs with the up and down comfort of training. Chatter and good manners went hand in hand, bite to bite, and all helped with the clean up except Tess, Gene, and Raffaele whom Tess insisted sit and enjoy her day of rest. A rare and gracious time, for in striving to compensate her family for having less, she was guilty of spoiling her two youngest with doing for them no matter how exhausted. Tess saw it immediately.

The Prezzemolo family quickly learned of Gene's many embarrassments at home. With his entire brood at home, pleasant chaos usually reigned, and the "who" in their names tended to elude Gene, coming out in the absent rather than the present. Marian became Beth, Millie became Angie, and Beth became Millie. Perhaps Gene mixed a father's desire to keep his girls young with a family resemblance that had them looking alike in the many stages of growing. Neighbors and friends were always confusing the girls.

The two families, though cut from the same cloth of heritage, were from very different bolts of life and destined to grow closer and closer.

Early on, Tony growled in his gruff voice, "Hey, JJ, want to help me show Prezze a good time?"

JJ beamed. *I'll be with the older guys.*

The teenager was now so good-looking his sisters teased him mercilessly. At this age he couldn't take full advantage of the gift that would soon dismay neighborhood parents.

Joe's good time was to be a trip to the Manfredi cellar and its world of culinary delights.

At the bottom of the narrow staircase descending from the Tess's kitchen, Joe lived a social shock. He was standing in his palate's dream of heaven.

Tony winked and JJ said, "Joe, help yourself. Tony says we're going to have a party."

"Jeez, guys, are you sure it's okay?"

"Heck, Joe, it was Pop who told me to tell you that you and your momma can help yourself whenever you need something. He meant it too, but he wanted us to have something just for you."

"I know about that. Your mom told mine, but it's really too much."

"No, it's not. Pop does things like this for people." Their was pride in Tony's voice. "Tonight, Pop wants you to have a good time. So try everything." Tony laughed and put the utensils, glasses, and dishes he was holding on a nearby table.

Joe was a drooling puppy entering a store where everything had been put on the floor where he could reach it. The loaves of bread under JJ's arm now made sense.

Joe explored. He found barrels of potatoes, apples, pears, and onions. Remnants of when the cellar housed horses, halter hooks in the rafters, supported slabs of dried bacon, provolone cheese, salami, pepperoni, and prosciutto. Beside them hung varied sausage-like meats he'd never had and couldn't name.

A rectangular wine press triggered Joe's active glands, as he envisioned the Manfredi girls crushing the grapes barefooted, skirts pulled high and tight around their hand size appealing cheeks. It was a family trait that many a young man wanted to fondle.

The publicly endangering thought was overpowered by the temptations found in an icebox containing two blocks of ice and perishables. Childlike enthusiasm subdued Joe's normally good manners. A wayward finger dipped into his most favorite dessert and came out dripping with rice pudding to relieve his mouth of its impatience.

"Oh, God, Tony this stuff in terrific." Suddenly, he was embarrassed by his lack of etiquette and almost stopped licking his fingers. When he realized Tony and JJ were enjoying him enjoying his excitement, he looked around for the dishes.

JJ said, very seriously and in his best adult voice, "Here, Joe, it's the biggest bowl we brought down."

Tony and JJ howled with laughter, as Joe took the bowl and filled it to the brim and said, "Thanks, JJ."

Two stories up Raffaele heard a son's boisterous laugh and smiled at his hard-earned pleasure as Tess said, "Raffaele, you are very lucky. Joseph loves you dearly."

"Si, Tess, I very lucky. Fine, healthy children and amici." She squeezed Tess's hand as she said it and watched her lean back so very tired, and her eyes filled with a strange sadness she'd learn about as days went on.

As he ate, Joe looked to the rear of the cellar where Gene kept several fifty-gallon casks against The Hill's cool granite wall. The temperature there was just right for chilling the wine and liquors he made.

"Joe, would you like a red, a rose, or a Rhine wine?"

"Can I try them all?"

"Sure. I'll get them."

Joe peeked into large ceramic crocks and found eggplant, hot and sweet peppers, cauliflower, carrots, cucumbers, and pickles.

Holy smokes, what do I pick first. Pop Manfredi is a great guy. Jeez, how'd we get so lucky? Joe dramatically raised eyes skyward and said, "Thank you."

Jugs of tomato paste joined shelves of canned homegrown tomatoes from Gene's large garden in the backyard where chickens and turtles roamed freely. The tomato stores kept the sauces for macaroni in good supply, and though the boys would eat macaroni three times a day, the parents in this home enjoyed a more encompassing menu on their table.

For Joe, the coup de grace was the furnace. He couldn't resist a serious moment. "You know, guys, it's such a good feeling being warm. This is the first time we've ever lived anywhere with steam heat. It's great."

By now, the boys were making sandwiches of their own design, so Joe grabbed a loaf of bread to join in. Their wedges would have made Dagwood Bumstead proud. With everything in reach, they lounged by the still.

Later, Joe made a second sandwich of pepper, cucumber, salami, pepperoni, and cheese on Italian bread. While there, they talked and laughed at words funny and not funny, as young men will. Eventually, the wine had its way with Joe, and he heaved everything he ate and then some.

Tony and JJ wanted to laugh, but Joe was so sick they didn't. Tony all but carried Joe up four flights of stairs while poor JJ took a deep breath and had the honor of cleaning up the mess or answer to one of his parents or worse his sister Marian who had a way of making him feel bad when he'd misbehaved.

Gene caught Tony on the second floor, cleared his throat, and warned, "Raffaele should take a switch to both of you, you chioffos (donkeys)." And quietamente, Momma is not feeling well."

Tess would never truly be well again.

Raffaele eyeballed Tony as he helped Joe into bed. "Wio, whatta you do to Guisseppe?"

Though Tony knew her gentleness, he fidgeted through, "I'm sorry, Mrs. Prezzemolo. Honest, we just wanted him to have a good time."

Raffaele nodded in affirmation, as she brushed the damp hair from Joe's brow and decided to leave a growing young man to learn his lesson. Tony hightailed it out the back door as she said, "Grazia, Tonio." With a half smile, she fetched a basin and placed it next to Joe's bed.

Joe didn't stop throwing up for days but went to work sharing the misadventure with his customers to salve the sick feeling, but as they tittered or roared, he inevitably sprinted to another expunge. One long hurting purge vented an earnest plea. "Dear Mary, Mother of God, let me live through this, and I promise I'll never get drunk again. Never!"

Gene, the typically confused father of girls, watched the entry of his oldest into the dating world where she dated, and he worried because his shame was so obvious even when Angie dutifully kissed him. Gene could do nothing about a silent Poppa Pento who could not help but favor Angie for being so like Tess while harboring thoughts against Gene so like his own.

It was a world of doing where his older girls found favor, not only with young men but also with their many uncles who enjoyed opening social doors for them to safely pass through. It was a safety that hopefully allowed good judgment to be chosen. Their uncles were a protective bunch buying them time to weigh the merits of the younger men of their specie. The young women were quickly learning both the good and bad in the male herds of their generation while still very naïve in the bigger world. However, The Hill offered more than their own heritage. Still the closed doors of closed minds were active everywhere.

In talking to the girls, Tess knew she had to prepare Gene and did, but she was limited to her own values and experience in the time in which they lived. She was able to help the girls with, "Gene, we already have all but lost Angie, and none of our girls will accept arranged marriages. And quite truthfully, I can't see it for them, and I agree with them. Please do not even consider it." Gene kept a close eye on them but realized he could not rule their choices but still believing they would pair with Italians.

Upstairs, the Prezzemoli family was going through a similar period, and Joe, being the man of the family, found his concern for his sisters was softer than Gene's but as a man of his own generation, without the commanding ardor of the previous generation, watched, but wouldn't interfere unless a real danger was present. "So help me, Mom, if anybody hurts the girls, they'll answer to me."

While the girls loved him for caring and knowing he would be there if they needed him, Raffaele would worry for Joe doing something violent. The look in his eyes when one of his own had been hurt had remained with her, and she prayed that nothing would ever happen again to anger him that deeply.

One day, at seventeen, Joe received a disturbing dunning letter from a collection agency. The items mentioned included a baby carriage, crib, and other household furniture.

Joe said, "Oh, shit."

"Guisseppe!" Raffaele startled Joe with her sharp tone.

"Sorry, Mom, but this is bad news." When that disturbed her even more, he smiled and said, "Not that bad. But I have to do something about it. I think some cousin and there are a few Josephs is using our address and not paying his bills, and the store is threatening to sue me. Mom, I work for a bank. I can't have bad credit assigned to my name. I could lose my job."

That Raffaele understood his lapse completely forgotten.

The next day, Jack said, "Who's the lucky girl, Joe?"

Joe blushed as his bank manager laughed and picked up the phone to call a city judge for an appointment.

In a matter of days, Joseph Louis Prezzemolo legally became Joseph Lewis Prezzemoli and changed all his existing records to protect his good name, his job, and his family. Then he called Louis in California who wrote regularly and visited Raffaele with his many children every few years.

"Lou, how are the kids doing?" After a few minutes, he explained about the change in name, and Louis said, "Damn, Joe, if they'd do it to you, they'd do it to me. We'll change too." Though separated by a continent, they remained a family. On the west coast, the family was doing quite well owning and thriving in private businesses.

Only then did Joe deal with the thieving cousins stating telling all, "If this happens again, there will be no loans for any cousin at any bank I work." That put an end to the problem for all time.

The Prezzemoli and Manfredi family members missed little within each brood.

A week later, Joe was waiting for Tony to finish dressing so they could leave for the dance at the Polish Community Center when a Manfredi misadventure rekindled his first visit to their cellar and he roared with laughter.

It was a rare day that Tess had again cooked with Marian's help, and missing Millie and Sossy, she asked Marian to find the too quiet youngsters. Just then, Gene came in from the living room and joined the hunt. Gene found them in the cellar unable to stand and moaning about their ailing stomachs right beside an empty bottle of delicious cherries that had been aged in his fine brandy. He called out, "Familia, they're in the cellar."

Marian flew down the stairs, came upon the scene, and burst into laughter as a reluctant father joined in. They carried them to the kitchen just as Angie and Beth arrived ready to say good night and leave for the dance. Tess—undisturbed by another of her children's misadventures—smiled, shook her still magnificent head of hair, and said, "Girls, take Sossy and Millie upstairs and put them to bed. The dance will have to wait a few more minutes. Poppa's brandied cherries were their downfall."

Both girls giggled as they took the ailing twosome and rushed to put them to bed before leaving. Marian stayed behind for its being her turn to be sure Tess had adult help but hearing Joe's roar of laughter said, "I'm sure Joe knows why the kids look so green." Now Gene and Tess joined her laughter for remembering his plight. The girls returned and Marian's smile disappeared as she sadly shook her head and watched as Angie left without kissing Gene good night and wondered, *How long can you continue the war with Poppa. It hurts everyone.* She and Beth had talked to Angie of it but nothing changed.

Beth was joining Tony and Joe and his friend Nick while Angie was meeting a young man neither Tess nor Gene liked.

Raffaele reveled in having close adult friends. A drab life had become more than work and children. Since moving in, Raffaele now listened to many sounds of home with great joy. A radiator's whistle was a luxury she thanked the Blessed Virgin for every night.

The limited time spent with Tess was a sharing of worlds particularly when illness forced Tess to bed. Now that was more and more frequent. They passed the time watching The Hill's children play on Orchard Street just above the yard. Sometimes during the summer, she would join Tess as she watched Sossy use the hose to give The Hill's children a bath in the yard. Sossy's clowning and majestic poses with the hose made children and watchers laugh as few could. Tess said, "Oh, Raffaele, he is my most endearing son, it seems no one can refuse him once he's charmed them."

She was destined to miss his growing into the man she had just described.

Both families loved music and spent evenings with the neighbors and their instruments that so reminded Raffaele of Gaetano. Raffaele, hearing Marian play the piano with the spontaneous bands, realized she had become a fine musician who ruined the men's fun because they could no longer tease her about her mistakes until she decided it was more fun to have an "oops" moment.

Over the years, great fun was had with a topless wine decanter. It had a long spout sticking out one side shaped like the tin man's cap. They would hold it high, lay their heads back, and tilt it forward while aiming for their wide-open mouths. A hit brought a cheer, a splashing a din of laughter, and when a young one asked to try, laughter multiplied because they let them.

At one gathering, Tess was in bed. Raffaele was there to keep her company. The ladies could hear all the fun, allowing them to pleasantly share the friends and music. Raffaele said, "Ah, Tess, Marianne plays so good, she remind me of my Gaetano."

"Ummm, she does, but she's good at anything she tries. She is somehow different, and yet all my girls are good daughters. It's a difference that will help her. She seems to understand so much more than I." Tess took a deep breath as though fatigue brought her other thoughts.

Raffaele smiled at the hint of concern in Tess's remark and said, "I very likea all your girls, but Marianne I likea best. She always do special things to make your day better and treat me with the same respect she offers you and Chiulli."

Tess could not miss the sadness in Raffaele's words and said, "Of course, she does. She knows you deserve so much more than that. And you do deserve so much more. Gene feels the same way about you—we all do."

The high praise touched Raffaele but the sad in Tess's effort took it away drowning the party sounds with troubling words, "For Gene, respect is so important. I've never been able to make him understand he misses much with our children because he stresses it in everything."

Knowing the story of Madre, Raffaele said, "Oh, Tessa, he likea animal trapped." When the right words failed her, Tess finished for her with, "His own doing!"

"Si, Tessa, si."

Tess's hazel eyes suddenly filled with tears that told Raffaele there was more to their talk today than light joyous sharing of proud mothers.

"Tessa" was all Raffaele could say, and not finding the words to ask, she waited and hoped for the problem's sharing and maybe ease her sadness.

The hesitation made Tess remember her friend understood far more than most, so she took Raffaele's hand knowing anything said would be private while thinking, *In days, everyone will know, and the telling will change nothing.*

"Raffaele, my Angie is pregnant of her own doing and will not listen to us about marrying the baby's father. We fear it will not be good for her or the baby."

Raffaele saw Tess's pain, remembered her Mary's mistake, listened and shared her Mary's folly agreeing with the danger of unhappiness, and told Tess of the greater danger. "Oh, Tessa, he hit my Mary so bad, even when with bambino."

Tears flowed from Tess, and they reached for each other. Raffaele held Tess as she cried her heart out for the grandchild she feared she'd never see.

Then they talked for a long time trying to deal with their parts as mothers in their oldest girls finding themselves pregnant. Both felt they should have done more, said more, as honest and imperfect mother's do. And as friends, they understood each other's helplessness.

Later that night, Joe's head flew up from reading his newspaper when he heard Margaret ask, "Mom, what's upsetting you?" Joe saw a tear and leaped up to join them, saying, "Mom, tell us."

It took only moments to explain to her two adults and dreaded the pain it could cause. Joe looked at Margaret and took Raffaele's hand, saying, "Cheez, Mom, I hope I'm never stupid enough to get a girl pregnant—everybody gets hurt."

Margaret nodded at him, kissed Raffaele, and left the room full of a searching silence women used to seek answers but thankful her child would arrive without blemish. She remembered her own decisions and accepting to understood the need for women to make their own decisions about the men in their lives.

Raffaele answered Joe's concern with, "Si wio everyone get hurt. Say nothing till you hear from others, Tessa and Chiulli hurt bad."

"Ah, Christ. Mom, what's gonna happen?"

"Joe, she will marry but—"

"Yeah, but I remember Mary too. Maybe it'll be better?"

"Si, maybe."

Joe went back to his paper but could not concentrate and instead made a promise to himself and whoever the woman would be that he'd marry. Joe knew the problem between Mr. Manfredi and Angie, but Tony had sworn him to secrecy. Both Tony and Joe had been concerned about her beau's drinking and wondered if Angie realized how much. He felt helpless but remained silent as expected.

This business of not reaching out to help is crazy, but I can't make decisions for other people all I can do if offer to help. Angie doesn't listen to any one. Tony tried, so have Beth and Marian. I'll offer to help, but I can't see it happening.

The days were passing little by little like a thick pudding sliding slowly down a spoon, as Tess's gaiety and giving diminished.

The families missed little within each brood.

Angie's rebellious corners stirred by her hateful anger for Gene left her refusing family help abruptly leaving home, pregnant and soon married. Tess continued to crumble under the loss. Tess's smiles and gaiety diminished further as Angie found more unhappiness for herself and those who loved her.

As usual, Gene and Tess had talked it through. "But Tess, he's Polish and see how he drinks. And how she spoke to us, to you, and she loves you more than anyone. Cara Mia, this cannot happen in this house."

"Oh, Gene, it has happened. I have no answers, and I'm so tired. I'm helping less and less. We forbad the marriage, and we offered to take the child and help her raise it. What more can we do? She's refused to stay within her own, and soon, we will have a grandchild, one I will never see now that you have disowned her." The last came out sounding like the accusation it was.

Gene's mouth opened, but no words came. His mind was spinning with the hatred, the disgrace, his own and his daughter's, all whipping him with more hurt. Now they had few smiles for anything. He felt the distance between him and Tess widening, as was the curse of Poppa Pento's disregard.

The remembering of what happened left him ashamed but still insistent on what he believed was right. The hurt continued as did the wall of silence.

In that place far away, a helpless watcher sadly understood the heartbreak between father and child for a father's mistake. Knowing neither would decide to change a watcher remembered his own misplaced guidance but could still hope. But time was no longer an ally.

Raffaele helped ease daily doing for the girls before and after her own work. And she was able to tease Gene out of his moods as few could. She had nicknamed him Chiulli after watching one of Tess's youngest visitors reach for him saying something unintelligible that sounded like Che-ool-ee. Later, she called his attention to the moment and found he enjoyed it. Then she added the sounds together, and it became Raffaele's nickname for him.

Gene enjoyed the teasing so much that Chiulli became an endearing term for him.

One night, Tony said, "Cripes, Joe, your mom's the only one who can really tease Pop like that. They've become good friends."

"Yeah, and it's terrific for my mom. She's never smiled as much as she has since we moved in here. I'll never be able to thank you enough."

Tony grabbed Joe's shoulder as others joined them, and Joe greeted them with a new joke.

For Gene, Raffaele's teasing was a way to share the little laughter Tess's illness allowed them, and Gene realized any kindness they had shown the Prezzemoli family was more than repaid by Raffaele's caring for them all, as was the respect and gift of laughter brought by a young man he was proud to know.

Raffaele's common sense world exposed her to the sadness in Gene's inability to change. Worse, he had begun to hide in his world beyond the house on The Hill at all male functions. Watching Tess waste away and losing Angie had tainted him with bitterness. Still they talked as friends do.

"Chiulli, my friend, I am seea Tess every day. I know you hurt butta you musta find a way to forgive Angie."

"Raffaele, my daughter sinned and worse married wrongly."

"Eh, maybe you talka nonsense? I no know much. But my Mary was with child, and she married this Italiano who almost kill her. You seea my Mary's lump? He kicka her while she carry Anna."

Gene gasped, "My God."

"You seea that in other Italiano, no? Angie no getting hurt that way by Polish wio. Chiulli, let it go."

"Raffaele, I cannot."

Raffaele wanted to say more of her thoughts. *You unable to let go of Momma and only because you made a promise that was wrong in the first place. Care for the more important things, amico mia.* But she couldn't, he was hurting too much.

Instead, Raffaele kissed him on the forehead and returned to sitting with Tess, saddened because she could not tell Tess he might change the situation. At night, she prayed to the Virgin Mary for her friends. Her prayers traveled to the world of the spirits, and though heard, nothing changed because the will of a man called Gene held the answers and those were mostly his alone.

The watcher's helplessness remained as he watched life's darkening shadow move closer to Tess.

Tess was grateful for Raffaele making days easier and became more and more concerned about the children she would leave behind. She looked down at her swollen legs and felt the end nearing on those days when the swelling moved farther and farther into her body to where she knew it would claim her soul. She could no longer avoid the thought three of her children would grow to adulthood without her. She was sadder still because Gene could not handle what was happening to her. She appreciated his trying to find ways to bring her pleasant times, but they were his ways not hers. He was handling her illness badly and everyone noticed, including Gene himself.

The time Tess spent with the girls was precious, and the best of times was when they washed her beautiful hair.

It became a habit for the girls to leave the window of Tess's room open because it looked out into the upper yard. It was there her other children, like Buster Muschak, would stick his head in and say, "Hi, Mrs. Manfredi," while young girls came through the open door to see her, usually with yellow dandelions in hand.

Meanwhile, Angie gave birth to Tess and Gene's first grandchild, and Gene had a granddaughter he would acknowledge too late.

Both families were growing as dating changed loving or needing and in most times they kept to choices within their heritage. Beth met Paul, and Joe's sister Margaret's belly grew bigger waiting for Harry's return. Both lads were American's of Italian blood bringing a softening to Tess's struggle.

Marian was soon to graduate and told no one, not even Tess, that she was planning on going to nursing school. It was time to deal with Pop.

About the same time Joe realized a dream, thinking it was good timing. *This should cheer everybody up at least a little, and we'll get to see Mary and the kids more often.*

When he arrived at Orchard Street, he stood above the house and called out, "Mom, Margaret, come down." Joe then leaned on the horn of a used 1927 Ford Class A Automobile. Anyone home at 92 Orchard came running up the stairs or were hanging out a window, not to mention interested neighbors and their children.

Raffaele was sitting with Tess, so they stuck their faces through the window to see Joe's surprise.

Joe's First Car

Seeing them, he yelled, "Hey, Mom, I'm coming down." Joe flew down the steps and into the house, removed his hat, and said, "Hi, ladies. I bought a car, and I want all of us to have fun going places in it. Right now, I want to take two of my favorite gals for a ride around the neighborhood." His voice, full of excitement, went through them like warm socks on a chilly evening. He rushed on in explanation.

"Mrs. Manfredi, I know you might not be able to come, but if you feel you can, I'll carry you up, right now!" Raffaele and Joe too knew she could not, but Joe's sharing with Tess gave her the feeling a mother gets when a son says, "I love you." Tess squeezed a smiling Raffaele's hand and said, "Raffaele, go with Joe but come tell me all about it when you get back. And yes, Joe, I will go when I feel better."

Joe said, "Okay, Mom, it's you and me this time. And the very next day you're up, Mrs. Manfredi, I'll take you wherever you want to go, okay?"

Tess's smile made him feel more the man as he took his mother's hand and led her away, but Raffaele was only "almost" all smiles as she asked, "Guisseppe, whatta you do? Cana we afford this machine?"

"Sure, we can, Mom. I saved a long time for it, and it only cost me twenty-five dollars."

Raffaela felt a surge of panic. In a very weak voice, she said, "That more thana you make a week.

Mom, it took me years to save for this, we sure can't afford a new one. That would cost $325. With all our hard work, we earned this." He watched her smile, sigh and she said, "Si, you right."

At the top of the stairs, the Manfredi youngsters and Joe's younger siblings had already piled into the car leaving just enough room for Joe and Raffaele in the front seat. Joe laughed and held the door for Raffaele in the style of a grand swashbuckler.

After a noisy ride with the kids, Joe brought them back near dinnertime and finally noticed Marian watching him from the door as she took the youngest kids back into the house to finish getting supper on the table. Raffaele went to sit with Tess to tell all. And, Tess told Marian, the Prezzemolis would eat with them. Untroubled, Marian nodded and headed for the kitchen knowing Gene, Tony, Beth, and Joe's sister Margaret would be home soon.

Joe, realizing he'd made more work for Marian and that she too would want a ride, came in behind her and said, "Hey, Marian. I'll take you first with Pop and Tony after dinner, okay?"

"That'll be fun, Joe, we'll see you downstairs."

Joe's fine set of wheels brought opportunities to broaden the world for both families. Now he planned Sundays around taking them to pick apples along the Saw Mill River Parkway or swimming further north on the Hudson and enjoyed helping Tony Manfredi shop for his first car. Most of all, he was thrilled with taking Raffaele to the Bronx to see Mary, Freddy, Anna, and his new nephew Tom Chelloti. He missed having them around, and his love for Mary in particular made them special.

Socially, the car made dating a far more interesting event as the ladies were very pleased with a gentleman who called for them in his car. Fast becoming a man of many layers, he enjoyed life for all its adventures as long as people were a part of it.

The world suddenly dimmed as death took Tess. Before leaving the warmth of the children she loved she did hold and see her first grandchild because Gene had sent for Angie but Joe never got to share a ride with her.

Tess, bloated by body fluids, drowned in them surrounded by Poppa Pento, Gene and all her children for Gene had sent for Angie.

As they watched the doctor helplessly declare her gone; a struggling, Gene pulled an unfeeling Tess from the bed shaking her and begging her to stay, but she could not.

The young adults and children brokenhearted grabbed someone close as they watched Gene with mixed, complex reactions ranging from the horror of hatred to acceptance and understanding, all shaded in the measure of right or wrong homed in personal values.

Poppa Pento, droop shouldered, saw nothing of Gene's pain and walked away, for his own sorrow placed him on the edge of an abyss he was willing to throw himself into and yet could not.

Angie walked away disgusted for a father's actions and added it to the lonely and bitter thoughts that she had lived with since leaving the home of her childhood and losing much of herself never again to be found. The hurt and love for Tess so huge in those years was still a part of her but no longer had a mother's voice to bridge the distance hatred had created. Bearing her second child, she left forgiveness to others.

When Tess's eyes closed for the last time, she found herself without fear of the unknown, and her watcher smiled at her arrival and silently stepped aside for she arrived as a glowing child to stand before a beautiful lady in blue who took Tess's hand and guided her to a special place where loving spirits make a home for arriving children. This was a place Tess always knew existed and had strived to help recreate its presence on earth. She chose not to be a watcher or guardian.

Raffaele and Joe came down to pay their respects and to help with the arrangements. Joe heard Marian say to young Sossy, "I'm going to ask Tony to take you for a new suit early tomorrow since you've outgrown your Sunday best. And Millie, you'll wear the dress Momma loves on you. You'll both want to look nice for Momma. You know how very proud of you she is when you look your best." Then Marian turned and saw Joe standing nearby.

JJ could not hide his tears, so Marian pulled him close and told him things Joe could not hear, and the faltering smile it produced on JJ's teenage face brought Joe a cautious one of his own and a feeling he couldn't identify.

Marian wiped JJ's tears and kissed him before sending him on his way. Joe stepped closer and quietly said, "Marian, I'd like to take Sossy for that suit," he hesitated, "if that's okay. It'll give you, Tony, and JJ time to concentrate on what's needed here."

"Thank you, Joe. You and your family are making things so much easier. Your mom is taking care of Carmella Grace for the night."

Tess was waked at home, as is the era's custom, in the living room just the other side of Tess and Gene's room.

Angie stayed with Tess to see to the proper handling in preparing her for the wake, the right dress, the combing of her hair, and the chance to spend time with the mother she loved and had not seen in months. The weight of her loss was as crushing as a strangle hold, but at its worst, the bitterness of her values was greater. She relived the moments of her death, and black moments in times past. She had lost her way and refused any path back.

Marian had just graduated high school and gone to work at Alexander Smith's, and at fifteen, she had been happy to be near Angie. Her time there was short, for Tess's death immediately turned her to a future very different than any she had dreamed about. Her desired career, one she would have to fight for, was now further away than just overcoming Pop's objections. She loved her brothers and sister, and recognizing their needing her, set her own desires aside. At least until they were old enough to do without her care.

She was untroubled by the new responsibilities and Gene's request to take them over.

"Marian, Momma said you are best to take care of the children, is that all right with you?"

"Oh, Pop, I know that's what Momma wants, but we will have to talk about it because there are other matters to be considered."

"Si, familia si. Another time."

Marian worried for him, but with eyes filled with tears that could but would not fall, Marian started her new life.

Oh, Momma, what will we be without you and Angie too. At least at work I was able to spend time with her. It's not the same.

Her siblings knew Marian's prowess in the kitchen but recognized something they couldn't put into words that made Marian different, and all agreed she was the best choice to help not only the youngsters but for all of them. Even Poppa Pento and her many uncles agreed, though Poppa Pento never uttered a word directly to Gene.

Beth being at the carpet shop and Tony at the barbershop left Marian alone to combat the cruel loneliness of being wherever Tess would be. Caring for the children left Marian with no time for teenage activities because she was changing daily, becoming a woman far beyond her years. It was not unusual for her time in life. She was particularly talented in helping a grieving father who saw Tess in almost everything she did, and he soon realized the younger children thrived, having more fun than circumstances had allowed before.

The next couple of years passed with Raffaele and Joe doing what they could to erase the grief and bring more laughter back to the household.

Gene could not help but notice that Marian had young men who vied for her free time, and they were good wio's who appreciated what there was in her that would make a man happy. Some were not of Italian descent, but he believed she would know the good from the bad and did not push as he had with Angie. He also appreciated that though Marian enjoyed their company, she also had an eye on family.

The Prezzemolis always joined the family at a mass or novena for Tess and had watched the children find their way through the loss of their best friend to become much Tess wanted for them.

At twenty, Joe too had grown and learned much from the living of every day and spent time with many ladies in their social world just enjoying the fun. This year at Tess's novena, Joe was surprised to find himself watching only Marian. Her courage, strength, and compassion had taken a troubled father, grandfather, and children through a difficult adjustment; and he was surprised to find his friendship had turned to admiration wrapped in the fact she was no longer a kid.

My God, she's so tiny, and yet she's handled everything and everyone. I never really noticed how much she's changed. She's really something. I'm glad I've been helping with JJ and Sal. She's great with them all, particularly Carmella Grace. I'll bet Momma Tess is awfully proud of Marian. Mom said Mrs. Manfredi knew she would. It's a shame about Angie, but she can't let go of the whole thing. Mr. Manfredi refuses to do more. At this point, I can't blame him.

Gene had tried with Angie but failed, and as time past, he found himself ill-equipped for single parenthood. When he heard Carmella Grace crying for Tess, he would rock her to sleep or put her to bed beside him. The strain showed, and in other ways, he unthinkingly brought the younger children hurt that only lasted moments because Marian interceded and never hesitated to tell him how to handle it or how to undo it. Soon grateful for her ability, he relinquished

Carmella Grace to Marian and compromise became a part of his daily life.

As time took the Manfredi children to adulthood, the marks of Tess's death ran the gauntlet from festering or being buried to do no obvious harm or heal.

Though the loss of Tess went deep, Marian was able to walk through the hurt in her own way. One day, she was cooking and, without thought, began a conversation with Tess in the same way she had when standing beside Tess while learning to cook. Her concentration was on a variation of the tomato sauce Tess had taught her to make and, without thinking, turned and offered its new flavor for her to taste. Her mind stumbled over the mistake but was rescued by a sense of Tess's smiling approval.

On another day after a very busy hour trying to finish before the youngsters were home from school so she'd be free to spend time with them, she heard a knocking on the floor over her head and thought, *Momma*. She quickly wiped her hands, lowered the gas jets, and ran out of the kitchen through the dining room and started up the stairs, two at a time, and froze halfway up, sat down, and wept like a child wanting to be held by her momma. *Oh, God, Momma's dead. Oh, Momma, I miss you so. All this is so different without you to share it. Please, God, let me be strong enough to do all she wants of me.*

Marian wept herself to fatigue. It was the first time she'd cried since Tess's death only to realize, *Oh, I needed that, didn't I, Momma. Well, it's time to get back to doing, I hear Sossy coming. Oh, Momma, he's such a devil.*

She wiped her eyes and gave the children a big "Hi, you two." Millie took one look at her sister and knew enough to go to her and give her a big hug, while young Sossy said, "Hi, Mar. I'm gonna have something to eat," and rushed to the kitchen. Marian burst out laughing. "Leave that cake alone, and I'll decide how big a piece you get." She winked at Millie, and the girls went to join him.

One gorgeous summer day, the Prezzemoli and Manfredi families joined those going across the river for a day of swimming and picnicking at the beach below the towering Palisades ready to fully enjoy the river's blessings. Joe, Sossy, and Tony swam across the Hudson from a point further north of the ferry pier enabling them to use the currents to their advantage and to save the ferry fare. With Sossy between them, Joe and Tony took great care to keep Sossy safe from the unexpected threats of currents they knew well. The other frolickers boarded the ferry to meet them on the beach. Coming ashore they heard Sossy's cheers telling them how good a swimmer he was while Joe and Tony admitted he was really good.

Once on the Jersey side, everyone joined new groups to pursue the fun young people pursue. At one point, Joe stood atop a ferry piling casting a shadow upon the water. He was about to dive in again when he found himself watching Marian as she walked into the water and tried to swim.

I'll be a monkey's uncle. Marian's afraid of the water. I was beginning to think she wasn't afraid of anything.

A surprisingly protective but wanting surged through him, one that was anything but fatherly. He hesitated. *She might not want my help.*

Joe's View And Hope

Something inside him began to change as he realized he was seeing Marian as other men saw her, a sexy and sassy la Donna, and there wasn't a brotherly thought in his stirred mind. He was suddenly annoyed by Marian's seeing him as a family friend. *Gotta change that.*

He dove off the piling and cut the water with stokes that barely stirred the water heading straight at Marian.

He came up beside her, shook his head like a wet seal, and said, "Marian, would you like me to teach you to swim?"

The invitation was one she wanted, but she was really too frightened to chance and laughingly said.

"No way, Joe. Like my brothers, you'll try to drown me first."

For a moment, he found himself lost in her hazel eyes, something he'd been missing because he usually saw her with glasses, but he quickly said, "Come on. I won't dunk you, but you have to lean across my hands so I can show you how to float."

Marian looked from those long, interesting, tapered fingers to the big winning smile on his handsome face and was abruptly shocked by feelings she hadn't anticipated and lisped through, "No, thank you, Joe. I'll just stay cool and keep an eye on Sossy and Millie."

Disappointed she wouldn't let him hold her in deeper water, Joe spoke brashly but quietly, "What's the matter, Marian, afraid to let a guy hold you?"

The fierce look she gave him and the icy "Joe, go soak your head" was followed by her storming ashore looking like the proud lady she was. Joe swam away realizing the foolishness of his remark. *Oh, boy, I made a real mess of that. She's anything but afraid of being held. What's wrong with me? I did that all wrong. Marian has no trouble being held. She loves to dance, and I haven't seen her afraid of anyone. For crying out loud, I want to hold her close. It's me!*

He almost laughed out loud at himself for understanding why the small expanse of water between them seemed too large for him to swim. He was feeling like he had the first time he ever approached a girl for a date, until he remembered Andy, a friend they grew up with.

Holy smoke, Andy was serious when he said he has a special interest in Marian.

The humor gone, he rushed to a needed decision and started swimming toward Marian only to lose a stroke when hearing, "Hey, everybody, let's take a picture."

Marian walked ashore dealing with the anger toward herself for being too frightened to swim and had another of the conversations with Tess since her passing.

Momma, I enjoyed Joe wanting to help but not his wise crack. Did you notice how good he is in the water? He strokes and the water barely moves. I wish I weren't afraid of the swimming, and I don't know why I am. I shouldn't have gotten angry. Joe's a good guy, and he's right there when we need him. I wish—

She too heard the call for a picture.

The young men organized a pyramid with the Marian, Beth, Angie and Millie on top held aloft by many friends. Joe enjoyed holding Marian aloft as Gene pushed the button on a little black box called a Brownie Camera capturing memories for them all.

Before Joe could do anything about his decision, everyone was called to a finger-licking crab and eel meal that closed the day just as the sun disappeared behind the Palisades and surrounded them with a cooling shade.

Joe couldn't wait for the meal to be over nor could he take his eyes off Marian. He was sorry he had promised to eat with the children because he didn't break promises.

Geez, I must be as dense as the rocks on the beach. I've seen Marian eat dozens of times, but I'm just realizing she's as graceful as Pop Manfredi when she eats and she enjoys every bite. She's a lady I'll be proud to have on my arm. I hope I haven't waited too long.

Joe rode the ferry home under a beautiful sunset he wasn't noticing that took sky blue into steel blue smeared with orange and shades of bright violet. He was busy searching out Marian and spotted her at the ferry railing watching the sky. He approached her realizing he wanted to watch the sunset with her.

Finally some luck, both Andy and the kids weren't hanging on to her.

Joe moved quickly, took the space beside her, and said, "Beautiful, isn't it?"

Without turning to face him, she said, "It always is, we just forget to appreciate it."

"Marian, I'm sorry about my wise crack earlier. I didn't mean a word of it, and I'd like very much to take you dancing next week at St. Joseph's, if you'd like to go with me?" Now all he could hear was the *thump, thump* of the ferry's engine or was that his heart? Realizing he was about to ramble and she hadn't answered him, he shut up.

When she turned, he noticed she still didn't have her glasses on and as those hazel eyes took on the hue of the sky and he again found himself lost in reading them.

Her simple, unrushed answer, "I'd like that Joe, very much," made him lean on the railing beside her feeling relaxed for the first time since he dove off that piling to reach for the woman he saw.

Marian and Joe

Marian Manfredi, Joe's lady of choice, could sizzle words like an egg over a too hot flame, but an anger or hurt voiced was usually forgotten, unless you hurt one of her own. Then vehemence walked directly at you completely in control until the wrong turned right or until it prevented further ill-doing. Her entry into adulthood was full of dreams homed in a solid self-respect.

While Joe grew to manhood through his dating, he was unaware of Marian still so young. Marian was growing as an individual to whom people were the keys to a world that opened many doors others might fear to pass through. Even after finding themselves in the same social set, it was without reaching for each other except as friends who were extended family.

Tony and JJ watched her coming out, as brothers do, but more for the pleasure of watching her put any hooligan, foolish enough to treat her as less than lady being put in his place with quick, sure tongued verbal-to-the-point reality. Of course, they were always there as backup. And yes, she knew it.

Marian came to adulthood as a petite five foot two with a posture both erect and commanding. The creator had added to the picture those hand-sized Manfredi cheeks and a generous bust in a carriage just short of conceit. Exercise from tennis, skating, walking, and running The Hill had put marvelous curves in her legs atop an emphatic arch that gave her walk a soft rhythmic sway.

The day would finally come when she'd smile for remembering Joe telling her that her walk warmed him with an urge to run fingers from her toes to her close-cropped black hair over the temptingly long route.

Unfortunately, Joe also told her that its drawing masculine attention angered him. That, in turn, infuriated Marian making her a loving adversary to what he thought right and normal for a man. Marian had long taken a proud stand on what God had given her and determined that its disturbing Joe was completely wrong. Marian despised jealousy, and knowing this, Joe felt sure she'd realize the worth of jealousy after they married and that too brought her temper into full bloom. Anytime jealousy reared its ugly head, Joe received her anger's full scathe, but Joe—lacking full understanding—chose not to change this path.

Marian's first career choice, nursing, made at age fifteen, crashed when Gene refused permission to study for such a dirty job.

Marian knew Gene was protecting her and chose to fight this mistake immediately but respectfully. It was this handling that helped convince Gene, Marian was the one to take care of the children just as Tess has said. He listened carefully as Marian said, "I will do as you say, Pop, because you are my father, but I want you to know you are wrong and time will prove it to you." She also thought, *Well, I tried and Millie, Sossy and Carmella still need someone. When the kids are old enough I'll do what's right for myself.*

Marian had quickly found Gene's lack of fathering skills had become her advantage.

Marian knew Pop could forgive an error but not disrespect. And so she continued to tell Gene what she thought particularly when silencing a child and, as time passed, admonished him with, "Pop, don't you realize that your silencing Angie may be at the root of the distance between the two of you." And daring all, she finished with, "It had to be more than the slap, Pop, and it goes back to times before that."

Whatever his reaction, Gene persisted in silencing JJ and Millie, but Marian flew to their aid.

"Pop, I'm sorry, but I have to disagree with you about silencing JJ. It's too harsh a censure for a young man. It's better to talk to him about another punishment. You know Momma never wanted us silenced. It only leads to more hurt."

"Marian Sossy and JJ are to be men and they must learn but perhaps you are right at least about Millie, she is too quiet, we will see."

Sometimes, Gene listened and recanted. Other times, he just stood his fatherly ground. One thing Gene learned emphatically was that Marian was definitely Tess's daughter in heart and soul. The difference was a strength and love for thriving in the outside world he'd never seen in Tess. He privately acknowledged that, *If Marian chose to, she could take life on completely alone but that she chooses people instead is a blessing. I must do for her based on how she sees life.*

The caring decision brought a smile to his watcher, as the Archer sped an arrow of light to ease a father's pain.

Disappointment found no bed for rest in Marian's thriving spirit. Her vigorous taste for doings made many worlds possible. Stirred in this mix was her capacity for growing, and it showed itself in the courage to try whatever opportunity came her way. The everyday winning and losing of these battles had birthed a confidence that could turn a mistake into a success or accept the reason for not.

When Joe became a part of their lives, another corner presented itself, but it needed nurturing and other men before she could recognize she wanted to take life's corners with him.

Their dating turned into loving where they enjoyed figuring out what took them so long and laughed at concocting silly reasons. A courtship filled with lightheartedness and awareness fostered healthy friction between them that proved oral skills fluent in both, a fluency that usually eased troubling events, through discussion.

One night after a dance, Joe drove Marian home. A passionate groping in its natural way found them both in the same instant with hands, tender and exciting, exactly where they wanted them to be. Joe, as hard as he'd ever been, and Marian, impassioned as she'd never known, elicited spontaneous reactions. Joe said, "Oh, Jeeez, Mar," and pulled away so fast he slammed into the car door only to see her laughing nervously in the same position against the passenger door. Some quirk of their minds went from wanting to a full stop for remembering.

Joe blew his breath through pursed lips and straightened up.

"Mar, you know I love you, don't you?"

"Yes, and I love you, but I—we can't."

"Hush, hon, we're going in. There's no way in hell I'm going to have to tell your pop or my mom we have to get married. It's happened to them both, and everybody was miserable."

"I don't want it that way either, but I'm as much to blame."

Joe barely heard her for having leaped out and ran around to her door to open it.

"Thanks, hon, but you're one dangerous lady to be alone with." His caring smile made the jest all the more disarming. Joe merely put out his hand, and Marian slid hers into it. They gazed at each other for a long moment, and without further words, Joe walked her down the steps.

At the Manfredi door, Marian—in questioning herself—said, "Joe, shouldn't we talk about this?"

Joe studied her for a moment and whispered, "Yes, but not now. There's something I have to do. God, woman, think of the damage you've just done to my reputation."

Something different in his smile made her blush, and she suddenly knew how she'd be the night they wed and said, "Thank God you're not a blabber mouth." She watched those bushy eyebrows rise in pleasure as he backed up the stairs in spite of the discomfort of pants still too tight.

Not wanting him to leave but knowing he must, she laughingly said, "Joe, remember what we said about the things we want our kids to know?"

"Marian, you're merciless."

"Well, this is one you have to tell our girls about."

"Gladly, but only if you promise to tell our boys about it because they'll never believe I passed up such an opportunity." Grabbing a deep breath, he smiled and said, "Even I don't believe it." Now halfway up the stairs, he quickly said, "Night, honey," and ran already relieving himself of Marian's revealing impact.

Marian closed the door behind him, hoping Joe would be all right for his morning run. The marathon was months away, but he trained regularly. They had shared much about a man and woman's physical world, and both were anxious for their first time being together as man and wife.

The next morning after his run, Joe met Marian as he came down the stairs for their usual private moment before going to work. Both laughed through their embrace and promised to spend a quiet evening on the porch. As she walked away, Joe reached for her attention.

"Hey, pretty lady."

"What, Mr. Prezzemoli?"

"See you later."

Marian's breath quickened in reply, "You'd better."

As Joe took the stairs to the street, two at a time, Marian closed the door softly and warmed to the stirring of her innards for the tempting fantasy her mind suggested.

Later that day, she was taking lunch to Pop and Tony at the shop when she suddenly broke into a sprint to chase the trolley that ran north on Nepperhan Avenue all the way to the city line near St. Joseph's Cemetery where Tess was buried.

Despite looking like a lady, the trolley was easy to catch with a full out sprint, but once there, she had to shift the lunch pails to one arm to be able to reach out with the other. With that hand, she grabbed Sossy by his suspenders and the waistband of his knickers and pulled. Caught by surprise, Sossy yelped and fell backward while his sister ensured his skinniness fell against her to avoid his getting hurt. She took a quick breath and said, "Sossy, I warned you if I caught you hitching again, you'd be sorry." She was shaking him so hard he had to pee.

Though no match for Marian, Sossy wouldn't completely surrender. She wanted to wipe the hopelessly straight hair out of his eyes, but she never let go of the squirming hellion, causing the free-swinging lunch pails to swing like crazy bell clangors.

She dragged him fighting almost to the barbershop, looking like an engine pulling an overloaded caboose. Neighbors passing by laughed for she said hello to all as though nothing was happening. As they passed into the view of the window, Sossy's squirming stopped. She gave Sossy a look as she marched him through the shop's door and into a corner. Suddenly, he went quiet allowing her to lay out Pop and Tony's lunch on a clean towel. Sossy was now praying she'd say nothing about his latest doing. Marian joined the adult conversation without a mention of him, so he knew he escaped a stroking with the barber strap and remained quietly perched on stacked boxes filled with lemons and oranges. The fruit was another of Pop's gifts to neighbors and friends. The depression had not destroyed his keeping his promise to those who had less, and now he made sure Tess's other children had what they needed in a time harmful to them.

Old man Pacey, who was getting his haircut by Tony, said, "Marian, give up your banker beau. He's too young to know what he's getting."

"Thank you, Mr. Pacey, but Mrs. Pacey likes Joe too much for either of us to take the chance."

Pacey blushed at the responding laughter of his fellows and said, "On second thought, Marian, you're too smart for this old man."

Gene said to his longtime client, "Joe's also lucky that Marian is as fine a cook as her momma." He glanced over at the lunch and said, "Thank you, Marian."

Marian smiled quickly made a face at Tony, whose thank you was more a growl as she headed for the door with Sossy in tow.

As she left, Pacey said, "Gene, you'll miss her."

"Si, I will."

When Pacey left, Gene sat, ate, and had a widower's thought. *What I really appreciate is Marian's ability to stand between me and our younger children when I make mistakes. Her temper makes me think. Tess was right. She is the one best for the children. She holds us all together. She even keeps Angie in touch with what's going on, though it has brought change there is something missing.* The thought was brushed aside, and a new conversation started with Pacey.

Marian made sure Angie knew what was going on within the family for missing her and so that at home they knew how she, Micah, and the children were doing. She enjoyed taking the younger children to visit their now three girl cousins. That was unless Marian wanted private time. She still believed that with time Angie would forgive completely. She loved Angie and could not believe otherwise yet always stood up to her when she began a rant against Gene. At times like that, Marian never fully recognized her sister's depths as being all too familiar. Tony, Beth, and JJ freely stopped by to see her and the children but not as often as Marian. About now, she would find out a fourth child was in the making, and she loved being their aunt.

As Marian and Sossy climbed the hill to home after delivering the lunch, Marian turned to enjoy the Nepperhan Valley. Despite the spewing stacks of the factory, the background hills of rising green splashed with changing leaves were too pretty to ignore. Sossy caught her smiling, picked up a blade of wheat grass to chew, and said, "Bet yer thinking a somethin' mushy with Joe, huh."

"No, you fresh kid, I'm not, but I will." *And much more than that, Sos, much more.*

Sossy's mischievous answer was, "Race ya?"

Already running, Sossy heard, "No fair." Though laughing, Marian almost caught him. He rushed into the house, yelling, "I'm king of The Hill," his way of telling her he'd be on the throne in the downstairs bathroom with its toilet bowl resting three feet above the floor on its cement shelf.

The day was busy—several washes, ironing, shopping, and making sure Sossy stayed out of trouble after school while being there for Millie and Carmella. JJ was pretty much on his own but smart enough to check in with his sister to avoid her checking up on him. Marian would steal minutes for reading an Agatha Christy mystery. A maternal glance showed Sossy, the ceaseless scooch, laying candy on the table to torment siblings. Pop had given him a nickel to spend and knowing Sossy would charm away displeasure she returned to her book.

Finished for the moment, she placed it next to one of Joe's gifts, a wonderful little book telling of the founding of Yonkers. It reminded her of his love of American history particularly Indian folklore and the pleasure of their discussions on current events taken from the newspapers each night. The first time she saw him reading one, she laughed because his natural left-handedness had him going from the last page to the first, unless an article was continued. He enjoyed the humor around it and wouldn't change for anyone.

The economy of the 1920's had taught Joe much about banking, and he explained it all to Marian so that she had become his equal in the discussions. As he learned they shared his entire world with Marian, and she shared that world with Tess, as though she was listening in a nearby doorway.

Something deep within Marian knew that wherever spirits go, Momma heard the telling. "Oh, Momma, I enjoy using my mind and talking to Joe means thinking and growing. Look what I'm learning about the dangers of getting what we want through credit. He's so good I can forgive him anything, except his jealousy. I can't make him understand how wrong he is? It's our only real problem. Is it that he doesn't trust me? That's not true, and yet maybe it's something else? I don't know for sure, but it makes me so angry." She winced at her outrage reaching heights from which it had to crash dive. What frightened her most was the thought of losing Joe, but if it had to be, she knew she could and buried the defeating thought preferring to find the winning way.

Later, she escaped the busy of preparing dinner by playing at solving the Agatha mystery she had been reading. She continued training Millie and Carmella in the skills of cooking in the same manner that Tess had trained her. That lead to much laughter from her older sisters for remembering their own fumbling flavor fiascos. Carmella was being spoiled by Gene, but she was a good kid so much was overlooked. Marian doubted Grace would ever be the cook her older sisters were but only because so little was asked of her and she took full advantage of it.

Tonight, there would be roast chicken and potatoes accompanied by sausage for flavor plus spinach in oil and garlic, creamed carrots, and fresh bread and butter. Dessert would be simple: an icebox cake and whipped cream. Sossy and Millie fought over the whipping device to be able to lick it clean. Marian made sure Sossy lost this one because of his trolley hitch. Sossy grumbled but Marian's look of iron froze him silent for remembering he hadn't yet been punished for the fun ride.

He found himself only washing vegetables and taking out the garbage as part of his comeuppance, so he did it without griping.

Marian was glad Sossy had finally learned that when she said something she meant it. She stirred her tomato sauce for tomorrow's meal and licked the spoon smiling at the excellent flavor and thinking, *Thanks, Momma, for teaching me to cook. I love having everyone together. We have so much fun when they're enjoying the food. And Joe is so easy to please.*

She was looking forward to living with Raffaele and having a mother again. Raffaele had made Momma's death easier, but Raffaele's two youngest were another story. Raffaele had spoiled them trying to make up for having so little, and they didn't show the respect their hardworking mother deserved. Joe was angry about it but loved kids too much to be a mean taskmaster. Marian wanted to change the LaQuido children's attitude and tried every time they had dinner together.

She talked to Tess about it. "Momma, I don't think the kids will change, but at least I can give them someone else to be mean to, and maybe they won't hurt Raffaele as much."

Somehow, Marian's body clock always told her it was time to watch for Joe, though balancing out his accounts could vary his arrival greatly. More often, being late had more to do with his tendency to finish first and staying to help with any problem that occurred.

Marian had Millie setting the table as Tony, Pop, and JJ arrived from the shop in time for dinner, but JJ was in a rush for a date to play cards or with yet another lady in a very long list.

It troubled Marian that her male siblings were discussing taking numbers into the shop as a sideline concerned that perhaps Poppa Pento was encouraging this involvement, but knowing nothing about his Mafia connection except the whispering about the cars. She only said she hoped they wouldn't. They did!

Joe's day at work had a strangeness about it, but he couldn't pin down the feeling, so he concentrated on his customers and enjoying them, but he was continually saddened by the increasing difficulties they had each week as he watched their savings deplete.

Immediately after the day's cash was balanced, the tellers were called to the manager's desk to watch him pull pay envelopes from his drawer and turn toward them to raise his face showing them he was almost in tears.

Joe's stomach lurched as they heard, "I'm so sorry, but the bank is being closed. I know we all thought our bank was solid and sound, but I guess we were wrong. Today's our last day, and I have your pay envelopes for you. All I can do is wish us all luck and hope we'll all be back together soon."

Joe's feet felt like lead weights inhumanly heavy and accepted the yellow envelope. The shocked atmosphere left no time for anything except leaving to pass on the bad news. Crossing the bank's threshold, he almost tripped over it for his mind was racing ahead of him and sadly acknowledged the Negro guard's hand touching his arm with a tap from his shaking fingers without their eyes meeting for fear of its effect.

It brought a powerful fatigue comparable to his twenty-third mile when running the Yonkers Marathon knowing the worst hill was still to come. His legs were heavy with one part of him wanting to run home and the other preferring to run away. His lungs were wildly pitching up and down, not that he noticed because of thoughts just as powerful making him like a beast wanting to tear something apart.

This is insane. My world just fell apart. He stopped short and, for a moment bewildered, only to find himself at the foot of Orchard Street looking at the top of The Hill where Marian and his mother, unaware, were waiting.

"Oh, shit, how can I take care of them?" He turned the corner for home with his hands deep in his pockets.

He felt as though he was drowning in love's responsibility, yet he turned the corner, hands going even deeper into his pockets. He unexpectedly saw himself a very sad little boy he'd once been but couldn't remember why he was so sad and the fright became worse passing people he knew without being aware they said hello.

His torment peaked as he turned into the steps to go down to see Marian knowing she'd be in the kitchen giving dinner to Pop and the kids. Joe power kicked an oppressive rock. It didn't help. Now his toe throbbed with a strange warmth, as though a fond memory he couldn't find amid the chaos of his mind. Joe didn't know it, but that valued memory of gifted shoes, was a part of his mind hovering near to prevent his mind from closing down and help him to climb the hill he must, but couldn't prevent its crashing in on him again.

"Oh, God, where will I get the twenty-five cents a week I owe on our engagement ring?" He froze like a stone statue with bushy eyebrows creating a dark and threatening façade that would have made him a stranger to those who knew him. Only the laughter of the family passing through the kitchen window told him he was passing the field of peppermint outside that kitchen. He gritted his teeth but didn't take a piece to chew as he normally did before greeting Marian. The thought of losing Marian weighed on his heart, and breathing became more difficult.

Joe ran his fingers through his hair as he opened the screen door oblivious to the succulent aromas that had always brought him the joys of anticipation.

As he entered the kitchen, Marian turned to accept Joes affectionate greeting, but instead, he put out his hand and asked, "Marian, please come with me."

The heads of Gene, Tony, Beth, Sossy, and eight-year-old Carmella Grace came up in reaction to not receiving a greeting from Joe only to watch him lead Marian outside.

Gene said, "Hush, all of you, something serious has happened."

Once on the porch, Joe, unable to face Marian, stared at the cemetery on the hill. Marian brought him back.

"Joe, what is it?"

He turned slowly and, wanting to avoid her penetrating gaze, reached for her hands and looked down at them. That was more painful. All he saw was the ring.

He spit it out, "Marian, the bank is closing, and I've lost my job." Amid a deep breath, he continued, "We can't get married, and you may not be able to keep your ring."

His mouth was parched, and he thought, *God I'm thirsty and my lungs feel like bursting. Why doesn't she say something?*

Only a moment had passed.

The silence closed in on both sides of Joe's head like a vise, and it hurt bad.

Marian, finally sure there was nothing else to hear, said, "Joe, we either get married when we planned or you forget about it—completely!"

"But—"

"No buts, Joe. We get married, as planned, or not at all."

Joe looked straight into a pair of hazel eyes colored in fierce and unflinching determination until she added more softly, "We'll manage, hon, we will!" A slow smile lit up his face, and he took her into his arms.

Still startled, Joe worked through her words and all she was in that moment with an insecure whisper, "Marian."

She brushed his ear with the words, "Or not at all, Joe?" Now it was Marian's turn to struggle through the silence, her cheek next to his burned with concern for his well-being only to slip away as she heard his, "Dear God, thank you."

In their love's warmth, he suddenly felt human again and burst into laughter and softly said, "Honey, if a rock could speak, you were what it would have looked like. God, no wonder I love you until it hurts." He pulled her still closer as his mind turned agile and leaped to looking for options in earning a living.

Marian let go of her chosen battle to tender and snuggle, saying, "Don't you ever scare me like that again," and succumbed to the grateful embrace that she suddenly needed very badly.

Joe's hill to run was over with the sudden realization he'd known what she would say, remembering, *look what she did at the wedding interview with Fr. Agusto.*

"Marian, your friend Connie can't be your maid of honor, she's not Roman Catholic." The persuasive Italian accent lost all appeal.

Marian was strong in her faith, but a sense of conscience was the basis for decisions before man-made rules. There was no room in her life for man's foolishness, and Connie's being Greek Orthodox, so similar to her Catholic faith, riled her conscience's clearly defined sense of right and wrong. Marian stood, trying to be respectful and spoke clearly.

"Fr. Agusto, St. Joseph's won't marry us because it's an Irish parish. The fact we attended all services there and supported all activities and fed the collection basket every week doesn't matter. Now you tell me that because Connie is Greek Orthodox, she can't be my maid of honor."

Joe watched Marian's chest heave in determination. "Father, Connie will be my maid of honor, or I will not get married in the church." Joe leaped to his feet to stand with her thinking, *Good for you*, and waited for Fr. Agusto to erupt.

The priest had looked to Joe for understanding, but when Joe reached and took Marian's hand, he leaned back, steepled his fingers under his nose across his lips, and took their measure.

Marian was grateful her hand was in Joe's, but she refused to take her eyes off Agusto.

Agusto took a deep breath and said, "I think, Guisseppe, you will have an interesting life married to Marianne." He smiled and said, "I will see you both on the twenty-sixth of November at 4:15. You will be married at the altar rail, and Constance will be your maid of honor." His eyes never left Marian, and the corners of his lips had the slightest upward curl.

Joe's mind rushed him back to the porch and the lady in his arms. *I should have known losing my job wouldn't scare her off and she'll be mine on the 26th.*

Joe put some space between their pleasurable proximity, took Marian's face in his hands, kissed her, and said, "Come on, I have to talk to Pop."

In telling Gene the news, Joe expressed fears, financial and personal.

Gene was quiet but, wanting to encourage and reassure Joe, waited for him to finish and said, "What is important, Joe, is how you care for Marian—how you care for your family. You'll find work, you always have, and Marian does what she knows is right. And, Wio, as long as we're together, we will help each other just as we do now."

As they continued to talk, Marian drifted to the stove to fill her and Joe's plates while tuning into the exchange and wishing Pop handled his natural offspring with the same compassionate deference.

Later, Joe told Raffaele whose fear was calmed by the now self-assured approach of Joe's caring.

Joe continued to work part-time at Jacobs, held a second job as a soda jerk in a malt shop on South Broadway and some personal accounting jobs for former customers who were not good with their books, and felt stranded by the bank's closing. He took less where it was needed.

In free hours, he sought another full-time position and was thrilled when his former bank manager recommended him for a job to join the behind the scenes locally to reopen closed banks based on FDR's new programs to stimulate and reroute the economy. It was a painful but exciting year that included the end of prohibition. When the closed bank reopened, it was based on stringent rules, and each account would be insured to a fair maximum.

Joe ran in another Yonkers Marathon looking like a deck of cards with all the advertising signs pinned to his clothes flapping in the October wind. He had fun looking for friends and others he could wave at and point out a sign, often running backward to draw attention to them or to challenge a runner behind him to a sprint. Marian and the children, Manfredi and Prezzemoli, waved as he passed the corner of Ashburton and Nepperhan Avenues.

One payment for wearing a clothier's sign was the promise of a fashionable, perfectly fitted tuxedo for his wedding.

For all his busyness, Joe could not forget the promise to Marian to talk about raising their children, saying, "Marian, I want to be a good father to our kids, and I want to be like your pop in many ways."

"Don't let Angie hear you say that, she'd be so angry with you."

"Boy, that's an understatement if I ever heard one." They shared a wishful smile as he said, "I wish she wasn't so bitter. Pop isn't perfect by any means, and he never should have hit your mother, but Angie is so unhappy she's mixed it up with her other problems, and that's lousy because Pop's a good man." As Joe watched the sadness creep across Marian's face, he started to apologize. "Mar, I'm sorry, I—"

"No, don't. It's just that I have to hope you're wrong about Angie, even though a part of me has begun to dread some of my thoughts."

Joe kissed the hand he was holding and said, "So we'll keep trying. As you said, Pop's easier to deal with than he used to be. Heck, I'm sure she appreciates what Pop sends over every week." He slowed to think. "God, I can't imagine our being parents. Maybe I should be more scared."

"Oh, Joe, we're going to make mistakes too, and maybe they'll be worse." She chuckled. "At least they won't be the same ones."

Joe howled with laughter. "That's for sure, and it could happen to our girls, but if it does, we'll give her every chance I promise."

"If it happens to us, whether it's a son or daughter, we'll hurt just as much as Mom and Pop did."

"Yeah, a son can ruin his life too."

Marian nodded and asked, "How is Mary doing, I know you miss her."

"Yeah, I do. She's okay. I just wish her husband was different. But she's a lot tougher than she used to be."

"I know you worry about her, but I doubt he'd abuse her."

"That's not it, Mar. It's kind of hard to put into words, but it has something to do with his being Italian, you know old country values. They kind of conflict with being American, but as long as he's good to her and the kids, that's all that really matters, right?"

The impish smile on Joe's face told her he was reaching for her in a softer way and the rest of the evening, was lightened by wondering about the children they wanted and how different they would be as people, reminding Marian of Pop taking her to the speakeasy for beer… "And he wore his horseshoe diamond stick pin in a silk tie. I so love that pin. He looked so handsome, so worldly, and Momma made sure I looked perfect every day reminding me as she did all of us that your poppa loves you."

"Yes, he does and so do I." Joe's toothy smile made her warm and wishful that time would pass more quickly as Joe added, "I understand about his tie pin. Every time I see it on him, I kinda think of it as a mark of his being a good man who's helped my family when we needed it. I know I've said it before, but Pop's the only real father I've ever had." Joe seemed to drift away from the conversation for a second only to bounce back and say, "Honey, think you could arrange to have a girl first. I want one just like you."

"You're serious?"

Her tone of surprise caved to realizing the women in his life had raised him lovingly and said, "I'll see what I can do, Mr. Prezzemoli," and added a provocative tease. "You're either a very brave or very foolish man, thinking you can handle two exactly like me."

Joe burst into laughter proud that she could bring lighthearted thoughts to them with, so few words and their attention turned to just loving each other as the close of another day demanded a parting.

In the world of the spirits, heads discreetly turned to watch others in the household with hope for the father trapped in his sense of honor.

Some bad news reached the Manfredi household that impacted the situation. Angie's husband Micah contracted a disease from the wool at the carpet factory making it impossible for him to continue to work full time at anything.

Marian saw it as an opportunity to heal the wounds between Angie and Pop so after talking to Joe who asked, "Hon, can I help? Do you want me there?"

"Oh, I want you there, and I wish you could be, but Pop would die is he had to face your openly sharing the fact he hit Momma. He knows I tell you everything but—"

He placed his finger across her lips before she said the unnecessary and said, "Just don't hurt too much if it doesn't work out. Okay?"

"I promise. And I'll tell Pop I want you there when he and I talk family. I think he'll agree."

Joe and Marian felt the rearing of Sossy and Millie, and nine-year-old Carmella Grace was the key to Pop's capitulation, if only Angie would agree.

Marian and Joe planned to stay with Gene to see Carmella Grace and Sossy through their teens.

They knew Pop felt the kids were still too young to be without a woman's influence, and his fear of hurting his two youngest with his clumsy handling of growing needs made it a real concern.

Marian chose a time to talk to Pop when she was able to get everyone out of the house. Joe took both brood of kids to a free movie at Glen Park to avoid any unexpected intrusions leaving Marian free to say, "Pop, you know Joe and I are planning on staying here until Sossy, Millie, and Carmella are ready to be on their own, and I know you know about Angie's Micah being seriously ill from working with the wool. It's time to talk about helping them. We can't let them starve."

"You know I will not let that happen, and I've done what had to be done. I know what you are asking, but what of you and Joe who have done so much for the children? What of Raffaele and her children? There is no room here? I will not hurt all of you or help Angie more than I help you."

It reassured Marian to know he'd been thinking about it.

"Oh, Pop, Joe and I've talked about it. Actually, I wanted him here, but we'll be fine."

"Si, Marian, he should be here when we talk he's a good man, but tell me what you have decided."

"We know they need the help very badly, so we'll get our own place and take Raffaele and the children with us. It'll be tough, but you know I love Raffaele, and it's fine with her too. Besides, we'll still need your help in the same way you've always helped Joe and Raffaele and Angie and Micah, only now there's me too."

Marian saw he was remembering the severity of Angie's hatred through the years but appeared at ease with it. Marian noting he eased, decided not to push it any farther except to say, "Pop, I know you want to help Angie. But you have to ask her to come, or it won't happen. Besides it is what Momma would want you to do. And Angie's bitterness isn't just you anymore. Now it's more about what her marriage and hatred are doing to her and their children. She refuses to accept and acknowledge her part in it, so she won't make it easy on you."

Gene closed his eyes, nodded, and remembered. Marian went sad, kissed him, and left him to deal with his demons.

Next she had a sister-to-sister talk with Angie that threatened their very caring for each other, but it helped that Marian found enough strength to keep her temper in check even while Angie raged. It was now obvious. Angie would enjoy having a hold on Pop.

"So now he wants my help. It's about time. That's the least he can do after what he's done. He knows he owes me, and I'll make sure—" suddenly, she stopped.

Marian watched a strangely unpleasant yet familiar smile cross Angie's face, so like Tess's features, but in their mother, it had been sadness. In Angie, it was something Marian didn't like. Feeling it was wrong.

At this point, Marian wanted to scream, instead her thoughts ran angry. *How dare you after all Pop has done for you. Your kids would be starving without what he sends over every week. And you take it as though you were Momma and earned it. You haven't, but maybe now you will.*

Marian went into attack mode but reversed the reaction to understand her thinking. *My God, she's capable of doing exactly what Nonna did. What does she think she's won.* Marian found her answer and went stern, "Angie, I love you, but you can't do things that will destroy this family. If you do, I'll fight you, I promise I will."

Suddenly calm with realization Marian said, "Angie, Pop is offering you help. Just remember you're a part of this family and it's our home too. I have to go, Joe is due back." Suddenly, she just had to get out of there, so she kissed Angie reminding her of their last gown fittings.

Angie broke her strained silence with a hesitant smile to say warmly, "You're very lucky, Mar, Joe's a great guy. You'll have a wonderful day."

The next evening, Gene talked to Micah and Angie but never told Marian what was said just telling the family that Angie, Micah, and their four children would be moving in after Marian Manfredi became Marian Prezzemoli.

Gene was obviously upset, and Marian again feared she'd made a very bad mistake. But she shook off her dismay and went in search of a job.

It took a while, but she had the promise of a job the day after they married at a laundry near Getty Square.

An intelligent, tough concept of life made any job during the depression very acceptable. Compromise and the insistence on deciding things for herself set her apart.

Joe hated the choice, but life and Marian demanded it. He longed for the money to send Marian to nursing school but accepted it was wishful thinking.

November finally came. Turkeys for Thanksgiving swung from butcher hooks, but as long as millions of people stood cold in the streets over fires across the country, it was hard because all too many had was surviving another day.

In the meantime, Marian's immediate friends and family arranged a small bridal shower for her.

She was thoroughly enjoying the surprise that brought her a wash basket almost full of canned goods like milk, vegetables, and fruit all which Marian was thrilled with both for the caring and expense that went into it. Angie had something else for her. A beautiful, wistful print of a Collie sheepdog, his head high as he howled for help as he protectively stood over a fallen lamb in a seemingly unending deep snow. The print's subtle background tended to take you from wherever you were into the picture's cold barren place, and yet the emotions it wrought were warming. Those knowing Marian realized that Angie recognized Marian's true callings. Marian pulled it to her body and radiated the love for her sister without hesitation.

Marian felt it was an unspoken promise to take care of the children still at home or thanking her for doing just that after their mother died, which didn't matter. Angie's managing to find fifteen cents to buy the picture was very difficult, and Marian knew it and loved it. It would always grace her bedroom.

On November 26, 1933, neither Joe nor Marian remembered what was happening in the world around them because it was a rare moment in life where two people were the only ones that existed in their minds.

Marian slipped into her white, satin, softly flowing, floor-length wedding gown. A woman friend of Joe's had asked to make Marian's dress, and though the fittings excited her, today was very different. And she said, "Oh, Momma, it feels like silk."

The uninterrupted design of the gown flowed over that petite frame so that she appeared deceivingly delicate at ninety-six pounds.

A voile veil borrowed for the occasion fell behind her blue-black iron curled hair to cap those broad bright hazel eyes above a happy smile. Her hands rested on her glasses until she pushed them away with the decision they had no place in today's doings. Her hand went to her neck where her wedding gown fell in soft tufted ripples that curved gently across that generous bust to a slender belted waist, cinching the skirt to greet the subtle curve at the hips. The flow vaguely reminded her of a Victorian design yet crossed over to the fashion style of 1933 with its skirt floating just above the ground. The tufts that crossed the shoulders ran down the sleeves to peak in downward steeples above her fingers with a touch of elegance.

"Oh, Marian, you're beautiful," said Connie her deeply olive skinned Matron of Honor, meaning every syllable.

Marian threw her arms around Connie for sensing the bride's feelings.

A thrilled bride sighed, "Oh, Lord, I am. Thank you, Connie. Thank you for being my friend."

"Do the opinions of sisters count, we know you're beautiful too." Beth's eyes were full of tears of happiness as she spoke. She and Angie beamed at her as they peeked around the doorframe from the next room.

Marian said, "Oh, Beth, you'll be more beautiful next year when you and Paul get married. I'll miss you all."

Connie, still flushed from their private moment, handed Marian a bouquet of twenty-four white roses. The bridesmaid sisters entered the room to begin the merciless teasing with comments like Angie's, "Connie. Joe's a rather big man. Do you think we should warn Mar about tonight?" The ladies giggled as they closed ranks.

Gene returned minutes later from barbering Joe, having laughed through the hard time Joe's friends and family had given him. He finished dressing by slipping into his jacket and thinking, *Tess, when Angie brings our next grandchild into the family, Carmella, Sossy, JJ, and I will move upstairs so that Angie and our other grandchildren will have the room they need. I know you'll like that. Keep an eye on Marian and Joe for me. I'll miss them.*

He finished his own toilet by tying his tie and putting his diamond-shaped tie tack in his white cravat and then took a look at Tess's picture. That brought a sense of loss that included Marian's leaving and decided that a happy day had no place for sadness and joined his daughters.

En route, Gene chuckled at hearing her sisters razzing his toughest. It was good to hear Angie laugh. Though he feared she had no intention of completely forgiving him, the difference seemed good. Though Poppa Pento never let go of his hatred, Gene knew Pento always put his feelings for the children before it. He feared Angie was only coming to the house to help her own children, not even her husband.

Gene entered Marian's room.

"Are we ready? We mustn't keep Joe waiting. Filame, you look wonderful. Joe is a lucky man."

About the same time, Joe stood in the bedroom of the cold water flat they would call home. Raffaele and the children had already left for Our Lady of Mt. Carmel Church on Park Hill Avenue in the heart of a local Italian community that tomorrow would be home. Alone with his best man Nick, Joe stared at the elegant, handsome young man in the mirror and luxuriated in the feelings of finally having someone all his own.

Thank you, God. I never thought I'd find anyone like Marian. I promise I'll take care of her. I just wish other guys didn't go for her. She doesn't understand about how I feel, but I'm sure after we're married, she'll see a man needs to feel he's the only one. Losing her would—

Nick said, "Joe, you know that advertisement where that exquisite looking guy in the tux holds a violin in one hand the woman in the other?"

Joe leaped from his thoughts to hear most of what Nick asked and said, "Sure do."

"Well, you're looking grander and beat him by a mile. Too bad you can't play a violin. Just be sure you don't drop Marian, she's one of the best."

Jesus, he's reading my thoughts. "Nick, you are so right, and thanks. I'm lucky to have you for a friend. Since I can barely play a radio, it must be Pop's perfect haircut, shave, and facial." Joe's face actually glowed above the starched white collar and expertly bowed white tie.

"It's time to go, Joe."

A quick look to check the crease in his pants made Joe bellow, "Oh, God, no." He wheeled. "Nick, my socks! I have white socks on!"

The hunt began. Neither owned a pair of dress black socks, and the ushers had already left for the 4:15 church service.

It was 4:35, and Marian was doing battle with her feelings. Joe wasn't there. By now, they should have been husband and wife. Her concern had turned to fury, shame, and embarrassment, but anger took command. Suddenly, she pulled free of Gene's reassuring touch, turned to leave the vestibule, and found Larry Levy barring the path.

Larry knew Marian's dislike for him but met her desperate glare head on.

"Marian, Joe will be here. Trust him."

Marian wanted to scream at him, but his effeminate ways brought her an unwarranted threat making her recoil and striking her volatile voice silent. The knowledge that there were two brides waiting in the church hall because of Joe clawed at her mind like a wounded cat. Still her ferocity and unwarranted jeopardy mixed with the fear about Joe's not being there suddenly made Larry the perfect target.

As she opened her mouth to strike, she heard Joe explaining as he noisily headed for the altar straightening his tuxedo with a winded Nick right behind him. Fr. Agusto cut everyone short and firmly said, "Everyone, to your places."

Anger had illuminated Marian's freckles, but Joe's only thought as she came to him was, *She's lovelier than ever.*

Their Wedding

Joe's expression, so full of love, drained Marian of all anger. At the railing, Gene kissed her and stepped away. They immediately took each other's hand to turn the first corner of life together.

Mr. and Mrs. Joseph L. Prezzemoli visited the groom's sister Margaret at the hospital. The birth of a son, Ricky, had almost killed her. Ricky would be their only child. Marian and Joe kissed Margaret, their new nephew, and left for the reception in the house at 92 Orchard Street and spread out over all the porches and back yard once the formal studio pictures were taken.

More photos were taken when they arrived at the house, and as Pop joined Raffaele, she said, "Chiulli, you give the children a wonderful day. Such food and drink. I wish I could give you some money."

"Raffaele, have I asked you for money?"

"No, but you do so much." Gene noticed the pictures were done and said, "Dear Amica, our children are here, and they are in love, and we love them. What else could we want?" Offering Raffaele an arm, he called everyone including neighbors to join the festivities. Once again, all windows were open for all to join in the fun.

Gene handed Raffaele a glass of champagne, waited till everyone had their wine; then raised his own glass and Toasted the joining of the families. The air filled with the happy and echoing sounds of good wishes.

One Becomes Two and Three

Marian was shivering through the first minutes of their wedding night, but her eyes came up from her goose-bumped skin to meet Joe's warm smoldering orbs, and her mind lost itself in excitement, expectation, and hoping.

Both were remembering the open sharing of their dreams and were about to make some come true. In spite of the cold floor and damp air, Marian let her chemise drop to the floor.

Joe gulped at the sight and rose to the occasion, but realizing Marian was his now, he didn't want to rush. But his belt buckle caught in a new hole, and he had trouble pulling his eyes from her lovely body to deal with it.

Marian, both hesitant and wanting, decided to do it for him. The cold made shyness a waste while curiosity and desire made it easy.

Joe enjoyed her cool hands on his hot skin but realizing she was cold only allowed time for his buckle, pants, and underwear to fall away before sending his fingers over her cold skin to where he could lift and carry her to the warmth of their bed. Once there, he reached for the blanket and covered them before taking his cupped hand from her handful of Manfredi cheek to take his long strong fingers gently over the slow route from her legs to her hardened nipples where they began the adventure Marian had only thought about.

Later when her hands found his tender, silken balls in the way he had told her about, Joe's love for her remembering grew in ways he hadn't known existed.

Later with Joe asleep beside her like two books front cover to back cover, Marian was grateful for having a gentle but ardent lover. She had curled into his solid lean muscles to harness his warmth and looked forward to quickly passing from novice to full partner sexually only to find him awake again and gently turning her toward him feeling him harden reminded her of Beth and Angie's teasing and thought, *Pure jealousy sisters, pure jealousy.*

They were glad they had waited, and being inquisitive spirits, challenging experiments brought much laughter to the spontaneity of romantic fun though careful about the where, for the young were always near.

For Marian and Joe, it was a time of learning about each other while living in a new family group.

Of course, she kept Tess well-informed. *Oh, Momma, a cold-water flat is just that, cold and damp. And sitting on the throne out on the porch is like sticking my tush in ice water. I'm just glad it's not in the yard, we're three flights up.*

The people part turned out simpler for Marian than living in a cold-water flat, because after a childhood warmed by steam heat, her body betrayed her. From the beginning, she had colds and headaches difficult to ignore. Still her fighting spirit kept her happy and feisty.

As a family, it was a good time, except for the hostility of Joe's younger siblings. Thirteen-year-old Bart and eleven-year-old Louise were both bitter about their lot. The benefits of years at the Manfredi home left them both feeling deprived.

After dinner with Raffaele, Bart, and Louise, Marian and Joe would sit at the table to talk about what they read in the papers and the day's activities. Raffaele was thriving in the growth of ties with the young couple, and as adults, they hoped treating the teens like the adults they thought themselves might pull them closer. The teens wanted no part of it, or the fun games suggested for all to play during evenings at home they preferred maudlin lounging to doing.

Each morning, Marian and Joe would report for work full of energy and rush home despite the family's presence.

Not all went well. One day, both were rushing home. Marian was on Ashburton Avenue passing many early evening activities of others and acknowledged the many neighborhood people she knew along the way until she heard a familiar voice.

"Marian, wait a moment." A former beau and a school friend to both said, "Congratulations, Marian, I heard about you and Joe Prezzemoli. He's a great guy. Be good to each other."

Andy gently kissed her, and she returned it in kind and said, "Thank you, Andy." After this pleasant exchange Marian quickly headed home.

Being a woman who had learned to appreciate the worth of the individual man, she recognized the worthlessness of others without demeaning the gender. She acknowledged how lucky she'd been in her dating before Joe. She was smiling with anticipation at being with Joe and warmed herself with the thought she'd picked the best of the lot.

In the same moments, Joe too was on his way home savoring the romantic glow of having someone all his own. He too was on Ashburton when his stomach turned acrid, and disbelief swallowed common sense.

Marian's kissing Andy!

The sight propelled him across the street to rush at Marian.

A sensing made her turn to see Joe crossing the street, and before her growing smile could find a home, Joe impulsively yelled words that abolished Marian's warming.

"What's the idea of kissing another man?"

"What?" stammered Marian.

Unmindful of the surroundings, Joe yelled and pointed, "Him! Andy?"

Marian's features altered to the gray rock pallor of comprehension that turned her expression into a fortress of outrage.

Joe's emphatic arm waved with total disregard for the people watching the exchange. "How do you think I feel seeing my wife kissing—?"

Marian forcibly interrupted her voice hard.

"Our friend. One who congratulated us on our marriage and wished us good luck."

"What's that got to do with anything, you're my wife?"

The words were hammer blows Marian would not tolerate. She grabbed a harsh breath and said, "No, Joe. You're wrong. You're jealous and wrong. We've had this out before, and being married doesn't change anything. If you can't trust me, I won't go home. I swear I'll leave you. I won't live with a man who doesn't trust me. You know that! And I won't go home to Pop."

Oblivious to everything but his feelings, Joe started to say something else, but Marian, with a confidence bedded in right, whipped passed shocked, embarrassed onlookers like a determined soldier, her head high.

A waist length winter jacket allowed her rayon dress to wrap itself around her rear cheeks making Joe wonder if he were having a nightmare. Her vehemence steeped him in silence while her movements turned him on. Joe felt victimized, but a lonely vise closed on his stomach where the opposing acids of confusion and intelligence warred. The moment prolonged until some instinct responded to the people around him, human watchers who greeted him without smiles. A friend and shopkeeper standing with a customer at his store's entrance mouthed, without sound, "Go after her." Next, he saw one of his aging lady depositor shake her babushka'd head and say, "Oh, Joe." His mental dam broke even as he thought, *But she's mine!* His powerful people sagacity forced him to look around. *Oh, shit, I've made a fool of myself.* He pulled up his coat collar against the sudden chill and took off framing an apology to easily catch up with Marian. They yelled, they talked, and they walked. And did until Joe made promises Marian wanted to believe.

That night, he tried to show her how much he loved her with gentle and slow ministrations. But he lost the battle to a mutual surge of hunger that wore them out.

As his eyes closed, Joe knew he still felt the same way but knew he'd have to be more careful in the future. He knew Marian meant what she said, and any thought of losing her filled him with an uncontrollable fear. But that night, the young couple made a commitment to the life they'd begun by deciding to begin and end each time together with a kiss, no matter what or where and to test their own mettle forbad anger as an excuse to avoid a proper good-night kiss.

In the place of the spirits, the watchers were sad. So familiar with the problems of man, they knew that one like Joe, besieged by something all his own, fired with new love would learn slowly and perhaps not at all. Free will being what it is, another watcher said, "But Marian will fight for him and with him." Elsewhere a dark watcher had a moments pleasure in looking forward to Joe's next decision wrapped in Joe's not understanding.

The next morning, Joe was counting his morning cash drawer when Larry Levy left his cage and joined him. Before he could say anything, Larry stepped in close and whispered, "Joe, you were way out of line with Marian last night. What the hell made you do anything that stupid?"

Joe's nose flared, but Larry didn't budge an inch. "Joe, I walked up the hill with Andy, and when he spotted Marian, he left me to congratulate her on your marriage. I watched from cross the street. I'd have gone with him, but I know she's uncomfortable around me. At that point, I spotted you looking as angry as a charging bull. Marian's a great gal and didn't deserve any of that. And in public—Jesus, Joe?"

Joe, humbled by his words, said, "I know, Larry. I was stupid, and it'll get worse for me when Mr. Glenn and old Mrs. Hobbs come in."

Some humor finally entered Larry's tone as he said, "You deserve it."

"I'll make it up to her honest." Joe smiled at Larry, squeezed his arm, and said, "Thanks, buddy."

Larry looked back over his shoulder as he left the cage wondering if Joe knew himself as well as he needed to and found himself still worried for his friends.

That night, Joe told Marian what Larry had said to him and started to say what a good friend Larry was hoping to change her feelings, but she interrupted him with, "Joe, wait." She hesitated before saying, "He really is a good friend. Oh, Joe, you're not the only one who makes bad mistakes, I've made a big one in being afraid of Larry. Next time I see him, I'll tell him that, and I won't let anyone say anything nasty about him again. I used to hear all those bad jokes about him and his effeminate ways, and I believed them and became afraid of him. There's nothing wrong with him, and I should have known it. Oh, God, I'm such a dope."

Joe's face lit up with his toothy smile and said, "That's my girl."

Marian stopped at the bank to see Larry the very next day and kissed him on the cheek; and again before she left, leaving Larry grinning like a happy puppy. When realizing Joe was smiling at him, he blushed.

Marriage did not lessen Marian's ties to her siblings, especially Sossy and Carmella who freely volunteered Marian for school activities, like Alice Blue gowns for a school play or Robin Hood's woodland uniform. Later, it would be elf shoes and, still later, kilts and sashes made of crepe paper. It never occurred to Carmella, not to. Marian always made it so much fun, while Joe ceaselessly teased her to laughter and true to his memory of Tess called her Grace.

Whenever there was a problem, a Manfredi would show up at the apartment wanting to talk to Marian, and Joe would either join in the conversation or disappear only to hear every word once they left and then help Marian seek a solution and join her in implementing it. Joe's family were used to running to him. They continued to do so finding Marian always ready to receive them and help in whatever way possible.

Marian and Joe somehow were always able to set aside their current doing, good or bad, until later, as though it had never been interrupted, when a family need occurred. Like fine musicians, they rarely missed a beat. It was rare for them to be on their own.

Married to a woman who enjoyed people as much as he did slowed Joe's participation in sports because they flung open their door to friends and family. One more marathon and his energies would become wife, family, and work.

Just before Christmas, while in bed, Joe reached for Marian. They kissed, snuggled, closed their eyes, and crashed to the wooden floor. The sound echoed through the apartment giving way to filling rooms with laughter assuming sexual efforts had been to raucous. Marian and Joe laughed harder than anyone.

The holiday held all kinds of promise as Joe brought home a bonus check for one hundred dollars. They decided to get Raffaele something special and put the rest away for the future.

The time with Raffaele added to the genuine affection between Joe's ladies, but conflicts with a younger brother marred daily living. Marian and Bart were at war. A daughter-in-law could not, would not, tolerate a son's disrespect to his mother, and when Joe was out, the battle continued.

One evening, Marian beat Joe home, threw her handbag on the bed, and headed for the kitchen to help with dinner and walked in on Bart, saying, "Go to hell, Mom. I won't do it."

Marian crossed the room to Raffaele, stepped in front of her, and said, "Bart, don't you ever talk to Mom that way. Apologize now!"

"No! You can't tell me what to do. You ain't nothin'ta me."

None of them had heard Joe come in, but he heard what was said and passed between the two women with the speed and grace of an athlete but the mind of a furious man. Joe's left shot out and slammed Bart against the wall as he said, "You listen to me, little brother. The only reason I'm not beating the shit out of you is because you're a kid. But the next time you speak to Marian or Mom that way, I'm going to throw you out of the house, and you'll be on your own. Gabeesh!" Joe's other hand came to Bart's throat.

Bart had never seen Joe like this, but Raffaele had, and it was more frightening now than when he'd been young.

Neither had Marian, and though both women were frightened by it, Marian was determined the worst wasn't going to happen and placed both hands on his arm.

With anger trembling in his voice, Joe said, "I'm not going to hurt him," but he wouldn't look at Marian. Finally, Joe's hand dropped from Bart's throat to his chest, keeping him pinned, and said, "But this kid is going to work starting tomorrow." His eyes never left Bart as he continued with, "And if you don't turn in every penny to Mom to help out around here, you're gone." This was a Joe Bart didn't know, and he didn't dare move, not that he could.

Joe suddenly let go, turned his back on Bart, faced his ladies, shoved his hands deeply into his pockets, and was suddenly immobile when his eyes met Marian's. Silence enveloped the room until Marian turned to Raffaele, kissed her, and said, "Mom, I'm sorry Bart talked to you like that."

Grazie Marian, but Joe, he—

Marian quickly said, "It's all right, Mom." She glanced at Joe, saying emphatically, "Joe and I will talk." Then she turned to Bart. "Bart, I'm sorry you and I aren't getting along, and Joe is right, you have to go to work. But let's let it go at that and try to have a nice supper together." Marian turned to Louise, saw her hostility, and decided not to say anything further.

Marian again turned to Joe, placed a hand on his arm, kissed him, and then whispered, "You and I will talk."

He nodded, kissed her, and said, "Hey, I heard a great joke today," and pulled Bart close hoping he'd apologize. He didn't but Joe was more concerned about what Marian would have to say than anything his favorite ball buster could say. In a minute, the joke had them all laughing, even a reluctant Bart managed a shaky smile, while a big brother thought, *Marian's gonna take my head off.*

In the quiet of their room, Marian watched Joe sit on the edge of the bed waiting and calmly said, "Joe, I never want to see you like that again. You were out of control. I think the only reason you didn't hurt Bart was because Mom and I were there. What would have happened if we hadn't been?"

"He'd probably have gotten what he deserved. No one can speak to you or Mom that way and get away with it, not if I can help it."

"Joe, that can't happen again. Find another way. Don't you realize both Mom and I were terrified of you and what you might do? We were only angry at Bart, but we were afraid of you."

"Afraid of me? I'd never hurt either of you. Never, I swear it."

"I don't know that, Joe, though I believe it. I mean, I hope so, but life's proved believing isn't always true. Oh, Joe, you could hurt someone, and that can't happen." Both were thinking of Tess and Gene.

"Joe, please think. I've never seen this in you before, you looked as though you'd kill him. How would Mom and I live with that, how would you?"

Joe got up and started pacing back and forth across the room not answering.

Marian was worried that she'd said too much. He stopped in front of her, his hands again went into his pockets as though ashamed and hiding them, and she was deeply troubled by wondering what was causing this in him. At his first word, her mind leaped to listen.

"You're right, I could have killed him. But I love you both so much I just reacted, and please don't say it again. I know I can't let it happen. Hon, I can only remember feeling like that once before, and I was too young to do or understand anything about it. I just remember the feeling. It's strange but my stomach hurt both times. I'll apologize to Bart tomorrow, and I promise you I'll take my cues from you. I don't want to feel that way again. It scares me too. Okay?"

Her hesitation scared Joe even more, but her delayed "Okay" hit him with the relieving wallop of a breath he'd held too long.

It took them both longer than normal to fall asleep. For Joe it finally came as an escape from remembering. Marian took longer for suddenly feeling she was doing something wrong but couldn't figure out what. She realized she didn't know Joe the way a husband and wife must to succeed. In need of someone to talk to, she reached for Tess. *Oh, Momma, I know you saw how Joe was tonight. I know I'm doing something wrong. Please help me. I do love him so. Tomorrow, I'll talk to his mom, maybe I'll understand more then.*

Joe's arm came around her, and it felt good, as did the sounds of his deep sleep. Slowly, her mind gathered in the security and, through believing and hoping, joined Joe in slumber.

The fear instilled in Bart helped but was no cure to the bitterness so rooted in his personality so very much shared by his sister. Joe wanted so to help them but didn't know how anymore than why he was so jealous without reason.

The watcher caught in the quiet of concern could do nothing. It was Joe's to do, just as it was Bart's and Louise's. His was a search, where the living of a decision could infect or enlighten the hidden recesses of a mind's complexity, so much a part of being human, so the watcher turned his attention to other family happenings.

Madre's time to join the spirits came in a quick and merciful moment, but Madre went to a very dark place where no one was.

She spent a long time alone in the dark, but finally, the spirits came for her. One as malevolent, as the dark world, her decisions offered her. The other, as beautiful as she had been at fourteen, offered her hand to Madre, just as the child who had come to get her did. The choice to take that hand or refuse it was Madre's.

All Gene's children, Antonio and his Madre's second family gathered at the wake. To the very end, the child within Gene had kept the wrongful promise.

Gene helped Antonio and his half sisters clean out Madre's belongings. His mother's husband told them to take whatever they wanted. Gene and Antonio tackled a large closet planning on giving her clothes to the needy. As they worked, he made a discovery both about Madre and himself. After clearing the closet of clothes they found, stacked against the back wall, boxes galore of Uneeda Bisquits…unopened.

The sudden realization of Gene's caring prison of respect offered him an unobstructed view of the corner he was never wise enough to turn. Antonio both sensed and saw Gene stiffen and realized Gene was in trouble and firmly grabbed his shoulder. "Gene." Gene pulled from under his brother's hand, put his head high, and walked out of Madre's room taking nothing with him. Antonio left soon after knowing there was nothing he could say to his brother that would help. The brothers never discussed it.

The months spent with Raffaele added to the genuine affection between Joe's ladies, and in February, Marian was pregnant while continuing the fight against cold and sinus attacks without let up, made worse by the discomfort of throwing up for having day long morning sickness.

One day, Marian came home and bypassed everyone without greeting to rush to the kitchen sink. Joe rushed to hold her in the throes of expunging, took a good whiff of her deposit, and headed for the porch toilet to deposit his stomach's contents in compassionate retching.

When he returned to the kitchen a few shades whiter, Raffaele and the children could not contain their laughter, and even a pale Marian had to laugh at his sheepishly sorry expression as she and Raffaele cleaned up her mess.

A few nights later, a caring son and husband discussed Marian with his mother as she was adding greens to a soup. The sadness in his effort made his voice sound hoarse.

With his arm around Raffaele's waist and smiling sadly, he said, "Mom, I'm sorry, but I have to get Marian out of here. Between the baby and the headaches, she's getting too thin, and she insists on working. The doctor is worried about her. If we stay here, she won't get well."

"Si. She is ill alla time. I will amiss you bot."

"Mom, I haven't talked to Bart or Louise, but Louis called me at the bank from California and offered to take Bart and Louise into the business out in California. I don't want this for you, but he wants you too. Of course, I can change that feeling if you really want it, but I would miss you. You belong with us."

She turned and hugged Joe to say, "Barty and Louisa are not happy. I have not done well with my bambinos, but they are mine, I am their momma. We be okay, but mea going to youa and Marian or Louis? I'm a not know. Letta us wait to decide. My bambinos musta finish school likea you. They hatea school, but they must finish. We willa be fine. The children are both helping now."

Raffaele prayed, *Dear Madonna, look how I bring Guisseppe and Marian my bad luck? I must not go to them, and California is too far away look how little we see of mya Louis. Joe has longa been our anchor. Please find another way.*

Joe interrupted what he feared were superstitious thoughts. "Mom, you know Marian loves you, don't you?"

"Oh si. Cara Mia, she isa my daughta too. Her momma Tessa shares her witta me."

Joe fully embraced her knowing she was crying. "Your right, Mom. Marian loves you like her own mother, and we want you with us, no matter what. She wanted to ask you herself, but I felt it was better just you and me. Come to us whenever you want to, please?"

"Si, Guisseppe, si."

As Joe left, his shoulders slumped for knowing from experience Raffaele found decisions hard but once made; she was a tough adversary.

Still at the stove, Raffaele stirred a soup that became much saltier in the next few minutes because her eyes filled and shed many tears.

A watcher looked upon them and smiled as a lady in blue took note of Raffaele's prayer.

That night, Joe held Marian, as she cried for hearing what Raffaele had said.

"Oh, Joe, she's had it so hard, I hate leaving Mom behind. She needs to know she has a home with us. When she's with us we can spoil her, she'll be happy, and we'll take care of her the way she deserves."

"I tried, hon. She feels she's bad luck, and I've never been able to help her with it. She knows how you feel, but I doubt she'll change her mind."

Raffaele did not change her mind but found and took another route, public assistance.

Marian and Joe's new apartment was at the top of The Hill on High Street with both families' just minutes away. The first night, they shared a meal at their tiny narrow kitchen, sitting at the table they instinctively sat next to each other as they had during meals at Gene's and Raffaele's because they enjoyed being within reach of each other.

It became a lifelong habit wherever they called home.

Though money was short, Marian kept them well-fed with hearty peasant meals smartly made with much butchers threw away like neck and soup bones, chicken feet, pig skin, and many internal organs that generated good and healthy meals. Of course, Gene visited often toting edibles as part of his visit.

One night, Joe lay on the couch with his head in Marian's lap, his head against their baby's nest. "Whew, Mar, he just gave me a kick in the head."

"Excuse me, Mr. Prezzemoli, but didn't you order a girl."

"Yes, but I'm playing it safe. Oh, what the heck. Yeah, I want a girl."

"I'm sure that's already been decided, but I'll see what I can do." Joe's broad toothy grin had her mind drifting off to why she believed Joe wanted a girl. To her, it was Joe's world of poverty shared with a strong woman, his mother, whose capacity for loving him and doing without, brought her, his wife an undeniable first place in his life.

Joe made Marian laugh on the rare days they'd come home for lunch and he'd hope for macaroni. He loved her sauces but she'd smile, kiss him and tell what they would eat. His lower lip would thoughtfully lift to almost touch his awaiting nose only to smile after tasting Marian's instinctive and delicious meal based on what's best for humans. He soon came to appreciate and voice his pride in the many fine meals served in his own home by his terrific wife who had promised he'd have his macaroni at least twice a week.

Time and life were passing quickly for Marian and Joe. It helped that Bart now worked every day after school as his first corner to adulthood, and though he was as unhappy and sullen as usual, he accepted the need to help and the complaining became less frequent. But he was never truly happy, and his sister Louise mirrored his every mood but also chose to help by working after school.

Joe kept his promise to Raffaele and often picked her up after Marian got home to continue their habit of going down the Bronx Grand Concourse to visit Mary, her husband Carlo, Anna, Freddy, and her growing grandson Tommy. Joe made it a game to try to time the lights perfectly to avoid having to stop for a red light all the way to where they were parallel to Yankee Stadium where they turned left to get to Mary's. Keeping the car, important to his promises meant doing without, but they'd gotten very good at it. Joe gave Marian every cent he earned at the bank and kept only what he absolutely needed from the few accounting jobs he took on the side.

While Marian enjoyed a very loud, very big toddling Tommy, she also learned more about and enjoyed Freddy and Anna. Meanwhile, Joe talked with Mary's husband at the kitchen table. Joe considered Chelotti a hardworking man but one stubborn male in believing he knew what was best for himself or his family. His favorable leanings toward the old country and what was happening there created serious doubts about the safety of Mary and the children in the future.

In a few weeks time, Raffaele dealt with the excitement of a hello from her son Louis, who arrived with his four kids in tow and his very pregnant wife. They were planning on being here a couple of months and took an apartment for their stay. Raffaele was joyous. While here, their baby decided it was time to arrive much earlier than expected. In the ambulance en route to the hospital just miles away first one, then two, and then a third baby entered the world. But so quickly, the ambulance doctor could not attend them sufficiently, and one died in the doctor's arms. Once all were able to travel, Louis and his now family with six children returned to California with promises to come again. Next time, they visited there would be more grandchildren for Raffaele to miss.

Soon after that, Joe's corner to parenthood was a wish come true. A daughter was born on November 6, 1934. Joe ran all the way to Raffaele's and then headed to the barbershop while telling everyone along the way of his daughter's arrival.

As he passed the butcher shop on Ashburton Avenue, he quickly and breathlessly detoured to his friend Phil.

"Phil, I have a daughter."

"What's her name?"

Joe laughed and said, "God, I don't know yet." In minutes, he was heading down to Nepperhan and the barbershops.

Joe tried again to get his daughter named Raffaele, but even Raffaele told him, "Guisseppe mya name is no American, and I no wanna her to have a my bad luck." Joe didn't push.

Marian lit up when the nurse Della put her daughter in her arms even though she was still sore from the last suckling, but she was happy she had plenty of milk for her to drink. Later as she slowly, painfully walked the pediatric corridor before going to sleep, she heard Della say, "Marian, I'm sorry, but we forgot to have you bathe your daughter. Would you like to wash another infant?"

"Yes, please."

Marian unwound the bundled baby and laughed. "What a fine chocolate babe you are, and you're a boy. Be a good guy, and don't let the other boys get fresh with my daughter. Her father is a very jealous man." She nuzzled him and lowered his bare bottom into mildly warm water.

Della, one of Joe's many cousins, hearing the boy mewed out of crying, went about other duties knowing she didn't have to worry about Cousin Joe's new little girl. And worry she did. Any child she helped bring into the world held a special place in her oversized heart.

Before Marian could leave the hospital, her happiness was marred by learning a severely tilted uterus might prevent future conceptions. It kept intruding on her nicer thoughts, so she grabbed a movie magazine to get away from the harangue. She smiled as she saw her favorite actress on the cover and began to wonder about her little girl's name only to look up and see Angie walk in, saying, "Mar, I'm on my lunch hour and came to see my niece."

"You mean your godchild, don't you?"

Before she had a chance to say anything else, they heard, "Marian, stop everything. I have no name for your daughter's birth certificate, and you're going home." Della was all boss nurse, standing her ground.

Stymied, Marian stared at her laughing sister Angie who reminded her, "Mar, didn't you say you'd know what to call her as soon as you held her?"

Angie's gotcha earned her a quick "Grrrr" until Marian realized she was waving the movie magazine at Angie. She decided to put it down before it went flying but stopped for seeing her favorite actress again and said, "Jean Arthur." And she held it out to Angie for consideration, saying, "Oh, Angie, Jean Prezzemoli sounds good, doesn't it?"

Angie knew how much Marian admired the actress and thought, *It's a great name for a little girl. Too bad.* She cut hherself off and said, "Oh Mar it's a fine name for my Godchild. I'll see her before I leave, give her a kiss and whisper her name to her. I have to get back to work."

She kissed Marian and left. She did visit the babies and held her niece for a long moment and whispered in her ear. "I'm your Godmother, Aunt Angie. Your name is Jean and you will always be welcome in my home." She kissed Jean returned her to the nurse and headed back to work lickety-split.

When Della left, Marian thought, *Oh, darn. Even though she's Jean's godmother, Angie had a hard time with my calling her Jean. Momma, do you think you can get a message across to Angie. She has to stop the hating. Wounds have to heal. I know it won't change anything. It's just that she's so unhappy, but she'll be a good godmother and Mikah a decent godfather. Joe and I hoped it might help things get better. I guess we'll never have the answer to it. I should have asked Della what time Joe will pick me up. She'd never let a chance go by to make his day.*

That night, Joe's girls came home, and he volunteered to bathe Jean in the kitchen sink as Raffaele and Marian watched. His booming laugh filled the kitchen because he was getting wetter by the second while getting to know his firstborn.

"Hey, Jeannie's got a crossed toe just like mine. And it's on her left foot too."

Marian squeezed Raffaele's hand resting on her shoulder as she teased him. "What else could I give her of yours, she's a girl?"

Joe chewed on Jean's toe making her gurgle and bubble. Raffaele smiled at his happiness and put an affectionate squeeze on Marian's shoulder. She would spend many weekends with them to be with her new grandchild knowing Marian would spoil both grandparents.

That night, Joe kissed Jean good night and watched Marian and Raffaele tuck her in. Later, he began a nightly ritual all his own. He stopped reading his paper, got up, and disappeared into the bedroom where he stood over Jean and just watched her sleep. Then he ran his fingers down her arm and returned to his chair to finish the paper, back to front in his own left-handed way and discussed what he read with the ladies without a word about having checked on the new girl in his life. It became something he did every night.

That Sunday, Gene and the children came for dinner, and they took turns at holding, changing, and playing with Jean.

Gene had her while they ate so he stuck his finger into this glass of wine and put that finger in Jean's mouth. The babe sucked away and grandpa smiled and said, "Marian, she has Manfredi taste buds."

"God, help her if she's got my stomach," said Joe. He had no idea how prophetic he was.

Sossy and Carmella were soon babysitting for Jean and came often for dinner especially after bringing something Pop sent them to deliver. One afternoon, Carmella seemed too quiet, so Marian asked, "Hey, honey, is something bothering you?"

"I guess…"

"What?" Marian said softly.

"I had koodies."

Marian bit her lip to avoid laughing and asked, "And?"

"Lots of us had them, and Mrs. Edwins had the nurse scrub our heads with some awful smelling stuff and sent us home from school."

Marian caught on immediately. "And what did Pop do?"

"Oh, Pop was furious, and then he cleaned my scalp the way it should be done, dried my hair, and marched me back to school."

"Sounds like Pop, and then he did what?"

"Mar, Pop yelled at Mrs. Edwins." Carmella stood up straight and did a fair imitation of Pop and said, "You, Mrs. Edwins, are a teacher, but I am a barber, and I will take care of my children's hair. Do you understand the difference?"

By now, Marian was openly laughing and said, "Did she understand?"

"Oh yeah, she got awful pale, and I felt sorrier for her than I did for us who got our heads scrubbed. Pop did the right thing, didn't he, Mar?"

Now laughing out right, Marian took the unsure Carmella into her arms and kissed the top of Carmella's head, saying, "You smell good, and yes, Pop did just the right thing, and Mrs. Edwins is very lucky you didn't come to me first. Only I'd have included the nurse in my fit of temper." Marian could feel Carmella's giggle where their bodies touched and began to realize how well the cloak of motherhood fit across her shoulders and how well Pop was learning the lessons of father to child but had little hope for his handling of his adult children.

In later weeks, the couple's new friends began a draining battle to save their youngest daughter's life—a life that seemed to be slipping away like an outgoing tide. Born several months before Jean, Patricia Mulligan was dying. The couple, Madge and Jim Mulligan, lived on the floor above Joe and Marian.

The doctors could not stop Patty's bloating. When Marian held Patty, she always thought of Tess for Patty's death in her own fluids was imminent. Marian and Joe joined the praying parents at Sacred Heart's Monastery church that crowned the top of The Hill to stand beside them as Madge and Jim promised Christ a life of service to the church if he would help.

One morning, Marian and Jean visited Jim's Scottish wife Madge whose hair was an orange red that marked her heritage well. They walked in without knocking as both families usually did each day, only today, Marian found Madge weeping in the kitchen.

"Oh, Madge, don't give up hope, please." Marian rushed Jean into the living room, put her in Patti's playpen, and rushed to put her arms around her friend to hold her as she wept.

Madge's freckles were stark against her fear filled features as she said, "We're praying so hard. God has to realize we'll do anything to save her—anything."

As Marian looked over Madge's shoulder, she saw another fear in the eyes of Madge's older daughter and son, smiled at them, and gently reminded Madge of the others in her life.

Madge pulled away and went to her other children. When Marian left, she was remembering the impact a deadly illness had on a family and uttered a quick prayer.

Marian and Joe found themselves even more in touch with Madge and John's plight when Jean developed a croup that almost killed her. The time lacked needed medications to help children, and the violence of Jean's coughing episodes meant Marian did twenty-four-hour watches in their double bed. She laid beside Jean her hand on her chest's rise and fall rarely left its fevered skin.

Each time that tiny body convulsed with racking coughs, Marian physically pulled her baby out of the balling spasms determined to help her breath the medicated air wafting from the vaporizer and whispering, "Come on, honey. You can do this, breath."

An anxious Joe watched over both, standing in his shorts at the bedroom door. He couldn't sleep. The couch was too far away from them. He had a horrible thought. *Oh, Jeannie, you're like a caterpillar all curled up trying to avoid being eaten by a giant praying mantis. Dear God, please help Jean and Patty. They're just babies and babies shouldn't have to go through such pain. Please.*

He didn't feel the tears on his cheek, but the watchers in the land of the spirits collected them for the love they held.

Weeks passed and Jean was well, but Joe was also able to say to his friend Jim, "I guess the boss liked your deal, John. Patty looks wonderful."

"Oh yeah, she's fine, it's all gone away." And he laughed as he added, "And the doctor's can't understand, but we do." A lifetime promise made and kept.

Jean And A Well Pattie

Joe rubbed the stubble on his chin against Patty's pudgy cheek and felt her vibrate with laughter, and when her small hand grabbed Joe's abundant chest hair, she conjured his yelping, "Yeow."

Now both girls were sound, but Jean's threat, the croup, would come again and again until time brought needed answers.

When Patty and Jean were both two, the fathers took the girls to Pop's for haircuts. Jean's baby fine blonde hair, next to Patty's thick carrot-toned locks looked unhealthy because there was little of it.

Pop said, "Joe, a baldy will make Jean's hair grow and come in thicker."

Jean went home a cue ball while the bubbling redhead sported the latest fashion. Joe laughed while a daughter to young to notice the personal affront joined the laughter.

Raffaele came to the door and said, "Poor Bambina."

Marian winced. "I was afraid of this." But she was laughing just as hard as Joe and said, "Joe, you let Pop turn my baby into a cue ball."

"Si, Marian sheeza cutea ball," said Raffaele.

Marian laughed even harder and said, "Yes, Mom, you're right. She is cutea bald."

Joe said, "Mom, you made a joke," and they all roared with pleasure.

The Mulligan and Prezzemoli families spent evenings gaming, talking and listening to the radio.

One night as they watched the children play with Jim's collection of pipes, making like uncle Jim, Madge said, "Marian will you teach me to make a tomato sauce with meat?"

"Actually the only way to learn is to do it yourself, but I'll help you."

One Saturday they went shopping and then Marian guided Madge through watering the pan to fry the sausage, spare ribs and pig's feet. While she slowly, completely browned the pieces of pork she had to put a large pot on another burner. In that Madge had to simmer two cans of crushed tomatoes with equal amounts of water. Then she had to add basil, diced garlic, parsley, salt and pepper to the tomatoes.

Once the pork was fried and put aside, it was time to mix and fry the meatballs then tie the Braciola to be fried in the flavorful leavings of the fried pork. Madge had to flatten and line the thin Braciola steak with Romano cheese, minced garlic, parsley, salt and pepper. Then Marian had her roll it tightly short end to short end and tie it with sewing thread. Then Marian said, "All right Madge lets do the meatballs.

The chopped beef laid claim to a small mixture of pork. Madge had to add chopped Garlic, grated Romano cheese, parsley, salt, black pepper, softened stale bread and eggs.

"What's next Marian?"

"Now you mix it."

Madge reached for a spoon and Marian laughed.

"No, my Scottish Colleen this is where we separate the real cooks" and took the spoon away and acknowledged Madge's questioning stare.

"With your hands, ninny. You have to feel the texture and taste it to know what it needs." Marian had her fingers in front of Madge rubbing her thumbs across the tips of her fingers to illustrate the motion.

Madge looked at the mess she had to put her hands into and shook a chastising finger at Marian's laughter and her obvious challenge in stepping back and crossing her arms to wait for Madge to get to it. In answer to the goad, Madge plunged ten reluctant fingers through the slimy eggs, the sloshy bread, and cold meat to squish and squish until it was smoothly blended.

Marian earned a terrible glare for the next instruction.

"Taste it." Marian smirked and continued to stand cross armed to wait out a tarrying friend.

Madge finally took a small bit, pinched her nose in anticipation, and chewed. Madge's freckled face broke into a surprised smile, and she whipped back her red hair to say, "Marian, it's good."

"Of course, it is. And any of this you're doing is just basics. Once you learn it you can make all kinds of delicious variations"

The instructor then grabbed a fingertip full, tasted, and told the student how to improve it. Then at each juncture, Marian again had Madge taste the difference. Each time, the ladies washed their hands keeping towels over their shoulders to save time.

Now Madge removed the thoroughly browned Braciola and browned the meatballs.

Marian said, "That's it, brown them on all sides just the way you did the other meat. Good!"

By now, Madge was almost finished except for browning the tomato paste in the remaining meat oils until it was almost black in color. Then stirring it into the simmering tomatoes, she had to clean the frying pan by filling the tomato paste cans with water and boiling the water in the frying pan to capture the meat residue. After pouring that into the sauce with another can of water, she had Madge stir it deeply, saying, "All that's left to do is add the meat, except for the meatballs, which you'll add in about an hour and a half to avoid their falling apart."

Marian put her arms around Madge and said, "Great job. They'll love it. Just come back often to stir it, right to the bottom, so it won't stick. It will take about three hours to cook."

That night, the delicious aroma foretold the success of Madge's first sauce. The masculine devouring had Madge taking bows causing her freckles to glisten with pride. Madge and John's Irish/Scottish families would make her sauce legendary, and a day would come, many years later, that she would refuse the recipe to her children and when told her smiling friend Marian she heard laughter in, "That's not something I taught you." And Madge blushed the shade of her hair but would forever keep her secret.

As Marian's field of friends grew so did her culinary skills to include many ethnic cuisines, including corned beef and cabbage. Though she substituted tenderloin to save money, she served it with carrots, potatoes, onions, and an abundance of herbs that seasoned and seeped into the pots contents creating another eating sensation.

At one meal, Pop told her, "Figlia mia, coming to your home is like going into New York City for the many different flavors that please my palate."

Marian tucked the warmth of pride deep within her personal world. It would reach a potential where friends and Joe's business contacts offered her opportunities to open her own restaurant, but she would decline each offer, explaining, "Thank you, but I love cooking for family and friends with no one to answer to and I'm making stuffed cabbages for you on Wednesday."

An increase in rent forced Joe and Marian to move again, this time to Vineyard Avenue remaining on The Hill.

Once again, Irish friends looked down on the Italians.

Their apartment on the second floor had a closed in porch, a complete bathroom and a large room with a working kitchen off to one side raised by one step. Even after the table and chairs were set up, they were able to use the balance of the room as the master bedroom and two much smaller rooms facing the street, as a bedroom and parlor. A staircase off the large room took them directly to Vineyard Avenue. One feature had them thrilled with the move. "Oh, Joe, having a playhouse out back means Jean will be safe from traffic."

"It's terrific. She's already claiming it as hers alone."

Jean was beginning to flourish despite the recurring croup, but she seemed lonely. Even the attention of many cousins, aunts, uncles, and grandparents, thoroughly enjoyed, left her too quiet for Marian to feel right about it. *I want Jean to accomplish whatever she wants out of life without parents who hold her back, and that means she has to be very strong socially but very much a girl who respects others. Oh my, she's a baby, and I'm already pushing her.*

New York Governor Franklin Delano Roosevelt had become president the year before Jean's birth and his first term of office was beginning to show real changes. One day in 1935, Joe walked home on his lunch hour with his pay envelope untouched, kissed Marian, and said, "I didn't touch this because I wanted you to see it."

"It's started."

"Uh-huh."

She saw the FICA amount deducted on the envelope, and though there was less to run the house on, she smiled and kissed him.

"Joe, just think of what we can do when we're old enough to retire, especially if we can save more on our own."

"Hon, it's a great step for everyone. I hope Roosevelt can get more like this done. It's needed to get the public feeling secure enough to pull together and get the U.S. out of this financial cellar."

"I think he will."

"I'm hoping the rumors about a government housing project going up here in Yonkers will come true. We'd have a good chance of getting rooms there, if the rent's based on income. Keep your fingers crossed."

Joe kissed her goodbye and went back to work with only the change in his pocket because Marian continued to handle the finances with Joe as the prime consultant. He was proud at how quickly she learned and understood.

The playhouse out back was a full size room that looked down over The Hill's edge to Orchard Street, the top of Pop's house and the valley below. In it, there stood a crank Victrola about four feet tall, with a brown felt turntable, for twelve-inch hard-surfaced records.

Marian and Joe had enjoyed watching a growing daughter claim the playhouse. One afternoon, Joe leaned against the door while she showed him how to play the Victrola. Wrestling with a chair, she crawled onto it, a skinny fanny weaving in the air. As Joe quieted his chuckle, she grunted and cranked the handle until it would turn no more. Biting her tongue, she carefully tried to place the needle on the record.

Joe's laugh slipped out, and she turned an angry look on him.

"Uh oh, you didn't like that, did you, honey. You're going to be a fighter like your mommy? That's good."

Her insistent voice said, "Daddy, watch, it goes around and around."

It took several tries for Jean to get the needle on the record, but finally with a smile of triumph, she made music that made Daddy applaud and ask, "Wanna dance with Daddy?"

Her head bounced up and down with excitement, so she went to her tummy, slid off the chair, and stood on the toes of Joe's shoes the way Mommy taught her to again fall in love with the man called Daddy.

Marian spent an entire evening wondering and explaining to Joe about Jean's friend, who played with her in the playhouse. Joe didn't really understand the dilemma until she said, "Joe, she's invisible. Jean says she lives there and can't go anywhere else."

"Does her friend have a name?"

"Uh-huh, it's Penny."

"Think she'll introduce us?"

"I don't know, hon. It seems to be very hush-hush."

"Boy, what imaginations kids have." Neither was worried.

Many Sundays, the family gathered at Pops but in Angie's apartment downstairs. Tony was discussing his future with Pop while the girls cooked and spent time with their new sister, Dody, Tony's wife an unworldly lady but delightful to be with who fitted in beautifully and humorously.

Joe sat with Tony and Pop listening to Tony's arguments for a heart's desire. Joe was hoping he could help as Tony said, "But, Pop, I'm good. I can make a living on the golf circuit."

It wasn't going well, but Joe too felt Tony could do it.

Tony's conversation reeked with frustration rather than anger, though Tony's gruff voice deceived children and strangers who believed him angry.

Pop said, "Tony, it's the life of a vagabond, and there's no sure payback. How will you take care of a wife and children if you're not one of the best? If you travel all the time, when will you see your family? When will you be a father to your children?"

"Pop, you traveled."

"Figlio, I traveled once in a while and made mistakes, but your momma always had help. You, on the other hand, would be gone most of the year. Even if Dody agrees to go and she will, is it a good life for a woman like Dody? How will she fare while you are playing golf? How would you school your children? Could you really make a home for them?"

Tony looked helpless because family was important to him and he would not leave Dody behind. He knew Dody needed family, so he made the decision alone. When Joe had a chance, he tried to convince Tony to let Dody play a bigger part in the decision, but Tony had made his decision.

Later at dinner, Tony's quiet struck Marian who glanced at Joe. His look meant he'd explain later. Joe told a very cute joke, and all laughed heartily, except Dody who seemed perplexed. No one said anything until during a quieter moment Dody broke into laughter, all by herself. She blushed and said, "I finally got the joke." Then everyone howled with good feeling. Dody loved a good joke, but it took time for her to understand them and she was a good sport about the teasing from one and all.

Two seats away from Tony, a young man called Diz, his real name was Bernard, sat next to Millie. Another backyard wedding would soon be taking place. Only JJ—now a grown man—Sossy, and Carmella would still be at home with Pop. Gene, in missing his girls, saw that Carmella wanted for nothing, and as her beauty grew, so would his willingness to spend on her for she knew he'd refuse her nothing.

As for JJ and Sossy, though years apart, they both had a magnetism that drew female attentions. That something also curried favor in the average male for wanting its sameness with the exception of the fathers of tempted, attracted females.

Days later, Joe spoke to Pop about Tony hoping he could change his mind, but something Pop said softened his effort.

"Joe, did I say anything that was not true?"

"No. But, Pop, Tony has a real chance."

"I do not doubt his talent, but even at that, he must believe it above everything and in spite of everyone. Joe, I will honor his decision and help him and Dody as I have helped all of you. But tell me, if you were in Tony's place and I told you and Marian the same thing, what would you do?"

"Pop that's not fair. Marian isn't a quiet woman like—" He stopped for realizing, *He may be right, they'd have no one except each other, and Tony wouldn't be there most of the time and Dody is so—*

Joe went sad because he understood the difference someone like Marian would have made to their decision and could understand what Pop had done and knew Tony had to be his own man. Still he didn't agree but understood Pop's thinking, so he changed the subject. "Pop, you wanted to talk to me about a Cuban investment?"

They talked and Joe promised to check it out.

Marian joined them, and Pop asked, "Marian, may I take Jean to the woods with me tomorrow to pick mushrooms and greens."

Marian said, "Sure, Pop. She likes being with you except at meals, but she's learning fast. You won't fool her much longer."

"Yes, but only if she is very much like you. Many of my grandchildren find no pleasure in me."

"Ah, Pop, they're children, they'll come around."

His expression showed his resignation to the way it was.

Later, Joe told Marian the whole story, and she lost hope for Tony's dream.

In a few days, Joe told Gene that the Cuban sugar market was a worthwhile investment, added a few dollars to Pop's money, and arranged for the purchase of some shares but only after he had discussed its merits with Marian.

Joe hoped to build Marian a home someday and saw this as a first step. On his teller's salary alone, it would take forever.

Though Yonkers was now a big city, it maintained its small town leanings that blended its many ethnic sections. Even so, if you're lonely, you went visiting unannounced. Doors were open without knocking and what little you had you shared.

Over the years, both families had ridden the waves of dishonoring actions—as most families do—with drunkards, mental illness, abortions, lies, desertions, abuse, crime, and prejudices. As the families continued, Marian and Joe became anchors all could count on for honesty and caring even when not agreeing. However, they could be formidable adversaries when needed.

One spring day, Marian was on her knees at the bathroom tub romancing the scrubbing board with a wash. Jean was playing on the kitchen floor behind her. She turned at a sound behind her and saw Joe shaking a pair of roller skates overhead. "Come on, Jeannie, I'm going to teach you to skate." The thin five-year-old screeched with delight.

"Let's skate, Daddy, let's skate. Mommy, Daddy is taking me skating."

Joe hustled a piece of clothesline and grabbed a pillow from the bed. In minutes, they were out on the sidewalk with Joe struggling to tie them to an excited, squirming Jean's rump. Marian sat on the front stoop with her arms wrapped around her knees awaiting the first flop, enjoying how the sun bounced off Jean's gleaming blonde hair in its first signs of darkening. She smiled as two neighbor children came to sit with her, and she shifted her position to make room for them.

"Hi, Mrs. P., can we watch too?"

"Of course, you can, Jay. Jean would be disappointed if you didn't."

Eight-year-old Jay (Jean's hero) and four year old Jacky (Jean's shadow) Pringle, sat quickly beside Marian to watch their friend's adventure.

Jean And Her Shadow

Thoughts of almost losing Jean invaded Marian's pleasure. Jay, four years older than Jean, was her gallant knight because he had seen a man with candy leaning across the front seat of his car coaxing Jean to come toward him. Jay ran over and challenged him.

"Hey, Mister, you leave her alone." He grabbed Jean and held on. Not liking and frightened by the look the man gave him, Jay screamed, "Mr. Prezzemoli, Mr. Prezzemoli!"

The candy man bolted upright behind the wheel and hit the gas pedal.

As fast as Joe was, he could not prevent the man's escape, and while he notified the police, Marian held Jean's hand and walked the avenue to tell other mothers to be watchful so they could protect their children.

While anger left Marian chilled, confusion replaced it when Jay explained, "Mom told me to go out and play. She thinks I study too much."

Marian kissed him, and Joe shook his hand before going to thank his mother Molly Pringle who said, "Oh, that's strange. I was in the backyard, but I can't remember telling Jay to go outside. I have to admit I do yell at him for spending too much time indoors studying, but I'm very proud he was there to help."

The grateful parents found no explanation when Jay said again how glad he was that his mother chased him outside. Then they set about making sure their four-year-old knew enough to say no to strangers, not to approach any car and to scream her head off if necessary. It was a lesson repeated and repeated changing only to suit her as she grew to truly understand danger.

In the land of the spirits, the archer saw a family watcher return with a smile to say, "The evil one had unfairly interfered with the candy man's free will in his decision to take Young Jean. I had to act quickly."

Marian's chilling thoughts were banished by the poof of Jean's pillow bound rear hitting the ground replacing her thoughts with hearty laughter.

Jean rolled and giggled and said, "Again, Daddy, again. Mommy, watch me skate."

Joe lifted Jean with a hug. To him, Marian's peeling laughter was a sound of home, and he said, "Jeannie, we'll teach you to ice-skate like Mommy next winter, okay?" Jean nodded, though winded by the excitement an obvious effect of the croup.

Jay hollered, "Keep trying, Jean, you'll get it."

Young Jay said, "Please, Mr. P."

Marian put an arm around the boys and proudly watched Joe being a father and grinned at Joe's. "Sure."

Jean tried and tried undaunted by the falling and decided, "Daddy, it's fun to go poof."

The boy's cheers turned Jean's brown eyes bright. Joe remembered originally hoping she'd have Marian's hazel orbs, but she was given his deep-set globes of brown, and he really didn't mind. *God, I'm glad she didn't get my bushy eyebrows.* He tried to visualize it as he helped her up and burst into laughter to say, "Okay, honey, it's time to let Jacky try."

In 1939, a pleased Dr. Griffon watched a new lady patient rush down his stairs to find a perpetrator.

She was too late. The door was closed, so she knocked loudly.

"Is something wrong?" asked the colored guard.

"No, Mr. Benjamin, I just have something important to tell him."

Joe looked up, startled. "Marian! Hon, what's wrong?"

"Nothing, Mr. Prezzemoli, except you're going to be a father again, in October."

A stack of uncounted bills scattered, as he vaulted the teller's gate to throw his arms around her. In moments, they were surrounded. Larry Levy kissed Marian on the cheek, and she enjoyed their exchange. His effeminate ways no longer had any bearing on anything important, and true to the learning, said, "Larry, thank you for being such a good friend to Joe and to me. I'm so sorry you're leaving us, but the new job sounds perfect for you. She whispered, "We'll miss you, but you're coming to dinner this Wednesday or Thursday? Which?"

Joe heard his, "Yes, either one," and gave Larry a wink as Marian gave him a hug.

While Hitler's twisted fingers reached for Europe's throat, Marian prepared Jean for kindergarten and looked forward to the new arrival knowing her part-time job would again be put aside but it would help improve their financial picture until the baby came.

After school, Jean was to walk down The Hill to Aunt Angie's home with her children and would stay there until Joe called for her.

Jean's loneliness for being an only child had been easing, but it had been mirrored in Marian and Joe's wanting to conceive. As energetic parents, their only real concern for Jean was her recurring bouts with the croup that robbed Jean of needed strength. She was much smaller than her peers.

On their next visit to the Bronx to visit Mary and family, much happened that would leave Joe and Marian worried again about what could be another family corner in crisis.

Jean and her cousins played together in a room away from the kitchen, and while Jean followed cousin Freddy around like a faithful puppy, Mary, Marian, and Anna visited in the living room. Out in the kitchen, Joe and Carlo discussed politics, but Joe was wishing he was with the kids rather than listening to Carlo's usual one sided view of Italy's political grandeur.

Chelotti was explaining that he believed a man called Mussolini was bringing Italy renewed prestige and wanted to return to join him in making Italy a grand empire, saying, "Like it was in the days of the Roman Empire, Joe."

Joe said, "Carlo, there's trouble in Europe, and the peace processes may fail. How can you think of taking Mary and the children to Italy? Italy could be in serious trouble even now."

"No, Guisseppe. Italy has an air force, a navy, an army, and a great leader. Look what Mussolini has done for the country. Businesses flourish, everyone goes to school, and there is plenty of work. It can only get better with such a man, and if war is necessary, so be it. I have heard him speak. He is sincere and gets things done. He outshines your president. I am going no matter what, and I will join the army to do my part. Mary is my wife, so she must come with me, but you are Italian you should understand."

Joe winced both with his love of family and then with his own national pride. He wanted to defend his love for his sister but realized his emotions were coming in a dangerous rush. *You son of a bitch, you try to take Mary of the kids, and I'll—*

The brakes of his mind once again placed his hands deep in his pockets, where he surprisingly found some restraint and said, "Carlo, I'm not Italian—I'm American. I was born here, and what you're spouting is a load—of very bad judgment."

A sensing made him look over Carlo's shoulder to see Anna and Freddy standing in the doorway, obviously drawn by their raised voices. Both men took a deep breath, and Joe gave them a wink and a nod that told them to take their curiosity back to the ladies and lowered his voice almost to a whisper to say, "Carlo, Mary is my sister. She and the children are part of my family. I love them all including Tommy. I want them safe, and you plan on taking them to where they could be killed. Forget that nonsense about it's being my sister's duty to go with you, and don't try to force that on her." He turned to leave the room but stopped to say, "I'm going inside with the ladies. If you love Mary, rethink this whole idea, it's not what she wants. If you can't, then just go, alone! Then the only one in danger is you."

Carlo's stance seemed threatening, changing Joe's quiet demeanor to a strangely deeply different look. It brought with it an aura that confronted Carlo so strongly his first reaction to Joe's demand disappeared into the unknown maze of Carlo's mind that made him what he was. A short time later, Carlo would take his corner to a decision, one that could have been based on caring. The family would never be sure.

Joe left Carlo to join the family knowing Mary would have told Marian how she felt about it. Joe entered the room and sat next to Mary who took one look at his pursed lips and said, "Joe, I won't go with him, but what will we do if he leaves. We'll have nothing."

"Don't worry, sis, we'll work it out. We always have." He looked at Raffaele and saw she was willing no matter what.

That night, Marian and Joe wondered about the turns of world and personal events and the impact on them without finding any immediate answers, so Joe read everything in the papers regarding

Europe hoping to figure out what his brother-in-law might accept as the incentive to resolve his sister's danger. None of the stories read well.

The Prezzemoli and Manfredi ladies were close. Mary's Young Anna and Gene's Carmella were hanging out together and spent time looking for part-time work together or meeting young men. The girls were successful at all.

Marian, Joe, and Jean walked through the lives of a dual family as though in a revolving door that moved so slowly it allowed them to share both yet permitted stepping out into new worlds and step back in to continue the circle as needed. Time rushed by.

It was a confusing day in the Bronx for Mary and her children who came home to find Chelotti had left for Italy without offering his family any hope of his returning or leaving a penny's worth of help. His leaving did not bring the hurt all feared and was never again heard from. The decisions were made to change their circumstances, and the courts granted Mary a divorce.

Raffaele cried tears of joy and sorrow.

Holy Mother, I am so happy my Joe is going to be a poppa again. Lovely lady grazie and my daughter Mary and my grandchildren will join Bart and Louise and me. Coming together will make life better for us all. I am sorry my Mary has my bad luck, but we will do fine. I must tell Joe to call Louis and explain that his offer to take Bart and Louise is not needed.

Once again, a loving though poor home decided public assistance would help, but there was one who sought a way to avoid that. There was a man of the house to whom responsibility did not weigh like a grumpy ton.

Young Freddy decided to quit school to help his sister Anna and uncle Bart establish stability in their home by going to work full time in the furniture factory where he had been working as a part-time apprentice designer of bed headboards. His talent in carving meant he could earn a good salary.

Freddy

The home they created was visited often by Marian and Joe who made family a word they could rely on and Freddy wanted to mimic his uncle Joe's willingness to work for them all.

Joe's sister Mary's and Raffaele's life improved basically. The apartment in the Bronx housed them all comfortably, and they ate well. Young Tom, still a child, was growing into a giant proving they were doing something right.

Marian soon learned there were disadvantages to a husband who was a caring and involved uncle. It meant he worried, and that made her worry. Joe tried to talk Freddy out of quitting, but Freddy said, "Unc, I know you'll give up a lot to help us. I know you'd hold down as many jobs as possible to help but this way that's not needed. It's time we took care of ourselves, and I'm ready for it—honest. But, Unc, please stay close."

Joe could say nothing but put his arm around Freddy and told him how lucky his mother was to have him. In the moment, he held

Freddy the boy folded against him, but it was the man who slowly pulled away, smiling.

Freddy earned a good wage by using his artistic carving talents to create pieces for his employer's cliental.

When Marian heard what Young Freddy had decided, she was as proud of him as she could be and in the same moment worried about her own man of the house. Freddy's sacrifice made its way into her deeper feelings because she was sensing something inside Joe whenever he worried and it seemed to be getting worse with each problem. In reaching for ways to answer it, she weighted her insights wrongly. There was still much they needed know about each other and tempers flared for the lacking.

Freddy grew into "the keeper of cousinhood," and as Tommy grew, the young cousins combined their natural mischievous ways that Freddy channeled to pleasant active fun. But beware his absence. As in all kids, the potential of Joe's nephew Tommy rested in the mysteries of the future. He was a typical Bronx street kid, so jail was always an option. Freddy tried to be there in the same sense of his uncle Joe, and both hoped to cultivate the lad's need for real caring.

Joe's youngest nephew Ricky, the son of his sister Margaret and Harry, now lived in Mt. Vernon. He joined Tom in following Freddy around. Margaret considered Jean and her son twin-like. Luckily, the mischief so much a part of Freddy's love of fun had no need of parental concern.

Jean, as the only girl child on that side of the family, insisted on trailing adoringly along after Freddy.

Without hesitation, she considered herself one of the boys.

By volleying visits between locations, growing cousins got to know one another very well, and that led the boys to taking Jean on excursions and at this age being her protectors because Freddy would have it no other way. When Fred wasn't there, boys would be boys, and Jean was easily caught in their mischief and would be for some time to come.

On many Sundays, the commander-in-chief sat at the head of the huge dining room table reminding the now many grandchildren of much to do. Somehow, Jean and Manfredi side cousins remembered Gene's sternness more than the many good jokes Grandpa played. The one he favored was looking like he would slap their hand and deliberately miss looking chagrined at the offending hand.

"Jean, sit up straight and bring your spoon up to your mouth like this." Her lack of immediate reaction brought the longest arms in the world to show her how while Grandpa made a funny face. The many jaunts with Grandpa did not prevent Jean's teetering and cringing before the blow that she knew would never come, but flinch she did, and her eyes often went to her parents to see if she was really in trouble.

When it came to eating, Marian smiled without comment knowing Pop's training would someday enhance Jean's adult world and whispered to Joe, "She doesn't know whether to love or hate Pop. One moment, he has her laughing, and the next, she thinks he's going to hit her."

"She'll figure him out. He already dotes on her, especially since you've trained her to the point where *please* and *thank you* are her favorite words. Some of the older kids could learn from her."

"Only because it gets her what she wants."

"Hey, that's not a bad thing." Joe was still watching Jean as they spoke, and seeing Jean's spoon again trespass across the soup plate toward her, he wiggled his marvelously long nose at her.

Jean spied Daddy's message, giggled, sat up, and rushed her spoon to the outside of her dish. It was fun to watch Daddy squeeze his nose while he wrinkled his lips.

By now, the depression was being left behind, and America was embarking on a chance to grow like a healthy child wanting to be an adult before its time.

Joe was still taking one course at a time toward his degree.

Son of a Gun

P ublic School Number Nine's combination of human worth and
academics enhanced Marian and Joe's decision not to send their
children to Catholic school. In reflective action, they appreciated their
alma mater's teachings, and it replaced any guilt in not being able to
afford the cost of Catholic school. They had thought it through and
chose to avoid the stilted approach of the teaching church because it
lacked the open direction needed by a country full of people created
in all shades of God's sunlight. They even wondered about their own
shortcoming in that area.

School Nine housed any nationality, any race and combined
healthy students with those of limited physical capacities. Those
weak of heart shared the school with those afflicted by MS, MD,
or speech problems. The usual hurtful prejudices were as common
at P.S. Number Nine as elsewhere, but the school makeup and
teacher leadership sought out and challenged such problems very
successfully.

In the school yard, the children like Jean were the lucky ones,
able to run while others very different in capacities mixed in. Getting
to understand School Nine's many layers of people allowed learning
to sneak up on a student through people stimulation. Like osmo-
sis. Still it needed attaining adulthood to express its appreciation.
Kids instinctively doing right brought many a smile and adventure
to teacher and children.

School #9 rested atop The Hill, as though its roots had taken
hold. The Hill then lent the school its strength to help the children
grow, if they were open enough to accept it. The School Nine student
luckily had a chance to acquire compassion and camaraderie that
would help when dealing with the cruelty of the misled.

Jean's entering school allowed finding a world all her own. Though no one would know her better than Joe and Marian, Jean's finding her own world would soon include an unusual aura that at times would confound them both.

Part of their understanding was recognizing Jean as an especially curious youngster with insatiable wonder about the world and not only the one she was growing up in.

While they continued life's search with adult caution, Jean's seeking grew right alongside theirs, and without serious limitations, she was driving them wild with questions.

Months before Jean entered school, Marian had a mission in mind. She was moved by the publicity for a new movie aimed at children, one she was determined to take Jean to see.

It was the most talked about child's movie since movies had became part of their lives. Called *The Wizard of Oz*, it would follow its New York debut with a visit to Radio City Music Hall. Marian was thrilled at the thought that Oz's stars—Judy, Maggie, Ray, Bert, Jack, Billie, and Frank—would be on stage with her Jean there to see them.

Marian talked to Joe. Though he would not be able to come, he called his sister Mary and her brood, and it was planned that they would meet Marian in New York to wait on line with thousands of others. Marian had wisely purchased reserved seats. As though by magic, the seats were in the fourth row right behind the conductor in the orchestra pit, dead center of the stage. Marian, thrilled by their good luck, couldn't decide which was more exciting—watching Jean or reacting to the movie herself.

Jean sat on her skinny legs and stretched forward, fascinated. When Jean saw Margaret Hamilton as the witch on the screen, her eyes widened, and a little yelp left her lips. Enthralled, her attention never left the screen as the witch's face was surrounded by swirling black while she cackled as only an evil witch could. When the live characters appeared on stage just feet away, Jean joined in the cheering instinctively accepting the difference between screen make believe and stage real.

Maggie Hamilton, concerned that the "witch" badly frightened children, spent much time visiting schools and explaining the difference of real and make-believe to offset the fright her awesome characterization brought to the young. As told to this writer, lucky enough to meet the lovely lady during her lifetime.

On the jiggling subway home, Jean tried to move like her favorites. She fumbled like the scarecrow wiggling her legs, outstretching and waving her arm while screeching in imitation of the Wicked Witch of the West. When they reached Woodlawn Station, a laughing Marian watched Jean throw herself off the stairs into Daddy's arms. Poor Joe had a hard but fun-filled time trying to kiss his wife hello and listen to both his ladies tell him about the color, the characters, the laughter, and the mean ol' witch.

Early in the school year, Jean's learning included spending warped time in the kindergarten cloakroom for eating paste, which shied her greatly. The lessons found in being laughed at by her peers were honed alongside fascinating moments like listening to mommy's large belly for the sounds of her growing sibling.

In the time before sleep, Joe had often placed his hand on Marian's growing belly to catch the child's movement and began to believe it was a boy. One night, he said, "Mar, he's so active, it's bound to be a boy."

"Oh, hon, he might be a girl."

"Hey, it really doesn't matter, but this baby is so much more active than Jeannie was."

"Joe, do you realize you are the only one Jean she lets call her Jeannie. Angie tells me she heard her Mickey call her Jeannie, and she told him, 'Only Daddy can call me Jeannie.'"

Joe grinned and Marian said, "Okay, enjoy yourself, but I'm trying to teach her respect, and she comes out fighting."

"Hey, it's not me she takes after, and besides, it was another kid not an adult."

"Hmmmm. True."

Marian laughed as he put his head down on her belly and whispered, "Whatever, kiddo, you be good to your mommy, you hear?" Joe could almost swear he heard the baby's heart beat begin to race at his words.

With Jean safely in school, Marian looked five months pregnant rather than the full-term-due-any-day mother whose unborn was scurrying like a squirrel mimicking his mother in her busy schedule. Marian hoped that meant it was a boy. During this pregnancy in moments of stress, she talked not only to Tess but also to her child forging a bond that would grow tight.

Whatever you are, I hope you realize that your big sister Jean doesn't care whether you're a boy or a girl. She just wants someone who will play with her.

Early in the morning, on October 13, Marian went to Getty Square to shop. At one point, she stopped at Federal Bakery—next to the stocking store she worked in on North Broadway—to watch them ice the cakes in the front window, stepped inside, said hello to friends, and bought a black-and-white cookie for herself and two small cupcakes for her always-hungry, snack-loving minions. As she went out into the cooler air, she felt a short sharp abdominal pain. Noting that she just missed the trolley, she decided to head for home and, in minutes, had walked to Palisade Avenue for the upward trek home when another spasm forced her to lean against a nearby stonewall towering overhead with the homes of the area sitting atop.

Marian smiled, realized her time had definitely arrived, looked up The Hill, made a decision, and slowly headed for Yonkers General hospital, a right turn at the top of Palisade avenue about half way up The Hill. Confident she could get there in time, she maneuvered The Hill strongly despite some recurring pain. Better than halfway, she stopped, took a deep breath, and told the forthcoming child, "You stay put until I get there." She arrived at the hospital, thankful they had both made it, and recklessly decided this was a child who knew how to listen. Greeted by the chief maternity nurse Della, Joe's cousin, she heard, "Marian, I called Joe as soon as I saw you." Marian smiled her thanks and struggled through another contraction.

By the time Joe arrived, Marian and the child had joined forces in a battle for life that included bypassing a tumor blocking the birth canal with many long hours of effort. The untried child had to find his way through a narrower opening than Jean and suffered the pressure of forceps to make the trip more demanding leaving the doctor troubled by the complication.

As Joe did the expected paternal jog on the hospital lawn as the doctor set aside the forceps as inadequate and faced the complication. The doctor took a deep breath and met the child's need by cutting Marian acutely, earning the child's rambunctious howl of approval. Unheard by his unconscious, wanting mother, who was to waken to his life's wonderous moment and find a frightening challenge.

World events went unread, as Joe stood at the viewing window to watch a screaming son fight the restricted confines of his blue bunting. Joseph Jr. immediately became Joey.

It was now about midnight, and Della, doing a double tour, noticed Joe at the viewing window looking too serious for his usual joking self. His quiet prompted her to teasingly ask, "Well, are you going to keep him?"

Della's jest did not relieve his troubled mind. His intelligence was falling prey to Raffaele's superstitious influence, and he answered with, "I sure am, Della, but I'm worried. Joey's been born on Friday the thirteenth, I don't want him to have rotten luck all his life?"

"Joe, you surprise me." Della regretted putting it that way but wanted to laugh because it was difficult to ignore Joe's bushy eyebrow hairs standing straight up on his furrowed brow and quickly said, "Joe, you listen to me. You know I check on my children, don't you?"

"Of course, I do. I get a big kick out of the stories you tell me on payday."

"While I enjoy your jokes." She touched his arm and continued with, "Joe, believe me, my Friday the thirteenth kids have fantastic luck. Some angels of God must consider them their special assignments. They step in shit and come up smelling sweet. It won't be any different for Joey. I promise."

Joe flushed, bent, and kissed the diminutive nurse on the cheek and said, "Thanks, Del." With a toothy smile, he said, "God help Marian, he has my lungs. He screams louder than the rest."

In the place of spirits, a watcher hummed at Della's words being right about young Joey and wondered if Joey would use his gift wisely while readying for the unpredictability of his potential. He would know in moments for in a watchers realm seconds had no meaning in living time.

Dr Griffon who would be a clinic doctor until establishing his own practice, walked down the hospital corridor realizing Joe wasn't in the waiting room and found him on a small balcony overlooking St. Joseph's Church. He took a deep breath of air and explained much Joe needed to know, closing with, "Marian won't be conscious for hours, so either go home or go sit with her until she wakes up. Her pain will be bad, but we've given her enough to make her sleep through the worst of it. I'll be here a while longer, and then I'll check her again in a few hours. We'll all talk tomorrow. See you then, Joe." Griffon decided not to tell him everything preferring Joe had the chance to enjoy the birth of his son before hearing about the worst of it.

Joe watched Griffon leave, swallowed that choking fear of hospitals, and sat beside Marian until he had to think about going to work. He felt sad remembering Griffon said Marian again had an allergic reaction to the anesthesia and that was almost as hard on her as the birth. *I think the guy upstairs knew what he was doing making our ladies have the babies. Joey, your daddy knows a good deal when he's got it. If you're smart, you will too.*

About 6:00 a.m., he left to tell the family of Joey's arrival knowing he'd return after telling them at work. Once free of the hospital's confines, the excitement hit him, and the first person he saw was the nun who was principal at St. Joseph's School. He ran across the street and blurted out, "Sister Ascenta, I have a son. We're calling him Joey." And without waiting for an acknowledgement, he took off hearing her laughter as she shared his happiness.

Taking a shortcut through the construction site of the first federal housing project in Yonkers took him across the southeast side of The Hill to the east side to Poppa Pento's and then to Pop's house on Orchard. At each stop, his love gushed once again telling about a son called Joey.

He found Jean in Pop's front yard with her cousins playing before breakfast. Jean came running, so he picked her up, twirled her around smiling while enjoying the sunlight catching the blonde streaks in her darkening hair, put her down, and squatted to say, "Honey, Mommy's given you a brother Joey to play with."

That earned him a hug. As Angie's kids ran into the house to announce the birth, Jean said, "Daddy, can I see Joey?"

Slowly realizing it would be fun to sneak her in, he said, "I'll take you tomorrow, but you can't hold him until we take him home." He loved her excitement.

Together, they ran the stairs up to Pop's apartment and shared the news with him, JJ, and Carmella, telling her, "Grace, you have a new nephew to babysit—one with a great set of lungs."

Everyone laughed and Pop said he'd see Marian at the hospital, and then Joe headed downstairs to see Angie.

"Hi, Angie, Mikah." While standing next to Mikah, he realized his brother-in-law's coffee cup reeked with more than coffee, smiled, and said, "We've had a boy, so he's one more cousin for your four to chase around. Thanks for watching Jean for us, Angie. I'll pick her up tomorrow after I visit Marian."

"Tell Marian not to worry, Jean's no trouble at all." Joe kissed Jean and said, "I'm glad to hear that, honey, but be sure to wait for your cousins after school tomorrow and come back to Aunt Angie, okay? I'll tell your mommy you're being good."

In moments, Joe rushed off to Raffaele's and grabbed her in a bear hug to tell her of Joey.

Later in the day, another teller would take Joe's cage to allow the afternoon at the hospital. Joe shook off the hospital goose bumps by looking forward to having time alone with Marian and stopped for a box of Loft Parleys, a milk chocolate candy about the size of a big finger that she loved. The stop at Green's stationery was another chance to share his excitement with another good friend after stopping at the butcher to tell Phil.

At the door to her room, he saw Marian, Dr. Griffon, and another doctor in a huddle that shredded his growing muse. Griffon's word *tumor* loosed claws to tear at Joe's innards. Marian spied him and put out a pale hand to be held. And hold it he did, doggedly while begging, *Dear God, not my Mar.*

Griffon quickly brought Joe up to date explaining he didn't want to talk to them both until he'd gotten as much information as he could to answer questions. No explanation could stop Joe's mind filling with fear.

"As I explained, the operation means no more children."

Joe's childhood fear of doctors brought a mistrust of an operation that mixed anger with his fear and doubts began their insidious climb to self-jeopardy while thinking, *But if it's her only chance.*

His mind slowed when he heard Marian's voice.

The surgeon had discussed the options with Marian before he'd gotten there, and then she only listened. Now Joe was there, and she found the strength to say and direct her control. "The decision is really mine to make Dr. Griffon, so let's review what I need to know again, and I'll decide. Please." The statement was equivalent to a commanding order, and the look she gave the three men meant she had taken charge.

The surgeon took Marian's hand and said, "If you need me, Marian, I'll make myself available." Then he nodded at Griffon and left. Griffon shared a sad look with Joe knowing they'd bow to her feelings. Griffon sighed and answered with the options, including the dangers and closed with, "Yes, Marian, it is your decision. But the dangers are real and something we can't control."

"Thank you for being so thorough, but you did say the tumor is benign and contained?"

Marian was fighting for a dream.

"Yes, but, Marian, it will continue to grow, and it could become cancerous." As he repeated himself, there was a slight tremor to Griffon's voice. He was, at heart, a doctor of all, and in caring, he hurt for them.

Joe listened knowing Marian was thinking about the children they both still wanted. At least he had wanted them. Confusion entered the growing list of emotions attacking him through his greatest asset, his ability to love. Joe tried to convince himself—*doctors have been wrong*—but something deep within dropped into his stomach making it as tight as an iced snowball made only to hurt someone.

He saw a soft smile cross Marian's tired face. One bathed in believing as she said, "We'll wait." Their grasped fingers tightened. Marian read that as his commitment to their wanting a large family, but it wasn't.

Griffon heard the words, studied the couple, and realized Joe couldn't say no to her anymore than he could. *Marian, I wish we were sure—. I wish we knew more about this damn disease.* His lips pursed in frustration, but he nodded and left feeling he hadn't done enough and dreaded the corner her decision might force them to turn.

Joe worried out loud, and Marian's chuckled response, "Hon, we get to enjoy trying harder," didn't make him laugh. Even a wife's serious "It'll be all right, really" did nothing to ease Joe's shaken look.

Marian found herself more shaken about where Joe's thoughts were taking him than she was when she heard the word *tumor*. What troubled her most was the realization he was terrified. She stared at him once again thinking, *What am I missing*, and saw that being a wife had corners she'd never anticipated and recognized she still had much to learn about Joe.

When Joe reached outdoors, he stood on the stairs of the hospital dragging the edge of a shoe along a step, hands deep in his pockets, and continued a voyage he had started long ago. But as an adult, he did not recognize it. Only this voyage was on an older, leaky ship that would isolate him from those he loved.

Joe reminded himself how his $25.00 a week paycheck had not lessened their filial need and how his annual bonus of a hundred dollars helped them conceive some real dreams. Only now the dreams were turning into a sea storm Joe couldn't escape.

The beautiful October afternoon scented by falling leaves lacked any pleasant impact on him. Instead, his skin felt clammy and chilled.

Across the street, the side door of St. Joseph's Church opened, and the flickering candles siphoned his attention and called him inside.

One hand on the altar rail, he knelt and prayed, "Please, Dear God, I don't care about more children. Just let me keep Marian. It's no good without her."

The next day, Joe picked up Jeannie, and they snuck in the side door and tiptoed down the hall to the hospital-receiving desk. Jean kept saying, "Shhh, Daddy," as she tiptoed along the marbled floor. Then she enthusiastically yelped, "Oh, Daddy, look at the big clock. It's pretty."

A magnificent grandfather's intricately gold-carved faced clock graced the hospital's hall as long as most could remember. Joe agreed and shushed her as he "snuck" his excited daughter past the hospital's receiving desk while winking at friends who willingly never saw a thing.

Upstairs, Joe held Jean to the viewing window and heard, "Daddy, which one is ours? Which one is Joey?"

Della has been watching for them and picked up the howling Joey and brought him to the window for Jean to see.

"That's him, honey, the one cousin Della is holding—the one crying so loud."

It was almost two weeks before Griffon allowed Marian to go home, but she seemed well and looking forward to caring for her family again. It was a joyous evening shared with Raffaele before the apartment filled with relatives asking to hold Young Joey. After everyone left, they settled in for the evening, and Raffaele chased the last remnants of company insisting Marian do nothing. "Marianne, I doa these dishes and givea Joey his bath beforea you feed the bambino."

"Thank you, Mom."

Joe chimed in as he grabbed a piece of cake. "Mom, I'll give him his bath." He turned to Jean and said, "Jeannie, you want to help me give your brother a bath, and then after your mommy feeds him, you can hold him until he falls asleep."

Jean ran for a chair and pushed it to the sink and climbed aboard to watch Raffaele finish the dishes, clean the sink, and run the water for Joey. She even tested the water the way Grandma did, dipping her elbow into the warm water without falling in. Then Joe took a naked son into his charge, saying to Jean, "Honey, we may get a little wet."

Joe showed Jean how to gently wash him and then handed her the washcloth. Joe watched her gently rub Joey's leg with it, only to hear her screech, "Daddy!" as a stream of pee caught her in the face. Joe took the washrag from her, wiped her clean, and watched her anger flair as Raffaele and Marian laughed at her dilemma.

Through the laughter, Joe anticipated Marian's "Joe," reminding him to explain and said, "Honey, Joey's sorry, but he can't help doing that. He's too little to hold his penis to prevent wetting everything. He doesn't get to sit down to do pee-pee the way you can." Her understanding look filled with a five-year-old's frustration that lead to wanting to get down quickly, so he added, "Look, honey, I'm putting another washcloth on him so he can't do it again, then you can finish and hold him. Okay?" As he began to drop the cloth, Joey let another stream go that almost caught Joe and Jean burst into laughter lasting longer for Joe's wide-eyed, lip-raised, teasing look. In seconds, Jean reached for another washcloth. It became an activity Joe enjoyed with them both. In the short minutes that Jean held Joey, he slipped into sleep, and both were soon settled in their beds.

After Marian bid the children good night, he helped her to get into bed, kissed his tired lady, and spent some time with Raffaele who wasn't the least bit surprised when Joe disappeared into the bedroom to check on the children. Once again, Joe stood over his new born making promises as his father. Finally, he dragged his fingers down his son's arm, lingered a moment, said—"I'll see you tomorrow, Joey"—touched and smiled at Jean, and returned to Raffaele to bid her good night before joining Marian.

Franklin Delano Roosevelt's New Deal Policies found a welcome in Yonkers, bringing an answer to a specific depression ill. Homes for the poor built in four-story, brick structures to be nestled on the south side of The Hill facing New York City that would house hundreds of financially struggling families. Apartments high on The Hill would be able to see the George Washington Bridge and the beautiful sunsets peeking over the Jersey Palisades.

The project had small, dual-purpose playground parks between the buildings. The parks were edged with clotheslines the companioned the in-house laundries. There were four sectionss in each building, and every two sections of the buildings shared—four ringer washers and four large sinks in an open work area between two large storage areas. Tenants entered through steel fire doors, one for each section of the building. A garbage disposal drop slot was located in each building section with a drop door between the two apartments on each floor. The chute ran from the top floor down to the basement furnace area for burning by the newly created positions for maintenance personnel to keep the project running smoothly.

The apartments' rooms approximately 12 x 12 were filled with warmth from radiators built into outside walls of each room and homed a full size tiled bathroom fitted with bright chrome fixtures, a full ceramic tub with an shower fixture, and a rod for a shower curtain. In the kitchen, there was a gas stove, a general electric refrigerator with a tiny freezer and space for two ice cube trays, and a small fold away ironing board on the wall next to a section of wall cabinets for storage. Below them was a sink with both hot and cold running water. This wonder of the thirties, offered a gracious apartment the poor could call home, was graced with large casement windows with many panes of glass held in place by pliable putty that opened out like French doors and filled the rooms with daylight.

Watching the project rise took on a special meaning when Marian and Joe found themselves eligible for four rooms in the project and began to take walks down Vineyard Avenue just to take a look every few days. It was an exciting corner to take, one only months and blocks away.

The rents were salary based, and that made saving possible, though meager. The offer was irresistible.

While their excitement grew, they began learning about their son. Young Joey had a voracious appetite, and Marian's breasts were tapped many times a day to feed his healthy growing body. As the time to move came near, Joe watched Marian closely not only because of the tumor but also because this husband trusted his wife with all he had. He watched her budget for their future continuing to ask only pennies for spending. Right now, they wanted a radio, and Marian intended to have it soon.

As the day to leave Vineyard Avenue for the project approached, they found Jean didn't want to leave the playhouse. The morning they left, Joe took his tearful five-year-old for a last look. Joe tried to comfort Jean but found he could not, for realizing why she was sad. "Daddy, I don't want to leave my friend. I know you can't see her and Mommy told me she lives here and can't come with us, but I don't want to leave her." Joe stumbled through another corner to the many facets of being a father to a girl. Without fully understanding Jean's growing needs, he could only admit to the existence of the friend and his need to grow along with her when he could, so he waved goodbye just as long as Jean did.

With her eyes still tear filled, Joe passed Jean to Raffaele in the back seat where a superstitious grandmother stroked her, wondered, and believed in what Jean's young eyes saw while Young Joey slept through the excitement.

In Europe, a housepainter named Hitler had become chancellor of Germany, changed the face of the country, stole the minds of its people, and marched into Poland about the time Einstein told FDR of something called an atomic bomb.

Joe and Marian carefully read the paper and still discussed all they read before turning on their new radio to enjoy a program geared to laughter. Bed time prayers now included a wish to keep the world safe.

Marian had enjoyed breastfeeding Jean, but with Joey, it became something else. The very natural flow of feeding Joey was her refuge; a time when she could thoroughly relax that cared for her spirit as well as her child. And Joey? By now, Joey loved Marian's milk before all things, and her abundant supply left him round, chubby but robustly solid while Jean was lanky to the point of being too skinny.

Jean would sit cross-legged to watch Marian feed Joey while Joe watched them all. The only word they found for a five-year-olds expression as she watched Joey eat was *awe*.

Joe said, "Hon, he eats like there's no tomorrow."

"He takes after his father."

Joe enjoyed Jean's impish giggle, winked at her, and bent to kiss his son's head and Marian's bust and said, "He knows a good thing when he has hold of it."

Marian swatted Joe's nonexistent rear with Jean taking it all in. Though not understanding it's meaning to a child's sense of security, Jean tucked it into her mind's many developing directions.

When Joey was full, Marian gave him to Jean sitting on the floor where she could play with him until sleep claimed him. They enjoyed a sister's antics while she laughed at a brother's strange gurgling sounds and expressions.

Though the new surroundings of the project were not without problems, they adjusted quickly, and baby Joey grew phenomenally.

One of the problems they chose to ignore was the prejudice they found that they'd known as children that those on The Hill usually outgrew by getting to know each other. They hoped the same would happen here, but occasionally, it didn't. The neighbor who shared the floor with them refused all friendly efforts for not liking or trusting Italians. But many descendents of Italians did the same to other nationalities. Still they made wonderful friends of others, and life's good moments were many, though the dark shadow hanging over the world was getting bigger.

One morning, Jean stood at the bathroom door watching Joe and said, "Daddy, can I shave too?"

Joe was standing at the medicine cabinet mirror getting ready for work. He stopped his safety razor, smiled, and said, "Honey, only men have to shave. Girls are pretty and don't have hair on their faces."

In disappointment, Jean's chin dropped to her chest making Daddy push over one more time.

"But we can make believe." Watching a six-year-old light up made him feel as though he'd sunk a winning basket.

He said, "Go ask Mommy to give you the flat butter knife."

She ran and Marian asked, "Why?"

"I'm going to shave."

"Oh, you are, are you?"

Jean flew out of the kitchen back to Joe who stood her on the rim of the tub where she could see into the mirror of the opened medicine cabinet.

With a dramatic swish of his brush in his shaving mug, Joe made lots of lather showing it to Jean. "See all the suds?" She nodded quickly. "Okay, now I'm going to paint it on your face just the way Grandpa does at the barbershop." With deft strokes, Joe gave her a mustache, beard, and sculpted white eyebrows for fun. Then he scraped the butter knife over his cheek to show her how to shave. Then it was Jean's turn.

A curious Marian had come to the foyer to peek at the fun in time to hear Joe say, "Good job, honey. Maybe I'll let you shave me. If you tell Grandpa, he might put you to work at the barbershop."

Marian happily tiptoed away proud of Joe's patience. Her mother bond with Jean had easily come about, but that same bond with Joey was too tight. Marian could not leave him without his endless, loud crying serenading the neighborhood until she returned. The family resorted to comic subterfuge. Again and again, look-alike sisters donned Marian's housedress to pretend to be her but only after Marian fed him. A baby with a full tummy, ready for sleep was easily fooled.

Carmella, now a beautiful young woman, and Sossy, a handsome young man much like his mother, came to babysit. Carmella put on Marian's housedress to pretend she was Marian and give her a chance to escape for a few hours.

Minutes after Marian left, Carmella forgot and turned, and a sleepy Joey realized it wasn't his mother and wailing filled the rooms. Sossy tried to quiet Joey while Carmella ran to the window, calling, "Mar, come back."

A loving sister heard, but with the overwhelming taste of freedom, she blew Carmella a kiss and rushed away. The younger Manfredi germane wanted to throttle her. Joey's ability to vex those loving him started very early. He screamed the whole time she was gone.

Joey was chubby but so solid he creased at all his joints, with hair so blonde, it looked green. Many strangers thought him a happy German baby.

One day on a Jersey side beach of the Hudson River, Joe found himself following his baby around as he held on to whatever was in arms reach trying to walk on his own. Joe now found himself in a new land of worry, remembering the candy man's visiting Vineyard in a try for Jean. He knew it was reaching the level of irrational but couldn't seem to help himself. But this was a daddy's job, and his mind insisted.

While Joey hung onto a wire fence, passersby stopped to play with him, and one asked, "Is he of German descent, he sure looks it?" It wasn't the first time the possibility of Joey's German heritage had been asked and answered, "With a name like Prezzemoli, I doubt it." Still Joe's curiosity left him wondering, and when he returned to Marian, he said, "Hon, people are right. Joey does look like a roly-poly German baby. Who'd we mix him up with?"

A Young Joey

Marian, kneeling on the beach blanket, answered through teeth-clenching diaper pins and said, "With Pop."

Joe's classic nose curled as Marian handed him Joey's wafting remains, but he listened as she explained and diapered Joey's well-rounded, now sweet-smelling bottom.

"Seems we, the Manfredi clan, descend from a Northern Italian prince near the German border, so our Germanic influence is very strong. And Pop was very blonde until he became ill and lost it all. For some reason, it grew back in blue black like mine. It was before he married Momma."

Joe's eyes twinkled as he said, "Since Prezzemoli means Parsley, I guess my ancestors grew the stuff. I've married very well."

"And don't you forget it Mi Lord."

Joe leaned across the blanket to beard her cheek to cheek. When Marian leaned into his affectionate move, her welcoming smile became a grimace. She waved Joey's smelly load away and said, "Joe, he's your son in more ways than one."

A daddy's laughter roared in recognition.

In quieter, lonelier moments, Joe hovered in fear for Marian. The response grew even when making love in hope of another child. Guilt plagued him for wanting her more than he wanted the children they had hoped to create. He would often wake while Marian slept and just watch over her. Sometimes, he would place a hand on her stomach, a pinky resting in pubic hair wishing the evil away.

One winter night, the project woke to clanging fire engines, and people leaped out of warm beds.

Joey, too small to leap, understood waking meant eating and cried for Marian.

Joe leaned out over the wide windowsill only to realize the fire was in the area directly across from the end of their building, and it blocked his view but felt it was serious for seeing a bristling, dancing light where there shouldn't be one.

"Mar, I'm going out to check on this." Joe grabbed a winter coat to put over his underwear and struggled into a pair of boots.

Jean saw and said, "Daddy, please take me?"

Joe hesitated and looked to Marian.

"Take her, Joe, I'll feed Joey."

Joe dressed her warmly and piggybacked a booted Jean to the corner and immediately regretted bringing her. What they saw were raging flames consuming a wood frame house in a group of homes only feet apart. The homes stood on one-story high cinder blocks with a flight of wooden stairs rising to the first floor porches. The firehouse two and a half blocks away on Vineyard Avenue responded in time to contain the menace and had gotten the Negro family out, but a child was missing and the huge amounts of water from the fire-fighters did little to quench the insatiable beast. All they could do to prevent it's spreading, they did, and the lack of wind helped.

There was no wind, but the temperature was in the low teens freezing the water wherever it hit the ground, and the ice compli-cated every effort.

Joe put Jean down, holding her hand as they joined the small crowd directly across from the burning home. They heard the moth-er's scream for her child as firemen went into the inferno. Joe felt Jean's hand tighten in his, and her arm tightly wound around his leg. Still he didn't take her home something within compelled him to stay.

Dense smoke and hungry cracking flames left firemen only minutes to find the boy. Each returned empty-handed. One stayed longer. All eyes watched the greedy flames gnawing at the doorway. Finally, that hero fell through the doorway, arms empty and burned. Blackened hands, stiff before him, he stumbled and crawled on his knees.

His weight rolled him down the smoldering steps to where his rushing fellows pulled him away, hearing, "Oh, God, I couldn't find him. I heard him crying, but I couldn't find him."

A buddy's callused hand grabbed the crying fireman and gently held him against his slicker.

The ousted family huddling, struggling, and shivering in bed-clothes were further stunned by the sudden unbearable cries from a brother, a son causing love to pierce their hearts as he was eaten alive by gnawing flames. He was lost in a world of horror instead of the safety of his own bed.

The tormented mother begged, "My baby, please, oh, please someone save my baby."

As the flames fed on flesh, his agony filled the human spectators with the smoke of hopelessness.

His wail iced the already frigid air making Jean grab Joe's leg with both arms, and as she pulled her hand from his, he could feel her fear climb, so he lifted her to hold her close just in time for her to see the child's mother rush the burning stairs. Firefighters pulled the mother away, though she tried to beat them off. Finally, restrained, she let out a soul-retching sound and collapsed. Jean's hold nearly strangled him, but still he couldn't leave.

Another fire fighter dashed up the burning stairs only he fell through. Others rushed to pull him from the burning debris. Another tried from the truck's ladder to the second floor where the porch roof gave way. Only grabbing a ladder rung prevented his falling to serious hurt. Searing, unrelenting flames viciously reached for a pair of dangling booted feet.

Onlookers gagged on the scents of hell. Hose water frozen as high as two feet became grotesque shapes with shifting reflections as though hosting satanic spirits cursing and savoring a night theirs alone.

Suddenly, the screams were gone, and the silence became more unbearable as the house fell inward.

Remorse for the black family churned in many a mind and heart including Joe who wondered about the souls of the good and bad around them wondering if man's evil was relishing the horror hidden by veil of night.

Holding Jean close, Joe thought, *How do you survive such tragedy without going insane? A mother heard a son die, brothers and sisters heard a brother die. I heard him die, my Jeannie heard him. Oh, God.*

Loss pressed itself upon him in a strangely personal way where he couldn't escape the guilt of wrongful laughter he found on the streets of the city he loved.

His cheek was wet with tears. Jean's slender finger touched his cheek, and feeling the tear on her finger, she laid her head on his shoulder and felt him shaking.

Joe kissed her and returned sore and watery eyes to the stricken family. The youngest boy clothed only in underpants huddled beside a sister under a blanket for warmth.

Joe spoke hoarsely, "Honey, I'm going to put you down, but hold on to me." Joe moved forward, took off his coat, placed it around another of the woman's son, and pulled it tight to keep him warm.

He said, "Take care of your mommy." The boy's expression, dazed and unseeing, would stay with Joe a very long time. The boy's sister pulled the boy protectively closer, and the fear Joe saw in the girl's eyes deepened the sense of guilt.

He slowly headed home after picking up Jean, while others came forward to help as he had. He was shivering in his underwear. The sensing of Jean's snuggling against his neck should have warmed him but it didn't.

After the briefest explanation to a shocked Marian, he tucked Jean in, wiped her tears, kissed her, and—with his lips close to her cold ear—said, "Say a prayer for the little boy?"

Joe's breath felt warm on Jean's ear, but she tensed as she nodded and sadly watched him stoop and kiss a sleeping Joey and saw her fathers trembling fingers gently move along a sleeping son's arm.

In moments, Joe returned to the kitchen, and Marian filled with regret for letting them go and placed Joe's bathrobe over his shoulders.

"Sit down, you need something hot."

Oh, God, I shouldn't have let them go, I—

Unable to take her eyes off him, she saw he didn't budge and remained there anchored in troubled thought.

She forcefully said, "Joe!"

Bothered by his silence and Joe's strained look, Marian needed to say the right thing. It wasn't necessary to ask about his coat, but she knew he needed to talk about what he saw.

Joe was staring at the Nepperhan Hills opposite the fire. He remembered how the Ku Klux Klan had burned crosses on the hill above the cemetery beyond Smith's Carpet Shop.

"Oh, Mar, the Klan burned their crosses there, we've both seen them. How many times did I watch and then join in telling offensive jokes? How many times? That's the same hill Mom, Louis, and I used to climb to go see the Margaret and Mary at the home. Dear God, caring for family and friends isn't enough."

The kitchen windows reflecting the overhead light reminded him of the fire's glow. With Hitler threatening the world, the boy's death stirred his untended values about people different in God's design. Being a husband and father brought those values into sharp focus to take on the harder real world meanings of a good world. Joe was turning a forceful corner that added to his troubled voyage.

Marian put her arms around his waist to warm him and the iceberg of feeling broke.

"Marian." The hollow sounding voice startled her, as he added, "Our kids mustn't grow up hating anyone."

Exhausted, Joe sat at the table, and Marian quickly moved to the tea water and made a potent hot toddy while saying, "I know. The project's shown me how wide spread prejudice really is. But people here are good and would run to help."

Joe stiffened and she stopped herself for realizing her words lacked reality and added, "But the others are here too? And so much of it is like my mistrust of Larry. Oh, hon, do you think someone set—"

"I'd say so, but I don't know. No matter how much water they poured into that fire, it wouldn't go out. Marian, that little boy didn't stand a chance. Thank God the fire trucks were only blocks away or no one in that string of homes would have gotten out."

They were both struggling with the thought a killer might have been in the crowd feeding on the little boy's cries.

Over the warming tea, a husband and wife talked of loathing such horrors and of doing right. They decided their home would challenge the odium hidden in the recesses of un-American or uncaring dangerous minds. Hatred without conscience needs conquerors in every home. The best they could do was start with their own and hope the streets would not undo their efforts with Joey and Jean.

Joe's watcher saw the colored child's spirit—whole and well arrive in the arms of one of many who loved him.

As time passed, the project became a way of life that led to other kinds of battles for Marian.

The croup continued to plague Jean, and this time, when she was almost well enough to go back to school, Marian discussed the problem with Joe as they prepared for bed.

As she slipped into a soft-clinging nightgown, she said, "Joe, I'm worried about Jean. All the trips to the clinic and it still keeps coming back on her."

"I know. She seems to get weaker, even skinnier every time it happens. The next time we need a doctor let's go to Dr. Griffon. We'll ask him about how to put it behind her. He's proven himself to be a good doctor and he has a private practice now."

Marian sat on the bed beside Joe to say, "It means we'll be tighter financially because I want him to take care of Joey too."

"We'll manage. The clinic changes doctors too often, and they really don't know the individual patient."

Joe reached for her hand and the light switch only to hear Jean scream, "Mommy! Mommy, something's on my belly."

Marian leaped off the bed and ran. In seconds, she stood over Jean with Joe right behind her.

Jean was scrunched up against the bed's headboard white with fear and brushing wildly at the "whatever" that was working its way across her belly. Suddenly, tearfully Jean tearfully said, "It's gone."

Joey had joined the group with a half cry, but the deep sleep he'd been in easily reclaimed him, and Joe reached down to sooth him not taking his eyes off his girls.

Marian said, "Jean, get out of bed now." Jean leaped out of her way and leaned against her daddy from where they watched a furious mother tear the bed apart until she found the offending roach and did it in. But that wasn't enough. She washed Jean's offended stomach, calmed her down, put her to sleep on the couch, walked past a

242

tight-lipped Joe standing at the bedroom door, and explosively said, "Don't you say a word, Joe. I'm going to put a stop to this. I'm not the only mother angry about the roaches."

"Yes, ma'am." Joe's own fury slid away on the wings of pity for anyone standing in her way as he again checked on Joey, kissed him on the forehead, and went to bed alone knowing she wouldn't return until she'd checked the whole room.

The next day, Marian spoke to the neighbors and headed the fusion of mothers who exploded over the project administration. They explained how the beleaguered families in their building were more concerned with proper garbage disposal than the project personnel who burned the garbage.

When the fallout settled, the administration saw to proper preventive measures and handling of the garbage that fell down the chute and warnings of evictions to tenants causing the problem with following through.

That done, the problem was controllable with steel wool in any open space in pipes entering the apartment and killing powder along room borders and door. And yes, some tenants lost the privilege to live there.

Raffaele visited often to enjoy a night or weekend in a home geared to a good time. Marian always looked forward to spoiling her. At forty-one, Raffaele still possessed that handsome striking presence. Accumulating age and life's problems had not defeated her.

Joey and Jean were joys to Raffaele, but American differences in Jean's growing as a female troubled her.

Joe hid behind the paper from Raffaele's bother and whispered, "Mar, if Mom has her way, Jean will be the perfect lady."

"It's a lost cause. She gets as dirty, as her boy cousins, and now she has a brother to play with."

Raffaele watched over Jean cautioning her in many fine ways, but they included efforts to impart her superstitious nature and the language of her birth.

One day, she said, "Babina no leavea your new shoes on a table, it will a bring bada luck."

Jean had begun to understand Raffaele and the phrase superstitious, and a quick look at her parents told her she was right and said, "Oh, Grandma!" Jean tried to not to laugh, but remembering Joe trained her to sit at the table to polish her new shoes on newspaper made it difficult. And seeing Raffaele was serious, she lowered her head so Raffaele couldn't see, smiled, and mumbled, "Yes, Grandma."

When Marian looked to Joe for help, his paper was already covering his laughter, so she returned to crocheting a beautiful dress for Jean, unbothered that she would grow out of it in weeks. It would be easily passed on.

The children were important to Raffaele, but these days, it was Marian she watched with a serious serious study of Marian's body. For this daughter was getting thinner and thinner, and this mother-in-law, though uneducated in book knowledge, was worldly in everyday caring. She understood that Marian was not helping her own health with her conscientious feeding of a ravenous son. It was leaving her fatigued and diminishing in size. When she found out Marian was now less than ninety pounds, she spoke out.

"Marianne, you must stop a feeding the bambino. He take a too much. Please, it's no a good for you."

Joe heard and wondered why he lacked the common sense to stop her. "Mom's right, hon. It's time to stop. He's almost two, and he's got a great start."

All Marian said was, "You're probably right." As her hand removed her tit, Joey began a deprivation howl that seemed to last and last, but Joe's mind was filling with the fear for Marian's well-being and neglected to thank his mother for taking Joey and fixing a bottle for the hungry chub.

Dear God, Marian's so weak. Ordinarily, she'd fight us to keep feeding him because she loves feeding him. Up until recently, it's been a special time for her. I should have made her stop. Dear God, what am I using for brains.

As time marched along, his upset about Marian dug a deeper well into his mind, but he still managed to laugh at a comical son when he lifted bowls to his mouth swallowing in huge insatiable gulps. At meals end, Joey looked like a garbage heap, so meals end meant the tubbing and scrubbing of the grubby roly-poly. Young Jean, standing on a chair, had often helped, but having to use the wash cloth to catch his high flying wee, she began to feel he waited for her before letting it fly. Jean soon left the chore to others.

Unfortunately, Joe's ship of laughter, his vessel to home, was taking on water in seas that might be too wide and deep for him to swim to safety.

In 1941, while Jean prepared for second grade, Britain forces desperately repelled the Luftwaffe, and Joe and Marian read all the papers had to offer and tuned a small radio to the news before listening to programs they enjoyed.

The entering of the second grade in September posed an unusual problem for Jean. There were two second-grade classes. One was for slower students and another for average and advanced students. Some of the children clearly knew the difference.

Jean's social growth was primarily through playing, but her verbal entry paths with adults were restrained very unlike her parents, but she loved to copycat her folks. It usually served her well to hide a nagging shyness except in the need for class participation which it kept at a minimum.

Jean stood as she was told to join the Mrs. Taft's class. This was for the slower students, but instead of joining that group, she said very forcefully, "I won't go. I passed all my tests. I belong with my friends." Berta, Netty, Eddie, Jesse were already standing with the advanced group.

Taken by surprise by Jean's unusual openness and Jean's blunt and surprising young logic, the teachers took pause to think. Neither noticed the sparkling tears in Jean's eyes as they moved away to where they couldn't be heard. The tears never fell.

Having stepped aside to reevaluate the decision, the first-grade teacher explained that she placed Jean in the slower group based on the thought her quietness was immaturity. "After all, she is one of the youngest in my class, but she's never a problem except she doesn't participate sufficiently, but her marks are very good." It was obvious she was questioning the strength of her decision.

Jean gulped, hopefully looked at her friends knowing they were quietly rooting for her to join them. Suddenly, Jean was more worried about Mommy and Daddy being angry with her for being disrespectful, and those tears came closer to falling.

The advanced second-grade teacher faulted the decision. "Were you expecting Jean to have her parents' gregarious natures? We both had Marian and Joe, and we'd enjoy her being just like them. When she participates, does she make many errors?"

"No, when she answers, she's very sure of herself."

Since the teachers were good friends, the first-grade teacher whispered, "Oh, dear, it looks like I've misjudged Jean. I felt she'd benefit from the slower group. At this age, months can be a big difference. Apparently, she is just different, and she's just shown me she can hold her own better than most at her age."

In moments, Jean was told to join her friends not knowing she had turned a very youthful corner, alone.

Mommy and Daddy never said a word to her when they came to know about. It seemed her new teacher cashed her paycheck at Joe's teller window and had, for many years, enjoyed her former student.

Joe's cage was just one phase of the network this mother and father were establishing with small town attentions that would keep track of their children as well as family and friends.

The differences between Joey and Jean were very clear early on especially in personalities. Even at two, Joey had no such withdrawal patterns. Where Jean had always quietly taken in the world around her, Joey recklessly approached people and barreled through all situations. It was without vicious intent but, in search of laughter and every effort to mellow his enthusiasm, did nothing. He accomplished it with charming yet equally frustrating demeanor. Marian's most frequent thought when hearing friends comments was, *Heaven, help us, he's just like Sossy.*

The lessons about Jean were coming fast and furious as the world opened up to her in spite of the fact Marian and Joe were getting ragged running after a hyper active son who couldn't seem to sit still.

One day after school, Jean and friends—Jessie a colored, Berta, Beth, Eddie of Italian, Irish, and Greek ancestry—left school with a friend Betty who had multiple sclerosis.

They walked Betty to her pickup point before heading home. Betty had great difficulty taking curbs with her leg braces but managed the effort with cane. Her friend bid her "bye" and started home just as a group of youngsters wearing school jackets arrived nearby and the biggest yelled. "Hey cripple, think you'll ever get there? Can we get ya a cart? They surrounded Betty lauging meanly.

Eddy and the girls heard the cruel remark and ran back. Eddie got there first yelling, "Leave Betty alone, you jerk." Eddie didn't like the smirk on the kids face and saw his hand heading towards Betty and threw himself at the loudmouth bully. As the bully's friends came to his aid, Jean and Jesse flew at the other taunters, while Berta and Beth protected Betty from falling or being hurt in the melee.

Eddie, Jean, and Jesse suddenly felt their feet leave the ground as they were put behind teachers who had seen what happened and left the school yard to keep order. Too young to really know how to fight, no one was hurt in the shuffling scuffle. The bullies were sent away after a good talking to.

Jean came home proud of her friends and her ripped dress and answered all the questions Marian and Joe asked about the why. After telling Jean she did the right thing, they told her to invite her friends home for lunch on Thursday? Her smile warming them both disappeared from view as she proudly marched off to change to play clothes. Marian called out, "Jean, make sure they tell their parents where they'll be," and turned to ask.

Marian and Joe decided life with children was becoming very interesting and willingly began the constant trail of young people that would pass through their home to become their extended family. She smiled at Jean's "Yes Mommy" and Joe's "Sure hon."

When Joe sat in front of Joey to play choo-choo, he said, "Joey, looks like I have to worry about your sister's social life now, so don't you grow too fast."

Joey gave him a pursed lip wondering glance as Marian said, "I wouldn't count on that, hon." Joe smiled but it lacked his usual buoyancy.

It was the beginning of a direction that they would insist on for both children.

On December 7, 1941, they were frozen at the radio's speaker listening to the news about Japan attacking Pearl Harbor quickly followed by President Roosevelt's declaration of war. The day after Pearl Harbor, Sossy Manfredi enlisted in the Army, and days later, they got a call from Bart letting them know he had been drafted for the Army Air Corp. It was happening all across the nation.

Joe agonized over a need to join. "Marian, I want to go. Staying home scares me more than going."

"Oh, Joe, I understand but we need you here." She hated the look of disappointment on Joe's face, and she thought she understood. *Americans are dying. If they put a gun in my hand and the Japanese were here, I'd use it. But it frightens me that if men like Joe don't go, the war will reach here. Oh, God, I'm sorry I can't tell him to go. My God, he can't kill an animal and killing a person would destroy him.*

Marian prayed daily for Sossy and Bart using each prayer to deal with the guilt of not telling Joe to go, but she refused losing him before it was demanded.

Sadly, her emotions were shortsighted. She was yet to see it went much deeper, and she failed to find and understand the child within him. While she battled her body for a dream, more children, she weakened more and more. Joe watched and watched, and as the war worsened, his personal voyage took him farther away from his safe harbor to rough seas where his smiles dimmed even more.

As a couple, a dangerous corner was coming closer.

In the months that followed, America geared up to full mobilization where key activities to its internal/financial security fell to the banks with fewer bodies to handle them. Joe was assigned to work with treasury people and other Federal agencies specifically on counterfeiting and on war bond drives. His days became longer, and because his car was needed to travel from bond sale to bond sale, he was able to keep it while neighbors were turning theirs in for needed scrap metal.

With timely awareness, "Yonkers-ites" noticed that the Palisades created a strange rock formation in Hitler's deplorable likeness. About the same time, Gene's Carmella quickly married a coast guardsman assigned to the North Atlantic and Mary's Anna an Army man going to the Burmese jungles. Both would see action firsthand.

Young Joey's growth was magnificent, and Joe's being busy deprived father and son of their usual time together, but Joey latched on to any pleasing adult or playmate who he could follow, but mostly, he attached himself to whatever Jean wanted to do or wherever she wanted to go. School and the project had given her the friends she wanted to play with, and the original welcome of a little brother began to change to pesty and annoying.

It was 1942 when Marian knew she was too weak to ignore her steadily vacating health and went to see Dr. Griffon.

"Dr. Griffon, I should have listened to you. Keeping up with Joey is beyond me. He's so active, and I want to enjoy him and do for my family, but I'm finding I can't, but—"

Griffon touched her arm to stop the guilt, "Marian, this is my fault. We have to go after that tumor. I'm the doctor, I should have fought you harder. I'll call the surgeon and make an appointment, and we'll take it from there. I can arrange to stay with you through it all, if that'll help?"

"Please."

Griffon turned from her tear-filled eyes and made the calls knowing Marian's waning strength left her no arguments. After the phone calls were made, Griffon turned and realized Marian was more than just relaxed.

Catching his curious look, she explained, "It's your rocker, Doctor. This is the first time my pain has eased in a long time."

With the arrangements made, she told Joe what would be happening. His stomach railed, and his mind froze with panic under the obvious threat that warped his thinking while it garnered the guilt that manipulated his mind's directions allowing him to hide in the serious nature of his new bank responsibilities. Busy made it easier.

Marian instinctively felt the distancing between them while his hovering made him a contradiction in motion. Feeling depressed made her perception of Joe's stumbling into jeopardy a shadowy illusion she could not clearly define.

Amid the horrors of the war, the Manfredi ladies—Millie, Beth Dody, and Marian—since becoming mothers faithfully put aside a quarter a week for going out together with their spouses. It could be dinner or a show downtown or maybe burlesque in New Jersey. The enjoying of each other's company meant a fun-filled evening for all, which they enjoyed more for not knowing how long they'd be lucky enough to still have their husbands to share.

Just before going into the hospital, Joe cashed in their quarters, and the ladies and spouses went into Manhattan for the night and found Times Square was bursting with uniforms. The National Anthem at the musical they attended tied stranger to stranger in a union of passionate determination. The torturous ongoing violence left little for the American public to enjoy, and most were taking pleasure where it could be found.

During intermission, Marian pointed something out to Joe and tiptoed away only to reappear glowing while extending a playbill that said, "Thank you, Marian, Caesar Romero." The Manfredi girls strained to see the strikingly star in his Navy uniform more the excited teens than mothers of many.

Earlier that month, Jean's luck with school authority seemed to have deserted her for having clearly discovered her tongue in the third grade, and her verbal annoyance proved rather quick and unfortunate. Punishments were needed, but the worst, sitting under the teacher's desk, reaped a cruel embarrassment. Then she found her parents in the enemy's camp, her tears flowing as she heard, "Jean, you cannot continue to interrupt a class with talking. You've made a bad mistake, and sitting under the desk was your punishment. I'm sorry it happened, but when you're wrong, you have to take your punishment. I don't like what was done, but I promise it you don't behave, and if it happens again, you'll be punished here at home as well. Now go to your room and stay there, and that's what you'll do after school for the rest of the week."

Marian looked to Joe, and he said, "Jeannie, I know you're listening to your mom, but don't let it happen again, okay?" Joe hated Jean's expression, but enough was enough. Disrespect would not be allowed. That said, his mind rushed on to frightening thoughts soon to unfold.

The day before the operation, Joe, too aware of the changes happening to him, realized it was touching both Jean and Joey and wanted to be honest with the kids without frightening them. Though he didn't know how to stop the effects on himself, he wanted to avoid the same problem for them, and answers were eluding him leaving him feeling helpless.

The night he said, "Your mommy is going into the hospital tomorrow. But she'll be home in a couple of weeks. She has something in her tummy the doctor has to take out. In the meantime, you'll have lots of fun with Grandma, your aunts, and cousins because they're going to take care of you until I get home. Okay." Joe was glad to see Joey light up in what he thought was anticipation of all the attention he'd get, but Jean didn't smile and only said, "Okay,

Daddy." His mind being on Marian, he saw both as normal reactions and hustled them off to bed only to realize he hadn't let them say good night to Marian. Joe ordered an about face in time to see Marian's still surprised look. Marian's hugs and kisses were long and she promised to see them soon.

Later when Joe felt they were asleep, he went to their room and didn't notice Jean was feigning sleep as he traced his fingers down her arm, and then he leaned over Joey brushed the hair out of his eyes and did the same to Joey his valley of troubled emotions knew only a moment's ease.

After he left, Jean climbed onto the wide windowsill to cry and to get angry. The ledge was wide enough for an adult to use, and it was there she said her prayers and told God, "Daddy is so sad, and Mommy isn't feeling good. I'm scared. Please make Mommy better. I heard the word *cancer*, and I know it's bad, but please make her better."

She felt comforted by the stars above her, and the large tree that watched over the bedroom window that she believed was put there to protect them from bad weather.

The next day at the hospital, when Marian was settled and receiving a shot, she said, "Joe, why don't you go to work."

"Uh-uh. I'll be here, when they bring you back and when you wake up." Marian knew hospitals frightened Joe, but needing him there, she shed the dread of the growing distance between them wanting to believe it was her illness and that all would be well soon.

Pop and Joe were together in the waiting room with Gene not knowing what to say to a troubled son-in-law who kept getting up and down and suddenly had a cigarette in his hand, even though he knew he shouldn't.

Sensing Gene's watching, Joe said, "She hates my smelling of cigarettes, Pop. I haven't had one of these since the year we married."

Gene nodded looking as helpless as Joe.

As Joe crushed the cigarette, Pop thought about those now gone and prayed, "*Cara Mia, Tess, take care of Marian and Joe too, he doesn't look well. She says he is not eating.*"

Joe began a marathon pace fixated in self-recriminations. Guilt was imprisoning Joe in water so deep he felt he could not surface. *Why didn't I demand the operation sooner? I should have told her no more kids.* Like many a human in trouble, he didn't realize the personal tirade magnified his depression and sense of loss, something he easily spotted in others.

Hours passed before Dr. Griffon, in surgical clothes, kept her vigiler's informed, and when it was over, the surgeon and Griffon sat with Marian's knights in waiting.

The surgeon said, "The tumor was very large, so I removed a good deal of muscle and tissue along with it to improve her chances. Now we have to wait for the biopsy."

Dr. Griffon explained again after he left. "What he excised has to go out of town for diagnosis. The report that comes back will tell us if it's cancer. Unfortunately, it'll take about two weeks."

The word *cancer* again cut another wound with the impact of a dull saw in a mind futilely searching for answers.

Meanwhile at home, the Prezzemoli and Manfredi crews watched over Jean and Joey. Both were sent to bed and while Joey, too young to truly understand, went easily to sleep Jean could not.

They had spent that day after school with Aunt Angie and her kids, went home later, and found Aunt Mary and Grandma there with supper ready. The shift had changed and would again.

The evening hours belonged to Angie's teenage daughters.

Later, JJ or Tony was there to wait and walk them down the hill to home. Sossy was not to be told unless absolutely necessary. He was currently training in tank maneuvers.

When Marian woke to find a bearding Joe holding her hand, darkness quickly reclaimed her.

When her cousins found Jean awake, they did the usual. "Hey, cuz, get up, the adults are all gone." It was something they all enjoyed and Jean she had fun and would never snitch only tonight there was no fun. Jean was on a mission and asked them, "What's cancer I heard Grandpa say Mom has it." Any age difference was gone.

On that first night they waited together, Jean asked all kinds of questions and the cousins told her the little they knew. "Cancer kills people and sometimes Doctor's operate to fix it." She listened, learned, and worried even more.

The cousins heard Joe coming and rushed Jean to bed where she again feigned sleep. Joe looked in on the children and again ran his fingers down their arms. The touch sent a million wiggles through Jean that made her cry after he left the room.

As Joe lay wide awake in a lonely bed, a daughter left hers to again sit on the metal windowsill to cry and be angry. She was drawn to the rain and lightning that filled the sky as though it too was tortured that her mother was ill.

Marian's real memory of the hospital began with the nausea and room spinning allergic reaction to the anesthesia. It lasted for days, made worse by the operations painful aftermath. Pop spent part of everyday with her having his meals sent in. Gene lacked the will to be anywhere else while sharing chairs and crossing paths with a worried Joe who refused to eat more than a forkful at a time.

Marian was still there when the tumor samples were returned with the analysis two weeks later.

Griffon and the surgeon joined an anxious Joe and Marian. They had with them the bottled specimen and its completed report. Griffon spoke warmly and gratefully, "The tumor was only partially cancerous. Here let me show you." The tissue in one spot on the specimen bottle was significantly different from the balance of the tissue. "Marian, this will be kept here for training purposes for other young doctors to see and recognize."

Joe listened with a heart pounding in concert with the churn of bile that generated a growing pain in a hard at work stomach. Marian listened and squeezed Joe fingers as they listened to the surgeon.

"What I took out included as much muscle as I could take without incapacitating you permanently. I hating doing it, but it ensured our getting it all. Having done that, it means a long recuperation.

It'll be months before you're up and around." He smiled at Marian and added, "Marian, getting well will take time, but after you heal and the muscles will heal, you'll find other muscles will take over for what's gone. So please believe me and work with your body. Rest, heal, and be patient." He stood and took his leave.

"Are you sure about getting all of it?" Joe asked Griffon.

Marian brought his hand to her cheek to calm him with little effect, but it helped her to try.

Griffon looked to Dr. Simon who hesitated at the door to support what he knew Griffon would say. "Yes, Joe, we both agree he got it all. You've been very lucky, Marian."

She whispered, "I know."

Griffon watched the believer in Marian close her eyes as she said, "Thank you, dear Lord," only to glance at Joe wondering where his mind was taking him. She had an ally in Dr. Griffon but Joe refused to talk to him and Griffon knew it, because Joe refused help.

Intellectually, Joe was reaching for acceptance, but something within loosed a jumble of emotions centering on Marian and the war that raged both in his stomach and in his everyday world that made food the enemy.

Days later, Joe carried his frail lover up the stairs to the apartment past concerned project friends and neighbors and found Joey standing at the door with Carmella, Raffaele, and Jean.

Joey was the first to speak, "Mommy, where's my baby? When ladies go to the hospital, they bring home babies from their tummies."

With tearful eyes, Marian saw Joe's helpless glare and answered her crying son, "I'm sorry, honey. I wanted a baby too." Joey's eyes filled with tears as he turned away.

Carmella took Young Joey to the crib holding her new baby girl and said, "Joey, if you save a dollar, you can have my baby, okay?" Young Joey nodded, crawled in beside Carmella's little girl, and went to sleep.

Joe crushed the dangerous anger he felt at Marian's hurt and rushed to put her to bed. The raw trouble of his emotion flooded with ease when Marian cried out, "Oh, Joe, my rocker!" Something she had longed from the day she sat in Dr. Griffons was now hers.

She kissed his cool cheek, ran her fingers through his untended mane, and ordered, "Joe, wash your hair."

The smile in her command told him, "She's home."

Jean and Raffaele came into the room and carefully sat on the bed, beginning a long line of visitors.

The rocker would be Marian's home while recuperating, but she feared the long time passing, the best guess was at least six months before resuming normal family activities or being a woman for Joe and herself.

Joe hovered between being mother and father and thanking the Holy Trinity for the family's help. When he slept, his thoughts were dogged by the specter of illness and the insistent need of more to do on the job and at home. His lonely voyage deepened his sea of dread.

Carmella came to use the washing machines downstairs whenever she needed them and did the Prezzemoli washes as well. One day, she arrived and put her sleeping baby on the studio couch next to Marian's rocker in the living room. Before she could say much, Joey rushed up to her his hand clenched tightly and thrust out to her.

Carmella wasn't sure what he wanted until Marian said, "Looks like he has something to give you."

"Oh, do you have something for me, Joey."

"Uh-huh, Aunt Carmella."

"What is it?"

His hand opened, and he said, "For my baby."

Carmella turned a strange shade of green, Marian burst into laughter, and Carmella became little sister again and cried, "Mar, help!"

Marian swallowed the laughter when she saw Joey was devastated, reached out, and pulled him to her.

She wanted so to pick him up but knew she couldn't and knew he didn't understand when she didn't. Instead, he clung to her knees, and she leaned as far forward as able and hugged him as hard as she could even though she hurt.

"Oh, honey, you can't have your cousin, it would hurt Aunt Carmella very much to lose her."

"But—" his tears were so big Marian wanted to cry too, and she wanted to rock him back and forth, but it hurt too much. And Carmella said, "Oh, Joey, I'm so sorry, I didn't mean you could actually buy her. But in a way, she already yours, she's your cousin, and nobody can take that away from you."

That didn't work either, and the crushed three-year-old moped all day.

Joe heard the story and watched his son stay sad for days avoiding the fun Marian tried to interest him in. When Jean tried to join some activity with Joey and Marian, Joey turned angry. Joe wanted to yell at him.

Joe, torn as he was, made an effort to help Joey by bringing home a beautiful German shepherd puppy. But Joey pushed him away. "I don't want him." As angry as Joe felt, he suddenly found it was good fortune. The project did not allow dogs. As Joe's anger slipped away, he said, "Oh, Mar, I made a huge mistake."

"Hon, I think somebody up there likes you a lot." Joe cast his eyes skyward and said, "Thanks."

All parental efforts never changed Young Joey's mind-set, but the incident simply disappeared to travel Joey's road where he'd place his own values on life and money. And only time would tell where it would take him, because in this house, there was little to spare.

One weekend, Jean was learning to be helpful in the kitchen by making tea when Joey came up behind her. As she turned toward the waiting cups, she bumped into him, the boiling water poured over the pan onto his thigh above the artery, and Joey screamed. Joe rushed in and tore the pants off Joey, Marian tried to leave her rocker but could not, but Joe put a towel with cold water on the burn and rushed him to the hospital just two blocks away. Marian came a little later with Jean and a neighbor who got them there, all but carrying Marian. There was no keeping the worried mother and sister at home.

Joey developed blood poisoning, and though he was seriously ill, to all appearances, he wasn't and the young hustler made the most of the nurses falling for his charming ways.

No one blamed Jean because they knew Joey never left her alone and was constantly under foot; a companion she was chained to; one she now and often wished she could escape.

Joey's hurting took her around a corner that taught her one of the many sides of loving with haunting reminders of many unkind thoughts she had when annoyed by him.

Joe, worried about losing his son and his own thoughts of illness, became real in his mind and his stomach. The impact had Joe edging toward a complete nervous breakdown. The fact that Joey came home weeks later, healthy and well, was too late to change Joe's downhill rush because pressures at work continued to push him leaving him little time for a clear rationale. Currently, he was trying to help local agents of the treasure department in a hunt for counterfeiters in the area. The usual safe existence of a banker was no more because his activities robbed the family of more time together and yet he couldn't tell them anything about it.

As days passed, Marian became involved in much she saw going on and began to react much like the captain of a ship talking to those on the bridge.

"Joe do you realize how much Joey misses you? You spend so much time at the bank. It just isn't good for the kids, particularly Joey. I know how important what you do is with most of the bank's help in the service, but is there some way you can make him feel better about it."

Guilt ran the gauntlet of his mind adding to the confusion already there. Fully knowing there wasn't time to give him, he said, "I'll try to spend more time with him."

Jean's collisions with fate seemed to be coming very close to one another, and she passed into the fourth grade. Her teacher found her somewhat noisy, reliable, and likable, so when asked for messengers, she would tell Jean to report to the principal. Feeling a bid smug, Jean left her class and usually returned confident and glad for the doing, but those feelings soon fell away. Carrying a message from class to class and loving the freedom, she suddenly froze. Mrs. Peppard, the fifth-grade teacher, was screaming at her class, "You cannot behave this way in my class, and you will learn that quickly." She called out names and offenses scaring Jean to the point that she tiptoed past to the next teacher without acknowledging the lapse to the principal and not realizing there would be consequences.

In a couple of days, she was called to the principal's office. Marian and Joe were informed, and the disheartened look from the teacher she admired turned Jean inward to accept both school and home punishments. The punishments were bad enough, but her teacher's disappointment left her floundering and unforgiving of her stupidity, and she wasn't quite sure she understood it all. Soon, all had forgiven her, but each new responsibility became something she tried to wear like a warm coat in winter to undo her mistake, and it left her very serious.

Young Joey, seeing the difficulties his sister had with such efforts, left him confused and wanting to avoid whatever it was that made her unhappy.

One weekend, neither Prezzemoli nor Manfredi sisters could come to help, so Joe stripped to his shorts before rushing to the bank and began scrubbing the kitchen floor on his knees. The months with a recalcitrant and worsening stomach were taking a toll. Sweating, he turned to see his nine-year-old Jean thoughtfully watching him from the kitchen doorway.

"Jean."

"Y-Yes, D-Daddy." The stuttering, which had begun right after Marian came home from the hospital, seemed to anger him, yet he never criticized her for it.

"You're old enough to help Mommy. Come on over, and I'll show you how to do this." She made a face but followed directions for the first of many assignments. Young Joey listened quietly and was very glad she had to and he didn't.

Joe knew she didn't like it, but helping Marian was another matter. He stood there in his baggy shorts watching. *She's a good girl, but she's not strong. And that stuttering, it started when Marian went to the hospital. God, I'm doing everything wrong, or she wouldn't be struggling. What do I do now?* Joe sensed Joey standing next to him not saying or offering to help his sister with a strange smile on his face. When Joey looked up, Joe was stern and said, "Wipe the smirk off your face, Joey, or I'll find something unpleasant for you to do too." Joey quickly moved to the couch. A few days later Jean had the croupe…again.

Joe made a decision and checked it with Marian. "Hon, I want to take her to Griffon next week and see what he suggests. Maybe he can help us with her stuttering too."

"Oh, Joe, I feel so helpless, but it's the right thing to do, and we'll follow his advice this time."

Joe took Jean to see Griffon who suggested she begin to swim regularly. Joe liked that idea rather than medicines. Griffon added, "Joe, I agree, Jean's stuttering has to do with Marian's illness, so try to be patient. It'll probably go away when Marian's back on her feet. Both Joey and Jean are reacting to Marian's illness. It's only natural."

Griffon took a good look at Joe and saw he was not well wanted to talk to him about his not eating but couldn't violate Marian's confidence and there wouldn't be another chance. "Joe, is there anything I can do for you? I'm leaving soon for the army."

Joe went silent, finally nodded, and said, "Cripes Hank, you take care yourself." It was the first time Joe ever used his first name. They shook hands warmly and then suddenly hugged. Joe felt scared for and proud of the man. Griffon bent down, and Jean kissed him goodbye.

Joe arranged for Jean to swim at the YWCA pool three times a week after school.

A draft status keeping Joe safe while Griffon answered the call berated Joe's self-worth. It wasn't a good day for him.

That same day, Marian coached Raffaele through every step for making one of Joe's favorite meals: meatloaf and gravy. She returned to her rocker after supervising. The meal included buttery mashed potatoes, peas with onions with dipping bread, and butter for the gravy. Both hoped they'd succeed in helping him eat.

Joe tried hard, but the pain in his stomach just got worse until he was grimacing, and he just stopped eating. By now, his thoughts were running wild.

Raffaele's difficult childhood and years of poverty had deprived her of becoming a good cook for having next to nothing to really cook, and what should have elated her instead made her worry even more about Joe's well-being. There seemed no way she could avoid bringing others her bad luck.

Marian and Raffaele exchanged glances for having discussed his weight loss and the fact he wouldn't talk to a doctor. They were feeling more and more helpless.

A look at his ladies triggered Joe's. *Oh, God, I'm letting everyone down. On top of everything, people like those working in war plants, bring home so much more than I make, and now I'm worrying them because I'm sick.*

Joe's litany of guilt grew another notch with, *Am I selfish staying with a job I love when my family has so little? And why should I be safe while someone like Hank who is really needed here is called?* As his thoughts beat on him, digesting food became more and more difficult and repulsive, so he excused himself and left the table.

Later when all was quiet, the family listened to the radio, and Joey sat next to Raffaele and endlessly teased her about the programs she liked, but Raffaele loved him for it because he chased away her fears.

Marian tried to openly discuss Joe's pain with him, but he refused and said, "Too much of what has to be done now is too important to allow this to interfere."

Marian wanted to scream at him, but putting the children in the middle was too threatening to them, and she watched him walk away without an open challenge.

Her thoughts were self-recriminating. *Dear God, if only I'd had this done sooner, I'd be able to deal with this. Everything is so important to him, and he's to carrying so much of it alone.*

In the land of spirits, the Archer paused to caution the Prezzemoli watcher and say, "You are troubled for leaving Marian and Joe! Man's worst decisions have brought tears and anguish of so many all at once."

"I know, it is more that I will miss them."

The watcher slowed his leaving for the harder assignments of a world at war to say, "They are two who know we exist and believe."

The Archer could only agree.

In 1944, while Joey grew into mischievous, Jean continued to come home with tales that made them think her a storyteller. On an errand for Marian, Jean took a quick detour to explore something she was curious about.

It was a couple of days after a bad hurricane and there was no school. Her curiosity took her down a street where electrical wires were down. She understood the dangers based on conversations at home and carefully stayed on the safe side of the street. As she reached a corner across from school, she saw a repairman working on a ladder high above the downed line in heavy rubber clothing. She was mesmerized until she saw a younger boy reaching for the line as though trying to help the man, and she screamed, "Nooo!"

The repairman was looking too and understood even as Jean screamed. The curious boy, as quick as a child is, grasped the wire and began to shake like a rag doll unable to let go of the deadly snake he had foolishly picked up. The repairman slid down the sides of the wooden ladder on the arch side of his heavily rubber booted feet, ran to the boy, and kicked him so hard he must have broken all his ribs but saved his life. A second repairman had heard the scream as well, saw the rescue, yelled at Jean, "Go home!" and ran to the nearest house having service, to ask a call for help be made.

When a fearful Jean returned home, she told Marian who said nothing while listening intently to her story wanting to scream at her for her nearness to danger. It was just one of many incidents where Marian and Joe found the happenings were not lies.

Marian felt strange and let Jean go without a lecture on danger and merely said, "Honey, do you understand why your daddy and I tell you not to do things that place you in danger?"

"Yes, Mom, but I didn't go near any wires, honest."

Later when she told Joe, it was he who voiced the idea of a pattern, and he didn't like it. As time passed, that reaction was going to grow without a way to fight it.

Nineteen-year-old Freddy said to his mother Mary, "Mom, I'm going to override my draft exception." With Anna married to a soldier, Freddy had become sole family provider for Mary and Young Tom.

Mary wept her panic on Joe's favorite sweater. He tried to comfort her but fully understood Freddy's need to go and longed to do the same thing.

Mary's distress washed away when the draft classified Fred as 4F, unfit to serve. His father's childhood beating left him with a rib missing right over his heart. Mary's thought was, *That son of a bitch finally did something for his son.*

Freddy sought out his uncle Joe. "Jeez, Unc, I want to go so bad."

"Me too, kid. Me too. I guess our ladies need us here, or we'd be gone by now." The darkness of his mind would not accept that rational, but it was what his nephew needed to hear, but his stomach took a blow as though he'd been punched.

Freddy didn't like the way Joe looked and lost some of his frustration in concern for the only man he looked to as a father. When Fred went to kiss Marian, Joe wondered how sons could be so different from fathers and proud that Freddy was. Then he thought, *I suppose Joey won't be like me either.*

Joe's time away from home skyrocketed as he traveled to nearby cities where theaters, schools, and business districts opened their doors to bond drives. Any areas where a table could be set up brought lines for saving stamps and bonds. The smallest bond was $18.75, and it grew to a huge $25 in a few years.

Celebrity War Bond drives placed Joe on stage in theaters including those on Broadway. One night, he came home, sat on the bed beside Marian, and told her about the evening.

"Mar, she has a perfect body. Her outfit covered her all her curves as smoothly as kid gloves. It left nothing to the imagination."

His moving hands drew pictures that made Marian laugh.

"And her outfit was almost see-through."

With her head on a crooked arm, Marian matched his enthusiasm by hanging on to every word.

"Imagine having a chance to pin a bond on parts of her body based on denomination? Want to guess where they pinned the $10, 000 and $25,000 bonds?"

Marian was agog, and her voice shared the excitement. "They really got to pin them on?"

"Honest to God. Mar, her bond sales total was more than three other stars put together." The admiration for Gypsy Rose Lee's talents, as seen by the Quarter a Week Club at New Jersey burlesque halls, found grand new boundaries.

Marian was so happy to see him smile, she wanted to hug Gypsy Rose.

Raffaele visited more often to ease Marian's recuperation. The children loved having her around, and the few problems were always funny.

"Grandma, I can't pull these any tighter." Jean was holding on with all her might. Afraid to lose the gain she'd made, she hollered, "Dad, help!"

Joe rose from his chair remembering having the same problem when he was growing. So he reached over a scrawny, rear-end-sticking-out daughter's arms and, without taking the laces away, added his power to hers. And together, they tightened Raffaele's cinch girdle.

Later, while Jean and Joe were alone, he continued her lessons in behavior—in this case, the caring of a grandmother and a mother.

"Honey, I want you to hold the door for Grandma and Mommy too. Be sure to help them with shopping bundles and other heavy stuff."

At that point, Joey crashed into the room, and Joe said, "And you listen to this too, Joey. It's meant for you both. I want you to remember that Grandma is getting older and Mommy isn't well. You should always kiss Grandma hello and goodbye just the way you do Mommy and me. Just be respectful and take care of her when I'm not around, okay? You're both getting big, and I'm proud of you when you help out."

"Ye-yes, Da-Daddy."

"Joey, do you understand? You have to help." Joey nodded his head and took off to join a game of tag that had started below the living room window because he heard someone yell, "You're it," and applying what he heard wasn't his strong point unless it was fun.

Joe's requests, though kept simple, were mandatory. Joe unlike many fathers did not distinguish between that which was a boy's to do or a girl's to do. Joe didn't realize that in keeping his promises to Marian about the raising of children that he often sounded as though he were giving a lecture nor did he realize the way the workload at home was normally handled was a contradiction that he never addressed. Marian, in most things, was the disciplinarian meaning every word she'd say, without question and without meaning too, her Love of spoiling Joe, did not encourage young Joey to understand about a fair share. The weight of Joe's problems was being noticed by both children. The changes in him had caused a disturbing loss of patience.

One weekend, Joe took Raffaele and Jean shopping on Saturday after coming home from the bank planning on returning to finish up his counterfeiting report later. Joe parked outside the hallway door and reminded Jean to take some of the packages, and then Joe saw young Joey watching but not coming over to help.

"Joey, come over here." Joey came slowly over, and Joe added, "You take a bundle too. You can play later." A glance showed Jean at the building entrance holding the door with her fanny, with both arms package laden, and added, "Good job, Jean." What Joe didn't notice was the expression on Young Joey's face. He wanted to play, and an older sister who always seemed to be doing the right thing was favoritism to his young mind, while in Jean's young mind, his doing less made him the favorite.

During Marian's confinement, Raffaele often went to the movies with Jean, Carmella, or Anna or Angie's girls and Joey who was to restless to take with them stayed at Angie's until Joe could pick him up.

After picking up the tickets before the price change, the ladies went through the wide polished brass trimmed glass doors, through the well-lit lobby lined with large preview posters into the darkness that presented an escape into mystery, romance, love, fear, and any other feelings man and woman might imitate on screen.

Two theaters, Loews and Proctors, were beauties equal to many of New York City's finest.

One particular night, they were heading for Loews on South Broadway having passed by the Strand and Proctors on the number 2 trolley in hopes they had picked the best movie of the lot to see.

Once inside, they traveled deep red, plush carpeting in the wide back foyer that silenced footsteps to meet an usher who lowered a lit flashlight to prevent anyone falling as he led them down the aisle beyond the divider between the foyer lobby and the patron seats.

With luck, based on your preference, they found you a good seat beneath the now darkened upside-down, cone-shaped, crystal chandeliers that softened and raised the house lights as needed. The ladies by passed other patrons excusing themselves because it required they lift up their seats to stand to allow them to reach their soft, comfortable seats. With luck, they managed it without stepping on precariously placed toes of those already involved and absorbing the world on the huge screen before them.

The theater had balconies and scalloped box seats, hand-painted with polished brass handrails. Most definitely, a proper setting for Ginger Rogers and Fred Astaire to perform in all their finery, though

the audience might house the factory worker taking in a movie on the way home or the business-clad banker doing the same. There was a stage suitable for a large production draped in a velvet curtain by golden cords as much as two inches thick with the white, silhouetted screen set between them in a manner due it projected wonders.

The ladies loved the movies. They were in a place that wrapped itself around the abundant dreams its human benefactor's contrived. Such mental expanses included men escorts, perhaps reluctant to admit the power of the features where they could trade places or elaborate on the scenes of pretense found in the hero's efforts.

In the darkened theater, Raffaele's personal loneliness disappeared as she drooled over Tyrone Power. Tonight, he was playing a gambler. Raffaele knew it was a place where she fed the fodder of illusion to nourish her imagination and she intended a very full meal.

Raffaele

She whispered to Jean, "Cara mia, whatta they say?"

Jean said, "Ah, Grandma," and then explained with an occasional Italian word to please Raffaele who tried to teach her the softer language but Jean really wasn't interested. Like her parents, she felt she was American and should speak only English. Raffaele didn't really mind for Tyrone had her full attention.

After the movie, Raffaele told Marian, "Thisa Tyrone Power can putta his shoes under mya bed anytime. You thinka I could maybe clean for this, Tyrone?"

Marian loved Raffaele's romantic nature and the way her eyes lit up with the tempting jest. She admired her mother-in-law's courage and cleanliness and enjoyed the chance to tell her, "Mom, I could eat out of my toilet bowl after you've cleaned it, but I'm not sure Tyrone Power could handle you."

Raffaele's grin was almost impish. "Grazie Marianne. In your home, there is little to do. But witta Tyrone, it would be a funa finding out." Raffaele smiled and her handsome face filled with suggestive implications that had both ladies laughing as only ladies could when men were the topic for Marian it was mindful of the way Tess and the girls had enjoyed similar discussions.

One Sunday, Jean had to go to mass by herself and didn't come straight home after mass. Marian did her best to calm Joe, but she too was getting anxious. By the time Jean walked in, Marian was furious.

"Jean, where have you been? How could you worry your daddy like that? You know his stomach is bothering him."

A frightened Jean respectfully waited and said, "Mom-m—my, I di-didn't do anything wrong, bu-but I-I couldn't come home."

"What? Why not?"

Jean leaped into the explanation fearing she'd be accused of lying, so her words tumbled. "I couldn't come home because I ha-had to go to cate-catechism because Sister Agatha made m-me sit with St. Jo-Joseph students because I-I was alone. She wouldn't listen to m-me and told me to be qui-quiet 'cause I was I-I was in church. And then she wouldn't let m-me leave af-after mass and marched m-me into cate-catechism class. M-Mom, I had to g-go with them or get yelled at by you for saying somethin' t-to her you won't let m-me say."

Marian said, "Oh!" and burst into laughter while Joe smiled a very tired smile and walked slowly away to pick up his paper for the umptieth time, finally able to make sense of it.

Jean looked at her laughing mother oddly and said, "Mom, don't laugh at m-me. I-it was awful. And I had to go to cate-cate-chism twice this week."

Marian gave her a hug and said, "Next time, we'll send you with an adult or keep you home. Okay?"

Jean nodded and hung on to Marian's hug as tightly as she could.

Jean left the hug, sat next to Joey, bumped him over to find space on the studio couch, grabbed the Sunday funnies, and began reading just like Joe from the back page to the front, though she was right-handed.

Marian returned to her book, thinking, *Thank God it wasn't Joey or we'd have to pick him up at the confessional.*

A Voyage at War

Marian's recuperation fueled battles between her and Joe that matched the complexity of the Desert Fox finding an enemy's weakness when seeking a method used to wound and tear at the Allied front. Only their battles took place on an emotional desert, rather than the hot sandy dunes of Africa.

The Prezzemoli kids picked now in a natural pattern of learning to pit Marian and Joe against each other. It created a field of vulnerability springing the traps within a dangerous and exploding minefield. Marian's and Joe's vocal harangues were as painful as flying shrapnel.

The growing denizens would run to a believing parent make their claim of being wronged and leave that parent to argue with the other in a duel for the reins of their runaway team. When the upheaval quieted, the adults found themselves in neutral corners groping for a secure hold on their emotional reins.

After one such quarrel, a contrite Joe entered the living room where a perplexed Marian sat in her rocker, watched him bite his lip, and heard him say, "They did it to us again! What are we going to do, Mar? We can't keep arguing like this, not because of them. Shit."

When she wide-eyed his word, his expression hastened to, "I'm sorry, Mar, but let's face it. Half the time, they can't remember how it started, and we wind up at each other's throat. I don't know whose telling the truth anymore. They're just kids, but it's wrong." Joe paced as Marian sought calm by rocking to and fro unaware of matching his pace.

She broke the heavy silence. "You're right. Their foolishness mustn't turn into a quarrel between us." Marian's thought, *Would this be happening, if I were well?* was detoured by Joe's softened tone.

"Maybe this is like kids fighting outside? Maybe if we leave it alone, they'll work it out?"

"Oh, Joe, this isn't outside. And we can't let them do this to us. If we do, they won't learn to be responsible for what they make happen. Besides, we don't deserve this. I guess my being sick is part of it."

"No, Mar, it's not that. It's just that they're kids, but you're right, we don't deserve this."

Joe was battling his mind hesitating through his words. I guess we should act as one?

"Even when we disagree!" suggested Marian.

"Maybe because we disagree. Mar, it feels right to me. One thing is certain—we lose when they pit us against each other. How about one of us handling it and the other just going along with it until we can discuss it privately. I don't see a problem in changing our direction afterward, do you?"

Marian didn't answer immediately. She was watching his hand rub across his face and nose, more troubled than he should be.

She left her reflections as he added, "But if we do that, we'll be at war with them, won't we? And they're so young. How do we make them understand? I'm afraid they'll think we don't love them."

Marian hated the effect such thoughts and the word *war*, too much a part of his troubling, had on Joe. His tight facial muscles were devoid of his usual relaxed and smiling manner. She saw it but didn't truly grasp his growing disturbance, and since he couldn't explain what he didn't understand himself, she dealt with what she could.

"Joe, that's easy. We keep showing them we love them until they know it. But I don't think that'll be a problem. They know we love them, and this is a matter of respect."

The changes in Joe continued to frighten her, as was her guilt for not being the lover she knew she wanted to be, the lover he needed and she couldn't be. She fixated on, *My kids better know how lucky they are having him for a father or they'll answer to me.* Unwittingly, the children had forced Marian to use the fierce strength she avoided using in dealing with children for fear of doing them harm.

The next time the chaotic duo separated and ran to a parent telling a tale of woe, Joe took his child and met at Marian's rocker while she kept the other there, silent until they were all together. These parents were in an allied attack mode.

In a voice rebounding with anger, she ordered, "Sit down. We should spank you both because you make Daddy and I argue."

Eyes popped in Joey and Jean's skinny faces as Joe said, "It's bad and it has to stop."

Marian's harsh voice explained, "We love you both, but Mommy and Daddy also love each other. No one should come between a husband and wife, especially not their children. Now you listen to me. You're going to grow up and move away from us, but we'll still be here, so you mustn't do things that make us argue."

Joe's anger matched Marian's, but his voice had a shutter totally unfamiliar to the kids. "Mommy is right. A father puts his wife before his children, and a mother puts her husband before them. When Mommy and I do that, we can help you two better because we work together to do it."

Jean and Joey left after the family discussion without a word and the toy they'd been fighting over was never mentioned and went to their shared room. It was as though they'd placed a sign on the door, "Silence!"

Joe broke the silence. "Marian, I realize this is beyond the kids' understanding, but I hope the telling and doing will root the idea. God, I hope so."

"Me too, Joe, me too. But they're smart, they'll figure it out." The fatigue she felt was apparent, but her anger reentered when she said, "I won't stand for any disrespect, Joe, they will learn or else. Any problem with my taking the toy? I plan on losing it."

"None, and yeah, we'll just stick to our guns."

In the times to follow the growing, ever eating twosome, again and again, tested their parents united front. And just like the Allies, it began to have an impact. Only the future would tell if it was good or bad.

Near the end of the summer, Sossy had a furlough, and knowing made Joe feel better than he had in a long time even though the furlough meant he was heading overseas. Though he enlisted the day after Pearl Harbor, Sossy was yet to see action. A recent transfer to paratrooper had the effect Sossy wanted.

The family excitement was infectious, after a heated discussion with Joe about, "I want to be there to see him come home. I don't care how tired I get."

"Mar, that's not smart."

"I want Sossy to see me active so that he doesn't go away worried about me. I'll do what I have to, to make sure he's leaves with good thoughts."

"All right. All right, but you stay off your feet, your sisters will do the work. Do you understand or I'll tell him the truth."

"Joe, don't use that tone with me."

"What do you expect when you jeopardize yourself?"

"All right. All right, you're right, but I'm going to be there when he walks through the door."

The day Sossy was due, all the family knew was that he was on his way but had no idea when. Marian said, "Jean, come to Grandpa's for lunch and remember to stay away from your brother and cousins. Hopefully, by that time, Uncle Sossy will be here."

At lunchtime, Jean called out, "Grandpa, I'm here."

Gene bent for a kiss and pulled a chair next to the stove for her to stand on so they could talk. There wasn't a gray hair in his head at sixty, and mixed with that flawless unwrinkled complexion, his age defied reality.

"Filyame, how about eating lunch with me, we've no idea when Uncle Sossy will arrive?" Putting down the stirring spoon, he faked hitting her hand and gave her a hug.

Now that she enjoyed Grandpa's game, she feigned tensing, made a face, burst into laughter, and hugged him back.

Hungry and nosy, she shoved her snoot into the pot about to say yes and froze. Monstrous dead eyes bulged at her. The full face of a goat defied her to eat him.

Head down, she squeaked as she said, "Um, Gran-Grandpa, Mom said I-I should come up t-to say hello. I gotta go." As she leaped off the chair, the kitchen filled with mirth. Gene shut off the stove and followed her down to say, "Marian, you better look Jean over."

A tired but excited Marian turned Jean's freckled face toward the light to say, "You're right, Pop. Sorry, kiddo, you're not going back to school. Angie, we have another kid with spots."

"What's one more?" In minutes, Jean was in a cousin's pajamas and went upstairs with Marian taking one straining step as a time.

Young Joey had joined four of Angie and Millie's youngsters yesterday and was wrestling with cousins John, Joe, Theresa, and Bernie. Oops two Johnnys, two Joey's not to mention two Theresas, and shucks only one Bernie. Laughter was running amok with their young heads turning each time a name was called as Jean added to the arms and legs waving for attention. Though she hated missing school—said, "M-Mom, this is fun." It was almost unpatriotic to have the German measles, but they did. Separating the kids saved most of the older folks from catching their share of spots.

Joe appeared at the second floor's porch entry waving at the itching children but staying safely away from the frolicking captives. He'd just been to the train station.

Then a uniform of a paratrooper stepped from behind Joe, and the brood screamed, "Uncle Sossy's here." Marian yelped his name, and her sisters hearing their calls sounded like stampeding cattle coming up the wooden stairs. Marian had beat the competition just as she hoped.

Sossy dove onto the large bed grabbing and hugging any kid in range and yelling, "Come on, gang. If I get the swastika measles, I'll get another week's leave."

Joe glanced beyond Sossy and quickly moved away to avoid the trample of love's rush.

The Manfredi sister's barreled through the doorway as though taking the same step. Sossy leaped up grabbed Marian with one hand and opened his other to gather them like a bouquet of flowers and hugged them so hard they couldn't breathe but didn't care. Long muscular arms befitting a six-foot frame easily held Angie, Beth, Marian, Millie, and Carmella.

The Soldier And His Sisters

When they pulled away, Marian took a good look at the uniform with wings and boots of a paratrooper to once again recognize a heartbreaker. Tess's influence embodied his Gregory Peck looks with a terrific build hardened by his training into admirable muscles. That would have been enough, but God amply graced it with tight cheeks and a sassy carriage. With Joey looking and behaving like him more every day, the future promised to be very interesting.

Conversations broke out like the overlapping layers of cookies covered with multicolored sprinkles each on a different subject.

The cousins joined Uncle Sossy's platoon when Sossy said, "I'm going to teach you kids to jump like paratroopers."

He smiled as Jean fought the boys for a place near the front of the line with Joey right behind while climbing the path beside an old cinder brick foundation wall in the backyard. The wall stood at a height of about ten feet, and they were to leap from there yelling, "Geronimo," and land in the arms of their uncle.

His sisters knew the children were safe but stayed to take in all of Sossy that they could automatically taking turns monitoring the cooking meal. The two weeks would pass with Joe and others listening to every word Sossy could tell about what was happening on the war front from one soldier's view, though it was little because he was still stateside something that had prompted his latest transfer request.

The Soldier And His Troops

On Saturday, Joe set work aside. He'd work all day Sunday and the family took off for Rockaway Beach. It took three cars and a very early start. Once there, Sossy took the children on a roller coaster, two at a time. Jean had a crushing hold on Sossy's waist as the roller coaster plummeted toward the ground. After the ride, Sossy deposited Jean on the ground, watched her heave her breakfast, and said, "You poor kid, you have you dad's stomach." Jean just smiled, gave him a hug, and ran off to tell the tale. Next was Joey's turn, and he ran to Joe crying because he was too small to pass the height test for the ride. The sisters were on the beach with Marian under a large umbrella and covered with towels to avoid her tendency for blood poisoning from the sun and to rest as her siblings demanded.

Later, everyone met on the beach for a swim. While swimming, Jean and a friend Marilyn who couldn't swim were caught in the undertow. The family heard their screams, and the next second, they went under. Instinctively, Joe and Sossy dove into the breakwaters at different points for not knowing the currents exact location.

Jean and Marilyn had been holding hands as they ran into the surf and grabbed at each other below the surface and refused to let go as they tumbled further out. There was no air, and their breaths were getting short and their panic fiercer. While Marilyn could not swim, she realized Jean was hanging on and so did she. Jean kicked and kicked as a swimmer should, but she was tiring quickly because the current had its way with them, and just as quickly, it spit them out, and they came up well beyond the wooden pilings separating the beaches only the incoming waves took pleasure in slamming them against the wood pilings. Still the girls held on to each other.

When Marian saw Joe and Sossy hit the water, she heart seemed to stop as she struggled to stay on her feet and cursing herself for not being able to swim. Finding Young Joey's hand in hers, she felt his trembling or was it her own. "Jean will be all right, Joey. Daddy and Uncle Sossy are going to get them." *Oh, please, Dear God, let me be right.*

The girls struggled to hold on, but the pilings were greasy, and they were at the mercy of the waves. They were in deep trouble. Suddenly, a lifeguard was there, lying on his stomach atop the pilings to grab both girls by the hair. He'd run the pilings to where they were. Now he was holding on determined not to lose them. Sossy and Joe joined the effort in the water only seconds later.

The lifeguard yelled, "I need help." Sossy pulled himself onto the pilings to help while Joe swam to the girls, put an arm around each of them, and placed himself between the girls and the pilings to take the pounding of the waves. He was kicking harder than he ever had. His desperate strength kept the pilings from smashing into the girls. He was impervious to the pounding.

Sossy and the lifeguard quickly raised the girls to safety and then hauled Joe up.

Joe had noticed how Jean hadn't let go of her friend and feared she'd really have gone down with her, but the thought hurt his gut so much, he thanked God for their saving instead.

When things quieted down, Jean refused to go back into the water. "No, I'm scared."

Marian immediately reacted to it and said, "Joe, I don't want Jean to be afraid of the water the way I am."

Joe nodded and said, "Marian, sit down, you're pale as a ghost. He turned his voice to soft with, "Jeannie, come here. You did a nice job out there hanging on to Marilyn."

"Daddy, she can't swim. I can."

"We all know that. Now aren't you glad you can. Come on, let's go back in."

He saw the panic in her eyes and squatted beside her. "It's okay, honey, you don't have to be scared. I'll be with you, and I'll show you how to swim across that kind of a current so you'll know how to help yourself. Okay?" *Like that's going to help if it's not in the cards. But she needs to get back in there.*

Sossy called out, "Go with him, Jean. Then when I come home again, you, Daddy, and I can go swim in the Hudson. In fact, I'll go with you now."

Thinking about their arms around her made her smile, but she still looked to Marian for an escape.

Marian merely said, "Go. I don't want you to be afraid of the water the way I am." Overruled, Jean took Joe's and Sossy's hands, and they ran into the surf, yelling, "Geronimo." Young Joey just watched torn between caring and wanting to be there too.

Sossy's last night at home was his turn to take everyone in. He was a sponge soaking up memories to squeeze out, as he needed them. They sang, they danced, and they played their musical instruments as neighbors and friends came and went. Sossy watched and found it strange for remembering warmly a vision of Marian chasing him over the hillside. It let him forget where he was going. He could see his being home was too much for her, because after the trip to the beach, she had to go back to her rocker after Joe brought it down for her to use. Sossy walked over, bent down to Marian, and whispered, "Are you well enough to be here?"

"You've gotten to smart, I'm not hiding anything, it's just going to take time, but I'm a lot better already."

"Okay, Mar, but I needed to hear it." He kissed her and went to join others.

All the goodbyes were said that night, and in the morning, Sossy walked away waving at Pop. Few letters came after that returning the family to waiting and writing him to ensure he had mail every day. What letters they received had no real information in them until after hitting the silk over Belgium on D-day the next summer.

Marian again in her rocker worried openly along with Joe about Sossy but found laughter in the female adventures he had shared with Joe. Their concern drifted to the humorous side of their young hellion being so like Sossy. When they sidled to sleep saying, "God, help us. He looks and acts like Sossy more every day."

And Joe quietly said, "As a man, I hope he fairs as well with the ladies."

"In that case, you, Mr. Prezzemoli, will handle the shot gun toting fathers."

In the dark she didn't notice his "Will do," held no humor.

Joe thought, *Oh Christ...* Joe was too tired to realize he's losing his sense of humor.

One day, tired, Joe came home hoping for a good-night's sleep, only there was a knock at the door.

His sister Mary and nephew Freddy came in. And before Joe could kiss her hello, she blurted out, under tear-filled eyes, a voice heavy with the weight of fright, "Oh, Joe, I have to register as a foreign alien."

"What, why?"

As the words left his mouth fear for her being deported rushed through his now remembering and raging mind.

"Dear God, you never became a citizen and were at war with Italy."

Now the tears fell. "Oh, Joe, what's going to happen to me and the boys and Mary."

Freddy jumped in, "Mom, take it easy, give Unc have a chance to think." Freddy looked pleadingly at his uncle as Marian come out of bedroom, sleepy eyed, and holding her back.

"Hi, Aunt Marian." Marian smiled at Fred as Joe said, "Hon, there's a problem."

Freddy kissed Marian. She patted him on the chest and went to Mary put an arm around her and said, "I heard, it'll be all right."

Joe's stomach lurched at seeing the tears running down Mary's beautiful cheeks and quickly said, "Sis, nothing will happen to your kids. They were both born here, and you let that idiot husband of yours go back to Italy refusing to go with him. But what were you thinking by not getting your papers?" He felt Marian's hand on his forearm as she said, "Forget that, what do we do now?"

Joe read the letter from immigration and said, "It says you have to register immediately. Freddy, can you take Mom downtown tomorrow and stay with her?"

Mary squeaked, "What about my kids?"

"Sis, calm down. You're not listening. They were all born here. Take their birth certificates. Good God, relax, Mary is safe. She's married to a soldier fighting in Burma, and they know that. I don't think there's a real problem. Hell, it's obvious you refused to go with your bastard husband when he went back and you divorced him."

Joe turned back to Freddy. "Can you do that?"

"Sure can, Unc."

"You know where she has to go?"

"Yes," answered Fred.

Marian said, "Joe, doesn't it usually help to have affidavits and character references for this kind of thing."

"I'll have all you need by noon."

"Unc, the instructions tell you everything. She insisted we come see you."

"That's okay, I'm always here for you guys."

"Come on. I'll drive you back to the subway."

Marian bit her tongue to prevent saying, "But you need sleep." *This is Mary, and she's very important to him. Besides it's the right thing to do. Dear Lord, don't let anything go wrong. He'd die if she was taken away.*

Joe wasn't eating well, and adding the problems family and friends brought to them was making it worse. The bruise of his not relishing food, one of his precious pastimes had Marian more worried than other factors.

This is my fault. I waited too long to have the operation, and now I'm not being a woman for him. Look what worrying about me has done to him. But even that doesn't explain what's happening to him, and he won't or can't tell me what it is.

Marian called Mary and invited them all for dinner a few days later. A call to her sisters brought them to pull the meal together.

By then, the registration ceased to be a problem, but the damage to Joe was done.

Marian had her sisters ply him with his favorite desserts, but nothing worked, and though Joe was willing to take the children to the doctor, going on his own behalf was a battle she always lost to his fear and hated the impact.

If only I understood where all his fear is coming from. There's more to it than just his caring so much. Oh, God, if I don't understand it, how can I help him?

The next night, Joe sat reading Mary's foreign alien registration card under an application number on a six-by-four inches in size. It said, "Application filed in the Alien Registration Division. Copy filed with Federal Bureau of Investigation at N.Y., N.Y." It was followed by her mother's maiden name, Scanapico and had a print of her own right index finger beside her photograph accompanied by her signature. Though he'd been assured by his calls that she was in no danger of deportation, it terrified him that Mary was vulnerable without U.S. citizenship. He didn't want his fear to pass on to her and said,

"Sis, at least it's a cute picture." But all noticed he left almost all his dinner on the plate.

Marian remembered having called, Dr. Griffon to wish him safe and taking his suggestion to grind Joe's food if he got worse. She suggested it to Joe and he was willing to try.

Marian managed as much as her energy allowed from her rocker making sure their wartime food stamps were wisely used. After squeezing a capsule of yellow food coloring into a package of Oleo, a margarine substitute for butter, she tasted it and chose to do without. She slowly moved to the stove to stir the tomato sauce for macaroni her sister Carmella had made, along with cleaning the house she returned to her rocker tired and hurting while holding on the door knobs and furniture to make it there and praying, "How do I help him?" While passing the window, she glanced outside and saw the windowed service stars of neighbors who had loved ones fighting overseas and the gold stars of those killed.

How can I cry when they're doing without those they love, while I have Joe here with me. Prayers for her brother and friends who could die at any moment forced her to reconsider telling Joe to go. *I could tell Joe to go and get a defense job where I'd make more money than we have right now.* She lowered herself into the rocker, sat erect, and made her decision. *Joe will answer the draft, but I won't send him.*

Joey was sometimes very lonely with Jean in school and busy with homework, so as parents, some happenings were eye-opening.

One evening, Marian and Joe were reading quietly when Joey came out of the bedroom crying.

Joe put down a *LIFE* magazine. "What's the matter?"

"I can't find Jean."

"What do you mean you can't find her?"

"She's not here."

Marian put down the mystery she was reading, knowing Jean hadn't left while Joe went to look for her in the bedroom. Joey was right, she was nowhere to be seen. Marian realized she was hiding and asked Joey, "Why are you looking for her?"

"I want her to play with me."

"Honey, sometimes, people like to be alone." Then she called, "Jean, where are you?" For a moment, there was no answer.

"Jean?" The tone elicited an immediate answer.

"I'm under the bed."

Joe joined them and anchored Joey as he headed for the floor along with Marian who had struggled to get down on her knees to see Jean on her belly with a flash light over a book she'd been reading.

"Mom, Joey won't leave me alone. I want to read." Joe ran the gauntlet of what to do to a quiet laugh while a mother struggled to find a solution but took a moment to say, "Joe, don't you laugh."

Rather than create worse havoc, Joe left the room and took Joey with him attempting to explain the situation to a subdued son.

Meanwhile, Marian said, "Honey, I can't let you read under the bed. It's not good for your eyes."

Joe tried. "Joey, you have to let your sister have time to herself. She has to study, so use your head, or your mother will find ways to keep you busy."

Young Joey thought that over, but he didn't like some of the things Marian asked him to do but trying hard met with some successes.

Soon, it was September, and Joey didn't like the idea of going to school.

"Mommy, I don't wanna go to school."

She brushed the hair out of his eyes and said, "It'll be fun, and you'll have Tony and Teddy in your class. Your friends will all be in school, and you won't have anyone to play with here.

"Your daddy and Jean will take you to school, and then you'll come home with your sister, but after a while, you can come home with your friends. And I'll be right here when you get home so you can tell me all about it. How's that?"

Joey roughed his shoe against the floor, and Marian noticed the sole was loose again. "Well, what do you say?"

"Okay." Marian wished for more enthusiasm, but what she noticed more was Jean's lack of enthusiasm for the assignment. "Jean, he's your younger brother, so keep an eye on him whether you're coming home or going to Aunt Angie's."

Joe marched him into class with Tony and Teddy grateful they were there and thinking they were the only reason Joey would stay.

The kindergarten teacher told Joe not to worry, but in the days to follow, she recognized yet another kindergarten class requiring she be a track star. Sitting seemed impossible for Joey, and while she loved his harmless, mischievous nature to where she'd melt at his winsome smile, she knew there would be many days, she would pray for three o'clock.

As Marian improved, she and Jean took a first-aid course offered at the project in case of attack. They took Joey along to keep him out of trouble. It was tiring, but she watched Jean learn quickly while Joey played the fidgeting patient. When he wasn't a patient, he began collecting newspapers and old rubber in a rickety wagon, as his part of the war effort.

Joey was learning he could make others laugh by teasing, but much differently than Joe would, and it soon became a way of life with him, a way seemingly without end.

Marian and Joe told him how proud they were of his contributions and enjoyed the glow in his eyes. The load of papers was sometimes too large for him, and he'd often leave his the wagon because he was restless or tired and couldn't seem to keep his attention on anything unless it was fun. Staying centered and being difficult, his many efforts often took days to complete, but they did get done.

At night, the family tilled a Victory Garden with other families on the Untermyer estate grounds, atop The Hill where complaining became the kids favorite pastime.

Jean's continuous complaining angered Joe. "Jean, no more complaining, or I'm going to spank you." The words were harsh and hurting. "We all have to do this. Farm food has to go to our sailors and soldiers and this how we get our vegetables, so no more complaining." The complaining stopped, but the evenings were moody at best.

War, the ever-present umbrella full of holes, saturated each of them in very different ways. While Jean had problems with the garden she enjoyed other things. She studied every day so that she could spot planes.

One night, Joe said, "Marian, I think she'd enlist in a minute if she were old enough. Thank God girls don't get to go to the front."

"She is adventurous, and I want her to do what she can and what she wants. I especially don't want us to be telling her she can't do something the way Pop told us kids."

"You can't think like that when it's dangerous."

"Oh, Joe, I doubt she'll do anything that dangerous." She didn't know how to answer Joe's strange look but wondered if she could be wrong.

The love Jean showed for flying was obvious, and it scared Joe that she was good at learning about it, as good as any of the boys. He stopped long enough to recognize that the usual sexual biases of peacetime were absent during wartime. That war made all things possible for young women making it more and more impossible to protect those he loved. He didn't want to think about what that would actually mean to Jean as things changed after the war and could this hell last long enough to really be a threat to her. That he couldn't think about any more.

Jean faithfully memorized the Smiling Jack cartoon's silhouettes and checklists for flight preparation that appeared in the *New York Daily News*. She would take the paper to Joe, and he would quiz her on what she had studied and would until the end of the war.

The stories his brother Bart told Jean and themselves in his letters from England, most blackened out, about bombers he serviced, made her study all the harder.

On Tuesdays of each week at School Nine, the children were given a couple of dimes to buy savings stamps to put into a book they save until she there was enough for an $18.75 War Bond that would later be worth $25. They proudly brought them home to display a growing wealth to their Mom and Dad.

Meanwhile, Federal assignments like control and tracking of counterfeited bills forced Joe to bring normal banking work home.

One Saturday, Joe walked in with a box full of interest payments for individual accounts.

"Okay, family, if anyone wants to go out later, I need help with these. Marian, can you help too?"

"Of course."

"I'll show you each what has to be done." Even Young Joey stacked and banded interest slips after Joe, Marian, and Jean calculated them. Joey's attention span wandered from the kitchen table to the living room, to the bedroom, but he managed to finish the job. He just couldn't sit still.

Later, Joe took them to the park. Marian hated her imprisonment, so when Joe was able to, she chased them out. She hated her confinement being theirs, but board games proved enjoyable. Parcheesi was a particular favorite as was listening to the serial programs on the radio.

Too often, Marian noticed Joe was only going through the motions, but his love for children helped him make it all he possible could.

A favorite game developed when Joe walked in and waved a large rolled up piece of paper. It was a color map of the world, three by five. After dinner, they all sat on the living room floor and devised a game.

Marian said, "Okay, who wants to go first? Each of us will pick a place to find on the map, and we'll have three minutes to find it. Joey, I'll help you pick one, and we'll write down the letters of the one you have to find, and you get four minutes. Yours will be easier than Jean's, okay?"

Joey lit up with having an edge over his sister.

Joe added, "It'll be good for you to know where your uncles are and where other people live."

They fanned out on the floor surrounding the map. Each took a turn selecting a place and keeping the clock. Sometimes, Joey would get frustrated but someone, including Jean would nudge him in the right direction and he'd yell things like, "I found where Uncle Bart is. I found him." He'd found England. Often, they would grab a paper and find the locations mentioned in stories about the war.

When the kids were bored, Marian would send Joe on errands insisting he see his friends at the gas station, and she would give the children leave to go play with friends while she turned to knitting, reading, or writing letters.

Marian was proud of Jean writing to her uncles and pen pals something that started in school with allied forces. Jean would come running to say, "I got a letter from Uncle Sossy," or, "I got a letter from Phil, the British soldier. Wanna hear?" After correcting her grammar, Marian or Joe would say, "Open it up, honey, let's hear it." They enjoyed the fact she shared whatever she read, and in a short time, Marian and Joe realized she received more mail than anyone in the family.

They encouraged any worthwhile activity Jean could squeeze in. There was school, the book mobile, her love of reading, running errands, keeping an eye on Joey and war efforts that made her childhood very hectic. When she had downtime, Jean would reach for their *Webster's Dictionary* to have fun with new words. It wasn't long before Marian and Joe found themselves the recipients of youthful poems colored in Jean's caring and reaching out mind. The poems would continue through her teen years.

With Joey in school, it wasn't long before Marian had to go to kindergarten about him. The teacher's fondness could not prevent his disinterest in schoolwork, and while she enjoyed his ability to make the other students laugh, she feared for his studies saying," Mrs. Petrosine, I can't keep him interested in school assignments and I don't want to hold him back, so I'm asking your help to avoid it by keeping him up to date."

It meant Marian, Joe, and Jean too would have to help him get schoolwork done efficiently.

With Joey now in school, it was a time that both Marian and Joe saw the children begin to change so quickly bringing the years parents see changes in fleeting moments only to watch them disappear into their next transition unable to grasp the people they were becoming who disappeared before they could really be aware of them. A change was coming over Joey that irked them all. They'd be playing a game, and he he'd begin to cheat in whatever way he could find and seemed to enjoy getting caught and lying almost so convincingly that they would have believed him and did the first few times until they all began to notice he had a "tell." Joey's nose splayed whenever he lied, and his family decided to never tell him about it. The fun began.

Joey's continuing to tease began to irk many and prompted some unwanted reactions.

One afternoon the kids came in after playing and it was obvious Jean had been crying. Marian and Joe heard the explanation and not wanting Jean hurt decided, "Okay, if Joey didn't make it happen, but was teasing then he has to learn he can't or it will be his fault."

"Dad the guy's a bully and bigger than most and Joey was just teasing too much.

Marian said, "but he hit you!"

"Yeah, but I got in the way."

"Honey you can't be doing that. Neither of you should be fighting."

Joe said, "Jeannie we don't want you fighting because of Joey."

Marian gave Joe a look, and the subject was dropped as Jean nodded and left to go to the bedroom. Joey had already been banished there.

More a skinny scarecrow than pretty, Jean had a disadvantage in fights, and both Marian and Joe knew it.

Marian followed Jean to the bedroom.

"Honey, are you okay?"

"Yeah, Mom."

"Yes," corrected the mother. "I don't think you are. You're very quiet. Are you sure you're not hurt?"

"I'm okay, but I don't like being different."

"Different?"

"I can't outrun him. If I could have, he couldn't have hit me. I'm like that guy on the back of comic books—a weakling."

"You've been sick, Jean, but you're outgrowing it. The swimming is helping. You're faster now than you were." Marian wished she was as sure as she sounded. "You know, honey, there are many ways to be strong."

Joey sat there with a comic book feeling he'd already had his druthers and paid little attention except to the fact her might not be able to count on his sister in the future.

Jean's forehead pinched with lines meaning questions, and Marian took the cue with, "Take Grandma for instance." Telling Jean of Raffaele's hardships and losses made brown eyes soften in admiration. "Strength isn't always something you can see. Some of the strongest battles are fought here." Her finger pointed to her temple. "Not fighting when you're so mad you could spit is a strength."

Jean smiled.

"Sweetheart, you can be anything you want to be including physically strong, but to be a good person, you have to have a good mind. And there will be battles you have to fight, and that's the way you fight them. It's easy to get into trouble. It is a lot harder to walk away, so if you insist on being strong, do it the right way."

Marian kissed her and left but not without noticing the large black and blue mark the bully inflected on her skinny daughter's arm. Jean had taken her sweater off as they talked, and her short sleeve blouse told Marian he caught her with his fist and her anger railed but she said nothing more.

Jean took to her windowsill as Joey returned to continue with his comic.

Marian went straight to Joe and said, "I've changed my mind. I don't want the kids to fight, but there are times when they must. Teach them."

"Aye, aye, sir!" Joe's hand went up in mock salute, but Marian's hazel eyes were fired with a look that reminded him of a lioness he'd seen in *National Geographic*, so despite a troubled mind, he took on the challenge but not before saying, "Hey, hon, did you notice who defended his teasing?"

"Oh, Joe, what else would she do. For all his vexing, she still loves him."

Joey danced around sticking out his fists, but a sister held him off with a long arm resting on his head.

"Joey, grow another foot, and maybe you'll reach your sister," said Joe. "Now take the stance I showed you."

Once again, a pillow was tied to a daughter for protection. Both soon learned to box.

It was obvious Jean was learning to talk her way out of situations, because in spite of Joey's continued irking and teasing, bullies ceased to be a problem and Joey's catching a few right-hands didn't stop the teasing but he learned to avoid problem kids and chose less challenging targets.

One day, Jean came home all excited for having found a wallet. "And, Mom, it has lots of money in it."

"I'm sorry, honey, that has to be returned to Mr. Walchek."

"Do I have to?"

Young Joey was taking it all in and said, "Gee, Mom, Jean found it, why can't we keep it."

"Because it's wrong, it's not ours."

Joe had walked quietly in kissed Marian, listened, and said, "Because people work hard for their money and it may be all they have, so you have to return it. Think how you'd feel if it was yours and you lost it and the person who found it kept it."

Jean nodded and Joey frowned, went silent to keep his own counsel.

The wallet belonged to a neighbor living about a block away from the project, and Joe took the kids over to return the wallet.

On the way, Joe said, "Jean, Mr. Walchek may want to give you a reward, but you shouldn't take a reward for doing the right thing."

"I know that, Dad."

Meanwhile, Joey was thinking, *Why does Daddy make us do that? I'd keep it.* Since both kids were usually there for his lectures, Joe rarely repeated them assuming both were listening and absorbing.

Mr. Walchek was so pleased he pulled a five-dollar bill out of his wallet and started to hand it to Jean. "Oh no, thank you, Mr. Walchek, I can't take that." Young Joey's eyes went wide.

Walchek looked at Joe Sr. realized she wouldn't take it and said, "Thank you, Jean, very much."

With going to school, Joey found he was expected to do more chores. Drying the dishes was particularly offensive to him. Up to now, Jean washed and dried.

After a couple of days, a pattern appeared. Jean would be washing the dishes, and Joey would grab a towel, stand at the sink for a moment, and say, "I have to go to the bathroom." By the time he returned, everything had been dried and put away. Marian immediately became suspicious, and when it happened a third time, Marian said, "Joey, when you come out the bathroom, I'm sure the dishes will be dry, so you put them all away."

Joey's mouth opened and clamped shut because Marian was giving him a look that said, "Quit while you're ahead." So he went to the kitchen after his "now every night" bathroom tour and pulled a chair to the counter and climbed up to put the dinner dishes away. *Mommy's smart.*

On Sundays after mass, Joe now went to the main office on South Broadway to compile federal reports and usually took Jean along to act as messenger or fetch snacks for other workers having cautioned her, "Remember you're coming with me to help, so if someone asks you to get something, you do it.

"Knowing this gang, they'll probably offer you a tip, but I don't want you to take it because we're all doing work to help out with the war effort. Okay."

"Okay, Daddy."

Jean couldn't help noticing Joe rubbing his magnificent nostril orifice, a habit when tired.

The drugstore that furnished lunches and coffee was on the ground floor with the bank, so Joe knew Jean could handle it.

The main office was a showplace with two-story high marble columns, with polished brass cages for the tellers and even had a mezzanine from where bank officials watched parades down South Broadway. Joe and the family were often asked to join the viewing. They did but actually preferred being out on the curb with the happy crowds.

Just waiting to help bored Jean, so she played in the open vault separating piles of money and trying to count as quickly as Joe could. A bundle of bills slipped and flew into the air, and she grinned as the pretty green-and-white fan it created until they dropped on the floor. Joe and a teller were returning a drawer of records as the bills settled helter-skelter. A studious Joe said, "Looks like you're playing fifty-two pickup," while the teller laughed, saying, "Good game, Jean. That's all counterfeit is good for?"

Joe watched how carefully she replaced everything and thought, *Good girl.* Occasionally, Jean would find small change. For being closer to the floor, she immediately gave it to Joe who returned it to a teller's till. Joe's praise made it easy for her.

Young Joey's time with him on Sundays was spent checking out the teller stalls looking for loose change and somehow forgetting to turn it into Joe, something he missed for being busy and that somehow made Joey feel good and a tip was something he never refused.

One day, Jean looked at the counterfeit bills Joe was stacking into a pickup bag and asked, "Daddy, why can't we keep the fake stuff?"

"We could keep it, if you want to go to jail with me."

Her eyes went wide with curiosity as she said, "Jail?"

"Uh-huh. The FBI or Secret Service would take us both."

"Really?"

"Really!"

"Wow!" Her animation made him think she liked the idea. He wasn't sure he liked her leanings toward the unusual.

Around eleven o'clock that morning, the bank guard quietly advised, "Joe, Mr. Burlew is at the door."

Joe nodded, respectfully thanked the aging colored guard, and said, "Jean, honey, see if anyone wants coffee. Okay?"

"Okay, Daddy."

He turned to the waiting guard and said, "Toby, do me a favor and bring him back to the desk I'm using."

"Sure, Joe."

"Thanks, Toby."

As Jean had left to take people's orders, Burlew's arrival left Joe very nervous, and looking around, he wasn't surprised that everyone had gone into deep working mode.

We're all the same, they scare us silly.

Burlew's six foot four with ice-blue eyes and a serious, commanding presentment made everyone he passed go quieter. Even when you did nothing wrong, having an FBI agent around tended to make everyone very cautious and curious.

Jean ran back to Joe. "Daddy, I'm going to go for the coffee now. Do you want some?"

"Yes, honey, a large cup, here's the money."

Jean craned her long neck at the blue-eyed man and said, "Hello."

The man said, "Hello to you. You're Jean, aren't you?"

"Yes, sir."

"Could you maybe get me a cup too and you can keep the change?"

Jean shot a glance at her father. "Oh no, thank you, sir. I do this to help, but I'll get you the coffee."

Without a smile, the tall man bent, gave her the change, and said, "Thank you, Jean." His eyes very close to her made her feel very safe, and something about him reminded her of a cowboy she'd seen in a movie. In seconds, she ran to "Mr. Toby" who let her out.

Burlew said, "She's a good kid, Joe."

"Yeah, she is. So's my son though he's a hellion who can't sit still."

"I'll bet he is. Joe, all this has come to a head. Are you sure you want to take part in this?"

"Howard, with the way things are, who else is there?"

Burlew's glance went to the door, Jean went through, and his voice turned regretful. "Look, I could do it, but I have to admit, you can answer money questions none of us can. I just wish you weren't right."

"Me too," whispered Joe knowing he'd never tell anyone what they'd be doing except Marian, and he hadn't told her yet. After a deep breath, he said, "Dear God, Howard, I hope this goes well. At least this group of counterfeiters will be out of business."

Burlew listened carefully and realized he'd never forget this fearful man who knew how to help.

Finally, Marian was well enough for normal activities, and while still excited by their first lovemaking since her illness, they enjoyed a second coupling and realizing it felt different they cuddled and talked about the differences that Marian felt were less stimulating than before the operation. But Marian was full of enthusiasm, and Joe's spirits soared at least for a few days. She realized Joe's problem was far beyond, her just not being well, but it was enough to deceive her into believing. It was a short-lived reprieve.

While she took on more than a fair share of the family workload, she felt airborne and happy while the contrast worked in reverse for Joe. One of her first social nights out was a party with friends, servicemen, and family. Joe hadn't wanted to go and was sullen most of the evening. And though he had kissed her good night, the next day, while the children were out playing, sullen became argumentative and a fierce row erupted.

Their voices rose and left the apartment like a bird freed from a cage. A friend asked Jean and Joey, "Isn't that yer' mom and dad?"

The kids' embarrassment turned into panic, as cruel words tumbled on. They huddled helplessly on the front stoop hoping it would stop. Discords in the project were common but not with this couple. Joe was livid with jealousy and need while Marian raged from accusation.

"I simply had a good time," said Marian.

"With a guy in uniform!"

Cruel, hurting words went on until a door slammed, and Marian passed the children like a train with its throttle on full. Joe watched the rush from the window. The words accusing her of coming on to that soldier shuddered through his psyche. Then Joe saw Jean and Joey standing on the front step staring after their mother as she headed away from them without a word.

He called out, "Jean!"

Jean's head whipped toward him.

"Go after your mother and make sure she's all right." The caring didn't change his wretched feeling but brought his fear to a dangerous edge where a sense of terrible loss overwhelmed him. His problem had finally warped its way into a marriage busting violation.

Jean turned to Joey and said, "Wait here." In moments, she caught up with Marian.

Joey watched her leave and looked strangely up at his father while accepting something a youngster is beyond understanding but would decide upon anyhow.

Why is Mommy going away? Why is Daddy mad at her? Why didn't Mommy take me? Is she coming back? The fear spun an anger and disappointment into his image of the man he loved that dove unrecognized into his subconscious to surface in later times.

Jean put on the brakes and slid to a stop next to Marian and said, "Mom, Dad sent m-me to see i-if you're all right."

Marian stopped looked down with damp eyes and tearstained face to answer in a cramped, choking voice that rang true in Jean's young mind and terrified her.

"Go back. Your father is going to need you."

Something told Jean, "Mom's right." Marian walked away without another word, and Jean was filled with tears for a mother looking so alone while recognizing a real threat to their home.

Jean ran up the apartment stairs with Joey right behind her, his hand holding her loose blouse as though he feared losing her too.

A haggard Joe asked, "What did she say?"

Breathless and confused by Joe's drained expression, Jean answered, "G-Go back your fa-father needs you."

The children watched Joe, his chest heaving, rub his face, and say, "Stay in the house and don't worry." The children suddenly alone gave each other a frightened look and rushed to the window to watch Joe run down the same street as Marian had. She was nowhere in sight.

Daylight passed into darkness as two window sentinels hoped and waited. Neither Joey nor Jean noticed that they hadn't eaten because their stomachs were stuffed with full of doubts seasoned with the hot pepper of sinister menace.

In the land of spirits, a voice said, "She is mine, let me help."

"Go, but remember you can do nothing without the right decision and your opposite is already there."

Joe felt strange. He got to the corner and couldn't find Marian. He searched the avenue and finally came back to realize he'd missed the park. Everything he saw was distorted by guilt. The park seemed like a place he'd never been with ominous shadows moving about, though there was no wind to move them. Worse, they were welcoming him. Only spying Marian on a bench near the Gazebo took him away to quietly sit beside her but dared not touch her.

Through fouling fury, she lisped, "Why, Joe, why? You know I didn't flirt. I danced, I laughed, but I shared it all with you. What's doing this?"

Joe found the world within getting darker and swirling with the words he'd flung at her and felt them rise again, but sensing his grave danger, he silenced them to say, "Jesus, Mar, I don't know. I knew I was wrong, but I couldn't stop it once I started. There's this thing inside me. I know it's me, and yet it isn't. Am I going insane?" The darkness was complete, and fear hid any hope.

Marian turned away and played with her wedding band. A terrible battle raged within. *This can't go on. Oh, God, if it continues, I'll leave him.*

Joe couldn't take his eyes off her, and the taste of bile that rose from his stomach made him fear he'd choke on it, or worse, because in the moving shadows, he saw the axe rising and the darkness moved closer.

She's going to leave me. Dear Jesus, what have I done.

The sound of Marian's icy, calm voice terrified him further.

"Joe, listen to me very carefully. I mean every word I say."

"Mar—"

"I said listen! I'm going home with you, but you have a decision to make. You know I married you because I wanted you, not because I needed you?" She turned her swollen hazel eyes toward him. They were hard and demanding an answer.

He said, "Yes," and grabbed his lower lip in his beautiful teeth and bit as she continued.

"Right now, you have to decide how this will be handled the next time this happens. Do the children and I leave you, or do you go and live with your mother? Either way, I can get a war plant job and take good care of the children and myself. Either way, you will be able to see the children whenever you want, but we won't live with you, not if this happens again. You'll be free to join the service."

Pale, his lips quivering, Joe said, "I don't want it that way. My God, give me a chance. I know I'm wrong."

"That's not enough, Joe. I won't live with this anymore than I would a drunk or a man who abuses his family. This is just as bad, and it can't happen again. You can't do this to me, and I won't let you do this to the kids." She turned away with no place to look except at the ground.

Joe sat rigid, his hands clasped between his knees in undecipherable pain. Anger, fear, *"To hell with you,"* and *"Oh, God, what's wrong with me?"* ran through his mind's haranguing dilemma.

The gentlest of winds swirled the dry soil at Marian's feet to rise and touch her tear-streaked cheeks. The dust touched her mindful of Tess's large strong hands wanting her attention, and a new thought crossed her mind that slowly turned her toward Joe where she saw through the transparency of his eyes into a part of his heart never before open to her to find terror and—*what is that?*

Through a startled breath, she said, "Oh, Joe, Joe, you don't know how much I love you, do you? My God, you don't know how much any of us loves you." The second sentence was stated as a fact.

Joe couldn't lower his eyes. It was as though a hand had loosened one of the steel bands locked around his mind as he heard Marian's voice caught between plead and prayer.

"Hon, you have to know I love you. This can't happen again. Why do you doubt me, us, the children, all of us? I thought we showed you our love every day. I won't put myself through this again. Your jealousy or whatever it is will destroy us all, and that mustn't happen. You've changed so terribly. You no longer enjoy life or us. I-I-I don't know what else to say. You have to deal with this."

Suddenly, Marian's tears flowed. She had glimpsed the part within him in such deep trouble and found herself one step from hopeless while Joe sat there more confused than before because her threat emblazoned and echoed within his psyche as though someone was carving his heart into small pieces.

Her tears meshed with his fear and committed emotions. He brought his white knuckled hands up and slowly put his arms around her. All he could do was keep her close, pray, and try. He was tormented by an inability to control his situation or the why of what he had said that hurt her. He didn't understand, but he knew he had to find an answer and silently accepted, *she's right.*

The world conflict worsened, and Joe's bank responsibilities continued to increase while he fought to protect what he had in continued solitude, but now he began to understand it had stolen the part of him birthing the laughter that made life so much better for them all, especially him. But he had no real answers except to continue the effective doings of his important job.

Joe was headed for a nervous breakdown like a ball thrown hard and fast down a sloping hill.

Marian pleaded, "You have to eat."

"I can't."

Marian continued to mash everything, but Joe was getting thinner, and Marian had the feeling all the good of the world was under attack and not just by those seeking world domination.

On one Sunday, Manfredi females, young and old, helped in the kitchen while the boys were out running where Joey learned more of his kind of mischief making fun possible when teasing his cousins to laughter.

Meanwhile in the kitchen, Jean joined in the making of the meal, saying, "Oh, come on. Let's get them off the walls."

Her older cousins came back with, "You do it. You get them off. They're alive. I don't want to touch them."

"Don't ask me, I don't either," said her cousin Theresa.

"Jean, you do it," suggested the youngest of Aunt Angie's daughters. Jean, the youngest girl cousin in the room, tried and refused to quit trying until she succeeded yelling, "They ju-just don't let go, just pull harder. Co-come on, help m-me, you're all stronger than I-I am. I-I'm not doing it alone."

Sisters Marian and Angie filled the kitchen at 92 Orchard Street with laughter as they watched the girls try to pull the living, wall-crawling snails free from counter and wall surfaces to put them back into the pots not holding them. Marian said, "Okay, girls, we need them now!"

All hands got busy, and one by one, the snails were plopped into a boiling, delicate tomato sauce. It crossed Marian's mind that the older girls turned to Jean more often than not. *I want her to lead not follow and she spoke up. Good!*

That afternoon, a station on the radio blared a song that had people mimicking it and laughing for many a day.

Spike Jones and his band released the song "The Fuehrer's Mustache" with their usual verve and ear-shattering noise that nourished America's need for the courage found in a release through humor.

After macaroni with snail sauce succulently digested, Marian realized something about Joe. In spite of his problem, he sought laughter for others. He told fewer jokes, but sought better moments.

As days passed, Young Joey continued to bring adventures into everyday life that both infuriated and humored.

"Mommy, I can't go to school today."

"Why can't you go to school, you're not sick?"

Joey was a little wary of the wooden spoon Marian had in her hand in spite of the fact she was cooking.

Joey hesitated and said, "I can't find my shoes."

His head was down, and Marian wasn't sure if he was telling the truth, so she accepted they'd been misplaced, and the hunt was on. They tried closets, under beds, wherever they'd been left was darn hard to find. Perplexed, she went looking for an old pair that he could go to school in but noticed the studio couch was slightly away from the wall, so she pulled it further away and discovered both the old and new pair wedged between the wall and the upper portion of the couch. She turned to Joey and handed him his shoes and said, "Go to school now."

She watched a dejected five-year-old march off sullenly to join a sister who had kept calling up, "Mom, I've got to go."

"You'll wait for your brother. I'll give you a note if it takes to long."

About a week later, the shoes disappeared again, and Joey said, "Mommy, I can't find my shoes, so I can't go to school."

Marian waited and this time saw his nose splay and said, "Okay, Joey, you don't have to go to school, but that means you can't go out. It means no playing outside, and if you miss school, you can't play with your friends when they get home and you are confined to your bedroom. On second thought, shoes cost too much to be losing them, and you will go to school with no shoes on at all; the way you father did when he was your age unless you find them in exactly five minutes. And Jean will not wait for you."

Joey's feet started moving, and his mouth tried to find words, but his mother's anger was too scary, and he suddenly realized he had goofed and said, "I'll look again, Mommy."

"Okay, maybe you'll get lucky."

A few minutes later, she sensed him behind her at the utility closet, and he had her large carpet sweeper in his hand. He popped open the cleaning vents, and out fell his small shoes. Only admiration for his ingenuity saved him from punishment. Later, she told Joe, "Whatever his problem is at school, it's not being dumb."

The season of Spring made Glen Park a very busy place. The same park Joe used to run his full out mile every morning homed a citywide grammar school competition in field and track events. It was a miniature Olympics that received a small town response from the city's diverse population. Employers released parents while defense plant personnel switched shifts to watch their young do their "darnedest."

It was May, and a uniformed father on crutches led the Pledge of Allegiance with their hands over their hearts, followed by "The Star-Spangled Banner" amid tears for those in danger. The arm-out-overhead salute had long disappeared for being too like the Nazi hail to the Fuehrer.

The cheering soon began with the disabled youngsters from School Nine yelling louder than most because the games were on and their friends needed support.

Marian and Joe watched Joey taking part in kindergarten throwing events across the field and saw Joey's ball soar beyond the throw of other youngsters and smiled at him and cheered his next throw when it secured the blue ribbon. Next, they watched him in a race, but he lost to a School Thirteen youngster. He was near tears feeling he should have won and didn't want to race anymore. Young Joey collected his throwing ribbon and ran to Marian and Joe. Joe hugged him and explained he had to leave to see Jean run for School Nine in the fifty-yard dash and told him he did a good job in the race.

"I didn't win." He was unusually sullen, and Joe said, "Joey, all you can do is try, and you'll get better, but it takes lots of practice."

"I don't want to practice. Jean doesn't practice, and she wins." He was angry when Joe bent and hugged him, saying, "You will, it's more important you try your best. Look, I have to run to make sure I see your sister's race. Make sure Mommy takes her time. Hon, I'll see you over there."

Joey felt cheated that Joe had to leave but followed his father's path holding his mother's hand still wondering why he didn't win the way Jean did and he only half listened as Marian said, "Joey, Joan didn't win all her races, that's something new. Besides, that was a great throw you made. Joan's going to be sorry she didn't see it. I'll bet it was as good as Daddy ever made." Realizing Joey hadn't heard a word she said, she added her gaze to his to follow Joe across the field worrying where Joe's mind was taking him and what a son was making of it.

Joe left on the run, got to the covered bleachers, asked a friend to save seats for Joey and Marian, and went down to where he could see Jean's effort more closely when they ran. Joe saw Marian sit with Jean's classmates Katherine, a beauty in her mixed racial blood beside Netty and Alberta Jean's friends who were getting prettier by the day. He'd been surprised to hear Jean would run for her school. He hadn't been sure her wind would hold up. It obviously had.

Jean and Jessie were in the fifty-yard dash for fifth graders. Jessie was larger and stronger than a still scrawny Jean, but the girls were in different classes at School Nine, and both made the finals. The four other lane runners came from other grammar schools across the city. Joe asked their times and found Jessie's seconds better than Jean's. He knew Jean would respond to the competitive mood and hoped she had the speed to win.

Jessie was one of the many friends of his two that traipsed through the house with Jean and Joey after school. Jessie, dark brown in her ancestry, was a striking comparison to Jean. Joe liked all Jean's friends for being polite, and because they loved to laugh, they were fun to have around. Alberta and Netty had remained Jean's friends since their days on Vineyard Avenue but were the real ladies of the group. Joey's young cohorts were still too young and wild for social functions.

Jean's still too thin, but at least something is going right. She's been swimming three times a week since Griffon suggested it, and it's making her stronger every day. Thank God she's stopped stuttering. At least that was Marian being ill, not something stupid I'd done.

Then his mind slipped to the way Jean looked at him since the day Marian walked out, too concerned and worried for her age. He didn't want to think about that, so he put his back to the stands and focused on the starting line to elude Marian's vigilant wondering. He still couldn't put his problem into words, but he and Marian were in a battle they were determined to win. He just wasn't sure he could do it. His eyes drifted to the wounded soldier and decided to talk to him before he left.

Jean kept shuffling her feet anxious to get started and wanting to win in the hope she'd make her father smile but feared she couldn't.

Jessie enjoyed teasing Jean who enthusiastically leaped into the distraction and joined in as Jesse said, "Watch out, skinny, I'm gonna beat ya." Jessie's beautifully wide, infectious grin made Jean chuckle as she said, "Not today, chubby."

They fluffed out their blue bloomer running shorts and placed their left foot at the starting line in the two middle lanes right next to each other and waited for the gun.

The gun cracked and girls pushed off causing their blue and white school ribbons to blow wildly in the rush they created. At the twenty-five yard line, the race belonged to Jean and Jesse. Both made their sprint to win in the same moment. Being shoulder to shoulder, the added bursts of speed caused the girls' feet to entangle and sent Jessie crashing to the ground.

Jean felt their feet hit and, a step later, realized Jessie wasn't next to her. She glanced backward and saw Jessie on the ground. She stopped.

Joe's mouth dropped wide open when Jean ran back to Jessie as the other racers finished the stretch by breaking the crepe paper tape to win. Jean grabbed Jessie's hand. As she rose unhurt, the girls walked to the finish line laughing at their big feet getting snarled.

The laughter ceased as they became aware of Joe's dark expression. Both girls slowed, and their smiles fled like startled birds from a nest.

Jean felt Joe's upset but didn't understand his why and was confused by her own feelings when realizing she had wanted to win to make him smile.

Joe said, "Jessie, are you all right?" Jessie nodded and stayed when Joe asked, "Jean, why did you stop?"

Jean saw his confused look and said, "Jessie tripped over my leg when we started to run faster. That wasn't fair."

She wanted so for him to smile, she missed his smiles. All their talks were so serious these days.

But she listened as he said, "Honey, you were running a race, accidents happen. You don't stop. You finish the race." Then he turned to Jessie. "Jessie, Jean is your friend, and I'm sure you're glad she stopped, but your school lost because neither of you tried to finish. Losing is okay, but you have to do your best. In this case, you'd have taken first place for School Nine, but now they've lost."

While Jessie looked at the ground saying, "We forgot," Jean pursued a point.

"But, Daddy, I tripped her." She was emphatic.

"Honey, you didn't do that on purpose, it just happened."

Her jutting chin softened as her young mind sought the answer that would fit her instincts—instincts Joe had helped make possible—and said, "Daddy, isn't Jessie more important than winning?"

Joe stared sadly for a moment his fixed mind easing around a corner saying, "Yes honey," placed his arms around the girls and walked to the stands. The girls missed the joking so typical of Joe but not as much as he did.

Young Joey watched his sister wondering what Joe was saying to her, and he was glad she didn't win and thought, *I'm glad it's not me Daddy's talking to.*

Marian surveyed the happening with a good idea of what Joe was saying but thought, *She's so like Joe. I worry about both of them being used every day. At least Joe knows his people. Jean has to learn to be tough. She still backs off with new people. I have to help her change that. She'll need to be independent, very independent, and the way the world is changing, she has to be able to take care of herself. She's got to be able to do what she wants without others controlling what she needs to do for herself. Joe wants to protect her the way Pop was always protecting us. And he's as wrong as Pop was. Joe insists on protecting all his women. I can't let that happen to Jean. It's a different world, and Joe has to realize he can't be there all the time to keep any of us safe. He worries much too much.*

She watched him leave the girls and join the soldier on crutches.

Joe's left him after discussing where he'd been knowing fathers with two children were soon to be drafted and he'd get his wish to answer the call but fear of losing Marian ran through his mind like the ants of South American devouring all there was before them.

That night air raid warning sirens blared across Yonkers reminding everyone of what could happen at any time. Joe grabbed Joey, as Marian and Jean came running from the kitchen. They rushed to the foyer bordered by the rooms they lived in that were constructed of cement blocks two deep between apartments. They closed the room doors and huddled together. Joe and Marian had shut the lights before they ran. The practice sessions of earlier raids both at home and school made it easy. They talked quietly but went silent every few minutes to listen for the drone of planes that never came. The beautiful moonlight filtering through the windows turned eerie and threatening. They knew the moonlight would help bombers find their mark.

Tonight, instead of discussing what to do if bombs found them, they played spelling games.

At the corner park, Joe took precious time to coach basketball for the boys whose fathers wore uniforms or worked defense shifts. Many impromptu games took place, and sometimes, they were shy one player.

Teddy Miller said, "We'll take Jean, if that's all right, Mr. P?" Having noticed a girl's eye-hand coordination was superior to boys at this age, Joe wasn't surprised by the request.

A daughter's world was broadening. His nephew Freddy had a girlfriend now but still stopped by with his mother Mary and took time to introduce Jean to handball. As time passed, they began to disappear to play against the park's cement wall. Though dating, Fred still enjoyed the company of younger relatives and mastered the mischief among them to assure no one would be hurt. Joe couldn't help but notice how Jean enjoyed being with Fred but then they all did.

While Joey and Jean learned more of sports from their father, Marian introduced Jean to the normal female requirements: cooking, knitting, crocheting, and sports like tennis and skating while hoping she'd acquire a call to gentle femininity, though it was like pulling a wagon in deep snow. The only household skill Jean really enjoyed was baking.

There were disadvantages to Jean being the only young Prezzemoli girl. One day, when Freddy was working, the boy cousins and Joey tried teasing her with frogs. That she laughed off, so cousins Ricky and Tommy aided by Young Joey locked her in a dark storage area under Uncle Harry's house on the pretext of playing hide-and-seek. Jean yelled her head off more hot-tempered than scared. Though tiptoeing spiders, had her doing some toe stepping of her own. Her quick temper made her a perfect target for many a tease, and the most ardent teaser was Young Joey who claimed the art as his own in the same way his father had chosen laughter.

When Joe and Harry heard Jean yelling, they let her out, spied the sneaky trio hiding in a nearby tree, and turned the garden hose on them. The boys laughed but didn't budge, so the men turned away to share the latest war news. Hearing, "Ready, aim, fire," Harry and Joe looked up catching a barrage of pee from the treed trio. The uncles turned the hose on themselves in surrender to a superior force for remembering themselves.

Buddies Rick Jean Tom

Marian was working part time in a stocking store in Getty Square owned by a Jewish family whose son was drafted and she became the full time manager and they quickly joined the Prezzemoli extended family.

Marian intended the money strictly for savings and worked through Saturday with Tuesday's off. With Joe working so many weekend hours at the bank, arrangements had to be made for the children in the afternoons. Gene and Angie helped during the week. Weekends were just Joe and the kids.

Since the onset of the war, afternoon movie houses were turned into cartoon festivals for children on weekends to help working and service parents. Monitored by older women, families felt it a secure place for children. Jean and Joey spent many an afternoon there. Joe would drop them off and say, "Gimme a kiss and be careful crossing the street to the bank. I'll see you later, and then we'll pick up your mommy." The Strand Theatre was within feet of being across the street from the bank's main office on South Broadway.

One day, Joe dropped them off, and Jean found them two seats in the lower seating section. At one point, they had to get up to allow one of the few adults in the audience to get to his seat next to Jean. Jean was laughing at Donald Ducks' antics with Huey, Duey, and Louie when she felt a hand on her knee working up the inside of her thigh. She turned to see a good-looking blond man smiling at her. She didn't know what to do. After all, he was an adult, but it made her so uncomfortable she rose from her chair, grabbed Joey's hand, and said, "Come on, Joey, we have to move." She found two aisle seats in the upper section. Joey was craning his neck to see the screen, so she was almost dragging him. She shushed him every time he started to complain. Everything was all right for a while until she looked up and saw the man again taking the seat next to her. He sat quietly for a while, but Jean felt frozen in her seat, and Joey was oblivious to the happening. Once again, his hand found her leg, and he smiled sweetly. Jean was so scared she wanted to scream. Instead, she grabbed Joey by the hand and pulled him out into the aisle.

"I wanna see the movie."

"Shut up, Joey, and hurry."

When he started to whine, she shoved him out in front of her pushing him toward the nearest matron and said, "That man up there put his hand on my leg and followed us up to the mezzanine when we moved and did it again."

The matron asked, "Where is he, dear?" She turned but he had disappeared. The woman had noticed an adult leave just moments before Jean got to her, so she escorted them to the front aisle, spoke to another custodian, and left as they were given better seats. The next weekend, a patrolman and the ladies walked the aisles to ensure the safety of the kids. Jean never told Joe or Marian, it didn't seem important to her once it was over, and she preferred to forget the feeling she had when he touched her. She was too young to fully understand the real danger, but remembering many cautions did the right thing.

Joey's youth and need for fun now homed in his psyche was out of touch with the situation, but their family knot kept him close in troubled moments. The incident became a part of Jean's subconscious world and would strangely touch her again.

In that place where spirits dwell, Jean's watcher glimpsed the happening and was pleased that the youngster did the right thing but feared the decision not to speak about it to others. This time the evil one had not intruded. This time, the youngster's mind was in control, and he had desperate souls to attend.

One night, Marian heard Jean scream out and ran quickly into her room and found her struggling with her sheet on the floor.

"Honey, what happened?"

"Mom, I fell out of bed!"

Marian sat down beside her as a sleepy-eyed Joe joined them.

She wiped the hair from Jean's face and realized she was moist with perspiration. "Jean, did you have a bad dream?"

"Yeah, I was falling and falling, and I couldn't stop. Then I woke up on the floor."

Joe, now awake, asked, "Did you hurt yourself?"

Jean gave him an embarrassed, "No—o."

"That's my girl."

Marian said, "Joe, go back to bed. I'll stay until she falls asleep again."

"Okay." He left slowly and backward until he couldn't see them anymore.

Marian helped Jean into bed and said, "You know, honey, that's a dream lots of people have. Do you remember anything else about the dream?" She feared she and Joe might be responsible.

"No, Mom." Her eyelids were still heavy with the disturbed need for sleep, so Marian said, "Honey, go back to sleep. I'll stay here until you do." She almost crooned the words as she tucked Jean in.

The next few nights, Marian stopped in to be sure she was all right and noticed how fitfully she twisted and turned.

After that, Jean fell out of bed again and again as the dream of falling repeated itself, but she didn't scream, she just crawled back into bed and went back to sleep. Much later, she stopped falling out of bed and dreams became less frequent, and finally, there were no dreams, except for very rare nightmares.

In their search for each other, Marian and Joe feared hurting the children, and they looked for ways to secure the world within the family, difficult for meeting the demands of work. But they found ways as one morning, a school day, Joe stuck his head into the children's room and said, "Dress quickly and brush your teeth." Then he smiled. "Hustle, you two, hustle. Your Mom and I have a surprise for you."

Hustle they did, and while brushing their teeth feverishly, Marian came into the bathroom and said, "You guys aren't ready yet?" Marian's impossible tease had toothpaste running down their chins as she added, "And don't forget to go to the bathroom."

In their rushing, they tripped over each other, and a laughing Marian said, "You're not going to school today. We're going to spend the day in New York. Visit a museum, have lunch at the Automat, and go to Radio City Music Hall. We have reserved seats."

In spite of his exhaustion, Joe picked up with, "But first, we're going to have breakfast at the diner on the way to the subway. How's that?"

The neighbors knew something was going on for the yeas reached many an ear.

Until now, New York City, as a family, was usually Aunt Mary and the Parades on Fifth Avenue. Joe's small raise completely set aside made many small things possible, and they were determined to expose the children to as much of an amazing world as they could.

Their eyes popped at new wonders wherever they went, but the thrill of the day belonged to the Automat. Having their own nickels to put into the slot next to the bright brass-trimmed, partial windowed door, where you could see the choice of food within, kept Jean busy lifting a younger brother up to see what he wanted. Their drinks came from a spigot sticking out of a large metal seashell. Marian could see Jean wanted to be annoyed at having to lift Joey so often, but she was deriving so much pleasure from the newness of picking and choosing that she forgot to be the pouty sister. Joe seemed to be enjoying them, so she relaxed and enjoyed watching her young learn while having fun.

Only advanced teen years and changing directions would stop what that day became; the first of their annual steal-away-from-school-with-parents' day to share the ever changing the excitement of New York City.

By now, the Allies were entering Rome raging from hill to hill, the long length of the boot after starting in Sicily. On June 6th, D day they landed in Normandy and Sossy jumped over Belgium. Their dread in not having contact with him fiercely held them all prisoners of caring. Still the family went on with what had to be done just like all the other American and Allied families with loved ones doing so much for so many.

One weekend, the Manfredi tribe planned a picnic at Beth and Paul's riding academy in White Plains, New York, just off the Hutchinson River Parkway. Joe filled the car with family after he and his home crew passed up mass to finish all interest tickets for the bank before leaving.

The men, brothers, and in-laws gathered their children to allow the sisters rare time together at Beth's home.

Paul, Beth's husband, herded the kids and fathers to his corral. He mounted Jean on a small unsaddled jumper named Pat and prepared the area for something special. He enjoyed Jean who seemed relaxed and comfortable. She was the one niece brave enough to try whatever he suggested but was never quite sure if she was excited or scared. He enjoyed the Prezzemoli visits and was glad bank business required a car that allowed them to come more frequently. He liked the fact Joe always brought whoever wanted to come unless his wife Beth insisted on time with her sister Marian without the rest of the family tagging along. One thing the family continued to do, as they did after Mama Tess had died, was believe and trust in Marian's ability to see things clearly. Paul sensed that would always be true.

Paul had decided to teach the kids how to ride a horse taking a jump, at least those that wanted to try. While they waited with mixed emotions, Paul put large portions of loose hay around the jump area.

As he did this, he heard Jean.

"Uncle Paul, what's all the straw for?"

"Nothing for you to worry about." Jean was somewhat suspicious of this playful uncle and found it hard to wait.

Gene's grandchildren sat on the fence surrounding the corral. Joe shook his head at Jean's insatiable curiosity but hated being annoyed at her without good reason.

He listened as Paul gave explicit instructions to Jean after telling the onlookers what to expect.

Joe called out, "Jean, pay attention to what Uncle Paul is telling you."

Paul said, "All you kids better listen to every word I tell, Jean, because you'll all get a turn." Paul helped her on to the horse and said, "Jean, keep your hands high and against your tummy for balance just the way you do when you ride without jumping. Only now, I want you to grip the horse with your knees real tight." He put his hands on Jean's knees, pushed them forcefully against the gentle jumpers sides until he was sure Jean got the idea, and asked, "Understand?"

Her eyes went wide with excitement as she nodded. Paul smiled and said, "Good, first, you tell her to go with the usual kick in the side, then tighten your knees and Patsy will do the rest. Go!"

The razzing and cheering by cousins started before Jean even kicked Patsy. A gentle Patsy headed for the foot high bar picked up speed, only to dig her hind legs into the corral's dusty floor just before she should have taken to the air. Meanwhile, Jean, unable to defy the law of gravity, shot off Patsy's back and sailed over the jumping rail where she landed in the cushioning hay.

Paul walked to where she sat up taking a strand of straw from her mouth and said, "Does this answer your question about the hay?" With her face red as an Indian, she made a contrite nod.

Paul gently took her arms looking her straight in the eye to say, "Will you do what I tell you the next time I give you instructions?"

"Yes, Uncle Paul." The merciless laughter of the cousins made Jean insist on trying again now. This time, she did exactly as told and screeched while she and Patsy were airborne. She was giggling for remembering she yelled, "Geronimo."

Instead of enjoying it, Joe was trapped in endless analysis looking for answers to why he was endangering all he had. He understood that too was wrong and decided to find a way to make others laugh was worth a try even if he couldn't. He smiled at the children, but without the enthusiasm or playfulness, he usually brought to them.

After all the kids had a chance to jump, Joe walked Paul and Patsy back to the barn. He had decided the riding was good for Jean, so he asked Paul how he could work off the cost of lessons.

"Joe, I like having her around. She's a good kid, so when she wants to ride, she can help my two with the chores around the barn." The discussion turned to the war, and both men knew their time was about to come for both had two children. Americans with one child had already answered the call.

"Are you scared as I am, Joe?"

"Probably more. Paul, you can at least shoot something. I can't." In his mind, Joe added, *But I'm more frightened that they won't take me.*

Paul was remembering teaching Joe to shoot for hunting. Joe had proved a superb marksman, which didn't surprise Paul, but whenever they took Joe hunting, he came home with nothing but spent shells. He grabbed Joe's shoulder affectionately, admitted to his own fears, and changed the subject.

A while later, Beth announced, "We're ready." That brought the many hands needed to heft the baskets to feed the twenty-one relatives. The baskets filled the trunk of the car with one basket left over.

Then twenty-one aunts, uncles, and cousins in diverse shapes and sizes s-q-u-e-e-z-e-d into the car with Joe at the wheel. It was only a five-minute drive to the Hutchinson River water hole. They were determined to make it in one trip to save gas. Hands, elbows, and knees were finding ways into the strangest body parts. The masses of human tissue confined to too little space muffled the childish and adult giggles between crush and push. Still all twenty-one and baskets squeezed into the four-door 1937 Ford Sedan. It was it's last trip. It was scheduled to be turned into steel for war machines.

The afternoon was spent in a creek no more than twenty feet wide at this point and just deep enough to swim. When a snake wiggled across the water, Joe was surprised to find Jean, dripping wet, hanging on to him. His little adventuress was afraid of snakes, and her needing him felt good. Joey spent the day teasing his cousins whenever he could in whatever way he could.

Another Sunday, cousins, ever Joey's targets, decided to strike back at the mocking youngster. At Grandpa's and Aunt Angie's, right after eating, Joey made his usual rush to the bathroom's throne seat when his teenage cousins, camera in hand, quietly grabbed the door and pop went the flashbulb. Laughter filled the rooms as the message passed from children to adult and the picture, once developed became a family treasure for they had caught Joey at half-mast his drawers below his knees and trying to hide. Joey himself could not stop laughing at it while not being allowed to forget it.

The next Sunday after dinner but before dessert, Pop begged for silence. Usually, quiet was hard to come by at Sunday dinners because the entire family showed up and noise reigned from Tony's booming voice, to multi-conversations and kids just being kids. Gene pulled a v-mail letter out of his shirt pocket. That brought immediate quiet. Everybody knew it was from Sossy and needed to hear it.

His long silence was the secrecy of D-Day preparations was told of jumping over Belgium and missing the harsher battles of the Normandy beachhead.

Joe's reasons for hanging on every word included his own hopes of soon joining him in uniform. His stomach made him believe it might not happen. The meal in front of Joe looked like three or four hills of mush. Marian carried her food chopper wherever they went without apology to ease the pain in digesting what he ate. If anyone had anything to say about it, the family knew Marian would chew them up and swallow them whole with anger they rarely saw.

After dinner, the cousins marched down the hill to the south side of the carpet mill and went to the Terrace Theater with the dime that Grandpa had given them and buying a pocketful of candy from the cubbyhole counter next to the theatre with their pennies.

The war worsened with more service stars appearing in windows, and far too many were now the gold of the warrior gone.

The call for steel bade goodbye to Joe's Ford, which was replaced by a wood bodied pickup with barely enough room up front for Marian and Joe. It was slow, but it added to the efforts of the neighborhood and work. They kept blankets in the rear for Jean, Joey, and anyone else needing a ride to grab a hitch.

One day, he read the paper, cover to cover, and said, "Oh, Jeez, Mar, so many men are dying. I want—" The softening look on Marian's face cut off his words. Both knew his day would come very soon. His stomach was getting worse, and his nerves were giving way.

One wintry Saturday, Joe worked at home on reports for the treasury department and asked Jean to go down and lock the pickup.

He added, "Be sure to put the keys in my coat pocket." The snow was falling heavily, and when Jean gave him her "why me" look, it earned a stern "go!"

At 4:30, he was ready to go sit with Marian until quitting time at 6:00. He worried she was in danger because Getty Square would be emptying early to allow people to get home by public transportation and because he knew Marian would be there alone for being the employee who lived closest.

He grabbed his coat off the bed and reached into the pocket for the keys. They weren't there.

"Jean, where are the keys?" His voice was filled with anger.

"In your pocket, Dad."

"No, they're not and your mom's waiting."

An unfamiliar but recognizable peril moved into the room spitting at Jean from Joe's eyes. Her own filled with doubt and alarm. Jean ran past him and checked the coat pocket again. It was still empty, and her eyes widened in disbelief until she looked like a skinny owl.

Joey took one look at his father and leaped up to help, sensing the danger to Jean and helped them search, but it proved fruitless. When he saw Joe turn to Jean, Joey suddenly moved further away from them because the room seemed to shake around him. He didn't know what to do, say, or where to go to be safe. He'd never seen his father this way, he was afraid for Jean and bewildered because something was very wrong.

That furious father asked again, "What did you do with the keys?"

Fear choked out the same answer. "I put them in your pocket."

"Don't lie to me." Joe's left hand slammed into Jean's face propelling her skinniness across the room into the metal entry door. She bounced off and ran into the kitchen crying.

The stranger in Joe pursued her as far as the doorway, his face red with violence. He said, "Don't you ever lie to me. He was so close, Jean felt he was breathing fire as he said, "Now your mother has to take a bus after being on her feet all day." Joe wheeled by a pale and cringing Joey, grabbed his coat, hat, and scarf, and ran out the door, struggling into his coat, intending to walk down The Hill to Getty Square

As he took the first flight of stairs, a strange jingle filtered through his anger like sound from a faulty speaker. He stopped. It stopped. Down the second flight of stairs, he heard it again. Now it was clearly a sound he had to hear. He realized it was coming from the hem of his coat. He shook the coat and heard them clashing together and felt his mouth go dry. He shoved a hand into the pocket, a finger into a hole of the lining and felt himself gag, and his stomach was hurting like hell.

For a moment, he couldn't move as he relived the twisted emotions of hitting a defenseless child, his own.

My God, I slapped her across the face for lying. Condemnation smothered him with, *You were out of control because it was Marian. What the hell's wrong with you? What are you turning your jealousy into, what the hell will you do next time? What if you'd had something in your hand?*

Joe rushed upstairs and burst through the door calling out, "Jean. Jean, honey?"

She was facing him but backpedaled as fast as she could until a wall stopped her.

"Please, Daddy, don't hit me again." Tears ran down her freckled cheeks with terror on her face, terror of him.

"Honey, I'm sorry. I made a mistake. The keys fell through a hole in my pocket, I—" His mind whipped at him.

Forget that crap. She's not coming near you. She doesn't want your lousy hands on her.

His eyes filled with the tears of sorrow that saturated his words. "I'm sorry." Remembering Marian, he turned past his confused son watched him cringe, and without knowing how to help either of them, he ran for the car cursing his vile temper birthed in an emotion he knew he had not yet learned to control.

Fortunately, Marian was alone, and as he helped her with her coat, he explained, "And now Jean won't let me touch her. I've terrified my own daughter. And Joey's scared too."

Marian was quiet until saying, "Oh, Joe, how could you hit her like that. I'm sorry but how else could she feel. She loves you so much, and you hit her in the worst possible way. Hon, she will forgive you. You're too good a father for her not too. But, Joe, you're going to have to give her time. Joey's harder to figure out, I don't know what he'll make of you. Oh, Joe, is this a part of what's going on within you that you don't understand?" He could only stare out into the falling snow.

Marian's words about Jean's love proved true, but Jean's look hounded Joe, and whenever there was a problem frothing his temper, he turned inward where Jean's look damned him never to be truly forgotten.

For Jean, loving Joe in ways a daughter doesn't understand the hurt vanished, but Joe would shackle himself to that memory just as he did others.

In the land of spirits, one said, "Will he find his way? He's so troubled."

You've watched over him for a long time. Perhaps you can sense the answer."

The spirit turned inward.

Because of his mistake, Marian and Joe carefully devised punishments for their denizens that would often mean they as parents spent time being grounded because their offspring were, but it was a prison of their own choosing.

Joey's cheating was becoming an ongoing problem, but he just thought it good fun and took any effort to change him as a joke.

Both Jean and Joey took their chances with lying; one serious in the getting caught, while the younger looked for other ways to accomplish the same thing. Ultimately, they both channeled their talent to fit their needs.

Without his anchor in laughter, Joe did find other ways to please children. A limping friend wearing an eagle veteran's pin in the lapel of his jacket furnished Joe with silent movies. He hauled them home and showed them both to his own kids and in an empty apartment to groups of children. Disney cartoons and Bud Abbott and Lou Costello were the big favorites. One day, the supplier offered him something unusual. He discussed it with Marian, and they decided to show it only to Jean and Joey. Too often, other parents were too cautious to brave a new door, and that, they understood and carefully selected the new doors for Joey and Jean.

This new door had Jean sitting on the floor with Joey between her legs. In minutes, both wore looks of astonishment. The blood and gore, bothered neither of them because the miracle of life fascinated them. They saw a child leave its mother womb and burst through her doorway to bellow into life. Joe and Marian found their children could accept much more than expected and chose to live life accordingly as long as right and wrong lines were not jeopardized.

The war-time use of telephones in the project limited them to four party lines, but it speeded doings over the grapevine like a rocket free of gravity and to many a youngster's dismay, a reward or penalty was waiting upon getting home.

Jean and Joey were no different. There were many such corners each would remember.

They had dishonoring moments, petty successes usually and luckily came to abrupt ends. Like a raid on Christmas gifts clumsily done, which included their cousins, sent Jean and Joey before determined parents for comeuppance.

That confrontation navigated a liar's wayward corner, and the lesson took hold in the young Prezzemoli minds. One Prezzemoli decided it was helpful in happenings where drama brought fun and honed the skills of an actress to bring pleasure and the other found it reasonable to use to win a battle of wits. Ultimately lying was channeled to fit their growing values.

Young Joey lost something without Joe's norm to count on and decided, "It's easy to get away with things when people don't know me." Many of his young friends were just as convinced, and though not bad minded, they were hell-bent on mischief, and being masters of their own ships without the mastery to do it alone gave peer power a stronghold.

Guilt's power; good and bad had entered their growing minds and the adults they would become would be guided by the decisions made along the way.

Within the Man

J oe's tormented stomach was like a ball thrown hard and fast down a sloping hill.

Marian pleaded, "You have to eat."

"I can't."

Marian continued to mash everything but had the feeling all the good of the world was under attack and not just by those seeking world domination.

In Europe, the Allies were making progress and had the Swastika mob on the run until a change in German strategy trapped the Allies in the Ardeen Forest in bitter cold weather. Horror stories began to appear at home that couldn't begin to describe the real situation. The Air Force was grounded by fog, and ground supply lines were thwarted by infiltration and the murder of Allied prisoners to prevent any delay to German mobility.

Joe was one of the millions who grabbed everything they could to read or hear from the terrible pictures in *LIFE* magazine and newspapers. Even the letters Jean normally received had all but stopped, and it looked like the American eagle and allied forces were bleeding hopelessly.

IN ENGLAND KEEPING THEM FLYING

IN BURMA

JUMPED OVER EUROPE

Our Men at War

Then they reported the answer of a soldier named McHolup trapped in the Battle of the Bulge when he was asked to surrender. Joe read it to Marian and the kids and when he said, "'Nutz' was the Yank's curt answer." Joe looked around and saw sadness and tears for our men and a quiet overwhelming for his courage, while stuck in the sadness of the men's dicey-no-way-out station.

When the entrapping fog lifted on December 22, 1944, the existence of God filled the churches for days, but then they'd been well visited for a long time.

As the skies cleared, the Allies took to the air, and the German attack on New Year's Day crumbled under the Allies fierce barrage. Though it took a dreadful toll of American and Allied lives, they determinedly continued the drive to bury the Fuehrer.

In the eastern part of the world, the Marines were landing on Pacific Islands and stateside relatives pining for news shivered at newsreel horrors of flamethrowers aimed at suicidal adversaries dealing death from depths within the ground. Terror filled theaters for the loss of life, while pride and heartbreaking gratitude touched those at home as brothers and sisters, the average American heroes, died to keep them safe and quaked with pride when five such heroes raised the Stars and Stripes on Iwo Jima.

Young Jean's reaction went so deep she cut the picture out of *LIFE* magazine to paste in the front of a notebook until it fell apart from use. The moment began her love affair with the Marine Corp anchored in the heart of a-soon-to-be-teen's imagination, fed by approaching womanhood.

Young Joey was moved as well. He decided on strong masculine heroes to admire while seeking the true measure of a man, at an age bypassing some of the deeper aspects of men at their best.

April 1945 brought the Axis Allies a day of joy that tore into and changed the pattern of American courage. Franklin Delano Roosevelt died. Harry S. Truman became president. A very different man now carried the flag passed to him but with the same sense of America to deal with even more tragic events.

As the death toll of American servicemen mounted, married men with two children were called to answer the draft.

One evening, Joe rushed to where Jean and Marian were taking an advanced first aid course while Joey was collecting papers.

Drawn but excited, he said, "Marian, I have to report for my physical." Marian took a deep breath that suspended her in somewhere that was nowhere. Being there changed nothing, and though a part of her was still reluctant to his going, she wanted and needed him well for none of it was any good unless he was, even if it meant his going to war.

As she turned the reluctant corner to awareness, she squeezed Joe's hand and, in a sad but firm whisper, said, "We'll be all right, hon. Go. I'm sorry I didn't let you go before. Just tell Mom before she hears from someone else."

In that moment, Joe loved her more than ever, but the threat of them not taking him was still very real and about to be faced.

Jean watched from a kneeling position over a dummy whose wound she was packing. Her parents' expressions froze in her mind, and she poured her attention into what she was doing as though it was the most important thing in the world.

When Joe told Raffaele, she touched his cheek and said, "We'll be a fine. Marianne and I have talked. She will work, and I will care for the bambinos."

On his way to Ellis Island, Joe thought, *My ladies are way ahead of me. Please, Dear God, they've got to take me. They've got to. They're safe now, and I've got to help keep them that way, no matter how scared I am.*

Joe reported to Ellis Island to spend three days eating and drinking rude and vile foods that just days before he couldn't even swallow. While they did extensive tests, he realized there were Italian prisoners doing much of the work on the island, and that made him wonder about his parents arrival here as immigrants. The men around him, some very ill and still willing to go, showed him his situation differently and without self-punishment.

On the third day, he sat beside the doctor while he reviewed his tests. Joe's foot visibly vibrated, and his hand kept rubbing across his grand nose. Looking at the tired man, Joe hoped Dr. Griffon was safe.

The doctor interrupted the thought.

"Which branch of the service do you want, Joe?"

In one marvelous expression, Joe went from fear to exultation and leaped from the chair into the air as though he had the winning basket at his fingertips and let go with a wild cheer.

The fatigued doctor smiled in this rare moment, glad for the job he had to do.

"The Navy, sir. I want submarine service." The joy in Joe's voice made the doctor's eyebrows pinch in disbelief, for he knew the dangers of underwater service.

Later, Joe found his wife and children in Pop's yard, threw both arms around Marian, and babbled about being well.

Her emotions soared at his well-being until he said, "I'm reporting for submarine service."

Then they crashed, and she vibrated in his arms, saying, "You're crazy. You volunteered for submarines?" Marian was aghast for he hadn't shared the decision.

Cruel disappointment spread across Joe's face making her throw her arms around his neck and bury her face in his shoulder. It was the only way she could silence a scream threatening to surface. After a deep breath, she said, "Oh, Joe. Oh, God, I'm sorry. Joe, please come back to us. I know this is what you need to do."

Jean and Joey stood on a nearby wall listening. A glacial cold froze their imagination with fear. Instinctively, they moved to where they could touch each other.

Young Joey felt cold and confused by wanting his daddy in uniform like other daddy's yet pictures of newsreels flew through his young mind and so confused he hung onto; Jean's blouse.

The strange isolation he felt made him lean against his sister knowing the thing between his mother and father made him feel safe was theirs alone sadly, his young mind could not understand his mixed feelings.

Meanwhile, Marian whispered, "How can you be this brave and yet frightened of so many things you can't tell me about."

He pulled her closer knowing he had no answers for her.

The children and the parents were turning corners faster than they could recognize them.

When Joe left, he went straight to Raffaele.

"Guisseppe, you be a fine. The Blessed Mother might let them take you from me but never from Marian and the children. She loves you so, and the children, they lovea you like you lovea yo Poppa."

"Oh, Joe, I missa you ahready."

Joe hugged her and huskily said, "You know, Mom, I don't remember Poppa, and I know I'll be all right. But, Mom, can I ask you a question about me?"

"Si." Her hand stroked his cheek as he sat in a kitchen chair in front of her and bent over to listen carefully.

"Tell me what you can about me when I was a kid. You know a little guy."

She watched for a long moment and couldn't miss how very important it was to him. Finally, she said, "Eh, you a like a your Jeannie, you were as quiet no—you lonely likea her you become like a your Joey later only you very different."

"How, Mom?"

They talked a long time.

The Navy yanked all of Joe's beautiful, cavity free teeth for having pyorrhea. The next few weeks passed quickly, and with indoctrination taking place at the Brooklyn Navy Yard, he came home frequently for only an hour or two at a time, but he was home.

V-E Day came as Joe started onboard training. Victory in Europe meant Ralph and Sal were safe for the time being and the people of the Hudson Valley watched Hitler's face on the Palisades crumble away a little more each day.

During Joe's training, Marian buried the threat in his going and made plans for now and when he returned.

As Joe trained, America dropped the atomic bombs over Hiroshima and Nagasaki that returned Joe to his family before any endangering.

A Broken Heart

The world learned some important lessons by the end of World War II but continued history's human errors by fondling madness in threats of destruction and separation.

But humanity also took an opportunity to put their finger in the holes of warring's weakened dike by creating the United Nations in San Francisco in 1945. In 1946, it founded its headquarters in New York and began to take some part in the future violence in an effort to prevent the same.

The world's governments continued to place people of the same heritage, even in the same family in positions of conflict as in the defeated city of Berlin, Germany. It was now a divided city where a sturdy stone walls had armed men upon them within the city of Berlin an abject separation between Allies who had fought a common enemy. It was a city that each ally had got his share. Berlin became like the human heart, was divided into four chambers, but unlike the human heart, it was unable to serve one mind.

It was a world in which the Communist became the omnipresent danger to democracy. The powers of that time set a future course both dangerous and complex for hidden intentions. A course that would one day touch the Prezzemoli family deeply.

By then, our soldiers were coming home as replacements were found to serve as occupying forces. It was a time when Joe's nephew Freddy was deeply in love and engaged, only to be jilted for a returning soldier. The mind of the twenty-one-year-old shut down, and when the tottering damsel kept the expensive engagement ring he had earned by working long hours, he hurt too much to even think about getting it back.

Though a loving family had much to say which he ignored, he found a place to avoid their loving but cruel reactions.

His big sister Anna, waiting for the return of her husband, still in the Burmese jungle felt the girl's behavior a slap in the face to all the gallant ladies who had waited alone and fearful for their men.

So one night, Anna took a subway across town, knocked on the girl's door, and—when she answered—said, "I'm here for my brother's ring."

"I don't have to give you anything. It was a gift." The girl's smiling arrogance turned Anna into an unfamiliar, threatening force that seemed to fill the doorframe bringing to the girl a sense of forboding that froze her on the spot.

Anna jammed her foot against the door and, with surprising strength pushed it, just far enough to touch the girl and leaned forward to say, "That's right, you don't. But if you don't, I'll take great pleasure in pulling a hair out of your head for every lonely day I've spent without my husband. While you, you bitch took advantage of a wonderful kid. A kid who would have willingly taken your sweetheart's or my husband's place."

A scalping was not the girl's style, so the ring left her right hand and found its way back to Freddy who found no solace in its return but joined those around him in search of rekindling the laughter in their ranks.

Joe was relieved of duty before going anywhere and returned home to Marian and the children more like the Joe who'd been missing during the war years. Joe teased the children with his ill fitted clacking teeth. A gift the Navy had given him to replace his beautiful white teeth. They were trimming the Christmas tree.

Joe was opening a Christmas gift. It was a companion for their eight-millimeter projector—a used motion picture camera. His excitement was dwarfed by a more personal box.

He slowly opened a jeweler box to find a gold pocket watch and chain. He fell in love with it and put a suit vest on over his undershirt to show it off. On his return to work, he wore it with the chain, worked through a buttonhole of the vest, and put the watch in his pants watch pocket or trailing from a belt hook into the left-hand pocket of his pants or passing through a button hole to a vest pocket.

He was having fun, but there was still a part of him that remained a stranger at least to Marian, and she was determined to find the answer to his destructive feelings before they surfaced again.

The sense of drama in the Prezzemoli crowd loved the formality of Joe's watch. For days, Joe grabbed for attention. "Anybody want to know the time?"

When Freddy came to visit Joe, he took the kids outside, and Freddy would play coach. "Okay, everybody, line up. We're going to have some races, and Uncle Joe will time us." Fred enjoyed Unc calling out the time and the seconds. No one took winning seriously, they just wanted the time, though Joe couldn't help but notice Jean was faster than ever while Joey clowned all through the races trying to hold her back any way he could and—when he couldn't—a teenage Tom would usually booby trap them both.

For Christmas, Joe had given Marian a sapphire ring giving her no idea how he managed it.

In 1946, Jean learned a lesson she didn't like. She needed glasses and hated them like most growing kids do, but it stopped some bad reading habits. It took a little time, but she adjusted.

Meanwhile, Marian and Joe were trying to deal with a son who didn't really hate school but had no intention of studying and who loved to tease but couldn't or wouldn't accept that it had a dangerous element enabling him to hurt someone even when it brought laughter to a moment.

Daddy doesn't understand. I want to make people laugh like he does, and then they'll like me the way they like him. He can't make me stop. I won't stop.

Joe's love of being with people and talent for bringing them wholesome laughter had been taken on by Joey as his own mantel of worth. Somehow, Joey couldn't isolate the level of use as his father had over the years and lacked the patience and watchfulness for being too young to find it on his own.

Now there were calls from teachers with comments like, "He's bright but refuses to apply himself." They reached the point Joe said, "Mar, maybe the only thing that will wake him up is being left back. If he's too young, time may help him grow up." He hesitated at her silence and added, "I hate the idea, but what do you think?"

"I've reached the point where I've considered it too. I hate the idea too. I'll talk to his teacher again and see what she thinks. We do have to try something."

"Want me there?"

"When the time comes to tell him, yes. Maybe it's not necessary."

Joe walked away realizing that as they got older, they were thinking more and more alike and stopped to say, "We're all spending hours every evening working with Joey just to get his homework done, and he always goes to school with it completed, but we're not making any headway. They're right he's smart. Smart to the point he knows, just what's enough, to get a passing grade."

Joey's third-grade teacher looked very troubled when she heard Marian say, "Look, Mrs. Edwin, Joe and I have discussed this and come to the conclusion the only thing that might still work is leaving Joey back. He's not going to like it, and we don't want to do it, but it's time he realizes he has to pay a price for deciding not to work, and he needs school for a good future."

Edwin's expression and hesitation made Marian think, *Maybe she doesn't want to do this.* "Mrs. Edwin, are you against this?"

"Oh no, Mrs. Prezzemoli, in fact, I'd really like to try it with Joseph, but I'm afraid we can't do it."

"I don't understand, why not?" Mrs. Edwin raised her hand and shook her head and tried to explain.

"Mrs. Prezzemoli, there is a new teaching format very much a part of our curriculum that's been approved called 'progressive education.' It firmly includes a premise built around not leaving a child back. The end result, whether a child does or doesn't do the work, they will be promoted except in rare and unusual cases. Apparently, the powers to be have decided that the emotional damage far exceeds the practical aspect of succeeding in life, and the students will adequately move along with their classmates. I don't agree, and it's probably threatening to my job to say what I've said, but it's true. Good teachers can offset the harmful aspects of being left back, but sometimes, we can't or don't. Forgive me, but it just frustrates me as a teacher."

Marian found herself bewildered as she headed home. *What can we do now to help Joey? Nothing that Joe and I are doing is getting through to him. Dear God, we're letting him down.*

That night, Marian and Joe realized something unexpected would have to happen to overcome this kind of a roadblock to Joey's learning. Joe's frustration showed in his closing words, "These idiots have created a great opportunity for kids like Joey and they probably did it to save money. I can't believe they don't recognize that they've created a classroom playground and taken control away from the teachers. It makes no sense, hon, none at all."

"Well, we'll keep after him maybe the unexpected will happen, you never know. All kids change as they grow."

"I hope so because he'll be one unhappy man without the education he needs to take care of himself and a family. He needs the capacity to find his way through serious personal problems. Without it, he hasn't a hope."

"Joe, he's not bad. So much of what we see in ourselves that we don't like we're afraid of seeing in our kids."

"Hon, I know that, but he has to be a man who can meet life on its own terms. I know he's got what it takes, but without trying there'll be too much he can't or won't find in life."

"Well, we both believe in him, so let's take it a day at a time. We have to believe he'll be all right."

Joe nodded and went back to reading his paper from his lefty point of view back to front after an informative scan.

The family efforts continued until Joey decided to at least complete his homework on his own but not much more, fun had become his god. He found he didn't like being punished or missing out on family doings, so he behaved just holding the line between foolhardy and acceptable.

It was a year that held awakenings for them all. Jean was old enough to stay home alone for private time and sit for Joey allowing Marian and Joe evenings out.

Jean's pleasure at being alone was as obvious as her dislike of responsibility. Marian gave her some pointers and a parental demand about being in charge. "Joey knows the rules just as well as you, and you're just to see that he follows them if he doesn't you're to tell me. Under no circumstances are you to change them. Okay?"

"Yes, Mom, but I don't like to snitch. No one likes a snitch."

"That's right Jean, but you aren't being a snitch, you're," she hesitated, "you're being a sister who cares about what kind of person her brother will grow up to be."

Because she was concentrating, Jean missed Joey's pleasure at the force of Marian's lecture, but Marian didn't so she faced him.

"Joey." Her switch in direction made him jump, and then he spotted his father watching him, closely and listened as his mother said, "You will listen to your sister, and if you don't, you will be punished. Now I want both of you to understand this. No one is to come in. Absolutely no one and that includes your friends." Marian swung back to Jean. "You are in control of this Jean, so I want you to tell me you completely understand."

"I do, Mom. I understand."

"And you, Joey, do you understand?"

"Ah, gee, Mom, I ain't no baby."

"I'm not a baby," corrected Marian.

Joey's humorous "got ya" presentation of "Right, Mom, that's what I said" almost made Joe smile as he slipped into his suit jacket.

Marian was shaking her head concealing a chuckle as Joe said, "Your mom and I trust you both, so don't let us down."

Joey and Jean nodded quickly. Joe winked and said, "Let's shake a leg, Mar, or we'll be late."

Joe touched Marian affectionately as they went back to their room to grab their coats and leave. Joey liked to watch that in his parents but took the moment to make a monkey face while Jean cautiously grinned at his silliness.

On the way out, Marian kissed them, pushed the hair out of Joey's eyes remembering how often she'd done the same to Sossy, told Joey his bedtime, and suggested Jean be nice about it.

Joey and Jean's first night alone was a surprise. There were no arguments or fights. Quite a feat since both thought nothing of wrestling over something. Joe had watched them physically grapple over many things including Joey trying to get Jean to say Uncle. Until now, she hadn't. The father waited to see how far it would go for he recognized his son was wrestling his darker side, but he was pleased to realize that when Joey knew he was hurting Jean he let go. The father said nothing for remembering his own demons, and he was grateful that his daughter who fought the same battle had the same result. The decision merely came faster to his growing girl.

Their first night together proved an adventure where Jean and Joey listened to the Lone Ranger, a mutual favorite, and then Inner Sanctum with its hair-raising, squeaking door. As it came on, Jean checked the door handle to ensure it was locked and quickly joined Joey who had propped himself against the radiator where they had a full view of the room and the rather frightening, darkened foyer. Alone and scared, having each other was better than not. Mid story, a sudden knock made them jump in surprise.

Jean stood and said, "Who is it?"

"It's Aunt Margaret and Uncle Harry."

Joey leaped up for he enjoyed this aunt and uncle and could not help but enjoy the fact it could mean some change from his uncle. He wanted to let them in, but Jean said, "I can't let you in. Mom said not to let anyone in."

Margaret asked, "But you know it's us?"

"Yes, but Mom told us we can't let anyone in. Not anyone." Jean voice had begun to shake with the weight of responsibility.

By now, Joey and Jean had their ears flat to the steel entry door. They liked their aunt and uncle, but they had their orders. Margaret, moved by the dilemma, said, "That's okay. You have to do what your parents told you. We'll see you another time." The fact they understood didn't especially help the kids because they heard Harry and Margaret laughing as they walked away. The kids didn't think it funny at all.

When Marian walked in, Jean blurted out, in the required honesty, "Aunt Margaret and Uncle Harry were here, and we didn't let them in."

Marian went ballistic. "Jean, how could you? Aunt Margaret and Uncle Harry traveled from Connecticut to get here. You should have let them in."

Joey's immediate gloat at Jean being trapped turned to pity. Jean was utterly confused, and Joey saw her bite her lip trying not to cry. "I'll deal with you in a minute," said the embarrassed Marian as she rushed to their four-party line phone and, finding it available, called Margaret and Harry.

Joe knew Marian was wrong but had to wait to tell her. He put his hands on Jean's shoulders and whispered, "Your mom's fast on her feet." Her eyes glistened with gratitude as he said, "It'll be all right." Except for Marian's upset about it being Joe's family, he knew it was funny. If a Manfredi went home without getting in, Marian would have laughed even though she'd be given a hard time by them just for fun. Joe knew Margaret would handle it and closely listened to the conversation.

"Margaret, I've called to apologize. Jean had no right to leave you out in the hall. I'm furious with her."

Margaret laughed. "Marian, didn't you tell her not to let anyone one in? No matter what?"

"Yes, but I didn't mean her aunts and—"

Margaret injected, "Marian?" Her tone intoned, think. In mid breath, a smile crept across Marian's taut features, and she raised her arm to signal Jean closer. Jean was cautiously slow but relaxed as Marian's arm pulled her close to stroke her tenderly. Joe and Joey tiptoed out of the line of fire in the girlie emotion.

335

The rules changed and centered on the trust to apply good judgment. Joe and Marian called the kids after school daily. They had a working plan and any unannounced changes came trundled in penalties.

Joey continued to irk and ire his peers with teasing that incited playground problems, where he'd come home dirty; and crying but now seemed to be holding his own.

Joe used his motion picture camera at Joey's first holy communion framing the family as lived.

Jean called out, "Dad, I think you hold the camera the other way."

Jean turned from his harsh look to laugh at a brother staying clean long enough to receive communion.

A week later, an excited Joe walked in with the film and set up the projector. "Lights out," called the projectionist. The machine clacked and whirred to everyone's laughter.

"You look good standing on your head, Joey."

"Thanks, Mom, but how come girls' skirts don't fall when they're upside down?"

Almost giggling, Marian gave him a gentle push.

Jean wanted to laugh but turned for Joe's reaction.

"Lights on," called the projectionist.

Joe rubbed the tip of his majestic nose, winked at Jean, and said, "I'm not so smart after all."

Alight with an idea, Joe clacked his teeth and hollered, "Lights out."

Again, the switch flipped, and the projector clacked, but the picture was right side up. All heads wheeled. Joe was sitting on the floor, with the projector upside down and braced between his knees.

"Don't make me laugh," he sputtered, "or your mom's and my sex life will cease to exist."

Joe's dangerous voyage was nearing home port, and Marian bust into enjoyable laughter.

Joe's successes during the war bettered his position, but it had to wait until after Veteran employees returned. That didn't bother him, and Marian's small income measured in smarts meant they were now saving a few dollars at a time and life was looking better.

The war's end had transformed the project. Friends having saved greater wartime earnings could now afford to meet the mortgages for a new home. While the Prezzemolis could not, Joe did earn an admirable reputation for reliable mortgage assignments, because he knew who could be trusted.

As friends left the project, their happiness for them was sorely mixed with disappointment.

As project faces changed, so did the behavior, dangerously. The American economy was sprouting like a healthy young'un, but many were unable to keep up.

Grandpa Gene left for Italy without telling anyone of feeling ill and met the symptoms with, *Ehhhh, they'll go away. They did before.*

"Buona Fortuna, Chiulli." Raffaele kissed her dear friend goodbye, and Gene promised to visit her hometown for news of her relatives. The animosity of her father could never touch her capacity to care because and it was her true nature.

As a father, Joe moved a son toward manly things by exposing him to his own good friends and now that his time was his again, by taking him fishing on the river and lakes of Westchester to talking of many things usually after dropping Jean off at her uncle Paul's riding academy in White Plains. A father's stewardship routed the manhood of a boy with honorable answers to questions too many men found troublesome or embarrassing to discuss.

Still there were pieces of Joey he couldn't fathom.

Geez, a boy's mind isn't any more readable than a girl's. I can't tell what his future will be anymore than I can Jean's. At least with him, I stand a chance, but it just isn't the same with him as it was for me, but as Marian says try. When I watch him with other kids he's proving to be a stead fast friend. He's nothing like that when he'd clowning around, but that's a great beginning.

On one fishing trip they were out on large lake as they discussed getting into real trouble with friends. Their excursion suddenly turned menacing for not paying attention to the weather. A squall hit the lake with demonic fury dumping waves of water into their dinghy where terror gripped both of them.

Joe battled the urge to make a desperate grab for Joey and put him beside him. Another wave hit. The dinghy pitched but did not flip. Joe was rowing for their lives.

He yelled over the wailing storm. "Joey, hold on with one hand and use the worm pail to bail. Hurry but hold on." The water was now over their ankles. Thoughts of being in the water even with the waves didn't faze Joe but thoughts of Joey... *Oh God, Please not Joey I could lose him. Please no.*

The prayer drowned in the need to survive. The crash of the next swell forced Joey's face to his knees while Joe jammed his leg muscles and knees against his seat to prevent being pulled backward and overboard. *I've got to keep rowing, it's our only chance.* His mouth and magnificent nose filled with water.

The swell inverted, and they rode up again as Joe yelled, "It's like a roller coaster."

Joey wanted to match his dad's courage but shivered with the effort. Young hands couldn't bail quickly enough with the water crashing again and again. Then a wall of water pulled Joey's hand from the seat and tumbling him into Joe. Desperation gave Joe the strength to hang on to the seat and grab Joey with his knees. Now Joey was kneeling in the pitching vessel with arms around his father's waist. Joe gripped the oars and his seat with the strength of survival. Again, they rose on a wave.

Oh, geez, another one like that, and we're in the water. Dear God, please.

As suddenly as it started, the storm abated, and the sun spread across Joe's face, and the water calmed. The magic of the warmth on their chilled skin had them laughing, hugging, and bailing.

Young Joey's mind, full of war heroes, placed his father's efforts somewhere among them to be revered or lost in his travels to manhood.

One day after catechism, Jean was running from person to person near their apartment, asking, "Have you seen Joey?" She had waited as long as she dared and, at last, was forced to make a phone call only it rang as she reached for it. After talking to Marian, she formed a project posse of friends and went looking for a missing brother only to return empty handed.

An old memory had Marian and Joe thinking the worst.

"Oh, Joe, what if?" She was remembering Jay and the candy man.

"Hon, don't! Please, don't even think it. He's a kid and time doesn't mean anything to him." Unable to hide his own fear his expression showed he wasn't sure.

A mother's mind came alive forcing a control on wild thoughts that might delay finding him. When darkness descended, hope struggled, and the police answered Joe's call.

Marian used a neighbor's phone to continue the search while Joe stood ready at home. Jean waited or paced feeling she fouled up in some way, though no one blamed her.

The police returned telling them they planned to widen the search when the door opened and Joey walked in dirty faced and unharmed.

"I played ball after school." His nonplused "what's the excitement all about" attitude infuriated Joe.

"That's it? It's been dark for hours, and you've worried your mother sick. Where have you been?" Joe fought the urge to grab him and shake him.

"We went to Mark's house."

"Mark who?" bellowed the unknowing father as he fought his temper while Marian, now aware it was a child's mistake, apologized and thanked the police and friends while keeping one eye on her normal boy who was in deep trouble but safe except from a father's at times dangerous wrath. She was remembering and her quieted fear came awake.

The gadabout was grounded from all after-school activities. There were no toys, no friends, and no going out. Not even hanging out the window allowed a respite. The promise of further isolation from the world kept him from the windowsill while his parents worked. Worse, he was at war with his sister who was the warden with them away. His feeling abused finally collapsed under the worst punishment, his separation from the family activities.

Marian realized how much her young son was like his father. The unseen was now there to be considered allowing Marian a real clue to Joe's troubling. As aloneness assailed young Joey, Marian realized the young can lack the security of that she had always seemed to have.

As they learned about their son, they laughed and lost count of Joey's trips to the bathroom from his side of the bedroom, where he could see in the living room and what the three of them were doing. Though they laughed at his predicament, the length of time they were all punished by keeping him home went full term.

Joey tried to coerce his father's sympathy and did but couldn't overcome Joe's knowing. Marian was right every time he suggested going easy on their son. The loyalty of his parents to one another left him without recourse, as long as they knew he'd "done" wrong. Oh how hurt young Joey was when daddy sided with Mom.

One Tuesday, Marian left an icebox cake to pull a date-nut bread from the oven to put it on the windowsill next to a cooling lemon meringue pie. She was taking a moment to enjoy the youngsters playing below when she heard a frantic knock on the door.

The ladies' arms reached for one another as Marian paled at seeing the blue, tell-tale lips on a frightened Raffaele as she heard, "Marianne, I am ill."

The vibration of Raffaele's trembling body passed into Marian with a searing sadness that tore the younger woman's hold with knowing; no matter how close she held Raffaele it was a battle they could lose.

"Oh, Mom, I have you, hold on to me. Oh, God, you walked all this way." Marian wrapped her warmly, called the hospital and Joe to immediately return to hold a woman she loved as close as possible. Now it was only her greater caring that kept Raffaele upright as they waited.

A son signed his first love into a hospital from which she would not return. Raffaele was laid to rest on the highest hill, which became a cliff with a sharp drop at her feet to overlook St. Joseph's Cemetery.

The soft winds from the world beyond were filled with gentle voices that kept her company until a beautiful lady in blue beckoned her. Raffaele, unafraid, took the lady's outstretched hand as she heard, "Come, Raffaele, your loved ones are waiting."

That Raffaele sought out Marian left Joe grateful and so very sad. Marian was able to deal with death's rue by knowing she had made Raffaele's life easier.

She held Joe as he wept over her loss, but it wasn't enough. Something deep within prevented all they had from reaching him.

Now she had a clearer picture of the problem commanding him still, though he now really encouraged her trying to help him deal with it. Still the pain was raw with hurt.

After the burial, Joe sat at the kitchen table while she hovered from the living room.

Jean said, "Mom, is Dad all right?"

"He'll be fine, Jean, but he has to learn to live with Grandma's dying. He misses her terribly." She watched Jean bite her lip and walk helplessly away.

Joey listened to the explanation at the kitchen doorway and watched Joe stare out the kitchen window at a cloudy sky.

Marian touched Joey. His upturned face held tears.

"Joey, if you want to be with Dad, it's all right."

"But Dad's crying? Men don't cry."

"Honey, men do so cry. Remember Daddy loves Grandma." Marian searched for words Joey could understand.

"He loves Grandma the way you love him." Her nod convinced the boy it was all right, perhaps clashing with his idea of a man supplied by movie screen heroes and familiar moments of heroism. Whether the two would meld, only time would tell.

Joey slowly stepped to the kitchen table and said, "Daddy?"

Joe turned and said, "Joey, do you remember when Grandma caught you with icing all over your face." Joey sat on the chair next to him, and they talked bending toward each other for a long time, and finally, Jean and Marian heard them laugh.

The grief went deep, and Joe took a lesson from it and put Marian behind the wheel, and in days, she had her license allowing her the ability to do more when needed.

Joe and Marian would think of Raffaele's romantic nature often about Jean explaining the love scenes and that lead to thoughts of Jean becoming a woman. Joe admitted, "Ah, hon, I'm not ready for this. It can't happen this quickly."

Marian only raised her eyebrows and smiled remembering how long it had taken Joe to see it in her.

⚬≪≫⚬

Joe was wrong. It was going to happen soon and the explaining fell to Marian. She carefully planned the discussion, did a tremendous lot of reading on the subject, learned more than she knew from small books now available. She was nonchalantly ironing clothes when she decided it was time to explain. For all apparent ease, she worried about mixing the latest facts with the everyday realities.

Wise Before Her Time

"And menstruating means you can be a mother because it allows your body to take the male sperm into your egg and you become pregnant and have a child." The silence made Marian wonder, *Is she really understanding me?*

She gave Jean a book to read and said, "Relax, honey, we'll talk again after you've read this."

While Jean read *The Making of a Child*, Marian held a conference with her instincts. *Did I handle it badly? Maybe she didn't understand? Maybe I should start from the beginning?*

Then it was time for questions. "And what can happen when a man puts his penis into you?"

The right answers left Marian undecided. *Should I be happy or worried?* She had watched Jean's mind at work, and the expression in Jean's eyes seemed to run wild. It was the same look she had in an exciting new doing.

Joe came in, pleasantly interrupted her thought—*Maybe we should have had all boys*—with a kiss and asking, "How'd it go, hon?"

She explained and then told him, "In a very short time, you're going to have talk to her about the bad in the male animal." She watched him nodding encouragingly as he said, "Why do they have to grow up?"

She met his obvious reluctance by placing her hands on his waist and saying, "I know it won't get easier. My part was kind of scary. Gosh, our parents knew next to nothing. Nodding Joe said, "I'm glad now that you gave me the books to read."

Days later, Joe opened the door to find Pop home from Europe. Joe grabbed him and gave him a hug. He was smiling grandly and said, "I have a lemon for your mother. I've carried it all the way from Sorrento." The look on Joe's face when he pulled away was enough.

"When?"

Chiulli's eyes filled with tears, as he fingered the fruit, and suddenly felt very alone amid a generation very unlike his.

In the days following, Gene watched a recurring pool of blood whirling in the toilet as mesmerizing as a snake before a strike.

"Why is this happening to me?"

Sossy, home for a visit, was now married and in business for himself as a carpenter. JJ had joined Tony at the barbershop allowing Gene to relax and see more of the world.

Sossy had taken Pop fishing and joined him at home for dinner. When Pop went to relieve himself, Sos heard. "Madre Mia, why me?" The anguish Sossy heard made him grab for the bathroom door to be shocked by the sight of bright red blood in the toilet bowl and a terrified Gene. He called Marian and rushed Gene to the doctor.

It was not Gene's first visit to a doctor because Gene was hearing the diagnosis for the second time, "Cancer of the bladder." Believing it had eluded him. It was no different than what the doctor in Italy had told him, but this time, he heard nothing else of the conversation because he let it evaporate like a pool of water in the desert and was suddenly a different man—a man dead in his own eyes.

Gene knew he was looking into the hollow eyes of the Grim Reaper, and he was demanding Gene's love for life during the time still left to him with the living, and Gene gave it to him.

An operation left a bag hanging between his legs that became a tormenting companion who murdered his manhood yet allowed him to walk around like a ghost of himself. An inability to deal with its degradation would hound him.

Jean continued to fall into strange and sometimes threatening incidents. At a very warm confirmation rehearsal, she fainted. Dragged from the pew by nuns unable to lift her, she awoke on a wooden bench at the back of Sacred Heart Church. The sister smiled gently and asked, "Jean, when did you last have your period?"

Jean answered in a screech, "I haven't had my first." But the gist of the question, the whispering of the nuns, and laughter of peers sent her home in a warped state.

The story told, Joe took a seething Marian to visit the nun. Joe was worried for the nun. A habit would do little to protect her from Marian's righteous tongue.

Marian allowed the nun to explain and then said, "My daughter hasn't yet reached puberty, and you laid a social mark on her before her time. How dare you? Wearing that habit gives you no right to hurt the innocent. I'd report you, except I think you meant well.

Either you call me or my husband when something is wrong, or keep your good intentions out of this mother's business."

Joe was transferred to a new bank branch on the corner of Yonkers and Central Park Avenues across from the local racetrack. He was not really new to the area for having filled in when the branch needed help. His new position added many more contacts to his already wide field of people that broadened and enlivened the family's day-to-day social pleasures.

There were events in New York City like circuses and plays at a frequency their finances could never allow because Joe's clients, soon friends, often passed on tickets for Joe and Marian to use.

The return of fathers, sons, and daughter brought an era of growth their world hadn't known since the industrial revolution. Joe loved being a part of it through bank activities and reading about it at home, but at home, they were trying to make the best of a worsening situation.

The project had turned frightening in its people aspects. Amid a growing fear, they too surrendered to the humorous mercy of black and white creatures trapped in small boxes in the living rooms as the boxes spread across the country.

Television claimed hearts and minds. As households bought television sets, households quickly shared with those not having one, reminiscent of Gene and Tess sharing their radio.

While saving for one, the Prezzemoli family accepted the invitation of a favored host. Franny, an army veteran, and his wife Ann lived below them with Ann's invalid mother Mrs. Ferrine. On free evenings, they joined them to watch TV, now a favorite term for the time-consuming entertainment media.

Joe said, "Jean, honey, here's the money. Go down to Mr. Green's, and get a quart of ice cream, and bring it back to Franny and Ann's."

Jean flew down the hill to the ice-cream store to fetch freshly packed Breyers flavors that Mr. Green always filled beyond capacity for them. Then she carefully hid the finger gouge and raced back before it melted. Only when she passed the alley at St. Joseph's School, she always slowed and whistled a tune that made her less afraid. Once passed the alley, she always remembered Raffaele telling her whistling made the Blessed Mother cry, and said, "Gee, Grandma, I bet you know the Blessed Mother likes a good whistler the way Daddy says she would. And I like to whistle those love songs you liked so much in the movie." Only then, would Jean run again as fast as she could.

Mrs. Ferrine became a surrogate grandmother, but Franny's wounds weren't healing, so a move to Arizona would soon have them leaving as so many others friends had already done, they moved because they could now afford a mortgage and the Prezzemoli family could not.

One evening, Marian opened the door to a handsome, young blonde male carrying Jean.

He said, "She fell off her bike. I didn't want her to put weight on the ankle in case it's more than sprained."

One couldn't miss a daughter's pleasure in being held or the reluctance to let go of the stalwart youth. It was time to discuss the opposite sex in a more intimate fashion.

This time, both parents braved the discussion. Though it looked comfortable, Marian and Joe felt like they were putting their fingers in a 110-volt outlet.

The romantic aspects of love were now on the agenda. Both parents intended to cover the expressions and dangers with the caring and uncaring male.

Joe opened another door.

"Jeannie, you do know how a girl gets pregnant, don't you?"

"Ah, Dad, of course, I do. You know Mom and I talked. A man has a penis, a woman a vagina, etc., etc."

The impatient shake of her head ended the review, except Marian insisted on a reminder.

Marian got it started. "Jean, I want you to understand any woman can get pregnant."

"Mom, that's not going to happen to me."

"No, Jean, that attitude guarantees you'll be vulnerable, and getting pregnant doesn't mean you're bad, but it is a brutal mistake during your single years. If it happens to you, Dad and I must be the first to know. We'll stand by you, but you can't expect us to raise your child. If it happens, we won't ask you to marry the father unless you're both really in love. Honey, there is a big difference between enjoying lovemaking and being in love. But not many boys or girls can tell the difference. Even when you're and adult, it's not easy."

Jean's eyes were getting bigger as the conversation went deeper. Marian continued, "So remember, we would love your child the way we love you, but we won't raise your child."

Joe picked up from where Marian left off. "Honey, we'll only be grandparents, not babysitters. If you have a baby, you can always live with us, and we'll always love the child because it's part of you. But you'll be more than a mother. You'll have to pay rent, just the way you would when you become an adult even if you live at home. And there's more. You'll be responsible for all your own expenses, and having a baby means the baby's expenses are yours too. And that means you may have to decide between what you want to do in life and what you have to do, care for your child."

Joe felt like he had a whip in his hand, and he hated having to make a girl soon to be a woman see that the real world can be very hard to live in. "I know this is all hard to deal with, but it's important to you."

Marian jumped back in.

"It means caring for a child in the same way your father and I take care of you, like when you're ill and paying the doctor bills. That's what being a parent really is. Sex is wonderful, but not if you're pregnant and don't want to be. Believe us, it's happened to many good people, even in our own families." She paused. "Now I want to know if you think that's a fair way to handle it?"

It took time to find that screechy preteen voice, but it gave them the answer they wanted to hear. "Yes, it is."

"All right, honey, but if it does happen, remember, come to us right away. Don't try to hide it. It's too hard to deal with alone. It will break our hearts, but we won't condemn you; anyone can make this mistake."

Joe watched the sad nod of Jean's head said, "Jeannie" and paused, "I'm a man, and I've been a boy, so I want you to listen hard to what I have to say. I want to tell you about us guys."

Jean's "Okay" now had a tremble to it but an attentive one.

Joe let out a breath and said, "Honey, a man or a boy will say anything to get a girl to take her pants down. I want you to trust people, but this is different. A man can wait regardless of what he tells you, and all men can take care of themselves without a woman, and he can do it with his own hands. So don't believe the lies they tell."

Jean's reactive "He can?" told him it's been discussed, and the light in her eyes told him she wanted to know more of the specifics. But he wanted a different reaction and shook her with, "Just don't be a tease. It's hurtful to the good guys and dangerous with the bad ones, and the word you're wondering about is called *masturbation*."

Joe waited a moment to reassure himself with a question and thought, *I hate that light that just comes into her eyes. Hell I'm discussing sex, but without understanding she's too vulnerable.* "Jean you have to protect yourself from bad guys."

After a few reassuring questions, Jean went to her room and soon left to meet friends, leaving her parents to openly decide if it went well. Joe said, "I just have the feeling that curiosity of hers might be a real problem later on. And Hon, we still have to do this with Joey. God, help us."

"That will be an adventure." Both laughed but genuinely dreaded the possibilities.

Marian was not surprised by Jean's question a few days later about "who" in the family had married because of pregnancy. Marian weighed trusting her and told her the truth and watched the news about her aunts settle sadly into her curious nature growing with every days passing. Jean's curiosity led to seeing Aunts and husbands realistically while coming to understand a family's caring and affections.

The project worsened, and leaving became very desirable. Dangerous incidents many involving troubled veterans became frequent. Violent arguments brandished souvenir weapons, and in one case, a young Veteran almost raped a friend of Jean's.

A decision had to be made and a way found.

Pop now lived at Rosary Hill, a home for cancer patients run by a wonderful nursing order of Catholic nuns. A beautiful tree-laden hill mounted by a stone hospital and chapel was reminiscent of a western hacienda.

That alien receptacle between Pop's legs filling with his body's wastes had proved too much for Gene, and he chose death by gas. Luckily, son-in-law Diz came to visit, smelled gas, and broke in. Pop's door had never been locked before.

Gene had believed the house empty and tormented himself further when they told him he almost harmed one of Angie's daughters who played hooky that day. Gene accepted his commitment and Angie's additional contempt for the close call because of the shame he felt for endangering a granddaughter.

The nuns at Rosary Hill tended the suffering while staunchly refusing recompense. Such unending caring left families with nil to do. Grateful relatives called upon ingenuity to find uncanny methods to offer the nuns any worthy thank you.

Joe tried again but already knew the answer.

"Sister Elizabeth, how can we thank you for all you've done. What can we do for you?"

"Joseph, you know I can't accept anything for what I do for our patients. They are my life."

The kind sisters lived in a real world and knew fertile minds could make earthbound angels invisible. Gene's family joined those ranks. His girls made large baskets of goodies, and Joe, Marian, Jean, and Joey found ways to sneak them in.

Joe knew timing was everything if they were to succeed. First, they hid the baskets around the back of the building behind bushes. Then they visited Gene, earning a smile from him when they told him what they intended to do.

Jean drifted away and outside to where the baskets were hidden. Joey did as well and positioned himself near the trees in the back to play chickie. It was after lunch, and the licking clean kitchen was empty. Joe ambled by, looked through the door's porthole window, and saw Joey wave through the rear door portal. Joe looked around and waved back. Joey then waved at Jean, and she rushed the kitchen's back door with both arms carrying baskets. Marian watched from Pop's first floor room and saw trouble coming with an empty tray heading for the kitchen. She stepped out and engaged the young nun in conversation that distracted her. A few more baskets and the deed was done, so the Prezzemoli rascals headed back to Pop's room. The young nun came running out the kitchen, excited by the wonderful things she found, while the family played dumb by lying, like the angels they weren't.

Sister Elizabeth didn't believe a word they said but admitted they sounded truthful. Asking the other visiting families gained the sisters nothing, and though they passed the goodies on to their patients, they had the joy of knowing people cared for them as well as the patients.

Gene's suffering took a couple of years while trapped with the melancholy of watching others succumb. Family visiting every week left them betwixt desperate to leave and tortured for the leaving. The courage and unfairness of all the jeopardized souls sheltered a common prayer among Rosary Hill families. To watch Pop was possible, but watching his young friend Michael—five years old, blonde and beautiful with a tumor hanging from his left eye, the size of a grapefruit—tore at their souls so that they begged and pleaded, "Please, God, take them."

The hopeless visit when they found Michael was gone, was the same one that put Gene to bed to never again get up. He was ready.

That day the Prezzemoli family left more quiet than usual and headed for a cousin's wedding reception.

Joe had to stop for a red light on the Saw Mill River Parkway near Hearst Street and did. The light seemed to become the eye of the devil holding them in place while the world turned upside down rudely and dangerously.

Joe's stomach felt weird as he thought, *Jean looks funny with that silly pillbox hat over her face.* Joe's mind was confused and disoriented.

Then he heard Joey crying and focused on returning to consciousness. He saw Joey was holding his bumped head and realized his driver's seat had fallen back and was leaning on the back seat. Luckily, Joey's legs were up on the cushion. He turned to find Marian lying very still beside him. As his mind began to clear, he asked, "Are you kids okay?"

He watched Jean push that hat off her face and heard her say, "I'm okay and Joey's okay too, but he did bump his head."

Suddenly fully awake, he whirled to the right and asked, "Marian, are you all right?" He reached awkwardly from his inverted V position.

Her response was faltering.

"Yes. How are the kids?"

"Okay."

Spotting a tear in Marian's eye, he checked and saw a leg wound oozing blood. Joe grabbed the wheel with two hands and hauled himself upright to look in the mirror. "Jesus, we've been hit by a big black touring car."

Joe watched the male driver stumbling out of his car. Thought became action. Joe kicked the sprung door open, swung himself out, and rushed the driver clumsily coming toward him.

The smell of liquor stung Joe's nostrils. He grabbed the man, forced him back onto the touring car and incensed; pounded him into the hood of the hissing car. "I'm going to kill you."

Joe bashed the drunk's head again and again with each blow worse than the one before. The man only whimpered. The dull, hollow sound of his head hitting the hood joined other sounds finally jarring Joe.

Marian was yelling, "Joe, no." And other voices were saying, "Damn it, Joe, let go you're killing him." The voice was familiar. Another even more familiar crashed through his thick rage.

"Let him go, Joe, let him go. He's not worth it."

Two troopers had locked his arms and repeated themselves, "Jesus, Joe, let go." Their combined strength defeated Joe's fixation set on kill. The taller of the two troopers placed himself between Joe and the drunk.

"Prezzemoli, what's the matter with you? You're scaring the hell out of your family. Calm down and go take care of them. We saw him hit you. He's ours."

Joe's rage drained, and he looked into the faces of two very worried cop friends and understood what he had done. The drunk was pitiful, and the alarm on the faces of his family froze his insides and his stomach hurt. Worse, as he returned to the car, Marian and the kids were already in the car, the seat up-righted, and Marian wasn't talking just waiting to go.

The ride to the wedding was silent. Joe's glance drifted to Marian's leg wondering why he lost it so completely and then admitted knowing why. His dread of losing her returned whipping him with his earned silence. The threat he'd come to believe no longer existed was suddenly back and threatening their loving. *Why, Dear God, why?*

At the wedding, Marian's brother Tony sensed a problem and hearing the story came back with four glasses and had them gulp it down.

"Uncle Tony, this is atrocious stuff. What is it?" Jean's facial expression had all the wrinkles of its overpowering taste.

"Only the best Scotch." The laughing uncle put an arm around the complainant and waved to his girls.

"Go have some fun with Sylvia and Terra." Terra grabbed Joey because the two were very much their own favorites. Then Tony eased a sister's turmoil.

"Marian, Joe was in shock. You all were and probably still are. Hell, most men would have done the same thing."

Joe came to Marian's defense. "Thanks, Tony, but I can't lie about it. Even if I hadn't blacked out, I'd have probably done the same stupid thing."

Marian finally smiled at his honesty, and the next few days, they talked of things deep within and learned more about his anger and loneliness but not quite everything. Luckier than Gene, Joe was finally dealing with the child within that so controlled his adult temper.

Time was traveling faster than the planes overhead, and as parents, Joe and Marian marveled at and battled with growing children's stumblings, though it created more mysteries only to be answered by the adults they would become.

Jean entered junior high and, in two months, celebrated her twelfth birthday with Marian who introduced her to live theater by seeing *Ten Little Indians*, starring Zachary Scott in an off Broadway Theater. Theater in New York became a new must in Jean's expanding world.

At family gatherings, the men continued to enjoy the exchange of jokes. At one, Angie's Micah blew his cork when Joe told a sex-oriented joke in front of his girls and Jean. A quasi-argument took place.

Joe coldly and calmly responded, "Your daughters should leave, if that's what you want. My Jeannie is staying. I want her to learn from me, not from kids in the street. There's a big difference in a healthy respect for sex and the snickering of youngsters who misconstrue what they don't understand."

Not yet a teen, Jean remained while older, midteen cousins quickly left. In Marian's kitchen, no one could tell Joe what to do. Any other place Jean would have joined her cousins if the host objected.

Marian and Joe laughed at their brother-in-law's naiveté. The same daughters brought jokes to an aunt and uncle understanding a need to share laughter and have fun, as long as the joke was meant solely for fun.

A gamete of happenings in junior high brought Jean into a shakier focus while widening that strange aura that followed her.

Joe reached for a ringing bank phone.

"Hey, Joe, it's Vic Jacobs."

"Hi, Vic, how's your father doing?"

"Great. So's the store, but I just saw something I thought you'd enjoy hearing."

"Shoot."

"I was walking old Mrs. Hendricks out to the trolley stop when a car traveling like a bat out of hell passed the trolley trying to beat the light. One of the girls from junior high was crossing and reading and didn't see the idiot coming."

Joe's heart began to race.

"Your Jean came from nowhere with a tackle sending them both clear to the sidewalk. The lunatic didn't even slow down."

"Is Jean okay?" Joe's voice almost shook.

"She's fine, but the girl yelled at her for ripping her stockings. I think Jean was pissed. Have to go. If her school had a football team, they could sure use her."

"Thanks, Vic." Joe hung up glad they were safe but wishing Jean wouldn't take such chances. Still it felt good.

An annoyed Jean told the story for effect.

"God, I was mad at her."

"Mad at what? You didn't expect something in return, did you?" asked Joe.

"No. I don't even remember thinking."

"Good, because when you do something for somebody, do it because you want to, not for what you can get out of it."

"Yes, Dad, I know. It's lecture three thousand twenty-two. The rest goes there is a lot more satisfaction, etcetera?"

Said in jest, Joe's shaking finger was a trifling gesture while Marian laughed at them both but wondered why the price of independence included such physical efforts in Jean's growing.

Netty and Alberta—Jean's friends since kindergarten, now beautiful in their arrival at young womanhood, in opposite Italian and Irish ways—usually walked home with the still skinny, "unbloomed" Jean. Jean's friends were very eye-catching in fashionable dirndl skirts and folded down bobby socks. Both were very much the social leaders that young men, some still boys, sought ways to approach. It didn't matter to the girls that Jean didn't fit their mold, they were friends.

At this age, the male gender, in their rush of hormones, generally picked the prettiest felines to make fools of themselves over so Jean's walks home with Netty and Alberta were eye-openers to her too curious nature.

One afternoon in the rush of leaving school for the day, a group of young men challenged one of their own immature, Sammy Macklin, to get Netty and Alberta's attention. In clod fashion, he took Netty's books and threw them to the ground, and as the girls protested, he turned to Alberta doing the same.

Cheered on by cohorts and having drawn an audience of students, Sammy enjoyed being the center of attention and turned next to Jean who pulled her books tightly to her chest. As he approached, her anger exploded, and she threw her books to the sidewalk, stepped over them, grabbed Sammy by the shirt, and pushed.

The surprise forced his skinniness against the school's fence where she lifted and his feet came off the ground.

"Sammy Macklin, you're an idiot. How dare you put your hands on us. Now pick up the books, or I'll really get mad."

Sammy was tall as Jean and as skinny. Suddenly muddled by the turn of events, he quickly retrieved the girls' books while Jean scooped up hers. The three girls quickly left the scene laughing and enjoying the popularity of the moment.

By the time the tale reached Joe and Marian, it had happened differently and humorously for leaving Sammy hanging on the fence.

Joey's "Gee, Jean, that's no way to treat a boyfriend" was followed by giggles as he gave Joe a knowing look, and they all burst into laughter for knowing Sammy. Confronted by their jocularity, Jean buried a blush and enjoyed the padded illusion even when it continued the next day at school in spite of flushes of embarrassment.

Jean's view of the seventh grade was full of such embarrassments and a growing shyness that left her knowing herself better. *Darn, I'm not like Mom and Dad, they're not afraid of people, but I am. But I do like them just as much as they do.*

When puberty found Jean, she was the very last of her friends to change, and she was alone. At the sight of her menstrual blood, she panicked and ran to her friend Dora's mother thinking herself dying. This strong communication link to a working mother stifled a laugh and called Marian at the stocking store.

The mothers enjoyed the telling, and then Marian spoke to Jean and sensed by the laughter Jean was blushing, "Honey, you've completely forgotten our conversations at the ironing board, haven't you?" A jogged memory meshed with an "Oh, gee," and adulthood began with embarrassment at the sound of her friend Dora's scoff. Dora too had crossed over months ago.

One day soon, Carmella awoke, startled to hear three knocks at the door and rushed to open it. There was no one there.

The next day, she took her laundry to Marian, and while it washed, they shared a cup of tea. While Marian washed the teacups, Carmella said, "Mar, the weirdest thing happened last night."

"What?"

"Something woke me, and then I heard three knocks on the door. When I opened it, there was no one there."

Marian leaned into the sink, felt heavy with sadness, jumped as the phone rang, and weakly said, "Pop's dead."

Carmella went pale and reached for the phone knowing Rosary Hill was on the line.

Joe felt that engulfing emptiness again. Though grateful, Gene's suffering was over he kept dealing with why the human contradiction hurt so terribly.

Soothing Marian's agony submerged his deep hurt like a diving submarine going too deep. Not until after he had held her and she slept did he slip from bed and allow his feelings to surface. Quietly, without putting a light on, he settled in the armchair facing the window and the night sky to mourn Gene's leaving.

His tears flowed at love's calling. As a soft stinging sob left his throat, Marian's hand covered his heart.

Covering her hand with his own, he said, "Hon, I miss him too. He's the only father I've ever had."

The funeral lacked typical Italian influence. Pop wanted an Irish wake with no wailing. Boisterous goings on, a well-set table, and an abundant liquor closet greeted the mourners.

Joe told joke after joke in memory of the man whose shortcomings had made him very human. At one point, Joe told Marian, "Check on, Jean, she's upset."

Marian touched her arm and said, "Honey, what's wrong?"

"Nothing."

"Come on, what is it?" A mother's loving voice was a gentle convincer as she asked, "Is it the drinking? Do you feel it doesn't honor Grandpa?"

"No. I know what Grandpa wanted, but it scares me."

Marian slowed and looked around. "Is it your uncles?"

A surprised Jean realized Marian understood.

"Yes."

"I hate the way they change too. Aren't we lucky your dad doesn't drink?" Marian kissed her and said, "Come on, give us a hand with the food."

Jean's helping had reached the point where she was turning into a good cook. Her baking was already there. Joe loved Jean's rice cake as much as Marian's. While Marian never liked the rice cake, her hubby and children were in a competition to get the most of the large-as-the-oven cake, they could get their drooling on.

Pop's going had unhappy repercussions. Neglecting to leave a will shattered the family's unity. Angie's hatred of Gene was more evident than ever. The brothers and sisters wanting the family to continue allowed the estate to be divided unfairly, giving Angie the two family house in Hope of healing old wounds.

In the place where souls wait and the Archer watched, Gene spent time in the darkness viewing things as they really were, and then his father rushed to him knowing a son was to long alone with an unfair vow.

One day, Joe found Marian holding a treasured keepsake in her hand. She was remembering her childhood visits with Pop to a local speakeasy with Gene perfectly attired.

Joe watched and decided he had waited long enough.

"Mar, do you think I could have one of the diamonds from Pop's stickpin? I'd like to have it made into a ring. You know, to have something of his?" Joe waited certain of consent.

The stickpin, horseshoe shaped, still held six small, matched diamonds in a gold setting.

"Hon, I'm sorry. I can't. I don't want to break up the setting." His look broke her heart as she thought, *Oh, God, I know I'm doing the right thing, but he's hurting so much.*

Joe felt like someone had taken his last piece of rice cake, but knowing the family squabbles had been difficult and the remembrances too few, he accepted the reason but felt left out.

Marian understood the hurt she handed Joe, but it didn't alter her decision.

The holidays of 1946 mixed with the bother of puberty thrusting femininity on Jean.

The public change came quickly. Growing taller gave Jean's long neck a proper pedestal. Jean's shoulders broadened to match a bust rounding voluptuously. While swimming kept the bouncy duo high and firm, they came to the subtlest pointing that drew attention that heightened her discomfort.

Marian turned, saw Jean, and swung her arm around until it landed hard against Jean's shoulder.

"Yeow. Mom, what did I do?"

"Stand up straight, and be proud of what God gave you." Marian hid the fact her hand hurt. She couldn't help but notice how dense Jean's muscles had become. Over the next few months, her hand would hurt often. Fortunately, Jean became ramrod before Marian injured that hand.

As Marian prepared the Christmas Eve meal, she excitedly waited for Mary's family and the Christmas tree Joe and committee of two were searching out. Her personal excitement was becoming difficult to contain.

When everyone arrived, they trimmed the tree and shared a wonderful dinner. Then they gathered in the living room to sing Christmas carols from the little books of carols the bank published and furnished free to their customers every year.

After, a round of songs with some reverence but mostly fun-loving hamming by varied songsters was accompanied by tasty demitasse savored with anisette. Not to mention an array of desserts that Marian and Jean spared no energy to create.

Joe headed for the kitchen to get more, and as soon as he'd gone far enough not to hear, the excitement and cajoling began with hurried pleas.

"Marian, give it to him. Please." Mary had shared the secret with her family, and all were anxious to watch Joe's reaction.

Freddy nodded at Tommy who understood and kept an eye out for his uncle Joe's return. Fred wary of spoiling the surprise asked Tommy to keep watch.

"Oh, Mom, please," added Jean who knew but Joey's "Please, Mom" joined in the excitement without knowing the why. A growing, excitable, inquisitive eight-year-old couldn't keep a secret.

Tommy, the chickie, leaned back across the floor to where he could look into the kitchen and watched for his uncle Joe through the kitchen doorway. Freddy leaned over and said, "Aunt Marian, if you need a couple of minutes I'll keep him busy out there?"

Tommy said, "Unc's still at the refrigerator."

Joe would eat more than he'd bring back. It was an affectionate battle, but for Joe, it was fair game to cheat each holiday. Even Marian's oven size pan could not satisfy the family's woolee.

Joe's niece Anna joined in. "Aunt Marian, we want to watch Uncle Joe's face." Her husband recently home from Burma smiled as he took in everyone's pleasure so tortuously remembered while away.

"Come on, Aunt Marian. How can you wait until tomorrow?" Fred's persuasive tone triggered the hope building deep within Marian, so she swallowed her usual patience like a wild cat about to take sips from a too full pitcher of cream. She nodded at Fred, and flushed with excitement, she rushed to the hiding place gripped the gift nervously, raised it to her lips, and uttered a quick prayer. "Please, Dear God, let him understand." And rushed back just as Joe returned with a large three-tiered dish and said, "Okay, guys, lets open some gifts."

It was a quick sharing of small, inexpensive presents, and as the last one was opened, a wave of heads turned toward Marian. Wondering why, Joe looked up at her sitting on the arm of his chair. The present came out of her apron pocket. "Hon, this is my Christmas gift to you."

The small package bewildered Joe, while Marian's tender glance had his heart beating faster. So much so his hand was both hesitant and shaky reaching for it.

"Come on, Unc, open it," encouraged Freddy.

"Yeah, Unc, do it." Young Tom's now husky voice came from a growing giant.

"Hurry up, Dad," cajoled Jean.

"Come on, Dad, I don't know what it is," was Joey's young wail.

Joe couldn't think of anything it could be, so he tore off the wrappings.

It was a ring box. Swallowing hard, he looked up at Marian and saw a warmth he knew but never truly believed because it never penetrated his fear. Their eyes held until she said, "Open it, Joe, please."

Something was happening to him, and he felt his hand really shake as he saw the matched diamonds, all of them mounted in a heavy gold setting that loudly and unmistakably told his mind, "I'm yours."

She's given me all of them. Joe's throat eased loosing the constricting noose of disbelief, preventing him from speaking.

All he could do he did. His arms encircled Marian lovingly. The tears steeped in the truth of Christmas wet her housedress and cascaded from Joe to Marian to the rest of the family. Young Joey had a puzzled look on his face for not fully understanding.

Joe sat back again with Marian's face atop his head and stared at his ring.

"Oh, Joe, put it on." A weepy sister Mary wanted it on his hand pronto.

Joe quickly lifted his hand, saw the shaking, and then realized, *Oh, jeez, I have to go*. He quickly put the ring on his left hand, a commitment and promise both he and Marian understood. He placed his hand in hers and saw the love traced across the diamonds in the colored lights reflecting from the Christmas tree.

Joe suddenly stood, whipped Marian around, kissed her unabashed and long in a lover's enveloping embrace. Then, laughingly, he softly dropped her and ran for the john.

"Open the window, Unc, or you'll asphyxiate us all," admonished a laughing Freddy.

"Yeah, Dad, please." Joey didn't know why there were tears, but he liked the feeling it brought when everyone was happy.

Joe happily opened the window with his left hand, cherishing Pop and Marian's giving. From the throne, he looked into the star-laden sky with vision clearer than ever before. While relishing the wedding band he'd never had, he marveled at finding himself loved in the deepest recesses of his soul and rushed to rejoin the family and a chance to express it.

A long dark voyage anchored in homeport, and Joe, the child within, joined Joe, the man who had struggled so long to understand.

The horseshoe ring joined the pocket watch as part of every day, while the couple talked about adults who kept a child within like Pop and Joe and found understanding of their truth.

Sharing their complexities led to a simple wisdom that no one has all the answers and wisely took new battle positions for the next time they would challenge each other free of love's doubts.

Joe had said, "I only remember the ache of being left every time I lost someone and it all twisted itself into loving you."

This long awaited corner left the danger of fear twisted into jealousy behind them both. At one point, Joe laughed so hard the bed shook and he said, "I wonder what other trouble I'll get into now that you'll be able to flatten me for." In the next instant, he winced at Marian's quick right jab to his ribs and securely wrapped his arms around her knowing her his but never really and welcomed her head on his chest and thanked God for the corners they would share in the future.

From that place of the spirits, the night winds carried a whisper more like a smile. But the lovers had no need to hear because both slept deeply bathed in a love safely imbedded in their souls.

Whew

As Jackie Robinson redefined the fielding of major league baseball, Jean's new set of enticements redefined her figure. She nicknamed them "boom booms," and the obvious tension completely vanished. Now her athleticism needed the kind of hardware that would permit running with little flip'n flop.

"Mom, this brassiere is so expensive, can we afford it?"

"We can afford one. You'll wash it every night, and take good care of it until we can buy another. It's the only way you can continue playing your sports without hurting, not to mention avoiding some rough comments."

Jean nodded, kissed Marian, and said, "Thanks, Mom."

"You're welcome."

As they prepared to leave the store, Marian quickly said, "Jean, look?"

With a big smile, Jean said, "Let's."

In a few steps, they were at the millinery section, grinned and headed for the most outrageous of hats, put one on, turned to each other, and burst into laughter. It was a ritual they performed when shopping in a department store. While Marian loved the shopping, Jean hated it but looked forward to popping hats on and off. Marian was a beauty in the small chic chapeaus while Jean needed a man's tailored or big southern belle floppy to frame and highlight her changing features. But they put those on only after putting the most inappropriate on their heads and turned to one another to howl at their silliness. They laughed all the way to the car and delighted Joe with the story while Joey read his *Superman* comic book to ignore the necessity of being there even though he and Joe had snuck off to grab a potato knish.

Joe wanted to help Joey get involved in a sport to assure he'd not have free time to spend on more troublesome doing the came so naturally to growing boys in an environ.

"Hey, Joey, how about we look at sports equipment? We can't afford much, but I can get you started on something you'd like. So what'll it be—baseball, basketball, track?"

The disinterest was so mystifying that Joe went quiet for a moment. Young Joey realized Joe was waiting and finally said, "I don't know, Dad, I like to play ball but not everything like Jean."

"Joey, this hasn't anything to do with your sister. You need to find something you enjoy. Come on, I'll help you get started. I'm sure you'll be as good, if not better than your sister at any sport."

"Nah, Dad, I don't want to be on a team."

"Okay, but I want you to find something you enjoy doing and stick with it." Joe reached out and touched Joey hoping to reassure him he meant what he said.

"Okay." The one word response lacked a convincing chord, and Joe wondered what he was doing wrong that he couldn't interest his son in a sport. As usual, he was beginning to worry about it.

As the growing continued, Joe's control was tested more than once by Jean's story telling personality used so easily in parlaying the events of her day. At dinner, they each took unrehearsed turns, but somehow, Jean's always took the longest.

One night, she had Joe's temper flaring and Joey's eyes popping. The telling of three bruisers trying to feel up a daughter by backing her into a wall at school made Joe move to the edge of his seat, but he remained calm of feature because he'd come to realize she would clam up, if his temper let fly, so he listened and thumped his foot to the increase of his heart beat as she continued.

"I waited, and when I pushed off the wall, it took them by surprise, and I was out of their circle and running."

Marian was considering mayhem on them but smiled as Joe said, "Would you like me to go to school and see that doesn't happen again?"

"Thanks, Dad, but Netty told Eddie what happened. Seems there was a welcoming committee when the idiots got to the gym."

Joe's thumping heart slowed, and his harshest thoughts washed away for knowing male friends carried her banner, but he was curious. "Were you scared?"

"Scared? I guess, maybe. I know I was furious, and my temper took over." Pausing, she said, "Maybe it's silly, but my temper scares me."

Joe's memory turned cold for remembering and said, "That I understand." *It better not be like mine.* The thought made him miss the quick look both kids gave him. Joey's look went to his sister, and he wished he'd been there. *I'd have gotten at least one of them real good.*

The emergence of Jean's somewhat mysterious and driving personality touched both father and son.

Young Joey took it all in wondering what the big deal was, but without truly understanding, he always wanted to punch guys when they made a remark about her changing body. Even though he found his sister's awakening interesting and somewhat bothering, he enjoyed teasing Jean about it, about anything. The five years between them made a big difference.

Joe later told Marian, "That part of her that takes her into dangerous territory has both a strange appeal to me, yet I dread it too. I'm proud of her, but cripes now, I have two brave women to worry about."

"I don't think we have to worry too much. That thing that appeals to you is her growing up because she's learning to take good care of herself and she proved it today. But I'm not sure our hearts and minds will survive what she does. She calls them adventures, but she does tell us about them. That's a plus while our son is telling us less and less while his nose continues to spread and give him away."

"Yeah, it kind of surprises me that with Jean there isn't a hopeful boyfriend following her around the way they follow Alberta and Netty. While with Joey, all we have to do is watch that nose and never let him know how he gives himself away."

"Oh, you just like to worry about Jean the way you do all your girls, but I've thought about it too. I'm grateful she doesn't have a beau." She was chuckling.

"Oh, I'm grateful too." But he was simultaneously shaking his finger at her knowing humor because his fatherly tone had given away that his feelings were a lot stronger. "Now if we can only convince our son that his teasing has to stop. He thrives on it, and no matter what we say, he doesn't grasp it."

Jean continued her hormonal bloom by complaining daily, the whining beginning at breakfast.

"Mom, I have nothing to wear. Nothing fits. Look at me. All my blouses have gaposis."

Both Joe and Joey burst out laughing, but Marian shushed them.

After sticking a tongue at them, Jean whimpered, "I don't fit into anyone's clothes anymore."

Now the tallest of the girl cousins, Marian said, "No more hand-me-downs for you. Joe, we have to pick up some clothes for—"

"My zoftic daughter." Joe quickly gave a mouthy son a cautioning look.

Joey shoved Rice Krispies into that growing orifice, and the milk ran down his pulsing, snickering chin. It was the best he could muster.

Marian said, "Joe, let's go to Alexander's in Fordham right after work."

Joe nodded and added, "Jeannie, you're beginning a beautiful figure. Please, enjoy it."

The word *beautiful* chimed in her growing mind, but she didn't let Joe know because she really didn't believe it.

Gee, that sounded so nice, but Dad's so prejudiced.

She couldn't resist looking in a mirror and said "Nah" to her general looks and "Ummm" to the way she was developing. Certain very sexy movie stars came to mind. *Esther Williams, and that new star, Sophia Loren, the Italian.* Part of her mind liked that, but another part turned away so quickly she never noticed it.

Before the end of her first pubescent year, she stood at five foot eight inches tall, a half inch taller the Joe, and the tallest of her friends. For 1949, that was taller than most, and that bothered her so she said so.

Joe chuckled. "Honey, most guys get tall later than girls. Besides, a man's height means little and even less in bed. Just pick a good guy."

Marian helped with, "Jean, Grandma Tess, my mother, was much taller than Grandpa."

Jean was pleasantly surprised, and she began to turn the corner to comfortable with what she had become though who she was, was a mystery she chose not to pursue while public acceptance of her apparent assets and genuine confidence took hold. It began a relaxing with new people and a new seeking of people in her every day. As her socializing began, it perplexed Joe's protective instincts for not knowing what was enough. His respect for Marian gave her an edge in all decisions about Jean. Joe began to recognize he'd just have to sweat it out like all the other fathers.

Both wanted Jean to lead rather than follow, but they felt it too soon to expect complete adult behavior. Still they pushed her in that direction by involving her in appropriate decision making and gave young Joey the same privilege.

Again and again, they cautioned Joey about teasing in general. They were bothered by whatever it was that prevented his taking the warning, and it continued as time passed taking him closer and closer to young manhood and the age that impressing and pleasing young ladies would become a young man's whole world.

A chowhound, Joey continued to remain skinny and not very tall, growing just as his uncle Sal had and Marian had to remind him of how tall Sal was when Joey complained about being the little guy.

Time was moving more quickly. Weekends came to mean, "Where could we go?" Sundays went quickest from mass to the bakery, get the newspapers, and go somewhere or share a day with a family gathering.

On one trip to the bakery, a thoughtless demand for buns from the kids brought, "Is it all right if your mother and I get a cruller for ourselves?" With a shaking head, he took Marian by the waist to cross the street.

Marian said, "I could buy you a sugar bun?" The deliberate tease reminded him they're only kids.

"I'll settle for the buns I have." He dropped his fingers and tapped out the message. Neither could see their daughter following the action with an appreciative smile just as she did when they kissed hello or goodbye with their coming and going. Young Joey enjoyed it too and began to build on the security offered without applying its true value to future understanding.

As time passed, locked in Jean's development, it began to lead to an amusing wide-eyed fascination in Joey with snickering that imposed on parents the speaking about care and feeding of females you love and its physical expression.

Joe and Marian once again stepped into the breach too many parents of their generation chose to avoid in discussion's loaded with emotional stressing.

They enjoyed his eye-popping-trying-to-look-worldly expression as they explained sex and a male's part in the act of conception and how he had to protect himself and, yes, the girl too. Then they explained the woman's part in it. Menstruation turned his look into something less appealing. The sound "yuk" made it obvious he appreciated being a boy and its edge over the ladies.

His mind was turning corners faster than he could completely comprehend. True to his gender, he thought, *Wow, have I got a lot to tell the guys?* It quickly disappeared when Joe put it on the line.

"Joey, if you are careless enough to get a girl pregnant and it can happen to anyone, we are not going to tell you, you have to marry the girl unless you truly love her the way your Mom and I love each other and, more importantly, only if she loves you too. A bad marriage will serve no one well."

Marian added, "Instead, you will accept responsibility for the child and support the child because you are the father. That means whatever you do to make a living must be shared with that child. Just the way we take care of you and your sister. Even if you later have a family you want, this will still be true."

Joe came back in with, "Joey, do you understand that a mistake like that isn't easy, but that this is fair?"

Joey's "Yeah" to the serious moment, left both parents uncomfortable, thinking, *Maybe we've hit him with too much too soon.*

Joe added, "Look, Joey, this is important to being a man, so your best bet is to control yourself and protect yourself when you have sex."

All this yak. While he answered, "It's okay, Dad, I understand."

Their approach lacked Joey's flair for fun but they both felt Joey would grow to be a good man, and closed the discussion.

Time passed and Joey reached an age ready for the more personal subjects of prevention and frustration, so Joe and his son shared feelings and problems on a man-to-man level. It went well, but Joey never shared his deeper values or his growing needs because outside influences and misunderstandings limiting his reaching to a parent and preferred sharing with good buddies. Except, his thorough enjoyment when bringing home a joke he could only share with dad.

When Joey decided he'd make sure he'd never get a girl pregnant, he was definitely in the Prezzemoli ballpark but perhaps on the wrong base. No one could be sure, he even confused himself.

Marian had her talk with him after Joe to share a woman's point of view and closed with, "Joey, it's okay to tease your sister, but going from childhood to womanhood is something you can't understand. At least not until you've made the change from boy to man. Even then, it's so different. Just go easy on her, you might need a friend, and you two should always be there to help each other because you are brother and sister."

As time passed, the sibling lesson took, particularly on serious levels, but seemed an insurmountable void in day-to-day dealings as brother and sister.

Time seemed to have no impact on Joey's rash teasing, and the parents feared he was missing much intended for a male to see and feel, especially in an enlightened generation. But right now, he had plenty of time to grow, and the humor in a time of a sister's body changes made it hard for the Prezzemoli guys to behave.

Once during a parental hot exchange, Jean wanted to test her own mettle and took sides with Marian, only to find herself out on a limb, with both parents rudely powering the saw that cut the limb off behind her making her fall to a bruising and very remembered bump.

Without missing a word, Marian turned to her and said, "Don't you ever get into an argument between me and your father!"

Joe added, "You heard your mom, Jean, never."

She ran for cover into her room while they continued the argument in perfect strokes.

Joey waited until she got comfortable on her bed next to him to offer a rather adult comment for his age.

"That was dumb, sis." Joey couldn't take his eyes off her.

A mortified Jean grabbed a book while her brother who had disappeared into their room the minute the argument began enjoyed her dilemma, feeling very smart for always avoiding such situations and things that he found hurtful. Success at such efforts felt like a skulking fox avoiding the hunters, and he enjoyed being the winner and the safe distance it offered him lofted him above trying's serious depths.

When Jean was declared junior high's athlete of the year, Joe was proudest of her, thinking that she wasn't that good.

"Gee, Dad, I think Jessie should have gotten it. Do you think I got it because Jessie is colored?"

"Honey, I'm glad you're aware of the price Jesse might pay for being colored, but I know Mrs. Delancy, she wouldn't do that. She's young but an excellent teacher whose thinking wouldn't prejudice her that way."

Jean turned to Marian for an opinion and heard, "If you have doubts, find out." Marian continued to push Jean to open doors to go through.

Jean did. Embarrassed by her teacher's short and sweet answer, "No, you're just a better athlete," and asking Jessie how she felt about it brought a friend's laughter, squelching Jean's question into a blush.

"Jeez, Jean, I can't keep up with you anymore. I agree with Mrs. Delancy. You're good, and you're the only one who breaks up fights—I don't. You didn't even rat on the new gal who took the ball away from Dee and knocked her down. The gal was colored like me, but I didn't mix in even when you did. You put her in her place because she was a bully, not because she was of color. I suppose I should have, but I didn't. You earned the award."

Jean smirked to say, "Gee, I thought being an athlete was playing sports and you hold up one of my dumber moves as an athletic accomplishment."

Jessie looked down her nose and said, "What are friends for?"

On a parents' day off, Jean and Joey would barge into the house with friends in tow as though it was a revolving door, and Jean would talk at Marian without taking a breath in a voice filling the room as though she was at a game.

"Jean, I'm right here, you don't have to yell." The apology came quickly but seemed to change nothing.

Meanwhile, seeing Joey and his cohorts disappear into the bedroom, Marian took some fresh cookies to them to assure herself no trouble was brewing.

When Joe was there, he was usually a silent watcher who occasionally would leave what he was doing to take a quick tour.

Jean's growing strength caused her to break a friend's hand during an aggressive volleyball game, and she was so upset she wanted to quit playing sports. That earned her lecture four thousand and twenty-one.

By now, Joe had decided a young woman was a heck of a lot more complex than changing from boy to man, so he attended another game concerned her fear would stifle her game playing.

He wasn't at a basketball game more than a few minutes when it was obvious Jean had made a change in her playing style.

She's switched from an aggressive offense to a controlling defense, and she's keying the team. Whew, she's really good, that was a perfect blind. It gave Jessie time for a clean two pointer. He watched her move down the court while giving signals. *My God, she's actually graceful out there, but at home, she can't walk through a room without bumping into a doorframe. I have to tell Marian about this.* He laughed out loud when Jean deftly maneuvered an opponent into fouling her.

Jean heard his familiar laugh, called time, and ran over to kiss him while the other girls called out, "Hi, Mr. P."

He congratulated her on that last move and headed back to work a little prouder than before, still wondering why he couldn't interest Joey in the any sport only to finally realize having a sister this good might be part of it.

I'm going to have to help him find something else he's good at. But what?

Joe didn't attend any more of her games.

One Sunday, Jean ran into the kitchen, skate box in hand, and bubbled through. "Mom, is it okay if I go skating with Dora and Janet?"

"It's all right with me if it's all right with your father."

Joe was reading and answered with, "It's all right with me if it's all right with your mother."

She trudged back to the kitchen.

"Mom, Dad said it's okay if you say it's all right?"

Marian blistered. "I said it's all right if it's all right with your father."

Jean winced and tried again.

"Dad?" He wasn't listening.

She puzzled out what to do, and remembering her boo-boo the last time they argued, she plopped on the floor right over the doorjamb between the two rooms, crossed her legs, and cracked the sound barrier.

"Will someone please tell me if I can go skating?"

Both parents came to the doorway. In moments, Jean was gone, and Marian and Joe stood there looking at each other not knowing whether to quarrel or laugh.

An enjoyable sensation nudged at Joe like the feeling that always sent him looking for Marian when a band played the first dance at an affair, only Joe immediately found himself in an exhaustive tug-of-war.

"Jean, relax. The man leads. You can't do your own thing."

"I'm trying. Please, don't yell at me."

Her eyes filled with tears, and he remembered screaming doesn't help.

One weekend, Freddy was visiting, and Joe tried again.

"Hey, Unc, let me have a try."

Fred's love of dance often took him to Roseland to amble in Terpsichore, and his polished moves drew Jean's athletic grace to the feminine side she was seeking.

Joe was miffed because Freddy was the first man Jean recognized as treating her like a lady. Wondering why a father's efforts didn't count, he found himself again glad she had no real beaus.

Joe hated admitting it to Marian, but he did.

"Honey, get used to it. I have the feeling many a guy is going to enjoy taking her out on the dance floor."

"God, help me." His laughter quickly died when he considered maybe, she doesn't enjoy dancing with him and thought, *Because she's still afraid of me?* That hurt.

Joey worried Marian because she longed for him to be more than being a good man. That she expected. She wanted him to grab at the chances she and Joe never had.

His disinterest in school had Marian checking his work daily at the kitchen table making him redo what she couldn't read. Such reluctance in a country where he could be anything he wanted drove Marian crazy. The current benign education system offered no anchor to his drifting, growing mind, and his settling for permissive passing grades and having fun made her try harder. Over time, even his handwriting had deteriorated. His games were those where laughter and fun reigned while his preferences in friends were taking him further and further from sports efforts. Still he finally tried track and did well. As his friends changed, so did his wonderings about girls.

Unexpectedly, a few weeks later, Joey stood at the side of the quarter-mile track cheering on his peers, but he wasn't having any fun. He liked the coach and joined to please him, but coach was all business, and he wanted more fun from what he spent time doing. Even winning didn't seem to be enough. The running and training were boring, so he made a decision.

To heck with this, I don't want to do this anymore.

Dropping the sport was fine, but the hanging out that was filling the same space was a caution his parents had to address. For Joey it was a dark shadow over his view of himself. One he doggedly meant to keep for the fun while its limitations had Marian and Joe struggling to help him.

The fifties geographically separated the family because many had bought homes around and outside of Yonkers, but Ma Bell knotted the family ties through the frequent use of a now private line, inspiring many wide ranging events, and encouraged a family picnic, annually.

Joe and other male family joined forces in making the picnics grow in pleasure and size. It was a guy thing, and they planned it all and did all the work. The guys had to finally rent a park to handle the attendance. A family picnic was attended by at least two hundred which included relatives to the fourth level from Connecticut, Long Island, New Jersey and Westchester points north.

It was a day the ladies treasured for just being there and enjoying while the guys did all the work. The parks were usually alongside the Hudson River with tree lined groomed fields for sports.

On a typical picnic day, Joe left Marian the car keys and then grabbed a ride with a brother-in-law.

The food was typical Italian/American picnic fare enhanced by such palate pleasing items as clams on the half shell, peppers, sausage, and onions on fresh Italian bread or rolls, corn on the cob, crabs, even macaroni with muscles, when the mood to really cook hit the guys who were as talented as many of their wives. The early birds included Joe and the kids who showed up with the fixings for coffee, rolls, and buns of all types. They usually picked them up at a large bakery in Mt. Vernon before any other bakeries were open for business. Over the years, the menu seemed to keep growing with more cars arriving even for the early shift.

All they had to do was get on line. No profits were made. The price was set at cost, but many a dollar was lost as games of chance sprang up in good fun wherever a table was available.

Even going to the San Gennaro Feast in the Bronx could not surpass the taste awakeners. The fathers made sure the day was full of activities—races, prizes, softball and games adult versus kid or partnered games.

The day came when Jean no longer raced because it belonged to the younger set while Joey, being one, continued to collect winnings and counted his horde lighting up with his good fortune and then sought his multitude of cousins for he was now one of the older boys and fooling around was the best thing on his menu.

At one such picnic, the males both Manfredi and Prezzemoli decided on a contest with their backs to female accompaniment.

Millie said, "Oh, God, don't tell me they're—"

"They certainly are," injected Marian.

Angie, Margaret, and Mary joined them in chortling as their mates and sons went about the adult game.

"Mine's longer than yours," said one.

"Hell, it is not," answered another.

Joe said, "Wait a minute, guys, don't count your chicks. We haven't measured Freddy's or mine yet. Right, Fred?"

"Right, Unc."

"Wait until you measure my brother's." Tommy, now taller than all his cousins, spoke proudly with Ricky, and Joey squeezed in beside him.

Freddy stepped forward with a wink for his brother and uncle. In moments the ladies heard, "Holy smoke, Jesus, we didn't stand a chance. Where'd you get that snozzola, kid? Jimmy Durante would be proud."

Home

In 1948, Joe discussed the news nightly because Americans were at risk flying the Berlin Blockade, their air cargo fuselage bellies licking the rooftops of Berlin homes. A high school student in the house with in world affairs enlivened the dialogue and equally caught the admiration of a son who watched it without a word.

Marian said, "If I were sitting in the plane, I could reach down and touch a roof."

Joe said, "My God, it's about as dangerous as it can get, but through some miracle, no one's been hurt."

Jean added her two cents, "As much as the idea of flying excites me, I'd never be able to do anything like that." She caught Joe's look and said, "I know, Dad, you don't want to fly ever."

Joe gave her a smile and thought, *But you'd want to try, I know you would*, and turned to watch the next plane make its run.

Joey was too enthralled by the real life heroes to tear his imagination away for discussion. His love of the macho male movie and TV versions was impacting his view of life but without the violent nature of the bad guys. At this age, he learned to avoid confrontation and knew how to avoid a lecture.

Joey was now a ball buster who had already developed the art of teasing to a point that many of his targets wanted to throttle him. By now Jean had hardened to Joey's teases. Both being stubborn they succeeded in placing an unrecognized wall between each other.

Good buddies were important to him and girls became a focal point, initially very hush-hush but oh how he liked that direction and poured his youthful energies into making girls laugh with humor and mischief. Hey, if he could make people laugh, they'd really like him.

With TV showing them what was happening, the caring millions across the United States watching the news multiplied the Prezzemoli concerns for the safety of those nesting in homes below the flying warehouses to bring them their needs for survival while understanding the growing danger to Americans at home. The world was getting smaller and smaller because new military weapons could reach almost anywhere and anyone.

Yet, courage of these airmen showed it a time of wisdom and kindness not always given at the end of a war to the enemy. The Russian blockade of Berlin, a human crisis, flourished hope.

Joey's watcher between his charges took time to ask the archer. "Joey's mind refuses life's options. I fear there will be few times I can help him. Still it offers a kind of strength that could go either way."

"You have learned much, but all have the capacity to go either way, so the decisions must be theirs. Growing's impact leaves all kinds of reasons to go in many directions. You watch well, he has time, yet we are able to do so little."

Jean at fourteen had reached a time when a girl fills with fantasy and dreams. There was a book she started, poetry written for those she cared about and for herself—a fantasy lover. A Marine called Bob, in search of answers of her future. While her hopes to fly were heightened by the air machines of the Berlin Blockade they remained a dream, as growing turned her mind to real world possibilities.

At fourteen Joe and Marian decided she wasn't to young for adult decisions, and the rushing world made it necessary if Jean and the family were going to build some of life's castles for themselves.

Jean in her private mind was ready to meet the real world. At least the part she was aware existed.

Parental directing required a family meeting.

Marian wanted to be sure they were ready.

"Joe, I know we've discussed this before, but let's be sure."

"It's all right, Mar, I'll help with anything she wants to do." He read the question mark in her eyes and added, "Even if it's something I hate."

"I'm sorry, hon, I know how you worry, but you and I didn't have the opportunities our kids have. I want them to have every chance at what they want."

"You know I agree with that, so relax and let's get it done."

Marian raised her voice slightly. "Jean, please come into the kitchen. Your dad and I want to talk to you."

Marian led off with, "What would you like to do to earn a living, Jean?"

She was quick to answer, "I'd like to be a gym teacher."

"Honey, that means college." Marian's voice was heavy with limitations.

"I know."

"That means money we don't have," added Joe.

"I know that too."

Joe continued with, "It means you'll have to work your way through school, and that's not easy, and it can take a long time. Look at me, I'm still at it."

Jean smiled and said, "Maybe I can go to work now. I can put my money away, and then maybe I won't have to work at school."

Marian and Joe shared a look. "There aren't too many jobs that pay well at fourteen," reminded Marian.

"Mom, I don't look fourteen. I have friends who look older like me and they're in better jobs. Why can't I be?"

This pair of parents had to think about this hard, so they put off the discussion for a few days.

Young Joey heard these conversations and knew his turn would come and drifted away to avoid any lecture applying to him.

"My God, Mar, she looks at least eighteen, and as much as it scares me, she's right. She could probably work anywhere."

"I know, and worse, I think she can? Either way, don't you play father protector. She needs room to grow and spread her wings."

"Marian, some guy could—"

"Joe—" The tone of Marian's voice reached for any threatening remnants within him.

Joe answered his watchful woman with a warm smile. "If any guy touches her, she'll split his head open or sic her mother on him."

"Then I'll cripple him. Though I really think she can take care of herself. She has this capacity for talking herself out of the worst messes. I worry more about those unending energies she puts into doing new things. They always take her to an adventure. Something she seems to be seeking more and more and one side of that coin is always dangerous."

Joe could only nod, so Marian skipped that to get to a direction-changing question. "Hon, can you find a good-paying job for her? Maybe with a friend who would watch out for her?"

Joe's lips crooked under his marvelous nose.

"I think so. Yes, I can make that happen, but we better not get ahead of ourselves. Let's get all the information we need as to what's involved in her getting into college."

"She's going to the counselor this week, and so we'll have a better idea afterward. Obviously, she's checking it all out on her own. After she talks to the counselor, she'll need to discuss extra studies with her teachers."

"That's as good a way as any. Hon, all we can do is help her see the hard side of what has to be done."

The counselor visit brought another problem; there were no jobs for new gym teachers. The older teachers were going to be around for a long time, and the baby-booming generation was nowhere near school age to change that need. Jean decided on a general education degree, and she alone could deal with not being prepared for college by her current courses. She decided to take extra math courses to qualify and came home prepared with a list, but it still left her sorely unprepared without the academic curriculum of a preparatory high school. Well liked, her teachers did what they could whenever she approached them. They even allowed her to take charge of classes when possible.

Marian and Joe could not help but notice. "She doesn't ask for much help, Mar."

"I know, and that bothers me too, but she has confidence in being able to do it, and her grades indicate she can. I don't want to discourage her, do you?"

"No. She could fail, but no sense belaboring the point. I don't want to discourage her either." His voice carried the question to her mind, and Marian nodded her agreement. "There's no way for parents to be sure, is there?"

"Afraid not, hon, but it's with us every day."

Marian looked at him realizing more strongly than ever that his caring was a constant danger to Joe's well-being just as it had been during the war, and he could not change that part of himself.

Other matters hit home as Jean made her way into high school's social structure. A commercial high school lacked female sport teams.

"Cheez, Louise, Mom, it's no fun. I miss basketball. I have to run just to feel good, and it is so boring."

Joe came to the rescue. "Honey, you could just go out and run, or you, Ellie, and Jessie can organize a team and play at the Y taking on all comers. That way, you'll play regularly."

The girls took the suggestion and found the caliber of players worth it, but Jean also ran more to keep fit but found herself very disturbed by the masculine very deliberate raw comments in time when a woman almost never ran the streets, but learned to ignore them. As time passed she taught herself to enjoy the running more but hated the comments it drew.

Joe didn't see the girls' games but delighted in his dueling denizens playing one on one. Joey was growing, and Jean was beginning to take some lumps because she didn't want to hurt a still small brother. Joey showed all the signs of being good, but he lacked real interest while beating his sister was high on his priority list.

Joe found Jean a job at an ice-cream chain store where one of his customers was the Franchise Manager. Jean worked after school until eleven evenings and daytime hours on weekends. The adult wage brought a fuller bloom of confidence that led her to do more and more and doing it well.

The job also fostered a deepening love for all the ice cream she could eat. Ice cream and running soon became synonymous for she was truly aware of her physical enticements and meant to keep them.

The store closed during three winter months allowing her to catch up socially and athletically, but little time for sports meant early morning runs before school. It kept her hustle hastening, but she still found it hard to handle the crass adult remarks guys found easy to make, only now she felt anger not embarrassment. Oh, the things she concocted to say but wisely did not, because it was accompanied by a very uncomfortable feeling that made her skin go taut. When it began to feel like something other than anger, it was so low key she lost it in her hectic schedule and didn't seek out its answer.

As parents, Marian and Joe weren't satisfied with just having her work with someone Joe trusted. Joe played chauffeur, and both parents called her daily. Jean's growing independence didn't rasp at the calls, she enjoyed the attention. Joe, as chauffer delivered Marian's hot meals to an eager and hungry daughter but rushed back to have dinner with his number one lady.

Jean usually opened up and worked alone on weekend mornings, without problems until the day truck after truck pulled to the curb on the almost endless Central Park Avenue. She watched unbelievingly as soldiers poured out and rushed the window. All Jean saw were heads and more heads bespeaking all at once.

Panic harassed her, so she grabbed five cones and began filling what she thought were right orders. When they crushed in her hand, she turned off the spigot, froze for a moment, then turned back to the counter. Then she looked for and found some rank and yelled, "Sergeant, get them into a line of threes or I go on strike."

"Yes, ma'am? You heard the lady. Line up, dogfaces, in threes."

Hey, I'm no ma'am. "Thank you, Sergeant." She was beginning to enjoy herself.

That night, she told of the fun and nonsense of uniforms waiting for three hundred licks while Marian and Joe mouthed their own gooey sundaes while waiting for her to finish for the day. She talked as she flavored two, hip high, full milk cans for the next day.

With that done and the cans capped, Jean opened the large walk-in refrigerator door and stepped between the cans. She grabbed the handles and hoisted both fully off the ground. Four steps later at the refrigerator door she simultaneously lifted them, bypassed the entry step by turning sideways and lifted one can at a time through the entryway without taking her grip off the other.

Cold ice cream dripped off a spoon onto Marian's hand, freeing her of being startled by Jean's strength. *Just how strong is she?* About to say something, she heard Joe's quiet, "Wow! Whatever happened to our ninety-pound weakling."

Happy, she was finished Jean missed their reaction.

It reminded them both of Jean coming home excited that she'd set a high school fitness record in required PFI tests. She ended the teasing with, "Dad, just remember I'm a tomboy because you threw me into a swimming pool."

"You're not a tomboy, you're an athlete."

"Thanks, but Mom and I know better. You know, for all this strength, I still can't climb that darn gym rope hand over hand. It's weird."

Marian didn't hear the last part. The touch of regret in Jean's voice had revealed a daughter's deepening concern for femininity. Marian also remembered she hadn't thought about that but did now and decided to say no more about voice and noise except when absolutely necessary. It was Jean's problem to solve.

High school had some humorous shortcomings.

Jean's typing teacher looked over her shoulder at her typing exercise paper as her fingers snapped back and forth up and down. The teacher softly said, "You certainly don't take after your father."

"No, Mrs. Morrissey, I don't. I'll never get close to his 117 words a minute. My sixty words a minute is about my best level. I'm sorry." Mrs. Morrissey laughed, tapped her on the shoulder, and moved on to the next student.

Jean slid down in her seat, as Ellie poked her and said, almost dumbfounded, "117 words a minute?"

"Yeah, 117 and he lost the state championship by one word a minute."

One awful night, a troubled veteran tried to break down the door of their project apartment and screamed threats at the huddling Prezzemoli tree. He thought he was upstairs at his apartment door.

Joe was working late and arrived home to find everyone shaking. The sounds of a beating above them triggered a rage he hadn't felt in years, but the child no longer ruled the man. The frightened faces of his family stepping between him, and the door brought him a small grin as he put and end to any danger that way by heading for the phone and calling the police.

The decision to move came easily, but when they looked at houses, their limited funds proved exasperating and discouraging.

After talking to a reliable customer, a builder, Joe rushed home with a house offer. Though the house was a small box, cape style, they wanted it. It was near the branch where Joe and Jean worked, while Marian and the kids would need transportation to get to cross town to Getty Square and school.

As purse keeper, Marian knew they lacked the money to do it. The small cape at $12,500 required $3,000 down. They only had a thousand to put down.

Joe knew it could be done by borrowing from friends but hesitated, so he discussed it with Marian.

Marian prodded, "Hon, we'll pay them back. The worst that can happen is losing the house, but we'll have tried." Her face alight with enthusiasm made Joe's confidence soar.

Joe carefully chose friends to ask. A boyhood friend, hearing the problem, gave Joe $1,000 interest free, saying only, "Pay it back when you can."

Flabbergasted, Joe grabbed him.

Another gave him a thousand interest free with ten years to pay. Again, he gave a friend a hug and rushed to the store to pick up Marian and happily put the checks in her hand.

Excited breathing announced what she held, but she had to see them to believe.

"Oh, Joe!"

"Hon, both Phil and Vic gave us the money, interest free. No due date on Phil's and ten years on Vic's." Near tears, they slipped into a strong hug.

They wished Jean and Joey didn't have to share a room at fifteen and ten so it was time for a family conference.

"Look, you two, we can do this, but it means doing without things you want." Joe hesitated wondering what reactions they would get.

Marian gave specifics. "There will be no sweet sixteen birthday party for you, Jean, and there will be next to nothing for school. Joey, you get no bike and other gifts this year."

Joey blurted out, "The house can be my Christmas gift." Excited, he turned to listen to his sister.

"I don't want a party. I want us out of here, and I already have the $600 I need."

Marian and Joe exchanged a glance, and Marian said, "One more thing. You will still have to share a room. We just can't afford another room." Marian wasn't apologetic, just honest.

Joey and Jean looked at each other. Separate rooms hadn't occurred to them.

"If Jean had her own room, whose gonna pick on me?"

Jean grabbed for him, but he was too wiry.

"Heck, Mom, it doesn't matter. I'll be off to school and then I'll trade in a couple of years, and then I trade him for seven other roommates."

Marian nodded at Joe.

"Okay, people, the Prezzemoli family is buying a house." The cheers shook the project.

Joe said, "Marian, I want the house in your name. I don't want you losing our home because inheritance taxes would take too much if I die."

Joe crossed to the sink to catch her reaction as she said, "Hon, I only asked it be in both our names."

"Look, I don't want you going through what Mom went through with us. It's a horror."

"Joe, I expect us to be around to a ripe old age. In a few years, the kids will be gone, and it'll be time for our dreams."

"That's a date, but it still goes in your name."

Her wet hand resting on his shirtfront played with a button as she said, "Thank you."

"Oh, lady, you know you don't get off that easy. I'll claim my reward later."

"No problem, Mr. Prezzemoli, no problem at all." Her hand moved up to his face.

The Prezzemoli family was strewn around the open wooden frame of the house soon to be theirs. Marian pictured a house full of people and formed new hopes. "We could turn the dormered attic into a room for one of the kids. The builder said there'd be a floor up there, and then we can enlarge the kitchen, but first, we repay our friends."

Joe's meandering found a place for his favorite chair and a section of the yard for a garden with tomato plants. He did a 360. *Great, there's plenty of room for family picnics, Mary and the boys will love it here.* It was on a corner city plot one hundred by fifty, but its cornered layout shattered the boxed in feeling of the homes lining Edgewood Avenue more in keeping with their people liking. Out back was a young maple tree soon to honor them with the comfort of shade during the hottest weather. Joe loved the tree so much, he promised to plant another outside the kitchen next to the road to gather shade for the kitchen and did.

The design of the house had one unexpected problem that challenged their safety. A box dropping from the level of the first floor, right in the middle of the house, furnished hot air heat. Joe, the first one down the cellar stairs, crashed into the box and voiced appropriate slurs, so Jean ducked but forgot the first day they moved in and yelled, "Sugar, plums, and apricots too."

Since "Shit" was not allowed, it was a phrase Marian and Joe smiled at often. Marian at five foot two would always passed under the box, but Joey had to wait a couple of years before he would make his ouch mark on the box.

In a few short months, they were in and faced an immediate problem. One neighbor proved a user and a fence had to be put up to end his trucks rutting their backyard. He had used the undeveloped plots to park his trucks overnight. They kept the fence's expense at a minimum, and in months, the neighbors were gone, apparently forewarned since Joe left no doubts in the neighbor's mind in neighborly confrontation.

The situation was more humorous than painful since the other neighbors were happy to see them leave while making the arrival of the Prezzemoli clan an occasion much enjoyed.

The Brunos, to the back of them—had five mostly adult children, two younger still at home, Louis and Mattie, a daughter in a convent, and the other boys in houses on the same street with their families—came to welcome them. They were soon joined by the Scatoways with three youngsters in the same age range as their own. The Lorraine and Ed Scatoway shared a two family home with her parents, the Marishs. Their lovely home facing Marian's kitchen was built by her contractor Father Ned Marish.

The Marrishs had a son Cliff, the same age as Jean, who quickly became a friend who let her fill the rumble seat of his car when she needed a ride to school. Joe knew these neighbors as customers at the bank and appreciated them as fun-loving people. He was told that one of the wives was insatiably curious about neighborhood people but it was not a problem. She took the teasing with a smile.

Marian and Joe were delighted with the reception and, without hesitation, accepted the new friends and their penchant for the arts of joke and prank.

Joe challenged their first efforts by responding to Ned Marrish's joke about a wop with, "Ned, do you know why the Polock bought half a toilet?"

"No, why?"

"Because his half-assed brother was coming to visit."

Marrish came right back with another joke making an Italian the fall guy, then Scatoway joined in with another. Both had Joe's raucous laugh reaching across the street to Marian's ears as she rushed to fix coffee and pull out a homemade cake to take to the yard while talking to other wives who had sent their young to fetch chairs. Hearing Joe's laugh was like a great meal's aroma drawing her to him.

Antics became an everyday thing, but the Scatoway's had the edge for having twins who drove the Prezzemoli crowd crazy by changing places.

Behind them, the Brunos were the first to invite the Prezzemoli family to a yard picnic where lights were strewn through the overhead trestle of grapevines.

The lights filtered down through the ripening grapes so that you had to duck hungry bees occasionally, but the good time was worth it, and one party turned into many where their touching yards saw all kinds of great Italian meals pass back and forth.

Jean became close to their youngest girl more the tomboy than Jean by virtue of having four older brothers all living on the same street, except for one, a police officer who was at war with his sister as much as Jean was with Joey. There was also another sister who had chosen a life as a nun who arrived with a nun companion in time to share that first meal together. Both Joe and Marian responded to Mrs. Bruno for her similarities to Tess and her husband Carmen who was a giant of a man who loved a house full of people as much as his wife and new neighbor Marian did.

Young Joey, as young boys will, enjoyed the Brunos but had a secret feeling about one that he kept to himself.

Having left the bad of the project behind it was splendid to find neighbors like Ned Marrish who was a skilled contractor who answered calls for help unselfishly particularly around the house, which delighted Joe since his around-the-house skills were nonexistent. Marian's culinary skills turned any plea for help into a well-fed social occasion that the guys were always glad to work off.

The house became home, and the yard began to fill with people. Mary's Tommy and Freddy delighted with having a new place to go frequently visited, and the bonds between the young cousins deepened even more as they grew with young Tom looking like a teenage Giant dwarfing his cousins.

That first year, Joey started a tradition of his own. Each day coming home from school, he and Jean had to pass the bank while Jean would tap on the window, wave at Joe, and turn the corner to walk to work. Joey did his own thing.

Joe usually had a customer when the banging began. Joey's sad sack face pleaded through the window for a quarter. Joe recognized the ploy and always said no but had to succumb to customer prodding again and again. His personable son was a natural winner.

While a son faithfully enjoyed bamboozling a father, a daughter stubbornly began to refuse help. Joe mixed loving Joey with wanting to throttle him while a daughter disturbed him by forsaking the simplest of monetary gifts. The personalities of his kids were defining themselves very differently.

One winter day, snow fell gently and deeply, all day and all work ceased, and students were sent home.

Joey and Jean went to the store after school to wait for Marian to close up. They began to realize Joe wouldn't make it. The pedestrian view outside the store was everyone walking while traffic was disappearing. By the time Marian was ready to leave, there were no cars on the streets except slow-moving public work vehicles unable to keep up with the deepening snow.

"Well, kids, I'm almost ready, and it looks like we're walking home. We'll probably meet your father on the way." Marian was pulling on boots when a snowman appeared at the door. "Anybody here want to walk home with me?" Joe had walked clear across town to see his lady home, as he always did and would. Joe's long nose heaped with snow looked like a ski jump.

It was a beautiful night for a walk. The traffic free road was the path home. A plow passed tooting a hello. Joe dropped a waving hand, saying, "If we still had trolleys, we'd be riding home." They all laughed in agreement. Many of the nicer old-fashioned modes were disappearing one by one, but tonight, they had one of nature's old-fashioned storms to enjoy rather than fear as many would. The isolation softened by the snowbound grandeur had them savoring the cascading lights from streetlamps too pretty to ignore as it filtered down through the bough work of the now bending tree limbs... viewing delights.

Joey's yells shattered the pretty silence proclaiming his unleashing a series of snowballs. All were ducked, and Jean ran at him and tackled him sending them both into a snow bank where Marian and

Joe joined the fray to pelt him with loose snow. Joey loved the laughter he generated having chosen laughter and its importance to life as his father had but by a very different path.

The change of address had torn him from his cohorts, and he sought friends of the same ilk.

That eased when Joey transferred to school four just up the street from the house and occurred just as his ladder to manhood reached the first rungs challenging authority. One day, he unwisely smart-mouthed Marian.

Joe slowly came out of his chair, grabbed Joey by his polo shirt, and—with deliberate control—lifted him high against the door-frame until they were eye to eye. Joey felt like a rocket leaving its pad.

Once Joe was sure he had Joey's attention, he said, "Apologize to your mother and Joey, you best remember something. You will never be too big for me to take down if you hurt your mom. So watch your step and your mouth."

He lowered a contrite son who was apologizing as he came down, only his polo shirt slid up revealing black and blue marks all around his milk white body. They resembled a beating.

"Oh, God." In the rush of guilt, Joe dropped Joey to the floor.

Marian laughed at Joe's torment. "Hon, he's not hurting."

"But people will think I took a cat of nine tails to him. Joey, does it hurt?"

"No, Dad."

The vision of hitting his daughter raced through Joe's mind, and though he could suppress it, no one could make Joe feel better. *I hurt my son.*

One parents' day at School Four, Joey and Marian found déjà vu in his teacher's words.

"Mr. and Mrs. Prezzemoli, I love having Joey in my class. He's a good boy, and he's enjoyable. He does relentlessly tease the girls but isn't mean about it. The only serious problem is that he has no real interest in learning his subjects. He does just enough to pass, but he doesn't really apply himself. I feel like I'm failing him."

Marian said, "No, it's not you. We all help him, but it's a constant battle."

"Unfortunately, some students are like that, but if there's anything I should know to help, I'd appreciate knowing it."

Marian and Joe shared what they could about Joey hoping between them they could find an answer, but solutions seemed to elude them or were repetitious of earlier efforts.

Even using the dismay of his teacher whom he liked and admired changed nothing.

Neither noticed the pleasant walk down Winfred Avenue to the house as Joe said, "Mar, it's time he began to outgrow this fooling around he's turning eleven next week."

"I know but he just doesn't like school and learning while he loves being with his friends and creating fun in everything he does."

"I must be doing a lousy job with him. I can't seem to make him understand."

"Oh, Joe, parents aren't to blame for everything. Each child is their own person." She suddenly stopped.

Joe thought she was going to cry, but she held it back to say, "He has a chance to be whatever he wants to be. If he doesn't change, he'll be throwing that away. Remember how both of us couldn't have what we wanted most. Me nursing and your four years of school. He'll have the chance at anything he wants but not if he keeps this up."

Joe took her hand, saying, "I know. I wish I could figure it out or that we could blame the friends he spends time with, but it's not them. They're good kids too. This is the way he is, and he refuses to change. It's either money or fun right now, and he can't see beyond that. But he's still a kid, and he still has time. Who knows maybe the right girl will be his key."

"Maybe, but that's too far away to count on, and I liked it better when he thought girls were—what's his word?"

"Yukky," answered Joe.

"Joe, what are we going to do with him?"

"Keep trying because he isn't bad, but he's always going to the edge of too far and crosses over so often, he's always in trouble. He's like Jean in some ways, only her adventures can only hurt her. He doesn't realize the harm lurking in his approach to having fun."

"He just doesn't seem to hear us. I have no answer, and worse, it's begun to pass into other things he does. One minute, he loves being with us, and then he's unhappy with everything. I dread full blown puberty because I can't help feeling we can lose him."

"Hon, any kid can get lost, but he's just a kid. He has a long way to go, and he has to find his own way. You're the one that's always reminding me of that we can't do it for them."

Once home, Joey listened respectfully what was said with no real plan to change the situation.

Joey listened respectfully to their results of their school visit, but he knew deep within himself that he didn't want to change.

When fun crossed this growing boy's travel through puberty's corner, he'd often detour. The luxury of firm but gentle parents left little to fear in severe punishment.

As time passed, Marian often wondered where Joey hid the barber straps and a four-foot-inch-thick stick kept nearby hoping proximity would make Joey think before acting.

Neither offspring had felt physical punishment in years, though Marian's wooden spoons had a life expectancy of two weeks with Joey's antics. She would yell, "Joey," and her wooden spoon would come down on the surface nearest to her just to caution him. For a short time, the sound still carried some power more in reflex than in fear, but a part of him just couldn't recognize she meant business until it was too late. What saved him was mother's love and the fact Marian couldn't hold a grudge against the normal misdeeds of growing.

Joe remembering his own youth watched Joey carefully and stumbled upon Joey having a secret he was holding ever so close that none of them had picked up on. Often getting home before Marian, Joe began to notice Joey left no change of clothes strewn around his shamble of a room in a rush to play.

One afternoon, Joe was talking to Poppa Bruno before going to kill time at the gas station with a friend before picking up Marian. While talking to Bruno on his back stoop, Joe could clearly see Joey's reason for not leaving a mess every day while Joey could not see him.

He decided to wait until tomorrow, Marian's day off. *She'll get a kick out of this.*

Joe rushed home the next day, sure he'd catch his offspring in action enjoying every moment of it.

He kissed Marian and then stood by the window as they shared their day. Once Joey arrived at the corner, he said, "Mar, I see our son has a crush." He watched her head come up from washing vegetables and rush to his side, asking, "Who?"

Joe put his arm around her waist, pointed, and said, "I can't fault his taste, can you?"

Marian leaned into Joe's holding to enjoy watching her son wheel Roseann, Bruno's granddaughter passed the corner while looking up at the tall, beautiful brunette mother with young love, hopefully well hidden from teasing family. The first day he saw her in the park across from school with her youngest he chose to escort her home and kept it a secret.

Marian said, "Oh, Joe, he does have good taste, but we can't tease him, he'd never forgive us."

"I won't but he'd certainly deserve it considering he never stops teasing everyone else."

"We've covered everything with him, so from here on in, it's up to him."

Joe's sudden smile gave way to, "Everything, except a mother's giving him her view of what pleases a woman and what threatens her."

"You would remember that."

"Uh-huh, and I remember how hard it was having that kind of talk with my daughter—oops, our daughter. But I sure learned why a lot of father's never get around to it." His grin widened grandly under a nose that seemed to emphasize his gotcha.

Her understanding became, "Joe, that sounds of sweet revenge?"

"Have no doubts, lady. I'll be as happy as you were to sit in on my conversation with Jean."

"I dread this more than I ever worried about Jean."

They watched him walk Roseanne to the front entrance, hold a pleasant conversation, and then ducked away from the window laughing as Joey turned to come home knowing they'd say nothing when he came in.

Later that week, they cornered Joey while Jean was working and Marian told her son the good and bad of sex from her point of view and not to expect any woman to be same as the one before.

He listened well while what he would do with the knowledge as he grew to manhood was a mystery to be solved while privacy made never knowing already a fact.

Marian's feeling of foreboding would prove accurate.

As time passed in their new home, the kids stayed closer for feeling slightly out of it without familiar haunts and nearby friends and because it was nice just to hang out.

One evening, the phone rang, and Marian, sitting right next to it in the living room, picked it up. All eyes turned toward her from the chairs and floor. Hearing it was Catherine, all eyes went back to the television until hearing, "Catherine, you're kidding?" Disbelief filled Marian's phone voice.

After a moment of silence, she again said, "You must be kidding." Only the words were slower and without the emotion and animation, typically Marian. Confused by her reactions, the family had turned away from the TV to listen.

All were befuddled by Marian's awe and inane responses to whatever Catherine was saying.

Marian finally put the receiver down and sat there looking blankly at something beyond a family's waiting curiosity.

"Marian?" Joe sounded both anxious and demanding.

She answered with a voice lacking punctuation. "I've just won five hundred dollars in St. Joseph's raffle."

In shock, she watched the family go wild, throw pillows, and romping around the room. Moments later, she stood laughing and joined them in a silly victory dance.

Marian took her winnings, called her brother Sossy, now Sal,—more appropriate for a master carpenter—and began conversion of the attic into a dormered bedroom, sitting room for Jean. Joey lost a roommate and took over the smaller bedroom downstairs to call it "mine". He showed the first signs of becoming a gentleman by not commenting on anything he heard through the thin walls to the room of loving parents.

Marian and Joe had finished the room exchange by making their bed when Joe pulled an imaginary handlebar mustache and said, "The better to chase you around, ma-dear, and I won't crash into the wall anymore when I roll over. I'm going to miss those black and blues." Marian smiled and threw him the pillow for his side of the bed.

Marian soon turned the simple rooms into beautiful arrangements with the making of eye-catching bed and window dressings.

The mistress of the house leaned against the doorframe, evaluated her handiwork, and said, "Thank you, Dear Lord, we have a lovely home." Joe—hearing—stood close behind her, took a peek over her shoulder, and said, "Wow, look what you've done. It's great. Thank you."

Marian leaned back into his field of warmth knowing what really made it a home.

Joe's depth of experience applied to his job had further developed that smart, conscientious people instinct benefiting both he and the bank. Over the years, as he learned, he passed it on to Marian, and she shared her growing with him both finding strength through the doing.

Other people recognized it too, and from time to time, marvelous job offers would come to Joe while Marian's awareness brought people to her to find confidential answers or new directions.

One year, the neighborhood trotter's track, only four blocks away, offered him the money room manager's position at night, but the bank frowned on any employee taking it thinking it menaced the bank's reputation. Joe said no, only to see a friend, a department manager, take it without repercussions. It hurt but he enjoyed the rewards of his job, and wise choices allowed him to accept favors without compromise, so he said nothing. Since Marian preferred him happy to the torment of insecurity for making the wrong decision for those he loved, she was content to be with him wherever he was happy and always told him the truth when angry.

The downside was his accessibility. Joe placed no limits on when or who. Marian did but he refused it. Too often, telephone calls came during dinner or when he was ill. A thwarted wife who recognized he worried about everyone argued, "Joe, you are not a priest on call or a doctor handling emergencies." She recognized his nature to worry and care as the villain in Joe's aging much too quickly and she wanted it to stop.

With a hand over the receiver, Joe insisted, "Marian, shhh." Joe's dinner turned cold while his Mrs. silently fumed yet listened to the advice and promises of help that Joe freely gave.

Joey asked if Joe was all right and was annoyed at just being assured he was and whispered, "Mom, why does Dad do this?"

While Joe was engrossed in explaining the complexity of certain type of loan, Marian quietly tried to answer Joey's obvious annoyance by setting aside her first angry thought as derogatory and found the right one. "Because your dad in a position to help people who need it. He wants to return some of his good luck, though he earned every bit of it." The anger had slipped back into the last few words, and her eyes had never left Joe.

Though young, Joey's reaction to her words went deep he didn't miss her anger and gave it the wrong value.

Well, I'm not gonna be like Dad. If people like me the way they like Dad, I'll get everything I want from them and make lots more money, and my wife will never be unhappy. I'll always make her laugh. Staunchly refusing other questions Joey's self-image continues to get stronger.

The decision made, Joey's watcher moved on, unable to bring the help he wanted so to give him, but the decision left no doubt he was going his own way. He feared the dark one's temptations would claim the youngster since Joey had opened this door.

The years not being good to Joe, health wise, had impacts on Joey very much a part of his growing creating a rift not intended. The very things Joey wanted might never come if his own values take him around the troubling corners he was courting.

Shortly after, an ever-concerned Joe said, "Let's get Joey a dog."

"Joey?" The response filled with laughter.

"Okay, I want a dog, but you do too. It'll be good for him to have something his alone. Maybe an animal will get through to him."

"I agree, but Joey will love having him while we get the work. The walking, the feeding—"

Joe, knowing the list, jumped in with, "He'll do his share, and we can all help."

"I hope so." Her doubtful tone softened to a purr under the lure of having a puppy to spoil.

Joe's visit to the pound meant visiting with a childhood friend, who showed him the best prospects. Those who growled lost a home.

Nearby a four-month-old pup was whimpering, and when Joe—the human—entered his cage and hunkered, he said, "Come on, fella. I won't hurt you." The pup backed away, so scared, he wet himself.

"Hon, is that the only pup you could find?"

"No, he's the only one I'd trust with kids."

Marian looked at the shivering lump and took him into her arms, asking, "What will we call him? Whiskers might do? I like his."

"I guess Joey should decide." She nodded.

The plan to hide him in the cellar fell away. The pup stood frozen with terror at the top of the stairs, so they closed the door, put down paper and leashed the pup to the knob, and waited.

Joey walked in shrieked with joy and wrapped his arms around the startled, shaking puppy unused to affectionate humans. A right-behind-him Jean said, "He's so homely." Yet, she was stroking his head and yearning to hold him.

Joey took a good look.

"Gosh, he is funny looking, but I like him."

"What will you name him?" asked Marian.

"Well, he's black and brown with a big really white spot on his chest." A happy voice declared, "I'll call him Spot."

"Spot, it is."

Marian shot Jean a look knowing she thought the name too common. The snuggling companion licking Joey's ear deemed it a good choice.

"Hello, Spot," crooned Jean, brushing Spot's ear between two fingers and asking, "Dad, has Spot's ear been broken?"

"Maybe? Benny believes the first owner beat him."

"Sounds right. Maybe they kept him in a cellar because ours terrifies him." Marian's words were filled with the fierce anger one carries for one of their own.

Joey, still beaming, said, "I'm gonna take him to bed with me."

"Not tonight, honey," said Marian. "He needs a bath and flea powder before he can wander the house."

"Dad, please."

"Sorry, Joey, Mom is right. Set up a bed and papers out here in the kitchen and leash Spot to the door, but first, I want to try something. We all have to train Spot to handle what people and kids do unexpectedly to animals that make them bite. He has to know he can't bite kids no matter what."

Joe put Spot on the floor, stepped behind him, and suddenly grabbed his tail and pulled. Spot turned and bared his teeth, but Joe quickly grabbed him and gave him a light whack with a newspaper. Each member of the family did the same thing. By that time, they were ready for bed. They could grab Spot quickly, and he'd turn and put his head down refusing to go for whoever did it. The loving he got after each whack was worth waiting for in the four-month-old's new world. He accepted his first lesson as family member.

No one was looking forward to cleaning up the mess the next morning, but when no one had to, Joey took him for a walk. That night, they all came home, and again, no one had to clean up after him, and he leaped for the door and his family.

"He's already house broken," said a proud Joey. "I've got one smart dog." Next came his bath, and Joey and Jean were sopping wet when they finished and watched enthralled as Spot shook himself clean and then laid down to clean himself, as a cat would only to suffer the indignity of a flea powder dousing so like Grandpa Gene's as he entered the United States of America. That night, Joey took his new roommate to bed with him.

Once in bed, Joey said, "Come on, Spot, put you head on my pillow the way I do. Atta, boy, that's the way." A loving hand on this dog's body made training easy.

Jean had given partial notice at the ice-cream store to try something new for the summer daytime hours while continuing to work from six-thirty to eleven at night, and when she and her parents got home the next night, they heard Spot whining behind Joey's closed bedroom door.

Spot loved his master and went faithfully to bed with him, slept with his head on a pillow, and made a decision all his own. Once Joey was asleep, Spot wanted to be with the rest of the family to share a couch, lap, or rug, which ever a family member would share with him not to mention snacks.

Joey's love of Spot brought him home after school, and his puppy love joined a boy rushing to puberty and not noticing that his crush on the beautiful lady next door passed into lustful imaginings of many types as challenging hormones gained momentum through the forceful dreams leading to manhood and realities that his maturity would hasten fathers to reach for their baseball bats.

Joe looked down one night and saw the growing dog with his head up on the baseboard snoring like crazy.

"I'll be darned. Spot's so used to a pillow he has to put his head on the baseboard to sleep." His girls confirmed and chuckled at the dog's growing human side.

This terrier type mutt with a chest of pure white, paws brown and black to his long tail's end, quickly absconded his fears and made these four his own.

Spot's almost human capacity to learn took him to being a fifteen-inch high terror, a lover, trickster, and babysitter who only once favored the dogcatcher with his presence. A typical male and chaser, the family expected his incarceration again and again for it was a time when dogs were allowed to go out alone for a run. A bitch-owning neighbor explained why it never happened again.

"Spot was among the four-legged studs courting my lady, and they were still milling around when the dogcatcher arrived. Your mutt saw the truck and crawled with his belly to the ground to hide deep in the hollow under our blue spruce. Through the mayhem of catching the other dogs, he never made a sound. I didn't have the balls to snitch on him but finally told him, 'Go home.' I could swear he asked, 'Any chance, Mister?'"

"I said, 'No way, fella,' and he left swinging that cocky ass of his. Joe, I wish I had half his brass when I was young." The men enjoyed a testosterone filled moment.

Spot's claim to family threatened both animal and human daring unauthorized entry.

Spot

One night, Joe and Spot took the garbage out to the cans not knowing a large hapless rat found a way into the yard, probably from the disappearing marshlands. Joe dropped the bag into the can, and the rat leaped on his arm, Spot sprung, grabbed the rat's vulnerable throat and took him to the ground killing him. Joe froze fearing for Spot…but it was over. Joe bent and held Spot steady but Spot breathing fiercely looked from Joe to the rat as though wondering what he did wrong.

Joe thanked Spot but said, "No boy, Well done." He all but dragged Spot to the hose, washed him down thoroughly and apologized as he held Spot's mouth open and scrubbed it clean with a handy piece of cloth. Then he got rid of the evidence, found another cloth, and wiped Spot down. Then he bent and thanked him again and, when Spot licked him, said, "Atta, boy. Thanks. Come on, let's go in."

After lauding Spot's deed, he made a phone call to have a cement structure built around the cans and passed the word to the neighbors, and all findable holes were poisoned with their pets housed until the job was done.

Another night, a human carefully opened the gate limping heavily. What Spot heard, Marian and Joe could not: the opening gate, it's closing and strange slumping footfalls climbing the stairs. The family sentinel moved to a position near the door almost hidden by a Hutch where he silently waited. The door soundlessly moved from the frame, and the person stepped in.

Spot's furious growl and leap carried him to the intruder's chest. The intruder screamed, and Spot's bared teeth stopped at a contrite Joey's throat to lick a very pale, former sneak.

Spot loved being with Marian on Tuesdays, her day off, especially when preschoolers called, "Mrs. P., can Spot come out to play?"

Marian enjoyed listening to the sounds of the children as Spot played by leaping high into the air to catch the thrown ball. Occasionally, Spot preferred tag and wouldn't give the ball back. Marian would referee from the nearest window. She would call out, "Spot, let go of the ball," and he'd relinquish his prize to start all over again.

Parents knew their children safe because coming to claim them found Spot standing between the grownup and their child, politely holding the adult at bay until Marian answered their call, "Marian, tell Spot it's all right. It's time for them to come home." Spot came to recognize the parents, but paving of the streets spoiled the playground with traffic.

The corner bringing this last member of the family aboard for the growing years rushed on to new ones.

Joey's focus even with Spot around was changing, and his activities brought him attention in a way he didn't appreciate.

One night, while Jean was working, Marian's delicious pasta fagioli lost its appeal.

Marian was saying, "Joey, you're not old enough to be completely on your own out here. There's no one who can keep an eye on you with all of us working."

His buttered piece of Italian bread stopped at his lips, so Marian smiled for having his attention.

"Ah, Mom, I don't need a babysitter." He caught his father's cautioning look and started chewing again fast.

Joe said, "You need something more after school to keep you busy, so it's time for you to make some spending money for your own use."

"Gee, Dad, I'm too young to work."

"Not really. We've thought of a few things you can do."

"There's too much of that we don't know about where you are and what you're doing, so think about running errands for people who work, cut grass or maybe a paper route or any of these things." Joe paused for a moment and said, "You decide and we'll discuss it again tomorrow, and we'll make it happen. Living here isn't like the project, a house isolates you, and I worry about your mom and sister as much as I worry about you. It's just safer if you're busy."

The next day, Joey told a buddy, "I guess I'll get a paper route. It's sure easier than working for people who might not like the way I do things. Heck, I don't want to push a lawn mower around, I don't even want to do it at home. And I sure as heck don't want to take orders from any more adults." He omitted that revealing phrase when telling Marian and Joe what he decided.

In contrast to his thoughts, Joey never missed his paper route unless sick, and Joe backed him up whenever there was a problem and those were few. His confidence seemed to grow and yet teetered with unchanging attitudes.

It was a delightful first year in a home. A promotion and raise put Joe in a financial bracket higher than expected. Marian planned a tight budget committed to returning the generosity of friends and decided she could save more by buying food on sale in quantity, so she suggested a freezer.

"In a few months, it'll pay for itself."

Joe's sly grin indicated a hard sell wasn't necessary and answered her with, "There are other benefits too."

"That means strawberry for me," said Marian.

"And I'll buy the five-gallon size to save money."

"I'll give $5.00 a week toward it." Joey had just offered most of his paper route tips to give reality a push, so Jean added half of what she kept in spending money. The day Marian plugged in the freezer, Joe bumped through the door with Breyers chocolate and strawberry five-gallon tubs.

As he ate his first of many sundaes, he said, "This needs really good chocolate syrup."

"Yeah, Dad, yours." Joey's mouthful, though sloppy, was seconded by all.

"Yup, I think I want a mix master for my birthday."

September 12, his birthday, Joe made wonderful sundaes but surprised them with thick milk shakes. The sundaes oozed with Joe's syrup made the same way as he did when he worked for Mr. Jacobs.

Summer was over school had begun, and Spot learned to be alone for long periods of time.

Jean's high school years kept her so busy that changes were too many and so swift it left her watcher with little to do because she had one goal in mind. The three years filled with the busies of learning and earning. Meanwhile that odd pattern of danger was giving her a frightening look at her temper when threatened and a peek at life's more humorous side. Her schedule helped her avoid the usual teen delving into teenage relationships leaving much of her self-undeveloped.

Changing each year of High School summer jobs took her to learning about children, young gangs, parents with power, winning the respect of young hoodlums and ego bending when she found she lacked her father's financial genius and turned wimp to gain his fatherly help when her bookkeeping kept her at her desk much too long. While her people knowledge and instincts grew her contact socially with the male gender was dormant. Yet she easily maintained male friendships at school actually preferring their company. She was too busy to even notice she was not like her peers.

Summer days as a park counselor at Mark Twain School brought Jean a good taste of what dealing with a class full of youngsters would be like. She won their respect the hard way with the help of Spot. The summer months were full of adventures that seemed to find their way to her. The children of all ages came from many backgrounds including young gangs often recruiting members something she found rather frightening but could not turn her back on.

Jean's sixteenth birthday came, and Joe was spending time helping her learn to drive. He couldn't understand why, with her eye-hand coordination she was not passing the tests. It was not until Ned Marrish asked, "Hey, Joe, what are you doin' to Jean. We can hear you yelling at her when all the windows are closed."

"You're kidding, aren't you?"

"No, Joe, it was raining like hell, and we all heard you."

"Oh, shit," decried the still learning father.

Ned saw Joe's reaction and quickly said, "Calm down, Joe. We all make mistakes with our kids. I'm a perfectionist, so I really drive my kids up walls. I know they've told you that, but I can't stop myself."

Another corner turned, Joe would go easier on his son a few years later for heeding the lesson.

A few weeks later Jean finally passed her fourth driver's test when a wise tester challenged her fear. Jean was forced to set her fear aside to avoid the immediate crash opportunites the tester forced her to deal with. A lesson learned and applied could not help her to duck Joey's never ending reminder of her many failures. Only she wished she could duck Joey's never letting her forget her four tests.

Joey entered junior high, and Joe put an end to his banging on the window. He got him a job right next to the bank in a malt shop saving a quarter a day. Joey worked well but was very unhappy with the small pay working really brought to his pocket and wanted more from Joe which Joe couldn't give him because even now he gave all his money to Marian keeping only some spending money. The kids often heard, "Mar, I need some money so I can take us to the movie tonight."

On parents' day at Jean's school during her senior year, one of her teachers voiced what might be a valid criticism.

"She doesn't involve herself sufficiently for top grades."

"We're surprised at the criticism, Mr. O'Neill. Your marking hasn't reflected a problem, and other teachers give her high grades on participation." Marian's instinct called for doing battle while Joe quietly studied the man.

O'Neill ignored her response and said, "In this class, her grades will suffer. Particularly, since she has chosen to go to college."

A regent's scholarship in this class was a real possibility, so this was a disappointment. If won, it would mean Jean wouldn't have to work at school and could use the time to stay on top of unfamiliar courses. It was disappointing to have the teacher challenge performance in her senior year. Their gender awareness made both sense something more between the teacher and student.

O'Neill said, "You know there's a regents scholarship in this subject, and without the right attitude, she won't get the best mark possible."

"Mr. O'Neill, we know that."

Jean jumped in on her own behalf, leaving Marian's scathing unvoiced.

"Mr. O'Neill, I will get the best mark possible."

"Not if you don't get involved."

"Sir, why don't we let my regents mark show whose right?"

Jean's firm voice remained respectful but surprisingly adult. Marian and Joe's direction suddenly turned silent because O'Neill's expression had changed sharply and he brought the meeting to a close. "So be it, Jean, I tried to help, and I have other parents waiting."

As they walked away, Marian asked, "Jean, did any of that have anything to do with not being one of his followers?"

"I think so, Mom. I've told you how he loves the leading girl students to sit on his desk talking to him and I won't do it. It embarrasses me, and I think it's unfair to the rest of the class. I think his class pets get better marks."

"You're sure he doesn't bother any of the girls?" asked Joe the father looking for dangers.

"No, Dad, it isn't like that, and he is a terrific teacher. He just loves attention, and it's not my thing."

Marian laughed. "Quite an ego builder for a little man." O'Neill was shorter than Marian.

"Honey, you did all the right things, but in the real world, you may have to play the game or take what comes."

"I know, Dad."

Joe recognized the glint in her eye and leaped in with, "Don't you dare tell me the number of my lecture," and put his arm around his ladies where his girls laughter rendered Jean's disturb, nonexistent.

One night, Jean ran to the car with sundaes for all, and they shared their day while Spot took licks. Joe finished first and drove off only to see a police car in the rearview mirror. Its siren demanded he pull over, and everyone was baffled by the need. An exceedingly neat, unknown officer approached. The kids in the back went silent as the officer spoke.

"Sir, you're driving without lights. I'm going to have to give you a ticket. May I have your license please?"

Joe fumbled, found it, and passed it out the open window.

The officer put a hand on the door, Spot sprang through the darkness, Marian lunged, caught his collar, and stopped the danger right in front of Joe's face. Spot's jaw missed the window just inches from the officer.

Joe pulled Spot's whiskered face to his. "Jesus Christ, Spot, he'll throw me in jail?"

The officer said, "Some animal. He knows how to take care of his own."

Joe, holding Spot by the jowls, added, "I'm sorry. He's a protective son of a mutt?"

Nodding, the officer bent and picked up the license he dropped and perused it.

The officer asked, "You the guy at the First National Bank?"

"Yes, sir."

The officer went silent for a moment.

Jean spoke tentatively, "My parents just picked me up. I work at Manning's Ice Cream. They won't let me go home alone."

"Yeah, they do it every night," said Joey.

"I guess we were too busy talking to notice the lights," offered Marian in an apologetic quiet tone the officer met eye to eye.

Then the unsmiling officer handed Joe the license and said, "Get the hell out of here, Joe, and put on those lights. I'll be in tomorrow to transfer my accounts to this precinct. The guys told me to see only you."

The officer gave Joe a crooked grin as Joe said, "Thanks, thanks a lot." Joe pulled away, and his harsh breathing became a chortle. "Spot, you saved me a ticket." Spot put his head into Joe's lap as laughter filled the car.

The regents' exams marked and approved put the two highest marks in New York State in O'Neill's class. The class was in an uproar of happiness, and losing the scholarship to a classmate whose mark came in two points above Jean's hurt but only a little.

Jean smiled at O'Neill who seemed to glance away, so she said to Ellie, "Guess he's not too happy with me."

"Yeah, you'd think he'd say something to you directly. He's sure proud enough that the top grades are in his class."

It never occurred to Jean that one of his favorites was the winner, but she was surprised that it was won by the most used essay topic, while Jean had chosen a financial topic much tougher and newer to their age group.

At home, she said, "Oh, well, at least I proved my point. I did get the kind of grade I knew I could get."

"You certainly did." Marian's tone made Jean feel good, and finding Joe's arm around her startled her, but she relaxed, and it felt good. Joe had felt her tighten and gripped her more tightly hoping it made a difference to the hurting reflex—his.

Jean thoroughly enjoyed her accomplishment.

Joey found her intelligence a stabbing, competitive drag as most younger siblings would, only it didn't make him want to succeed more but rather convinced himself trying so hard only to lose was too hard and not worth it.

Jean had permission to join the class graduation trip to Washington. Joe initially said no but relented when Marian made a point.

"Be fair. Jean hasn't had a vacation since she started working. It will be four more years of school and work before taking one. She's going to school at a disadvantage, as it is. Let's not add being strung out."

A couple of weeks before the graduation trip to Washington, Jean came storming through the door and slammed it so hard the woodframe house shook.

"And what did that door ever do to you?" said Marian.

Joe's paper dropped, as his daughter's wrath spilled out.

"You know our colored class president, Lionel Toomey?"

Marian nodded for realizing something was very wrong, and Joe said, "Uh-huh. He's a good kid."

"Did he do something wrong?" asked Marian.

"No, it's been done to him. They won't let him into a hotel in Washington because he's colored. And because of it, Lionel offered to resign as class president."

Jean was so angry; she was almost spitting until she grabbed hold of a fresh breath.

"And?" asked a curious mother.

"The principal called an emergency assembly. When Lionel told us what happened, we all yelled no. We yelled all kinds of suggestions from the floor. Only one was right. None of us want to go to our fine National Capitol." In her upset, she was pacing. "My God, we live in a free country, it's 1952, and Lionel can't stay at our hotel. It's a disgrace. It's so wrong, we unanimously voted to cancel the trip, and I hope they choke on my deposit."

Jean took the upset to her room while Marian and Joe discussed where such unfairness would take their beloved but imperfect country. There was no need to question the class' decision, but the path for a nation of mixed people loomed ominous in the cruel hatred of other races. To think of her as free of such thought wasn't true. Still Jean managed to set aside many first thoughts preferring to do what's right or considering how to handle them, at least that's what Joe and Marian hoped for. It was a pattern of reaction that slowed Jean's decisions except in physically dangerous situations.

Graduation day's summer heat kept the speeches short. A guest politician made the closing meaningful for the audience from a scaffold raised for the occasion and, in opening, said, "Having attained the age of thirty."

A loud, mocking laugh burst through the expectant silence.

"I guess"—he raised squinting eyes across the sun washed crowd—"somebody out there knows me for the liar I am."

Chippy Glynn was once again looking down on an Italian friend wishing he could aim his response right at Joe but couldn't. Chippy had become the politician he planned on being, and Joe was his banker.

On the stage, Ellie poked Jean in the ribs. "That's your father laughing."

"I know." Jean slid down into her seat laughing hard and joining the audience as they hee-hawed the mayor, who was about to run for the office of state senator. The two friends had grown up to realize their work plans and the hope of being good men.

Love and Failure

While a United Nations Police Action raged in a Far East Country called Korea, there were many American young in the fine company of other United Nations troops in serious jeopardy, while in Yonkers, the prom date Jean wanted brought flowers for her and a set of hand carved cowboy boots three inches tall for Marian. Cousin Fred looked magnificent in his white jacketed tuxedo.

Prom Date

It was a beautiful sunny day that made everything and everyone glow. Joey took pictures, as Marian and Joe watched six laughing couples load into cars and leave.

"Mar, I hope Jean doesn't love Freddy too much."

"Oh, Joe, she'll outgrow him. He makes her laugh and treats a woman very special. She needs to know that, but it will come. Personally, I wish Fred had someone all his own who appreciated him."

"Me too," said Joe wistfully.

Home in time for breakfast, Jean told of fighting off female friends insisting on dancing with Freddy.

"Especially after they saw us waltz. He's so good on the dance floor, and he's taking me to Roseland where we'll practice on my waltz." After a quick grin, she added, "I've been practicing in the cellar." She called out the steps, "One, two, three, cross over, one, two, three—ouch!"

The small kitchen filled with instant laughter because the effort looked anything but graceful. "Careful, sis, you're gonna break a wall."

The confining size of the tiny kitchen was definitely in the way of every move she made. Oh, how Marian wanted to change that kitchen.

Joe's laughter did not prevent his recognizing a daughter setting of masculine criteria that gave rise to the nagging concern that Jean wouldn't settle for less than what seemed a perfect man, and he wanted to warn her about the search for perfection. When that brought the thought, *Then she won't get married*, a wry fatherly smile graced his features, and he set lecture 6,440 aside. *I don't care is she never gets married.*

With Jean away at school, Marian said, "Joe, the house is too quiet, Joey has no one to hassle."

"I miss her too."

The college student changed rapidly, but the changes weren't bothersome, and young men began to call. None lasted long, and Marian and Joe could not see the dark cloud that had found its way into Jean's subconscious. Jean sensed it was there, but she could not see it clearly and saw no way to change it.

One homecoming involved her joining a backyard controversial discussion with male relatives until Joe spoke sharply, "Jean, will you please shut up!"

More furious than hurt, she left, stormed into the kitchen, took a deep breath, and respectfully said, "Mom, am I old enough to have an opinion and express it? Dad sent me packing for one he didn't like."

Unrushed, Marian finished tasting her batch of fried mushrooms but met Jean's gaze and reached for more fresh garlic.

"You're an adult. Handle the situation."

Marian added garlic and drifted to the window to listen.

She heard Jean say, "Dad, I'm sorry, but I'm staying in this conversation. My opinion is as good as the next person's."

Joe heard her words free of hostility, grunted, nodded, and continued to listen to a brother-in-law's dialogue while uncles and cousins took in her win without a comment. Jean suddenly had the feeling she'd been participating in an unexpected class exam and received a passing grade.

Boy that was easy.

Marian decided the mushrooms were almost ready and wondered if Jean understood. A father needed to know she can hold her own and an adult daughter needed to know a heated exchange with him was okay. Observing the same softness in both, Marian felt no guilt for mothering Jean's persistent independence. Without it, the needs of others would deprive her of much she had the right to seek. Independence meant going through life alone would not be a disadvantage and choosing a mate would be for the right reasons, so would bedding with one. She shuddered with recognizing the changing times in that thought and rushed to stirring the mushrooms refusing to deal with that very real possibility.

Joe adjusted quickly to the changes in Jean and continued to watch her world grow through applying her widening curiosity to what she learned about herself and the world around her with the same love he'd always held for her.

Joey tried time and time again to claim the same freedom's Jean now had, but watchful parents gave nothing more than what he earned as each year came.

Jean's visits home narrowed for joining new friends in uncommon doings that she freely told Marian and Joe about in quick letters. The honesty often left Marian and Joe close to losing their parental cool, but the distraction of Young Joey's antics kept them in balance for much he did made them laugh.

Confidence fueled Jean's forward charge, but that confused area in her mind ballooned darkly and remained very private. She was whipping around life's corners with seven chatty, very different roommates that embroiled her in decisions and steeped her in a deep dye of independence where she challenged many thoughts as though in a debate. The eight different roommates relied on each other as being family of a new design and often referred to Jean's oratory as, "Uh-oh, she's on her soapbox again."

All seven were the same for doing battle with the person "I am versus the mystique," the developing mind traveling and growing through an unconquered atmosphere.

On one occasion, a literary course required a short essay on an emotion of their choice. Jean was embarrassed by the teacher's comments after reading hers aloud to the class.

Jean had chosen fear as her powerful emotion. After reading the piece, the instructor complimented her on making it felt by her readers but reminded them that it only got a C+ because it lacked the grammatical accuracy while the feeling was "right on."

Jean used to the A's of high school was embarrassed by the mark and by the realization she'd put so much of herself into the piece and vowed to be more careful and yet didn't understand where the fear so very present came from. With increased dating it was becoming more and more controlling.

As part of speech class, Jean made a test tape of her voice and played it back. It made her grimace, and then roommate Maureen said, "Hey, Jean, that's hard on the ears. Lower it."

Jean said, "Do I really sound that loud?"

"Sure do," answered Abby.

"Oh, Lord, I'm a female Uncle Tony. No wonder Mom hassles me." True to a search for perfection, Jean began disappearing into a sound booth nightly in pursuit of a personal mission.

At home, Joey said, "Mom, I have to decide between shop and cooking as an elective." Joey was now attending Mark Twain Junior High and needed to make a decision.

"Honey, why don't you take cooking? With Jean away, you could help out a lot."

When his parents liked his pork chops better than Jean's, he took delight in public reminders to a sister's usual "Grrr," something he loved to hear.

One day at school, her last letter to Eddie came back marked; Return to sender. It had been months since she heard from her grammar school friend. She was ashamed she hadn't noticed. Touched by his death she began to fear for cousins who had donned uniforms. Aunt Angie's son served in Navy blues, Joe's nephew Ricky was an Army MP in Korea, and cousin Tom a Marine was on board a vessel off Korea. In fear for them, she tightened that firm family bond by writing to all.

Something was very wrong. Freddy was ill and couldn't keep food down, so Jean rushed home for a weekend and insisted on a visit where she tried to help him eat only to join the family in dread. She sat at her Aunt Mary's kitchen trying to coax Freddy to eat and had to shed the losing effort as to hard on him, so she reached out, touched his mustache, and said, "What say we try Roseland the next time I'm home?"

At Fred's warm smile, she moved closer, letting her hand drop to his arm as he said, "I'd like that, and if you want, I'll shave it off for you." He enjoyed her ability to be affectionate, but his words ended in a grimace, and though he recovered quickly, he longed to detour her frightened reaction and asked, "How come you're so quiet, cuz?"

Focused on his pain, it took a moment to answer, and then Jean followed his lead, "What quiet, I've been talking a blue streak."

"I mean your voice, I don't think we've ever had such a quiet personal conversation." He said it so softly, she hesitated.

"Oh, darn. You don't like it!"

"No, I like it a lot."

Her face lit up. "You're the only one that's noticed, I've been working on it for months. I heard my voice on tape and cringed, shame on you for never telling me."

He winked and smiled as best he could, and that scared her so much she felt like she'd been dunked in freezing water, so she hid in feeling special. *He would be the one to notice.* Some of the chill quieted.

Soon, it was time to leave, but Jean took Freddy back to school with her in the same way the Second World War had been a part of Joe; she was different.

That week in Psychology I, her instructor, a handsome man with the bluest, see-through-you eyes, asked if the class would like to perform an experiment in hypnosis. He would perform the actions needed to hypnotize the class. The excitement ran high, and a part of Jean wanted to try it, but since it was a choice each student had to make, she chose not to join in. She was afraid of what she might do, even though the teacher reassured her she'd do nothing against her will.

The experiment was successful, but Jean and a few others in the class did not allow themselves to participate and would not open their minds to any loss of themselves even to an innocent, learning experience. *I don't know what I'd do. I can't do it.*

Instead, she watched friends and classmates reactions and realized how important controlling the fears aroused by dating were, but without the knowledge of where it came from, she dared not and began to understand that freedom and learning at college could be both wonderful and dangerous to all who go. She honestly shared her thinking with her classmates but not the real reasons behind it.

It was 1953, the United States of America invested sixty million in France's Indochina War while a college sophomore initiated a war with the gray cloud bombarding both her conscious and subconscious mind. The more she dated, the worse it became because she couldn't understand her abnormal reactions to masculine advances while preferring their company to the average female friend.

Young Joey, almost fourteen, asked Joe once too often for more money and found his pockets closed to him.

"Joey, I just gave you money the day before yesterday. It's time you made enough money to pay for all your good times."

"But, Dad, I'm only fourteen."

"Hold it, kiddo, your sister did it and so can you. You at least you have a chance to work at something you want. She didn't get that break."

Joey felt like he'd been slapped in the face, and realizing Joe meant it, he began to walk away to rejoin his waiting friends outside the bank.

"I'll see you at home, Joey." Joe was disappointed that all he got was a nod of a son's duck-assed hair in acknowledgement.

Joe discussed Joey's attitude with Marian, and since he had just entered his ninth year in junior high, they decided it was time for him to earn a good wage, set up a budget, and begin really taking care of himself in time for entry to high school and that he should do it knowing what he'd like to take on as a career.

A few days later, Marian and Joe sat Joey down and had a heart-to-heart just as they did with Jean.

Marian started, "Joey, you'll be in high school next year, so you have to decide what direction you want your studies to take you in."

All they got was an "I know." There wasn't a part of him that wasn't moving as he sat there. The amount of energy leaving his body was tiring to watch.

Marian looked to Joe who said, "Joey, relax, this is something you have to deal with. Look, you know we don't have the means to send you to college, and I'm sorry about that, but if that's what you want to do, you can work your way through, and you can earn enough now and save enough to make it easier on yourself. We'll be able to help a bit but not a lot."

Marian jumped back in, "Honey, you can be anything you want, but you have to make up your mind, and you have to try."

"I don't want to go to college. I'm not like Jean."

"Hold it, Joey." Joe's voice was tightening. "We're not asking you to be like Jean because you're not like her and you don't have to go to college, it's just a smart move if you do." Joe began to back off for seeing how upset Joey was getting. "Look, we know college isn't right for everyone, but either way, you're the only one who can decide that. You have to make your own way in the world just like the rest of us. Jean is doing what's right for her. She decided that for her, it's all about school. She's not having fun. It's called growing up. Only in that way are you're both alike."

"After school, you may want to move out, most guys today do, because they want to be on their own, and that means you have to earn enough to take care of yourself. But we're not saying that to you. This is your home as long as you want it, but you have the responsibilities of being a man whether you leave or stay. And because it is, it means you'll have to pay a good rent and meet all you're own expenses. You can't do that on an after-school type of job. You need a good wage."

Still Joey said nothing.

"Joey, Dad and I are talking to you now so you'll have time to think about what you really want to do. We'll come back to you to see how we can help in the same way we did for Jean. You might even want to go into business for yourself and what you save now you'll be able to use to get started. We hope you decide on something you'll enjoy doing, so take your time, but give it a lot of thought, and if we can help in any way, just tell us. Okay?"

Joey's mind was running at full speed. *Ah, jeez, I don't know what I want to do. I sure don't want to go to school. Why me? All I wanted was a couple of bucks. Jeez, I hate school.*

Joey's guidance counselor was a little quicker than Marian and Joe had anticipated, and Joey was forced to make the decision and he decided, after a lunch period, on carpentry. The thought about his uncle Sossy, now uncle Sal remembering how he admired what he'd done to Joan's room. *Hope I can hit it off with the ladies like Uncle Sal.*

When he got home from school, he saw Marian was home. *I forgot, it's Mom's day off.*

He walked in and explained. Marian hated the lack of enthusiasm but said, "It's a good way to make a living, Joey, and if uncle Sal comes back from Florida, I'm sure he'll help you learn more about the trade than you can get in school."

Joe waited for Joey to get home from his stock boy job at Safeway and said, "Mom said you signed up for carpentry with you guidance counselor for high school. That means Saunders High. It's a good school. You'll learn a lot there."

"Yeah, I was gonna tell you."

"That's good. Now I can help you get a position in that field, and you'll make enough to take care of the cost of your growing social life."

Joe soon found a couple of construction customers more than willing to take Joey on their work force for the summer. After he and Marian discussed it, they decided Ned Marrish was the best guy both for training and keeping an eye on their overactive son.

"Are there any ways we can help him here at home to encourage his enjoying the work?"

"I had Joey call Sal, and he's sending Joey some on-job journals that will help. You know illustrations and that sort of thing."

"What else can we do?"

"Well, Jean has the better room, so let's do something for him along those lines. He'll come home filthy and need the bathroom.

You know how long it takes for him to comb his hair and all any of us do is rush him. How about asking Charley Leone to put in a bathroom down downstairs with a shower? Joey can come in through the cellar entrance, make as big a mess as he wants, and tie it up forever if he wants too and with no one telling him to hurry up. "He'll need a small closet with a rod for his changes of clothes."

"I think he'll like that. You tell him."

"Is $10 enough rent when he first starts or should we ask for more?"

"No, that's enough to start. We can increase it after we find out what he clears."

"Okay, hon, and while Charley's here, I'll have him hook up the gas line to where you want the stove for your summer kitchen." He watched her light up with appreciation and went back to reading his paper in his left-handed way.

Joe looked up from the letter he was reading, "Now it's mountain climbing. She's going to make us old before our time."

"Don't forget the swift water canoeing. I want to laugh Joe, but I don't like it either, besides there's no stopping her so try not to worry."

While they winced at the hazards, they had no idea the secret troubling within Jean was seeking other ways to feel good about the person she was. Her quick growing obscured any hints and being away allowed her space to avoid their keen knowledge of her reactions to problems. A part of her was learning to keep secrets well beyond the norm.

They were deluded by her growing womanhood because it was very comfortable to those watching. Jean was torn by the realization that she could draw men with the ease of a newly greased gear. The way she carried her lovely build made it worse, and her adult appreciation for its value made it a love-hate relationship.

Meanwhile, the lessons at school continued about people, politics, manipulations and relationships. She involved herself at depths proving Marian right to fear her softness. Watching Jean use what she learned forced Marian to recognize parental influence, mostly her's, and though it made Jean's independence fiercer than ever, she enjoyed Jean's sharings. Meanwhile Joe noted other traits and worried about the dangerous turns she took. But, Joe always worried for them all.

She had chosen a wrong path. Joe was right, Jean's search for personal perfection was a harmful corner she chose to take alone. Her choices prevented her seeing the available scholarship help and wrapped herself in isolation that added another trouble to her hidden concerns. Unfortunately, still young, she was blinded by the fierce light rushing toward her called the future.

The three dollars a week Marian and Joe gave her had been big money among some classmates but left her zilch for fun, so she took a job at school as a waitress. Joe offered her more money, but she refused and he wasn't happy with the stubborn stance. Joe's quick raises and stepping into management had made the offer one she should have accepted.

Her first visible sign of real trouble was physical in nature, but she did nothing about it because the troubled college junior was thinking of Fred's slow seemingly endless deterioration. She came home to join the family in his hospital room. Anna held her dying brother, as Mary and Tom touched him just to be near. Tom's enlistment was over, and he was now a police officer. How Jean wanted to hold this man she loved but couldn't make her body move to do just that.

Joe stood nearby needing to hold Freddy and did in the few moments allowed with him, but that comfort belonged to his mother Mary, Anna, and brother Tom who could not stand to be away from him for more than moments at a time.

Brothers

Joe squeezed Tom's shoulder knowing the brothers were spending hours together rooting a transition. Unable to watch any longer, he moved to Jean only her sorrow deepened the pit within him. As he put his arm around her, he felt her wince again, but her hand claimed his and stepped closer. Marian and Joey joined them creating a common circle of helplessness.

Young Joey found he couldn't approach the bed managing only hello and goodbye from a safe distance though Marian encouraged him to reach out. Her son's face reminded her of Joe as a young husband who found entering a hospital so painful it almost paralyzed him. She doubted Joey would recall the similarity.

Joe stepped away from Jean to put his arm around Young Joey recognizing the emotion that prevented his own sharing at such moments. Loving his nephew Fred in the same way he loved his own son made hanging on to Joey very important.

Joey didn't sense the power in Joe's loving touch because his mind, fending off the horrible hurt and fear of death's power over people he loved, took him to where he felt safe, deep within his mind. He was too young to realize that it would also render him helpless to reach out and aid those he really loved. It was the same place that prevented his understanding the faults in his incessant teasing and the value of a father.

And then Freddy was gone, taking with him many family sunbeams, but he had clearly passed the baton of responsibility and continuation of mischief to Tom.

At home, after the goodbyes Marian said, "Jean would you like the cowboy boots Fred carved for me. He'd understand giving them to you?" With the boots in hand she hugged her mother and went upstairs, snatched a framed athletic award from the wall, threw it away, found a snapshot of Fred, filled the frame with his handsome likeness and placed it next to her bed. "This is the nicest picture I have of you." Next to it, she placed the cowboy boots and said, "Be talking to you, cuz."

At her state university, things became worse as her marks and health locked on the path to collision. One evening, she passed the empty gym and saw the climbing rope hanging free. It was calling out to her like the anchorless rope of *Arabian Night* tales.

Without thought, she went to it, reached up, and—in moments—touched the ceiling. Something she'd never been able to do before made her cry. There was so much in life she didn't understand. *Dear God, what are you telling me? What's wrong with me?*

Sadly, she didn't mean her physical health.

In the land of the spirits, a student realized all the changes in Jean and wondered about what she could not understand and, now with adversity staking a multiple claim, where would her will power take her.

Her physical illness soon became apparent to her, but she still said nothing, and her marks plummeted to the point of failure. She had never truly failed at anything before and really didn't know how to handle the shame that accompanied it. Every feeling worsened for hearing the news. "Uncle JJ has the same bladder cancer your grandfather had. On top of that, Uncle Micah, Aunt Angie's husband, died of a heart attack, so you'll have to come home."

Oh, Freddy what's going wrong? Is it our family's turn to take its lumps all at once? First you, now my uncles, and what's happening to me? I'm scared. I'm not doing anything right.

Still she said nothing, but Jean rushed home acutely aware of family responsibilities to join the paying of respect and visiting an uncle facing certain death. It was something her mother did every day. The Manfredi clan seemed faced with a curse born solely by the men of the family. Though Marian had beaten the odds of her cancer, her father and brothers' bladder disease was a death sentence.

Still Jean said nothing.

Meanwhile at home, Joe, saddened by the family's problems, began worrying until his health began to deteriorate. A worried letter from Marian about his refusing to see a doctor brought a scorching, deeply hurting one pager from Jean.

In dealing with her own problems, she lost sight of the man Joe was. She had taken one of those mind-twisting corners where she knew his love and how he cared, but she ignored them and misplaced her own caring in writing and framed a letter full of anger. "Dad, you don't love us. If you did, you wouldn't be such a coward."

It never occurred to Jean that she was being the coward in not seeking help to come to understand the problem within while Joe was only guilty of caring too much and wearing his fear openly and for being so very human.

Unfortunately, Joe could not dismiss the hurt of Jean's wrongful words, and though Marian reassured him of a daughter's love, he never discussed it again. Instead, he stored the feelings in the secret place a man holds for his girl child where no hurt could destroy his love and where the ship of his mind, though anchored and harbored was battered by waves of doubt rooted in that old remembrance of being an imperfect father for slapping her wrongly, *why else would she flinch when I touch her?*

Jean's illness finally forced her home to find Joey had made a career choice. Her too brief recognition of it did not offer Joey any harbor to share doubts and thoughts.

Jean finally started visiting the doctor and Marian's lovingly administering how water enema's while she and Joe began to suspect a nervous breakdown.

The doctor concurred and said, "Jean, you're fine, but you're working too hard. I'm giving you some vitamins. The pills, a mild sedative, made her sleep when she needed to study. To her, it seemed her body's complete betrayal.

"Freddy, what's happening to me? I can't stay awake, and I don't have time to study."

The next weekend, she came home for a friend's wedding studying for her chemistry/physics course en route. Without warning, she fell asleep and woke to the peel of the conductor's "Yonkers, last call for Yonkers." She awoke startled, grabbed frantically for her belonging, and leaped off the train just seconds before it continued to New York. Only after getting home after the rehearsal dinner that same night did she realize the loss of her course study book and notes. Frantic calls to classmates who might have come home were fruitless. Panic set in and upon returning to school, to take the exam, her explanation to a disbelieving professor resulted in a feeling she'd never before dealt with, and she took the exam cold and handed in a blank term-end exam. Failure crept into her mind like a fog across a fine evening blotting out the sun's rays that light and warm.

Semester end sent her home to receive a telegram bringing the news of her expulsion. The telegram fell from her hands as she dropped to her knees and swallowed her struggling self-respect in one gulp while tears flowed heavily.

"Oh, honey, I'm so sorry." Marian knelt and held her weeping daughter while Joe and Joey stood behind them wishing for ways to help. The sadness Joey felt weighed more heavily than he understood giving rise to paralyzing shock leaving him with nothing to do to help, but then none of them could.

Jean pulled free of a mother's warmth to deal with it alone.

A stunned Marian recognized the first step into a world she could not enter. That the independence she had craved for Jean and led her to was a die with many sides. She leaned against Joe as they watched Jean go to her room while Joey floundered, saying nothing, isolated by whirling emotions within.

Joey was confused by his sadness for her and worried what it might do to Joe. *Dad can't protect her from this, but he'll try, and that might*—The feeling of concern crossed over to, *Shit if Jean couldn't make it at school. I sure as hell can't.* In his eyes, her failure proved him right, narrowing his already depriving directions. Suddenly he felt his father' eyes on him. Seeing Joe's feelings were the same, Joey shrugged his shoulders helplessly and his dad mouthed, "me too." But still, in strange balance Joe was glad Jean was home.

In the days to follow, self-contempt and life's routes gnarled by mental blockades strangled Jean's everyday, but somewhere from within, she refused the abyss of a nervous collapse and grabbed another of life's belays to climb above their confinement and, within two weeks, found a good-paying position with a communication company. Only it was a sad victory because she hated the job. The good-paying job meant offering excellent customer service when handling queries and complaints.

As her world narrowed, she was slow to notice the huge change in the world around her home. The swamp just north of the house had disappeared to become the first outdoor mall in the United States, just two blocks away. Jean, so like Joe in not liking to shop, took little notice. She had far more important things on her mind.

A teenage Joey tried to help, but his teasing never worked, and that was the only way he was comfortable. In an unfortunate way, he did prove to be a distraction. Though worried about a sister's anguish, his path to confrontation traveled to dangerous places within his growing mind. It was as though something was rushing, pushing, and shoving him into a river violent with water that could engulf him. His struggle with manhood seemed to lack a preserver that would allow him to swim ashore.

Unable to cope with what was happening in his mind, and at home, he sought escape in doing with his friends. Some were a few years older and others his age. The older young men reveled in the admiration of the younger lads and easily fell into mentoring them.

Sometimes, Joey would go to one of their homes. But mostly, they just hung out wherever they wandered, or he took them home with him, and they adorned the cellar furniture, which could freely be abused where they ate Marian's fine company goods and talked of their versions of adult input on females—sexy actresses, budding lasses their own ages, and wishful conquests. Though Joey had begun to attract the attention of his own girly age group, the girls seemed to enjoy his sense of laughter particularly when he found the words that made them feel sexy.

One evening in the cellar, the young men chose to discuss things like futures and family. Marian had called down to remind Joey he had a couple of chores to finish. She hadn't yelled, just simply reminded him, and he turned surly and said, "I wish she'd leave me alone."

One of the older boys asked, "What's up, Joey?" The game stopped, and Joey unloaded as he had before only this time he left little out and adding, "Now I have to pay rent every week. Ten bucks."

In this group of retail stores employees or not yet working friends, ten dollars was a lot of money. One Jimmy Santini laughed. He always seemed to have plenty of cash. Once Jimmy saw he had everyone's attention, the slightly older young man gave his best performance at worldliness.

"I don't pay rent. Never will. In fact, my mom cleans my room and puts away all my clothes after she washes and irons them."

A couple of other joiners immediately agreed that they too had this arrangement at home. Bravado or truth was rarely recognized.

Joey was doing a very slow burn and asked, "Don't tell me your father lets you get away with that?" Joey's forehead was wrinkled with consternation.

"I sure do. Hey, it's easier for my mom than all the yelling and screaming that I paid no attention to."

One of the quieter buddies said, "Your dad really lets you get away with that?"

"Sure does, he's the man of the house, and when he says that's the way it's supposed to be, that's the way it is. He hates the yelling too. So I get what I want when I want it. It's easy."

Joey was sizzling at the unfairness.

"Yeah, well, it isn't that way at our house. If I even look at Mom the wrong way, Dad puts me down. You heard my mom. It's expected." Joey didn't see the hidden looks of two friends who were of different ilk than Jimmy but to keep peace said nothing.

Jimmy, wise enough not to lose a friend whose mother welcomed him, let it go at, "Maybe you can change that."

Oh, shit. Why are Mom and Dad doing this to me? These guys don't have to do half the things they want me to do.

Joey spent the summer working in construction, the field he'd chosen for his future. The summer's tenure as a tapper, hammering nails into rough unfinished floorboards proved carpentry wrong for him, narrowing his world forcing him back into a local chain store to have money of his own. Now his confusion, massaged by the foolishness of youth, became marked in strain and arrogance with Joe Sr. as a target. In his thoughts, he battled with, *He's a fool. He lets people walk all over him.* This dim view of a father, who eased concerns for people including his son, held no value in Joey's teenage view of life.

In a short span of time, Joey broke two inviolate commandments of a usually fun loving abode.

One night, Joey was squeezed in with family friends in Marian's good-smelling, tiny kitchen. Only he was feeding a foul mood rather than enjoying a scrumptious, male-pleasing meal.

His surly tones and impolite grabbing of food forced Joe to take action.

"Joey, I've had enough of your lousy attitude. Apologize and leave the table."

Joey spat his answer, "Why the hell don't you shut up."

The air filled with the breeze of a hand passing over the table, catching Joey across the face and almost knocking him out of his chair. His head snapped back from the harsh blow, one he hadn't seen coming from his now standing mother.

Marian was breathing hard as she said, "I apologize for my son's behavior, but no one, not even my son, can talk to my husband that way." The guests, two couples', peers of Marian and Joe were frozen in various positions looking like statues entitled "Stunned."

With his hands in his lap, Joey bent a stainless steel fork. Jean was sitting next to him, saw the danger in those hands, and quietly pleaded, "Joey, please don't make it worse."

Marian's "Joey" demanded an apology from a wayward son.

His next words, both soft and brittle, came from a drooping head that made his uncontrollable hair fall into his eyes blocking those present from the fierce glare it hid. Then he quickly stood, politely excused himself, and left the table.

The evening went on without him. Alone in his tiny bedroom, the return of pleasant sounding voices reached his troubled thoughts generating more bitterness than he knew how to handle.

Though father and son had talked about anything and everything over the years past, growing seemed to slam those doors when opening others dark and hostile to his ideas of life, the future, and sharing. He continued to misread much that was still his to claim if he tried.

Joe was quick to forgive Joey as did Marian, but she kept an eye on everything Joey did realizing there was more to come. The realization Joey favored limiting macho images deeply worried her. It was a stance no one in this family found appealing, and it was a corner she had no intention of letting him take.

Joey's mind—filled with insolent, limited teenage ethics and expectations—laid claim too much not earned and drew him deeper into confusion.

It didn't help that school lessons were proving a waste that he met by doing nothing. Instead, he continued to work at local supermarkets draining any energy for other worthwhile directions. The security of being loved and he knew he was could not prevent the building of an abusive foul.

One morning, Joey was on the couch in wrinkled pj's, looking like a ragged hobo. Marian left the bedroom ready for work and said, "Joey, be sure to clean your room and take care of the garbage. You've let it go too long."

Without answering, Joey got up and headed for the kitchen. Joe came out of the bedroom hearing what Marian said and surmised Joey's lack of response from hearing her demanding, "Joey!"

The tone breathed anger like a smoke-filled breath on a cold day. The tone quickened Joe's step just as Joey whipped around to bellow, "Damn it, I pay rent, I don't have to do anything. It's your place to do it for me."

The words clubbed Marian with disrespect that turned her wounded heart bitterly cold. The expression on her face was one Joey had never seen. Joe, by now standing near the kitchen table, saw her face turn red and started to move around her, but she was too fast for him.

Joey stood defiantly and, without fear, stared at her. Then it happened. Marian took one step that braced him against the kitchen table, and the humor of his looking silly bent backward in droopy pajamas was wasted on the moment. The tiny kitchen left him no place to go and feeling ambivalent, as though he had nothing to do with what this stranger was saying.

And Marian coldly said, "You're $10.00 a week doesn't pay for one day of what you eat." Her voice seemed to come from far away, and he suddenly felt this was not his mother.

In that blink, Marian turned and crossed the threshold to leave but seemed to hang there as she said in a voice devoid of emotion.

"Pack your bottomless suitcase, and don't be here when I get home."

"Marian!" Joe's voice sounded raw. Marian faced Joe, and he understood what he saw.

Through clenched teeth, Joe put his palm, spread against Joey's chest, keeping him leaning backward over the table to hear, "You stupid idiot. There's no helping you this time. You're going to wish I'd reached you first."

Joey just stood there unable to speak. He was spared only Jean's reactions because she had left earlier while Spot stayed where he was not moving an inch.

As Joe drove Marian to work, he tried to change her mind but, unable to budge from her position, said, "My son no longer has a home with us."

Joe realized he agreed with her but hated it.

That night saw an immaculate Joey leap off the couch offering it to Marian who quietly walked away seeing and hearing nothing.

All Joey's chores were done, but Marian solidified her position. Joe didn't have to say a word.

Everything this mother usually did for Joey went undone. Joey washed his own clothes and cooked his own meals. Those he ate alone for Marian would not share a table with him. Even leftovers were off limits to him. Though Joe talked to his son, he followed Marian's lead in all other doing or not doing.

Joey knew he could bum meals with his aunts but didn't.

Marian no longer answered phones, furnished messages, or picked up cleaning.

It was an unhappy household, and Jean stayed out of it, but she finally spoke, "Joey, please try to apologize to Mom. My god, we're all miserable." The tone was begging and hid her urge to cry. That night, Joey stood to greet Marian as she walked in.

"Mom, I want to apologize for—"

Again, she heard nothing when passing through that void of cruel passion. Joey's unfinished sentence whipped about like a sheaf of paper at the mercy of a hurricane. He watched her leave the room and told Joe, "Jeez, Dad, you should have beat the hell out of me." He looked at Jean, sorry he'd ever listened to her, but saw she was almost in tears and that just confused him further.

Then Joey realized that Spot too had deserted him by no longer following him to bed and remaining on the living room couch at his mother's feet leading him to believe, *Even Spot hates me.* He had no way of realizing the animal's instinct told him Marian's anguish was greater than his and needed his presence more.

Seeing the damage, Jean wished she'd never said anything but never told him that. It seemed a betrayal to do so. The five years between her and Joey suddenly seemed a generation wide.

Still Joey didn't hide. The punishment turned into the worst he'd ever known by wrapping him in the same agony he heaped upon his mother.

Silence had never been an acceptable discipline in this home until now.

Jean worried about Joey.

Being alone with a problem when a family supports you is one thing. Without them, the world within is a depressing place and worse.

She worried he might wind up in the same place she was, a place she'd been since she began dating, and it was a place she knew as dangerous. Trained not to interfere in her parents decisions, she followed their lead and prayed for them all.

Jean's watcher waited for something that would allow him to help, but only Joey's sticking it out gave him hope for the future and said, "Can't his watcher help? Marian and Joe are concerned about both of them. Could the son too have a lesson as deep as Jean's to learn about?"

"No, the decision to challenge his mother was his. It is his to handle and remember he is not alone; now that it has become a family problem, it is their's to solve or not. Perhaps there is a deeper problem but Jean is yours so watch closely. Joey's luck has held in his mother's decision. Do not compare brother and sister. He has gifts she does not. He must decide how to use what he has been given and that luck that follows him."

A day came that Joe recognized, as the time to mete Marian's sadness. The calm knowledge of the husband, father and lover; faced together in their private world, unclenched a mother's fists of hurt and Marian relented and forgave Joey. In the living world, the silence for Joey ended as Marian finally relented and forgave.

His selfish, open approach to money went into hiding, but the incident did nothing to help him find a place in life. He still traveled the road of indecision but recognized the problem was his. Having had a clear view of the love his family offered him his vision cleared to the point he understood family could help, but his was the doing, and as his real-world needs rubbed against the frustrations of his sexual nature, a time so very full of youthful frustrations life became more difficult. A shadowy truth occurred to him. *Shit, I can't seem to tell the good guys from the bad guys. I keep making things worse.*

While his new approach brought much social fun and laughter back into their home, it only widened the void of his self-worth making his future seem bleaker than before his goof.

Joey had no way of knowing his sister's plight was as denying as his own or that manhood would find him soon enough for girls becoming women were to find him very tempting. The scope of life's promises were there for him to take in his own fashion.

Sadly, neither brother or sister sought the other as an ally in dealing with their personal development.

Amid family happenings, Jean continued to look for answers in a silent world shared with no one. It was a time that friends like Mattie Bruno became closer and eased the pain of her inner turmoil with life's doings allowing Jean to truly believe failure at school did not make her less of a person while her problem could destroy her.

The Prezzemoli and Bruno families passed time together continuing the neighborhood fun.

Another Christmas came, and the family chipped in for Joe's gift. His lament, "I don't get to watch anything I like on TV," was true. Joe was very much into American history programs but, outnumbered, rarely saw the historical and geographical programs he preferred. Joey had been drawn to them as well, but his antics and buddies took him away before his interest could really develop.

On Christmas morning, Jean and Joey carried a television into their parents' bedroom and wrestled the rabbit ear antenna into a receptive position. Joey yelled, "Hey, Dad, it's all set up. Come on in." And then Joey and Jean leaped on their parents' bed. Marian and Joe came, crawled up the center of the bed, and settled in to watch Joe's choice of station. About a half hour later, Joey and Jean slipped out, and a little later, so did Marian.

For days, Joe disappeared into the bedroom after dinner, but then he stopped.

On a night Jean and Joey were occupying the floor, Marian watched Joe come out of the kitchen and take his usual seat. She lowered her mystery novel to voice her curiosity.

"Hon, why aren't you watching your television?"

Jean and Joey turned at the question and waited for Joe to answer.

A sheepish look filled Joe's face as he said, "I miss you guys. It's too quiet, and I don't enjoy myself."

Jean and Joey shared a look and said, "Ah, poor daddy." Brother and sister had spoken in the same moment, smiled at each other, and leaped at Joe. The tickling began unmercifully. A laughing Marian intervened and kissed Joe, as he pulled her into his lap hoping to ward off further affection by two adults reverting to childhood.

Marian and Joe had done what they could to intercept the dangerous fallout in Jean's leaving school. But she remained a mystery. She appeared neither happy nor unhappy and kept in touch with college friends, made new ones, and refused to discuss her feelings. Her emotions were parked in neutral.

Escape into hard work paid off, but she hated the job.

"Okay, I've bragged about my raise, which means I need to know what you and Dad want for rent?"

Joe took the question. "How about 5% below the governments suggested percentage of salary for rent? Only you don't pay us, you put the money into your company's stock for your mom and me. Blue chip stock is easier to purchase as an employee."

Marian shared, "It will furnish income as we get older."

Jean's head tilted in appreciation as she decided to put some into stock for her own use, hoping one day she'd fulfill a dream to fly.

"Done and I'll automatically increase the amount by the percentage of each raise. Fair?"

Joe smiled and said, "Fair."

Joe's effort to help Jean find her first car one owner used was a mixed bag of feelings. He took pride in her earning it, so he found her a mint condition 1940, leaf-green Dodge with running boards and then sweated its affording her the freedom that furthered her unusual activities.

"Honey, take my car on your trip to school."
"Dad, I want to take my car."

"The weather is bad. It's been raining for days, and the roads are treacherous because of leaves. You need better traction."

Annoyed for realizing he'd prefer she'd stay home and knowing the weather was severe, Jean agreed, "Okay, Dad, I'll take your car." But her thoughts lacked gratitude. *Now I have to worry about Dad's car. It's bad enough he doesn't want me to climb, but darn, I'm only going to school to see my see friends.*

As her life settled in, she continued the dismal battle invisible to all while mixing adventures and friendship skillfully to avoid its revealing and found enjoyment where she could.

The trip to school was rougher than Joe predicted, and she literally bit her tongue for her strong language en route and arrived at the sorority house amid a relieved breath and realizing Joe had been right.

Abby and Babs greeted her at the sorority door where Aria joined them. They each kept in touch with Jean and joined her for two-legged hunting when home.

Once inside, Jean immediately felt the atmosphere flexing with nervous females.

Abby asked, "Jean, how'd you get through the radio, says the police are closing down all the roads?"

"Oh, boy, Dad was right!" She looked around realizing the ladies were dealing with the storm and clutching emotions as the girls explained how they were reacting to newscasts about the growing threat of a flood in the immediate area. "I guess I should let them know I arrived safely and was ahead of that being done."

Babs reached for the hall phone right nearby and handed it to Jean. Marian picked up the phone on the first ring, relief at hearing from her mixed with cracking and cackling sounds on the overloaded lines.

When she hung up, she said, "Now I'm worried about my father's car." They stepped away from the phone as a line began to form and asked, "Where can I put it that it'll be safe?"

The housemother heard the question and said, "Our neighbor is allowing us to put our cars in his barn behind his house at the top of the hill. It should be safe there." Jean thanked her and hustled her bustle up the street and came back to join the waiting.

Just hours later, the radio newscast declared them unreachable.

Jean seeking a brave front said, "Ah, shucks, ladies, I probably won't get to work Monday. Ain't" that a shame?" The friends shared a half-hearted chuckle. It was a small college town, and finding themselves unexpectedly cut off from the world was threatening to them all.

Abby, Babs, Aria, and Jean had to see to believe, so they walked to the river, but the usually chatty females didn't say much until—blocks from the normal Wallkill River bank—they found the water only feet away. Babs commented, "My God, we are cut off." The river and Mother Nature had filled the plateau west of the river right to the foot of the Shawangunk Mountains that housed a favorite hangout for the college students.

"How many miles away are they?" said Abby.

Jean said, "I don't know. It was quite a run." She scanned the dervish clouds dumping more and more on the new lake's rushing surface and added, "I wish I could move dad's car to even higher ground."

"Let's go back," said Aria. Her voice was shaking.

The sorority house had a generator for light, and an alert sorority sister had checked the cellar for flooding. It was.

The ladies organized a bucket brigade to prevent losing the generator mounted on a cement block fifteen inches high"I'll join the 2:00 to 3:00 a.m. shift with Babs, Abby, and Aria if that's all right?" asked Jean.

The house president threw Jean a "Thanks."

By now, all the ladies had taken turns calling home. Jean called home again. No one at the sorority house gave any thought to sleep. Instead, they huddled around the radio. The announcements applied to a local area and the nearby Kingston dam.

"Engineers believe it is only a matter of hours before the dam gives way." The radio explained the evacuation process for areas where evacuation was still possible.

It was frightening to all the girls. When they heard shots, the room filled with a true sense of horror. A phone call to the state police offered an explanation.

"Rescue teams have rifles. One shot means they found someone alive, two means they found a body." The girl hanging up was white with the telling.

The next girl using the phone turned whiter still.

"The phone's dead." The emotion charged atmosphere was immobilizing, the teams had been bailing water for hours.

At 2:00 a.m., the four friends took to the cellar.

As the girls stepped into the water, Jean said, "You gals can't get wet in shortly nightgowns. So I'm going to roll up my pj's."

Babs said, "Good thing there are no guys around Jean. Your see-through pj's leaves nothing to the imagination."

Jean quickly ducked the sexual implications. "Babs, if your bucket moves as quickly as your tongue, Aria, Abby, and I won't have to do very much." Jean stepped into the water and ugh-ed.

Jean filled a bucket and passed it to Abby who passed it to Babs, who handed it to Aria to pour out the cellar entrance to rush down the hill to mix with the rising river waters. The bucket brigade would have turned any healthy male into a panting bull. The water was up to their calves.

The girls hustled and made light of the effort but felt jeopardized. Abby said, "Babs, the last time we got into real trouble, wasn't Jean with us?"

"You mean the night the sheriff chased the lunatics you and I decided to go with and she tried to talk us out of it, failed, joined us, and then talked us out of being sent to the Hoosegow by the angry sheriff who stopped us? God, if he'd seen those liquor bottles she made us push under the seat, we'd still be locked up."

Jean chastised, "Don't remind me of my stupidity, but then I like being around for the fun."

"Ah yeah, fun." Abby's waving arms included the flooding cellar, as her small busts leaped around in comic collusion.

"Or," said Babs, "the day our clown dates insisted on the back trail down the mountain even when Jean told them it was not passable because she climbs there and we went off the cliff where the spindliest tree prevented our getting killed."

"Oh, come, gals, why is that my fault?" whimpered Jean.

Abby realized Jean was about to unload their escapades and leaped in with, "Sorry, Jean, you can't talk you're way out of this. We admit to our antics, but it never took us this close to the edge. One question will prove our point."

A quick look at Aria told Jean there was no help there as Abby asked her question while passing the next bucket along.

"Ladies, have these dangerous adventures ever happened to you before Jean joined our doings?"

The unified chorus of "No" made Jean wince at all the things that happen to her but saying, "Oh, what liars you are." Still knowing she couldn't explain, she ducked the discussion for having already lost it.

Relieved by a new bucket team, the felines, while drying their feet found places to listen to a portable radio where all the house members could hear. No one was sleeping. Abby and Babs rested at the large living room entryway while Aria left to make some tea.

Suddenly, feeling out of touch, Jean sat on the steps to the second floor. Not having slippers to warm her feet, she curled up facing the front door. Her thoughts traveled.

I don't belong here anymore. God, this is scary. I hope they're all right at home. The Kensico dam might go too. Saint Christopher, stay close. If the dam up here goes, I'll be able to wave as I float by.

Students with folks nearby, impotent by circumstance, began to crack under the strain.

The sound of two shots made everyone jump. Someone had died. Another two followed, and bedlam broke loose. Hysteria insidiously swept through the living room filling it with crying.

A girl screamed, "My parents? Oh, God, Mom and Dad, they'll be killed. I have to get to them."

The frantic female broke from the group heading for the door. Babs and Abby grabbed for her. A twisting bathrobe made her hard to hold while adrenaline gave her unexpected strength.

Abby's strong grip gave way as a rug went out from under her. Babs instinctively reached for a falling friend, while the desperate girl free of their restraint ran out the front door into the pelting storm. The violent wind crashed the door into the wall.

Jean watched the exodus feeling it a grade B movie but, without thought, left the stairs in a full run. The rain and wind glued her pj's to her body as she paused to see the stumbling girl heading for the dangerously swollen river through shin deep mud. The mud and bathrobe made it hard for the girl to gain ground, and then she fell.

Jean sloshed after her. Realizing her bare feet were an advantage, she pushed harder and got to the girl before she could stand again and reached down to help her up, but the girl—more a frightened animal than human—grappled like crazy. A pair of flaying arms whipped into Jean's cheek, but it only made her more determined, so she wrapped the girl in a tight bear hug and put her mouth to girl's ear, begging, "Please calm down, you can't do this."

The gentle effort did nothing. The girl fought like a trapped leprechaun, bumping and bruising Jean who was suddenly pissed. *Jesus, why me? I don't want this. Enough!*

Jean shifted her weight and grabbed the girl's arms in fierce handholds, shook her violently, and yelled, "Calm down, you fool. Calm down. There's no place for you to go." Her voice pulsed in harmony with the agitation that made the girl look like a shaking dust cloth.

The girl went limp and began to cry and said, "I'm sorry, I'm sorry."

Jean's long arms came around her with a whisper, "Forgive me if I hurt you, but your friends need your help to get through this. You can't get to your folks, we're cut off, but your folks would want you to help out here. Wouldn't they?" Suddenly, Jean felt like an insecure kid trying to make another scared kid feel brave, and she hated being scared.

A limping Abby and cohort Babs reached them took charge of the girl almost carrying her back with Jean sludging behind.

Abby glanced back, thinking, *I sure don't have to worry about failure destroying Jean.* And Babs, seeing Abby's expression, nodded her head in acknowledgement and relief. The girls, friends since childhood, read each other easily.

The rain stopped, the dams held, and Jean didn't get to work until Wednesday via New Jersey and the GW Bridge, twenty minutes south of home.

For Joe, the past hour had been stunning. Lunch with a couple of customer friends brought him a complex job offer.

"Joe, please, give this serious thought. You're our first choice."

"Thanks, guys, but move to Las Vegas? I don't know."

"What we're offering you to start, as our accounting head, is at least ten times what you'll ever make at the bank. Think what you can do for your family. We need your honesty and your abilities with people. Discuss it with your family. They'll change your mind."

Heading home, he recalled another job offer that had his head spinning. *It's kind of like that offer in the movie industry where we'd have had to move to California. I couldn't take that one either. Maybe I shouldn't tell them? No, I can't do that. It has to be a family decision.*

The past tied Joe to the bank and love of family to New York, but he remembered Marian's, "Hon, if you want California, we'll go. Just say the word."

Jeez, my earnings can never touch these offers still we're living better than ever. We take at least two vacations a year, and with the kids taking care of themselves, Mar and I will be able to do even more. Life's already good. Still Marian is working. I could change that. She could go to school or do whatever she wanted. She wouldn't be happy staying home, and I'd be home lots less.

Less than two hours later, Marian had listened, discussed things she would enjoy doing, and asked the final direction seeking questions. "Hon, this job requires far more time than you ever spent at the bank, right?"

"Yes, it always will."

"All right then, how do 'we' fit into this picture?"

Jean quickly received salary increases, bought a new Chevrolet to drive, and proudly took everyone to mass on Sundays.

One Sunday at mass, they had just received communion when Joe's face twisted like a wrung dishcloth while he gripped the pew desperately.

A horrified Marian watched a stroke threaten to take him. Jean and Joey moved forward both frightened by Fr. Ferme rushing from the altar to hear Marian say, "Joe, you've got to go to the hospital. Please."

Fr. Ferme tried but Joe refused and left the church to walk home leaving the family no choice but to follow him in the car, terrified the whole way.

The reactions to Joe's twisted cheek hit Jean and Joey very differently.

Jean had the benefit of being a full-fledged adult in managing her feelings of concern for her family, young Joey did not. Jean's thoughts went to Joe's needs, so she did not notice how young Joey could not look at his father and sought places and activities where he could hide from it. But everywhere he looked, he saw the threat on people's faces, and a part of his mind turned a corner no one, not even he could see happening, and he lacked knowing himself well enough to recognize it as fear.

Living with the knowledge, Joe was sick and faced with the thought of losing him as others in the family had been lost Joey dug a deep hole in his subconscious to bury those feelings, but those feelings took with them the warm memories of what a son and father share that express a father's true worth.

Marian tried but could not help Joe overcome the dread of doctor's or death, and that placed them on a bruising collision path. The emotional cataclysm left her willing to try anything and left a grow-ing son to flounder in his most formative years where the questions he would normally seek out his father or mother for were taken even further inside himself leading to paths foreign to the world he knew, the values and people he loved.

Nephew Tom heard about his uncle's leaving the church and refusing to go to the hospital. Tom left his worried mother Mary to rush to Marian and Joe hoping he could talk to his uncle, man to man, something he'd always relied on from Joe when he needed help.

Tom tried but Joe again walked out of the house past his son who had watched and heard and that part of his mind taking a new and troubling direction went further along the path harboring anger and disrespect for Joe's actions.

Joey almost said something derogatory about Joe to Tom but heard his mother say, "Thank you for trying, Tom, but you better leave, or Uncle Joe won't come back."

"I'm sorry, Aunt Marian."

Her hand went to Tom's arm in grateful measure, but she never took her eyes off Joe moving down the street. Tom cursed the failure and prayed, *"Don't take Unc, please,"* walked past Joey without a word for being so troubled himself, and said, "Jean, keep me in touch with this if Aunt Marian's not able to. Okay?"

"Sure, Tom, tell Aunt Mary we'll call and give her our love."

"I'm on night patrol, but Mom can get me in minutes, and I'll come straight away."

Jean nodded. "Thanks, cuz."

Jean saw Joey's troubled look but swung to her mother as she passed to go out the door heading after Joe Sr.

Watching her mother leave Jean was without a thought, to help a younger sibling.

Others in the land of the spirits watched as well. The student's focus changed from Jean to young Joey, and he asked, "He needs help or we may lose him."

"Has he asked for help or made an altering decision?"

"No."

The sad smile of the archer reminded the new student of the power of free will, and the student turned his attention back to the family in general.

Much of this stirred the spirits of the dark world to take note of Joey's directions to plan for taking advantage of every opportunity Joey's decisions offered. As his luck would have it, his avoidance of real decisions helped neither side.

It was a few days later when Marian said, "Joe, remember we're going to the Bruno's for dinner tonight."

He was glad for wanting desperately to return to normal. Worse than being scared was being lonely.

"Sounds great, hon."

Marian doesn't really understand, and I can't explain it to her. If things get normal, I can ignore these insane feeling that something is wrong. A night out sounds good, and maybe Marian and I will really relax.

When Joe entered the Bruno's familiar, good-smelling kitchen, he saw the table set for dinner and enjoyed Carmen's welcoming arm around his shoulder. In the moment, he turned to join Marian to say hello to his hostess Anna he took no notice of Carmen placing his six foot four, three-hundred-pound frame nonchalantly against the kitchen door. Joe heard a familiar voice, saying, "Hello, Joe. I hear it's time we spent some time together."

Joe turned toward the voice and became a trapped animal seeking escape, only there was none. Dr. Turco took Joe's arm, the arm of a friend, and said, "Come on, Joe, take a seat."

The heart specialist spoke softly and did his job.

His explanation of what he found helped very little. Joe's nostrils flared with feelings, too confused and turbulent to make sense, but Marian sat right next to him and listened carefully helping Turco to understand Joe's fears more fully and find the determination to fight with the best weapons available to an isolated lover, better habits.

When Turco finished, Joe was a different man. Under the weight of betrayal, the harbored ship within his soul began to flounder. Intelligence fought the emotions, and though he left his family no choice, he hated them for it. Worse, he hated himself. He accepted Marian's affection, but an emotional wall cut her off from their talking and sharing.

When alone, Marian cried but fought back with clear thinking and quietly left him to himself.

His battle with solitude won the first battle, and the wall cutting Marian off collapsed, but his survival meant regular doctor visits and worrying must stop. One proved easy, the other unachievable. Joe could not live without caring.

Other changes occurred. No more calls during dinner. Marian and offspring made appointments and judgments. Serious problems went no farther than Marian. In time, a lover no longer stroked his twisted face.

Marian had felt sure the kids would help because they were as scared as she was and wanted the fear to go away and would fight any battle needed. In time, as the muscles in Joe's face became normal, the Joe they knew, began to look ahead. Finally, Joe and Marian talked it out, and Marian knew she'd lost the important battle. As always, she would walk with him through anything that found him.

Young Joey did his best but misread much that was happening only to find more distress. It was a time when a young man needed the strength of a father to recognize and address his fears and confusion as he headed towards graduation from high school.

Siblings so Different

As time passed, Joe settled into the needed health routines, ever reluctantly but with the acceptance of an always watchful lover. Meanwhile he studiously followed the news on the government of Cuba as it passed from Batista to Castro after a deserved rebellion. When Joe found Castro had ominously played politics, to put a communist presence within throwing distance of "One Nation under God" he knew the threat was real. Then he bid bye-bye to the sugar investment he and Pop Manfredi made.

What remained was, *"And to think our Government supported him. How stupid can we get."*

He quickly put the upset aside and found himself thinking about Joey making fun of Jean's dates.

One thing I have to say for my son is he has a talent for laughter. I just had a quick flash of that huge, gentle guy she dated called Bull. He made our six-feet-four-inch Tom look small. Every time he called for Jean, Joey ran, got the kitchen step ladder, dragged it into the living room, climbed up on it, and—in a fair imitation of Bull's deep voice—said, "Hi, Mr. P. Is Jean ready?" Then he'd stoop like Bull had to when coming through the door and swelled his chest giving the impression of size filling the doorway. He was actually convincing, and Jean fought it but laughed as hard as we did.

I got a bigger kick out of how fast Joey leaped off the ladder and ran for cover when Bull rang the bell. The darn kid always timed it perfectly so that we were still laughing when we answered the door. I don't think he's missed making fun of any guy she's dated—a brother's prerogative. I wasn't easy on my sisters guys either. I wonder how long he'll be pulling that on her. He's a good kid, only he doesn't know when to stop. Well, not wanting his mood to change, he dismissed the deviating thought.

Jean noticed something was going wrong physically but believing in her strength assumed it would go away. And looked for ways to enjoy her new car. It was a light green. The color of New York Granny Smith fruit. St. Christopher had been its first occupant and she had taken to privately calling it "Freddy." St. Christopher was the car's first companion.

Joe's nephew Tom had earned a new respect from watchful relatives when he took the reins as man of the house after Fred's death to keep his mother Mary safe from hunger. Now a policeman, he had finished his high school equivalency and, with the coaching of a friendly police sergeant, had begun college studies obtaining higher marks than he had recognized himself capable of and he enjoyed the personal pride mixing with the expressions of proud family.

One day, without hesitation, he walked into the Prezzemoli kitchen very upset and without his usual respectful or fun-seeking greeting to say, "Unc, I need your help."

The couple set down their coffee cups, and Joe asked, "What's wrong?"

"Mom!" The one word made his voice squeak. "Jesus, she's making my life miserable because I stayed out all night. I can't take it. I'm moving out. She's going to have to take care of herself."

Marian didn't say a word, but her mind raced to Joe, and seeing him calmly listening took deeper heed of Tom's words. *He's really upset. Since it's about Mary, I'm sure Joe's the only one that can handle her. I'm surprised Mary didn't call Joe, but I think I see why. What is she thinking upsetting Tom to this point over this nonsense, no wonder she hasn't called. Tom's a good young man.* As Tom's words sank into the workings of her mind, they made her realize, *Oh, Lord, she's expecting Tom to behave like Freddy. Oh, Mary, that's so unfair.*

While Tom vented the anger he wouldn't loose on Mary, Joe patiently waited knowing this son loved Mary, however gruffly.

Joe recognized a young man's harsher, fatherless, city upbringing and the warping of police experiences fighting the emergence of a newer, gentler man in this latest mother-son upheaval. Tom, a man of feelings like his brother Fred, still had to learn to be comfortable with the softening of his exterior. Joe knew maturity or the right woman could do that for Tom.

Tom ran out of words and breathe simultaneously.

"Relax, Tom, I'll talk to her." Joe reached for the telephone.

Marian watched Tom pace from the tiny kitchen into the living room. With the stride of his six-foot-four, the small kitchen seemed the size of a dollhouse, but it was obvious he was listening to Joe's every word as he traveled.

Joe's voice was calm, soft, and filled with the loving caution one shows a person, too much alone, struggling with bruising emotions.

"Mary, Tom's here. Just hear me out, sis. Tom is a good son, but he is also the man who takes care of you. As a man, he doesn't have to answer to you when he spends a night howling with the guys or being with a woman." Joe uh-huh'ed and said, "Yes, I do. Sis, you have to get off his back. He doesn't deserve this. I know you worry about him, and with his job, you should, but you have to learn to handle it. If you don't and I hate to say this, he'll have to leave. Tom loves you, don't force that decision on him."

Joe listened to Mary and uh-huh'd for a few minutes. When the uh-huhs softened, Marian knew Mary was crying.

Tom stopped pacing and sat. Promises to Fred kept stabbing at his mind frantic with their responsibilities.

In the middle of a thought, he poignantly said, "Aunt Marian, I want to keep my promise, but—" An uncle's wink took Tom's mind to hopeful listening, and what he heard told him his promise to Fred would continue.

Joe persuasively continued with Mary, "Sis, look at some of my dumber moments. We're lucky. We both have good kids, so forget it. He'll probably be home in a little while."

A Son's Decision

Joe sought and found Tom's confirming smile and hung up to say, "Tom, it's hard on your mom loving you and being alone so much, but she does understand. Look, you don't have to, but consider calling her and telling her you won't be home. It avoids the worry because of that gun on your hip. If I were you, I'd consider it practice for when you get married. If you're smart, you'll let some pretty girl groom you the way Aunt Marian has me."

Tom studied his aunt and uncle for a moment and broke into a lascivious grin to say, "Fringe benefits, Unc."

"Definitely," injected Marian while Joe just laughed.

The nephew remained at home until marrying that pretty girl, and in the world of spirits, a brother smiled.

Marian and Joe made one decision that led to another that allowed them to select something just for the two of them.

One evening, Jean was in the yard shooting baskets above the garage door with Spot chasing the bouncing rebounds.

She caught movement behind her and spun around as a shining metallic gray car with red detailing pulled into the driveway. She grabbed Spot to keep him clear of strangers. She looked up to see it was Marian and Joe grinning like Cheshire cats. As they climbed from the gleaming vehicle, both extended their hands in exposing their brand new Chevrolet Bel Air coupe with red detailing that matched the red upholstery inside. It was one cool vehicle.

Jean come up wide mouthed and excitedly screeching, "Oh my God." and screamed excitedly, "Joey! Joey, come here quick. See what Mom and Dad have bought. Hurry!"

In seconds, Joey careened through the kitchen door, focused on a dream vehicle, and took all four steps in a wild leap.

Both young Prezzemolis grabbed their parents and danced around the new car. Joey let go to beat Jean to behind the wheel of the wing backed car only to hear Joe say, "Uh-uh, Joey, get out of there."

"Come on, Dad, I beat Jean fair and square."

Joe was laughing but said, "Out."

Joey looked to Jean who shrugged, saying, "I don't know what's going on either." A disappointed Joey slipped out of the seat.

Marian stood before him and said, "Joey, do you have a dollar?"

"Huh?" His muddle increased.

"I asked if you have a dollar." Her hand was extended towards him.

Joey was annoyed because Jean, now hanging out the driver's side window, suddenly broke into an understanding smile. He reached into his pocket and gave Marian a crumpled dollar bill.

Marian passed the dollar to Joe's left hand and, with his right hand, reached—jingling car keys at Joey—saying, "You drive your own car, the Mercury is now yours. This one belongs only to your mom and me."

Joey grabbed the keys and raced to the family Mercury sitting at the curb outside the fence. "It's yours, but no driving until after you sign the ownership papers and get your insurance."

Marian and Joe were chuckling as Joey said, "Okay, Dad, whatever you say." He slipped into his own still sleek black Mercury, saying, "Wow, this is one hot car. Hey, sis, see what comes your way when you pass your test first try."

Jean said, "Oh, Lord, he'll never let me forget he passed his driver's test first time out. And worse, now I'll have to listen to him about my 1940 dodge. What have you done to me!"

Marian and Joe laughed for Jean had already told them she was picking up her new car during the week.

Joey took the insurance money out of his savings account the next day and saw their insurance agent that afternoon.

Joey's graduation was less than two weeks away when Marian got a phone call to come to Saunders High School, so she walked from the store up Broadway to get there after telling the Jewish family she worked for. "My Joey has done something, and I have to find out how serious it is. I'll be back as soon as I can."

Mr. Schlesinger said, "I'll drive you there."

"Thank you, but it's a short walk, and I need to get a grip on my temper before I get there."

The principal greeted Marian and said, "I'm sorry I had to call you especially so close to graduation, but some of our kids have warped senses of humor, and Joey unfortunately is too willing to go along for the laugh."

"I know but what has he done this time?"

"He got himself locked out on the roof on a dare and created a small riot to get himself back in."

Marian and the principal both crushed the reflex to laugh, and he said, "I can't come up with any punishment suitable this late in the year, but I have to make an example of him for the sake of the younger clowns who participated in locking him out there. That was the bunch you passed coming into my office."

"Well, they seemed chagrined. Are their parents on the way too?"

"They are. Joey will be waiting for you downstairs at the door." Marian could say little that was free of anger and finally decided she could no longer find the answer to changing a son so full of—she didn't even have a word truly suitable for the young man she loved so dearly.

Joey waited for the ax to fall but kept quiet again enjoying and relying on the luck that never seemed to desert him.

Besides, he did have plans. He and two friends had their heads together over the last few weeks and had just about made a decision that none of them had discussed with their parents; they were men, and they were about to prove it.

Jean's path since college had turned several social corners and now crossed a personal one no one wishes to travel. An elusive weakness was slowly disarming her strong body. Her active social life had proven she had excellent taste in men, but each time, she declined marriage.

Marian and Joe were beginning to react to a disturbing reticence settling about her.

While realizing she lacked the selfishness of a heartbreaker, Joe shared a concern, "What if she doesn't marry?"

"Then she won't marry? Does she have to marry for you to be happy for her?"

"No! But I want her happy. She's not and it's not all physical. I honestly believe she needs someone." After a quiet moment, he added, "You know, I don't care anymore if she never leaves home. Actually, that's true of them both, and if they never leave home, we can leave the house to both of them, and they'll always have a home."

"That's not going to happen, and we both know it. We don't have to worry about her. If Jean leaves home, it'll be right for her. I worry more about Joey."

Joe laughed. "We haven't done so badly. Haven't seen any shotguns yet."

"But he's very confused, isn't he?"

"Very. It's probably too soon to tell. Look, I want to help, but I don't seem to be able to reach him anymore, and I feel that's my fault."

"Maybe that's only because, as you said, it's his to handle. It's the thing that makes the difference between being a man and a boy. Oh, Joe, you can't blame yourself for everything our kids do. I can't reach him either, and it hurts me too."

The discussion lead to mistakes made with the children, and they came to some honest conclusions. One in particular made them very human as parents, and they smiled at its truth.

"We favor Joey for his social winning way. He does have the gift of charm. Only he has to grow up. Still we favor Jean for her reliability and open caring, if only she would learn to be less controlled."

"You're right, she'll always step in where needed while Joey has begun to think the world owes him. That's got to lead down the wrong path." Marian could see Joe's mind take a turn as he added, "Yet when he drops the ball, even in a serious matter, his luck somehow saves him, and he laughs it off."

Only days after graduation, Joey came in after being out all day to boisterously announce, "I've enlisted in the Army."

Marian filled with exasperation, anger, and sorrow as an "Oh, Joey" escaped her now trembling lips, while Joe went silent regulated his breathing and with a voice full of regret and acceptance said, "Maybe it's what you need."

Joey was soon packing for a trip to Fort Dix, New Jersey.

The adventure chosen in haste reeked of waste. In their chosen direction, he and two buddies thought it would be fun to join up, but after a week at boot camp, fun turned to regret. Joey called home fighting the tears of loneliness and rue. He was where charm had no power except to make things worse, and time-wasting hee-haw had brought quick reprimand. No one rubbed it in, but Marian smiled and made her son a promise.

Only days later, a caravan of family, accompanied by enough food to feed a platoon, left Marian's kitchen packed in large thermoses filled to the brim with succulence.

They arrived to see Joey his face thinner with eyes worn by regret walking the picnic area with seven buddies hoping it would speed their arrival.

A skinny Joey in army green looked like a boy playing soldier. He rushed at his mother alight with adoring, out loud bragging about a mother's culinary prowess to his hairless buddies. "You khaki grunts never had it this good. Mom can have her own restaurant anytime she wants it."

Joey grabbed Marian, in a thankful hug, while Joe grabbed them both in a warm squeeze, and in minutes, he and his buddies were enjoying Joey's favorite macaroni fusilli, devouring three plates soaked in a rich meat sauce. Joey knew they were headed overseas and understood the ecstasy of a home cooked meal would have to last a very long time.

Months later, after a grueling ocean crossing that left Joey and others as green as their dress uniforms, letters from Germany began to arrive showing his world a bit brighter because he was seeing parts of the world he probably never would. Marian and Joe knew that had to be good for him. It was like having him at college.

"Mar, your son wants another fifty to go to some place I'm not sure how to pronounce."

Marian's tasting of stuffed pepper gravy slowed her comeback. "Amazing how he's my son when he asks for money and yours when telling us about the Frauleins."

Joe's grin was provokingly dirty. "He does mention that as part of the reason quite a bit actually."

Jean's illness was getting worse. Her sports surrendered to a body's weakening, and she initiated a doing that brought young Meggin into her search for personal worth and into the environs of her family's home hoping to help the child come to believe there's something of worth in the older generation. Jean was now a big sister again. Kind of left Marian and Joe wondering…was lil' brother missed?

The doctors could not identify the source of Jean's anemia and raised the possibility of cancer. The Manfredi family's tormenting specter scared them all as Jean took weekly iron shots to keep her functioning. Marian and Joe feared she might join the Manfredi men in a battle for life.

Jean and Mattie Bruno had become fast friends and about now returned from a trip to Washington to tell of many funny happenings and a good time. Later, Mattie stopped over with an invitation to dinner at the Bruno's table. She also told Marian and Joe, "We had a good time, but Jean's heart wasn't in it or at least her energy wasn't."

Mattie

Joe said, "Thanks for staying close to Jean, Mattie."

"Ah, Mr. P, she's a good friend and good for me. We laugh a lot. Did she tell you about our picking up a sailor trying to hitch a ride home? We felt safe putting him in the middle after we noticed there was no place to hide anything dangerous in the fine fit of his uniform." Seeing the slight frown on Mr. P's face, she quickly said, "It's a good thing he was with us, we got so lost. He was locally raised, so we took him right to his door." She quickly changed the subject to avoid Joe's lecture by saying, "And if she hadn't been with me, I might not be here to talk about it."

Marian said, "What happened, Mattie ?" Joe's attention immediately turned to concern for Mattie.

"Mrs. P, you won't believe this, but we were going over the Wilmington Bridge. You know how it kind of takes off into the sky?"

Mattie had Joe's complete attention, as Marian commented, "That's about the way I felt the first time we drove over it."

"Well, something happened to me, and I still don't understand it. I all but blacked out. Jean told me I was frozen at the wheel totally. She said she had to forcibly take my hands off the wheel to gain control while my foot was still on the gas. I don't remember our crossing until we were off it, and I asked Jean what she was doing virtually sitting in my lap. She burst out laughing and asked me to look around. I did and then I wanted to know how we got across the bridge and pulled over to the side. When she told me, I almost fainted."

Joe laughed and said, "I'm glad you're all right, Mattie, but the story doesn't surprise us. And don't worry about what happened except the next time you go across a bridge."

Marian was more reassuring. "Mattie, strange things like that happen to everyone during a lifetime."

"Well, it was a first for me."

They shared a laugh, and Marian said, "We want to thank you for being so good to Jean, and tell your mom we'll be there for dinner Saturday after I get home from work."

"Great!"

Joe walked Mattie out the door and watched her until she entered the Bruno home behind theirs.

As he returned, he heard, "Don't even say it, hon. Those things that happen to her are still happening and probably always will."

"Only now she's not telling us about them."

"Only because she's not feeling well. Don't make it harder for her."

Dinner at the Bruno's was, as always, an evening filled with good food, clinking glasses, and laughter in spite of Mattie and her brother's warring, very reminiscent of Jean and Joey. The house was, as always, full of cigarette smoke because the men of the Bruno family all smoked. It was the rare reason for being glad to leave the Bruno's for none of them smoked even Joey, though he tried as did Jean, but neither enjoyed the smell or taste on themselves while both chose to carry matches for others, as a rather weird way of fitting in.

Joey, in his new world, added carrying a pack of cigarettes to offer a lady one, as a means of opening a door for a new conquest becoming more and more frequent.

The next few months were filled with Jean, saying, "I'd rather not," to invitations from friends. The exceptions were these to the many dates with a lad named Bill Perry while refusing many an invitation from Marian and Joe to join them in a good time. Jean was too tired and seemed to be withdrawing further and further into herself.

Marian decided enough of this and put an end to it when an invitation from the Leones arrived inviting them to the dedication of their rebuilt Methodist Church. It had burned to the ground across the street from the Russian onion-shaped church in the area called the hollow on Joe's old running route. Neighbors, friends, and politicos of many faiths citywide were going to join in the festivities.

Jean's "I'd rather not" was met by Marian's "You are going. Staying home to mope doesn't help." Marian was at war with Jean's illness and its isolating, destructive impact on her lifestyle.

At twenty-two, Jean would not argue a valid point. Moping didn't help, but she felt so tired.

The overcrowded church poured people out the church doors onto two flights of stairs where they were unbothered by a gentle rain.

During one of the speeches, Jean said, "I'm going out for some air." She didn't admit that she felt dizzy.

Moments later, Joe followed her into the pleasant shower, saw her perched on the wall at the top of the stairs, and paused, knowing she'd be upset he was checking up on her and tried to fathom the nagging illness. Impatient for his return, Marian worked through the crowd, followed Joe's line of vision, saw Jean's eyes roll back into her head, and watched her pitch over the wall to the ground twelve feet below.

Marian knocked people aside including Joe to do a handspring that took her over the wall to land next to Jean who was face down and unconscious. Joe landed right beside her.

She rolled Jean over and removed the fresh manure and soft-top soil from her nose and mouth and tried to reach her with, "Jean? Jean, honey, answer me. Are you all right?" Joe was running his hands over Jean's legs checking for breaks with eyes jumping back and forth to watch over his girls.

Others rushed to help, including a first-day-on-the-beat patrolman. The officer gallantly took off his yellow slicker, covered Jean, and ran to the call box on the corner.

Jean's eyelids fluttered open to a field of heads holding up the gray sky on the stairs above.

"Oh, God!" she said.

Marian commanded, "Don't move."

Joe asked, "What can you feel?"

A clearing mind focused on toes, knees, and hips only to stop at a painful back.

"My back hurts. Nothin—'." She began to move.

"Stay put." Marian and Joe said the same thing in the same moment.

Jean laughed, only it hurt, so she shut up.

460

The x-rays indicated inflamed lungs that would heal completely, but the doctor warned of intense pain. The minute-to-minute hurt was nothing, and Jean refused to use the strong medication the doctor prescribed, and staying at home wasn't an option she considered. She easily withstood the pain and felt the doctor had exaggerated.

A few days later, at work and between phone calls, she sneezed.

The simple act turned violent, slapping her across the desk, her knuckles white, as she gripped its edges her breath gone and fear enveloped her as she near smothered herself with refusing to take the next breathe. It felt like something sliced down the center of her chest. The terror didn't help, and when nature forced the next breathe upon her, she prayed, "Please, Dear God, don't let me sneeze again."

Friends left their desks. One took her phone; another moved her chair to the side and stroked her back hoping it helped.

Jean recovered quickly and thanked them, and recognizing their faces were white with fear for her, she made light of it and plugged her phone back in. Their concern had made it easier, but the fear stayed with her.

Two weeks into healing with the medication within easy reach, the lungs were still the most serious problem. Another test showed them still enflamed but definitely improving.

One Sunday, Joe had taken Meggin, Jean's "little sister," home after she visited Jean and arrived back just as Charley Leone and the Methodist Church pastor came in the front door. Charley coming through the front door was a surprise to them all since he always used the side door whenever visiting, just like any member of their extended family.

Charley said no more than hello and introduced the pastor. The young minister, obviously upset, went right to the point.

"Mr. and Mrs. Prezzemoli, may I ask if you plan to sue my church? You have every right too. The overcrowding at the dedication gives you solid grounds."

Each Prezzemoli had the same reaction—surprise. Only it showed differently.

After looking at Marian, Joe spoke, "Reverend, we don't think along those lines, but"—he hesitated looking toward Jean who was poised to speak and said—"but our daughter is an adult. She has to speak for herself."

Everyone turned to Jean. Not even Joe and Marian knew what to expect because she was hurting.

The reverend fixed his attention solely on Jean.

Not feeling well left Jean edgy and defiant but hoping she hadn't signaled her vexation. *I don't need this nonsense. Why the big deal? I just want to be left alone. I just want to feel good again.*

She met the reverend's eyes and found herself studying him yet distracted by the lack of Mr. Leone's usual teasing. What she saw—upset and worry—changed vexing thoughts to a responsive utterance, "Reverend, I never gave that a thought. I can't sue your church. It was an accident. Please believe that I have no intention of going after you. My insurance is taking care of my bills."

The reverend's deep worry lines disappeared as he took a deep breath and said, "Thank you."

"You're welcome." Oddly, Jean felt better.

As the pastor left, Mr. Leone crossed the room to Jean, planted a kiss on her cheek, and said, "Feel better, kiddo. Marian, Joe, I'll see you guys later."

A parent's pride mixed with a good neighbor's leave-taking left Jean perplexed, as they stared at the closed door.

Jean turned and said, "Dad, did Mr. Leone really think I'd sue the church?"

"Some people would, and they had to be sure. At least the Parson obviously did, but—"

A sneeze wrenched Jean from where she stood, but Marian and Joe grabbed her before she fell. As it subsided, Jean reacted with, "I think the devil just had his way with me. They say revenge is sweet."

Joe said, "Ah, honey," and a frightened Marian declared tearfully, "I will never ask you to do anything you don't feel like doing again—not ever."

"Not ever, Mom?"

Joe couldn't resist a chuckle and added, "Sure, hon," mimicking Jean's knowing tone.

Marian, realizing what she said, recouped sheepishly. "Well, almost never, and yes, I will bite my tongue a million times."

Now they were all laughing. Only Jean was still hanging on to them.

After months of learning and moving supplies by truck from place to place to empower the army with the right equipment in the proper area, he was becoming a well-traveled man. Joey pulled into his home depot, thinking, *Man, I love driving a truck.*

He checked his watch remembering he had to report to the firing range to maintain his qualifying on the Ml rifle. It was hard to concentrate because he had just had a weekend that skyrocketed his self-image with the full realization of what the last months had done to his body. He'd joined a few buddies at the gym regularly lifting and looked forward to socializing with guys very like himself. It showed and he was doing both full out. Oh, how they loved the ladies.

The sergeant's command, "Assume a prone firing position, Prezzemoli," shook his mind free of the pleasing thoughts. He snapped to because he feared losing privileges, something his smart aleck ways of boot camp taught him to do, though he still tripped over his petard of humor.

"Prezzemoli, the targets are set, fire at will."

Joey jammed the rifle in place against his shoulder, regulated his breathing, and fired again and again.

The sergeant said nothing, just moved the target farther away as Joey reloaded and said, "Fire at will."

Again and again, the procedure took place from different positions, and finally, he heard, "Cease fire." Only then did Joey let a tired sore shoulder drop and found the sergeant standing tall above him hands on his hips.

Joey swallowed hard, suddenly uneasy.

"Prezzemoli." It came out a command, so Joey leaped to his feet, the rifle carefully placed butt down, chamber open and empty.

Now face-to-face, the three striper said, "Christ a mighty boy, that's damn good shooting. You belong in a rifle unit with that kind of a score."

"Gee, sergeant, I really like what I'm doing. Being in transport, I get to travel. It's important too. I have no idea why I'm a good shot, but I'd sure hate to be doing it all the time."

The sergeant, wise in the evaluating of a man and his skills, sensed Joey would not serve well in a rifle unit, so he dismissed him, though he had no idea Joey's macho image of himself would never have accepted, the sergeants view of him had he explained.

Joey had no idea that his skill on the range was a gift from his father. It too was part of that side of Joe he'd ceased to consider or refused to admit existed.

Joey returned to barracks a happier man recalling the events of the first real liberty of the weekend past for realizing and appreciating the potent body changes that required change in uniform size that genuinely made him a babe magnet. He was the spitting image of his uncle Sal, just under six feet, broad shouldered, tiny waist, and a well-endowed manhood sheltered between long well-developed legs, all this beneath a face, bearing Gregory Peck good looks. With a smile that said, I know it.

Grandma Tess's influence was very evident. Now as a man, he suddenly understood all the hoopla about his uncle and the ladies. Though these gifts were God-given, his ego and pride had taken great strides in a very short time.

It never occurred to Joey that his sister missed the chance to tease him, a perfect revenge, about shirts not fitting, buttons popping, pants a-crouching and socks a-falling below pant legs way too short.

He walked into the barracks, new uniforms over his arm, opened his locker, and said, "What are you standing there for? Get into uniform, the Frauliens await, let's not disappoint any of them."

One of his closest buddies Brad said, "Hey, Joey, are you planning on seeing the Frau, you made the date with last week? She's a beauty, but hubby's can be bothersome."

Before Joey answered, his mind took him to the moment his eyes met the mommas. He remembered how her beauty stunned him, reminding him of an older woman, a neighbor he could not approach for being too young to understand what he really felt. Smiling, he answered, "Hell, if I don't show, I'll ruin the lovely lady's day, and besides, we leave this base next week. I won't be seeing her again. As her daughter told you and she's your date, Momma and Poppa have an understanding that includes other 'intimates.' Hell, the Frau told me the same thing."

"Just watch your tail, my friend."

"With my luck, there's nothing to worry about. Right?"

"Right," answered the rest of the roving four, as they referred to themselves. The guys, having seen his luck in action, just laughed and finished dressing.

Joey had clearly joined the legions of men that good fathers spent wakeful nights wishing didn't exist. These fathers waited for their beautiful daughters to return home from dates with the charming American soldiers so much a part of a basically peaceful Europe.

Something within always insulated Joey from the effects of much self-knowledge, but he preferred to call, whatever it was, his luck. And now his luck was running on high, and he was becoming entrenched in believing nothing he could do would not be protected by the power of his luck and not only with the ladies. The consequences of his actions just didn't seem to catch up with him, and he loved the confidence instilled by the feeling.

In the land of the spirits, his watcher thought almost laughingly, *The ladies do like him, but it's not enough, and I can't help him. His decisions leave the door open for the dark ones, not me.*

The archer answered the thought with, *True, but they are as limited in what they can accomplish by the same decisions, and he has yet to choose true evil—fear his "luck" more than his decisions. Only the future and your careful watching may yet find a way to help.*

Jean was left with only an occasional crink in her neck from the fall and an instant of spasm that snapped her head backward to scare any viewer, but her weakness remained, and a new symptom occurred—a persistent sore throat. It seemed as though the come-along happenings she called adventures had been replaced by scary happenings in her body. The doctor tried but couldn't find anything wrong with the throat, and the slow downhill emotional decline continued. Jean's love of calf's liver and bacon was fulfilled five days a week and earned her a level of function that slowed the body's fatiguing.

A throat specialist explained, "I suspect a pernicious anemia." but neglected to explain the term, and she didn't ask. When she arrived home, she felt like a coward for not asking and reached for her dictionary. The word *cancer* made her shut the book without telling anyone, preferring to calm down and wait it out before panicking.

A few weeks later, Dr. Wolf again checked her throat.

"What the—? There's a tiny red spot in your throat. It wasn't there the last time I checked you, and I almost missed it now. Open wider."

Jean sat up straighter, as he put a suction devise down her throat and said, "Try not to fight this." Then he squeezed, she gagged, and it sucked. She fiercely grabbed the examining chair sides, trying not to fight it, but it felt like all her insides were coming through her throat. Wolf pulled out the device, and they both stared at a thin line of yellow in the glass bulb he held to the light for viewing.

Wolf gave out an angry "Son of a bitch! Your damn tonsils have grown in backward. Puss is poisoning your whole system." Then he unexpectedly smiled. "Jean, we just got damn lucky."

He explained with, "Without luck, we can't find this kind of puss infection, the body hides them too well."

Marian lost the debate with Jean. "Mom, don't lose a day's pay to sit at the hospital with me. Come up after work. It's only tonsils. Aunt Dodie said she'd keep me company."

Dodie, shy as always, sat in an uncomfortable chair and talked with Jean until the nurse gave Jean a twilight pill and took her to the operating room.

Jean's watching the preparations from the upright chair was short because Jean's eyes kept closing.

Then she screamed.

Wolf said, "What the hell's the matter with you?"

As his hand touched her leg, he howled, "Yeow! Jesus Christ, what's this goddamn dish doing here?" A kidney dish, now empty of boiling water, sat in Jean's lap. Wolf didn't wait for an answer. He tossed the dish aside, and as it clanged to the floor, he sent the sheet after it, saying as he pointed to different nurses, "You, get me a cream for the burns. You, get me a new cover sheet." In moments, Wolf had salved the reddened skin and waited. He was surprised at how quickly the pain disappeared and decided to continue, though as a doctor he harbored a serious possibility.

Back in her room, minus her tonsils, Jean was listening to an anxiously chattering Dodie when the world turned perverse. An overpowering quaking took possession of her. They were so powerful they attacked the bed and moved it across the room toward a now terrified aunt.

Jean brought all her will power into play, but it did nothing. Worse was watching Dodie contort in alarm. Jean yelled, "Aunt Dodie, get out of here!" Dodie raced from the hypnotic circumstance to return in moments with a nurse carrying a hypodermic syringe. Dr. Wolf had prepared for the worst, and Jean felt the needlepoint and instantly entered a void to nowhere.

The nowhere ended with fluttering eyelids viewing a cavalcade of male faces above her with Dr. Wolf softly, saying, "It's all right, dear, we're here to help you." The gentle words faded as Jean sank into a precarious slumber.

A return to the thinking world found Marian and Joe bending over her, and she slowly said, "This waking up to faces above me is getting to be a ridiculous habit. Ohh that hurt."

Marian brushed the damp hair from Jean's face while Joe held Jean's rather pale hand.

In a soft, hoarse slow voice she reached for humor. "Am I supposed to ask where am I or what am I doing here?" Her throat hurt and her voice was hoarse. She wanted to say, "Hey, I've got a sexy voice, but it isn't worth the hurting."

"How do you feel?" insisted Marian.

"Tired."

"Do you know what happened?" questioned Joe.

"I was burned, my tonsils were removed, and I started shaking."

"Not quite, honey. You hemorrhaged and they pumped your stomach to get rid of the blood." Joe bit his lip, visualizing what they had done.

"That's scary. I remember lots of faces and Dr. Wolf saying something nice. Then I went out again. It must have been serious he's never gentle."

Marian stroked her and told the truth. "You almost died, honey. They said your kind of shock isn't seen very often. The interns were here to learn. Dr. Wolf misjudged your burns because the pain went away so quickly but prepared for the possibilities."

Marian's hand felt good on Jean head. "Leave it to me to sleep through being the center of male attention." As Joe changed his position, she saw Dodie still sitting in that God-awful chair.

Smiling at Dodie, Jean added, "See, Mom, I told you Aunt Dodie would stay with me. At least it wasn't dull, Aunt Dodie. Thanks for being here. I'm sorry you had to see this. Dad, please take Aunt Dodie home before that God-awful chair cripples her. Jeez, my throat hurts."

Dodie walked over and kissed Jean. Joe extended his arm to Dodie and whispered a fervent, "Thank you, Dodie." He enjoyed Dodie's warm smile as she took his arm and said to Jean, "I'm going to call Meggin for you. I'll explain why you can't see her for a while."

"Thanks, Dad, and tell her not to worry." It was a real squeaky sentence.

With everyone gone, Jean passed quickly from "why me" to deeper thoughts and chatted with Freddy. "God, cuz, it's weird to know you almost die and not have any recollection of it. Boy, do I know when to sleep. This is scary."

Sensing the words, "Hang in there, cuz," she fell into a deep sleep.

The archer smiled at his student's use of family ESP.

The next day, the worst was over, but Jean felt ancient when the overly respectful student nurse apologized for the burning.

"I hope you'll forgive me. And I hope you won't have me fired. I want so to be a nurse."

The girl's sincerity rang true, and a tired Jean said, "I won't, but please, I want your promise to be the most careful nurse."

As the troubled but relieved young nurse left, Jean thought, *Would somebody please tell me why I keep getting into these messes?* Of course, there was no answer.

In that very far away place, her very serious watcher took heed of those words hoping to prompt the answers sometime in the future.

At home, Joe and Marian discussed Jean. A love for the unusual, they understood. What they couldn't understand was the element of danger that followed her or the people touching her life.

"Joe, what is it that takes her to the edge yet never lets her go over?"

"I don't know, but thank God someone watches over her. She won't let us do it. This was just life taking a mean corner."

"You know, hon, she's at least careful, while Joey ignores caution. With him, we've always expected the worst, and we're no longer surprised when it works for him while things come out of nowhere, trip Jean up, and then—but then that's her luck, isn't it?"

"Maybe, but I doubt we'll ever find the answers," he hesitated and added, "except that cousin Della was right. Friday the thirteenth babies have great luck. Too bad my son doesn't put it into other energies. He's a winner especially with the ladies, so say his letters and requests for more money."

"Oh, Joe, I worry that he'll go too far."

"I doubt that. He's not stupid. By the way, the Brunos want us over Saturday to show Jean a good time, and I suspect to spoil you as well. Okay?"

"Very okay. Jean enjoys them as much as we do, except when Mattie and Ralph go at it. I think it reminds her too much of her and Joey. They can't seem to understand each other."

"As we both know, age has nothing to do with a guy coming to understand a female, even his own."

Marian winked at Joe as he smiled.

Jean laughed her way through the night in the Bruno kitchen, only throwing a dirty look at Ralph after too much drinking had him picking on Mattie again. As usual, Mattie didn't let him get away with it. All went home wonderfully fed including Spot who happily took food from any offering.

Jean called Spot as they left and said, "Thanks, Mrs. Bruno. This is a great way to start feeling good again."

Later that night, Spot went crazy barking. He kept trying to get out the back window. Jean stumbled down stairs half awake to find Marian and Joe in the kitchen. Joe was in his baggy shorts, and

Marian was in a nightgown covered with her housecoat. Joe was restraining Spot who was fighting to get loose. They could see there was no one out there, but Joe looked and said, "My God, Mar, there's smoke coming from the Bruno's. I'll call the fire department." He reached for the phone next to the window, and Marian grabbed Spot and handed him to Jean.

Jean said, "Easy, Spot. Good boy, we see it."

Joe had just dialed when he saw Marian outside running toward the Bruno's. As he spoke to the operator, Joe, Jean, and a shivering Spot saw the Bruno windows explode outward, throwing the glass and debris right at Marian. The phone crashed to the floor, and the horrified three flew out the door unable to see Marian dive into the protection of the gutter.

What they did see was the flames seeking oxygen follow the debris across the street and then fold back inside the house allowing Marian to instinctively rise, unscathed and run to the front of the Bruno house with Joe, Jean, and Spot only feet behind.

Marian rounded the corner to find firemen already fighting the fire and ran to Mrs. Bruno throwing her arms around her. To other neighbors, the mother appeared hysterical, screaming in seemingly incoherent words. Marian realized it was panicked Italian and turned on the fire lieutenant. "She's telling you her daughter's in there, upstairs. She went to get the tenants out. Damn it, get her out. Joe and Jean joined them and Joe added, Ralph's not here. Jesus Christ get them both." Terror was burning a hole in their hearts. Spot huddled at Joe's feet.

Jean stood apart having heard what Marian had said. She stood directly in line with the hallway and found herself unable to move. The longer she saw nothing, the more her breathing quickened. Then they all saw movement, a fireman exiting the burning first floor with a body over his shoulder. The fireman ran Mattie clear of the fence and dropped her like a sack of potatoes and collapsed beside the fire hydrant hacking for air. Jean still couldn't move, she knew Mattie, bloated and ashen, was dead. Ralph was not with them.

Two Bruno brothers, having arrived from their homes down the street, became spectators to hell fearing the evil one had taken someone he had no right to take. One of Mattie's brothers, an ex navy medic, rushed to Mattie and fiercely tried to pump life into Mattie's bloated body. He couldn't. Finally, torn with sorrow, he covered Mattie's bare breast with the tattered pajama top and cried.

The upstairs tenants had escaped harm out a back window unknowing that Mattie was breaking down their door with her bare hands to reach them. The horror wasn't yet finished. Ralph was found on the back porch hidden from view by the steel garage so close to the house. He was burned horribly from the face to the waist. The only two Bruno adult children still at home was either dead or near dead. Ralph was en route to the hospital, as were Anna and her other children. There wasn't much hope, and neighbors collected their own and headed home.

All that had to be done was done, and the next day, the initial fire report stated probable cause, as an accident that started in the living room from Ralph's smoking cigarette.

Jean heard and filled with hatred for Ralph. She knew he was in unbelievable agony and had been fighting for his life for three days, but Jean chewed on cruel emotions without compassion for him. She turned cold and without tears since that moment with Mattie on the ground. The hate was spiraling Jean downward to a place a soul should never go. A place where thoughts too horrible to repeat fed on her soul like maggots in a festering wound.

She spent the days working like a mechanical device and passed by friends as if they didn't exist. By now, she was plagued by vicious thoughts of Ralph. By the third day, she'd begun to wish his death would take forever. After telling Marian and Joe how she felt and hating their reactions to her feelings, she clammed up refusing their efforts to help her see the situation clearly.

Elsewhere, a dark watcher moved closer to her helping to make her thoughts more at home. The door at a dangerous corner was wide open.

After a week in this lonely time, both Mattie and Ralph's funerals were over and it was time for Jean's fifteen-minute afternoon break, and she walked to the lounge and flopped into a chair dismal in every way.

She couldn't read, and she couldn't get her mind off seeing Mattie next to the fire hydrant and Ralph being responsible for killing her.

Just then, a friend came looking for her and said, "Jean, your mom's on the phone. I had it transferred in here."

Jean picked up the receiver.

Her voice, a cracking whisper, said, "Yeah, Mom."

"The fire inspector called your dad. The investigation is over. Jean, the fire actually started in the walls and was burning even while we were there for supper." The silence made Marian stop. "Honey, are you listening?"

"Yes." The answer sounded very un-Jean to Marian, as though said by a five-year-old.

"I'm sorry to call you at work, but you need to know this, and so did Dad and I. It wasn't Ralph's fault. Apparently, he woke up with his thoughts completely muddled by smoke inhalation and, yes, the drinking too, but he must have thought the fire started in the TV. He actually picked it up. Honey, it was burning, and he carried it out to the back porch. They found it at the base of the steps. Jean, he did what he could. He did all that his body and mind would let him. Honey, Ralph wasn't to blame. The fire was electrical and started in the walls."

"Oh, Mom." Jean gagged as though choking on smoke and no more words would come. The misplaced hatred tore from Jean. She cried and shuddered with pain for both her friends. It was Ralph who took to her last prom before she left college. That night, he had stayed sober and had been fun to be with, and they even talked of Mattie and him. Jean's mind went to Mrs. Bruno, and her body rocked with sadness. Jean's friend took the phone and told Marian what was happening.

"Mrs. P, Jean is crying. Is there anything I can do to help?"

"No, Pat, but thank you. She needs to cry, we all do. When you can, tell her to come home now, and thank you again for staying with her."

The friend touched Jean's head with compassion and arranged to have her desk covered by a supervisor so that Jean could leave to do battle with her demons at home.

That night, the mother, father, and daughter talked of gone friends and confused feelings. Jean hesitated and then asked, "Mom, was it like this with Aunt Angie and your grandmother when they hated?"

Marian closed her eyes, and finding Joe's hand once more in hers, she answered, "Honey, it was worse. They never learned to stop or forgive."

The silence and the unshed tears in her mother's eyes, and her father's sadness left Jean unbelievably wasted and grateful for arriving at some understanding.

It was time for bed, but as they headed for their rooms, Marian stopped and said, "Oh, God, we have to tell Joey." There was no going to bed until it was done.

Joey and Mattie

It took time, but Joey was fetched and returned their emergency call. It was difficult, but they had all grabbed an extension, Marian in the kitchen, Joe in the bedroom, and Jean in the cellar.

They couldn't hang up until Joey was handling it. Marian did the dirty work, and each took a turn to talk to Joey until he was able to accept a reality that until now had never taken close friends from him. That done, they went to bed ready to help the Bruno family in any way needed, knowing there really was nothing they could do and their hearts trembled.

The neighborhood mourned, and the Bruno's never called it home again, and the more than one-hundred-year-old house carried its sadness for years but would one day know another family as caring, very Irish, very much both family and friend.

Jean, now free of her illness, set about regaining her strength. She talked to Joe, and he pointed to the hill on their street and said, "Since you don't want to swim, start walking that hill and then run it. Between the lifting for your back muscles and the running, you'll be fit in no time."

An exercise starved body responded beautifully, and in a few months, she was strong as ever. One afternoon, she returned from a run to find the house full of people. Relatives and neighbors filled the kitchen and living room, so she began kissing everyone hello only to realize they were watching her. She was about to ask why when she heard, "Hi, sis."

An army uniform filled out with a taller, well-built Joey, the spitting image of their uncle Sal stood in the foyer. Words choked and tears flowed as she flew into his arms, lesser men would have landed on the floor with her impact.

Family laughed at the brother and sister, more combatants who cried as they held each other. His tour was over.

In a matter of days, Joey was again working at a food chain store because he needed money quickly for a very special event while he was still not sure what he wanted to do with his life. True to brotherly fashion he met Bill Perry and the teasing began. She ignored it, while little Meggin more the young lady then when he left was happy to have another Sir Galahad who showed her the better side of life.

Joey and Jean took over a family conversation. Jean led off with, "Okay, Mom, we're here to discuss what you and Dad want for your twenty-fifth anniversary. We can't make any decisions because you've always told us you know exactly how you want it to be."

Joey said, "So start telling us what you want us to do and Jean, and I will pay for as much of it as we can. No arguments."

The excited parents joined right in.

Marian did the planning, and though the young adults met most bills, she and Joe chose some expensive extras to honor their twenty-fifth anniversary. A planned trip to California to see Joe's brother Louis bit the dust so the couple could have everything and everyone they wanted. Louis, now the father of eight, would be unable to attend, but the contact was maintained. The family was doing enormously well financially in California, and visits did occur and both Joe's youngest siblings, Bart and Louise moved there.

Marian delighted in her extensive anniversary menu adding other special ethnic plates that complimented and added to the evening's pleasure. For weeks, Jean and she fried eggplant, filling the freezer and then prepared to supervise the cooking for hundreds at St. Michael's Ukrainian Church Hall and hired their excellent cook to handle the meal that night freeing Marian to hostess and enjoy their anniversary evening.

On the night of the party, they left the house acting joyously silly. When the music began, the celebrating couple led off a cotillion. Marian's uncles tap-danced on stage in true Fred Astaire style and held dance contests, and the celebrant couple sailed the dance floor in each other's arms.

Jean and look alike cousin Rick took pictures, motion and still. Jean's new thirty-five millimeter cornered everyone who came. Joey had arranged for an excellent band. They weren't big, but they played all kinds of music beautifully, and the dance floor was never empty.

Marian had said, "Jean, you take care that your cousin Tom and other predators don't get near the eggplant."

25ᵗʰ Anniversary

Jean burst into laughter and left, saying, "Sure, give me the impossible jobs. Talk about being outnumbered."

When Joey told those male predators what was on the menu, Tom organized a raiding party. The cohorts sneaked into the kitchen and outflanked Jean who hollered for the big guns.

Marian flew into the kitchen followed by a laughing Joe, and oodles of family and friends crowding the door to watch the antics. They found Jean and the Ukrainian cook and staff with wooden spoons trying to fence off the eggplant. Marian and Joe charged between the chowhounds to push them out of the kitchen, but they still left licking their fingers.

Tom said, "Aw, Aunt Marian, you know we love your food."

"Git" was about all the laughing aunt could manage.

The meal itself was delightfully unrushed and savored.

Later, Joey sang a love song to his parents leading to Joe taking Marian into his arms to do the honors. Joey smiled and felt special for having found his voice in honoring them.

Joey, the man, cheered with pride in his parents sharing, as the audience went wild at his father's unabashed showing of his love for his mother, as Jean wished for the same with all her troubled heart.

No one left the party before 3:00 a.m., and then the party continued at the house until everyone went to mass. An old-fashioned

American shivaree prevented the night of conjugal fancies the couple had planned. A pleasant corner that had long been anticipated out-did itself.

Joe continued to read everything he could find on Castro's Cuba and the nationalization of the sugar industry. Joe's disbelief of Castro's statement that he wasn't exporting revolution was as strong, as it was correct. ESP usually belonged to Joe's ladies, but this time, Joe augured the future. A strange foreboding beyond any reasoning gave Cuba an importance that was far more personal, so Joe pushed the fear far away.

The family watcher stymied with concern, breathed a heavenly sigh grateful Joe had dismissed Cuba. He knew where such knowledge would take this caring man and the dangerous future was almost here.

The Irish lad, Bill Perry, was showing up very regularly as Jean poured renewing energy into new doings and opening new worlds to Meggin with Bill's help.

Marian and Joe liked Bill and wondered if this was it while Jean's lack of excitement told them no.

The revisiting of Marian and Joe's family corners would soon be over.

Jean's watcher turned to the archer and said, "It really begins for Jean now, doesn't it?"

The Archer said, "You are learning well, pay heed. Your time to help could come suddenly if it comes at all. And her doings in this time, opens the doors of decisions, frightening, destructive or loving and giving. Beware the open doors for her dark watcher is ready and a quick adversary. I dread the real-world decisions where we can lose both Jean and her brother."

A Spirit's Love in Why

Caring's tentacles often wrapped this family into passion's homing. One night, the daughter of a close childhood friend of Marian and Joe's dropped by with a young man in tow, no one but Jean recognized.

Jean called out, "Hi, Sandra. Hi, Peter."

After a moment explaining the need to talk to her parents, Jean took the couple to the living room.

Peter, spoke first, "Mr. and Mrs. Prezzemoli, I know you don't know me, but Sandra and I need your help." He gulped. "Sandra's pregnant, and we have to tell her parents."

While Joe's eyes found Jean's realizing she wasn't surprised, Marian's never left the couple and calmly asked, "And what do you want us to do?" The question lacked challenge.

Sandra continued with, "Aunt Marian"—Sandra's voice was shaking—"I don't know what my father will do when we tell him. We want to get married, but Dad has such a temper he's liable to kill one of us."

Marian didn't say anything, instead she was studying Joe while remembering Nick so like her brother Tony whose temper flared like a gas torch. But seeing Joe attentive but untroubled decided to follow his lead.

Joe was as blunt as Marian had been and addressed Peter. "Marriage may not be your answer. You would be making a bigger mistake by marrying if it's only because of the baby." While waiting for an answer, Joe recalled the temper Sandra feared and looked to Marian.

Peter brought him back. "Sir, I care about Sandra. I can't say I'm ready for marriage, but it's time." His jaw slammed shut, for feeling clumsy. "I mean, I want both to have my name, and if Sandra's father has a vicious temper, I'd like someone around he respects. I don't want to fight him. I learned to protect myself in the shore patrol. If he's as bad as she says, I'd have to hurt him to stop him."

While Joe studied Peter, Marian spoke to Sandra, "Sandra, what are your feelings?" The softness of her words told her what Marian was really asking.

"Oh, Aunt Marian, I wouldn't be pregnant if I didn't love Peter. Please believe me, and please help us?"

Marian hesitated long enough to read Joe again. It bothered them both that Peter never used the word *love*. She understood this and decided.

"You've obviously thought this through, so we'll go with you. But you, Sandra, will have to tell your parents, not Peter. And you know your father would never harm you." A glance at Peter said she wasn't too sure about him.

Sandra nodded feeling a little safer. Marian then added, "I think Jean should come too. It'll help your parents to see that your friends are standing by you."

Jean thought, *Oh, s-sugar plums and apricots too, here we go again.* But her insatiable curiosity made it easier.

Sandra made the announcement, and her father turned to Peter and growled, "You son of a bitch!"

Peter didn't budge as Nick charged at him, but Nick never reached him.

Joe grabbed the angry father, just as Marian cut into Nick's path and took hold of his shirt.

"Look at me, Nick." Again, she said more insistently, "Look at me, Nick." Waiting a split second, she went on forcefully.

"You want to hurt Peter? For what?"

A puzzled Nick said, "How can you stick up for this son of a bitch? He got my daughter pregnant."

"If Sandra hadn't lifted her skirt, she wouldn't be pregnant."

Sandra's mother joined the wounding barrage. "Nick! Please stop. She's right."

Joe felt the fury in Nick's body collapse under the crippling weight of the truth. A daughter had made her bed.

Later Joe asked Jean, "Had Sandra told you? Did you Have anything to do with their coming here?"

"No, Dad, no. I just noticed the change in her figure. I hate being right." Joe nodded and Jean realized how sad he was and thought, *Oh, Dad, my God, if you knew that you don't have worry about this with me and knew what was happening to me, it would kill you. I can't and won't tell you.*

This corner in human time returned Marian and Joe's remembering to NOW and wondering about Jean's being with Bill Perry and the heart break the couple were dealing with.

Marian was about to ask a question about Bill, but instead went all mother to say, "She's home."

They watched a saddened daughter come through the kitchen door.

"Are you okay?" Joe asked softly.

Jean nodded.

"Will Bill be all right?" asked Marian.

"I think so. I hope so. I should have told him sooner. I can be so dense." Jean kissed them and went upstairs.

Her need to be alone was obvious. She went upstairs reliving every moment in a crucible analysis while Bill was pounded by it all.

When Bill saw Jean unexpectedly leave the house, he had to wait in the cold air and deal with it as best he could.

She's not waiting for me to come in. She's as sexy as ever, and all I can think about is she's angry. Just the way she's carrying herself—oh, shit, I'm in big trouble. I've seen her this way before. Whenever an unpleasant chore needed doing, this "thing" settles around her. It's like a shield cemented in place giving her complete control and there's no changing it. I tried it with her concerns about Meggin, but she knew what had to be done and was right both times.

Now only feet away, he reached for the gate and opened it for her. Jean touched his arm, saying, "Thanks, Bill." He could still feel it because her genuine acknowledgments of his small attentions had always made him feel good about himself. Today, the effort was chilling. Every molecule shivered in winter mode as he held the car door for her.

He slowly went around to the driver side, thinking, *She wanted me to find a place we could talk, so the park's our best bet. Oh, Christ, I love her but she's calling it off between us. Why, damn it, why? Not because I accused her of lying, though that's enough to do it, but then I blurted out I loved her—real romantic, you asshole.*

He slipped into the driver's seat reliving the numbing anger. *Jesus, Joseph, and Mary, how dumb can I get. But she didn't tell me about the change in plans? It was a stupid mistake. But that's not like her. Christ, I hope she didn't tell her parents. I don't want them to think I'm that stupid.*

As he started the engine, he said, "We'll go to Tibbetts to talk if that's all right."

Her "That's fine, Bill" had the slightest tremble to it.

God, I love her and she's calling us off. Why, damn it, why?

Self-abusing emotions intruded his unhappy reflections and offered an old answer, one that, for him, had yet to be proven wrong.

Minutes later, they pulled into a parking space in the same Tibbetts Brook Park Joe ran as a young man. It was pretty in hibernation under October's first scant snow, and the gazebo's storybook look Joe loved went unnoticed. Jean was cold, troubled, but determined as an anxious Bill charged into conversation.

"I'm sorry I accused you of lying, but what was I supposed to think? You popped out of the car window yelling hi when I thought you were visiting your uncle in the hospital. Jesus, you were in a car full of girls." He wanted to say clowns. "I never meant to tell you I love you that way, but I want to marry you, and I won't mistrust you again."

Remembering she hates jealousy, he added, "And I wasn't jealous, just mad as hell."

The words pounded on Jean like the blaring of a radio at full volume in a very small room. Feeling worse with each syllable, she labored to stop him.

"Oh, Bill, please don't. This has nothing to do with the other day."

His voice changed sounding almost hoarse for the trapped emotions, "Oh, God, Jean, I—"

"Bill, I'm sorry, I didn't know you felt this strongly about me. This is my fault. I've been stupid." Now she sounded frightened, but she dared not stop. "I mean, I can't marry you be—"

His control cut into her words to hammer home his reaction.

"Because I'm a bastard and no one is going to want me. Least of all, someone like you. It's all right for me to love you, but you can't love me."

The child he had been dismantled Jean's warping self-pity. Unsure which was worse, his look of hurt or his flush of shame, she grabbed his arm and pulled forcing him to look at her and prayed, "*God please make him understand I'm the problem, not him.*"

"Bill, listen to me."

The sudden calm of her voice reached Bill's harassed being.

"You know that's not true. Damn it, you're not knowing who your father is never mattered to me or my family, and it won't matter to anyone who loves you. Don't do this to yourself."

Her swearing pierced Bill's lifelong dishonor. He had never heard her curse, and her fierce grip upon his arm brought him the reminder of her caring so much a part of her that it took him from seeing her as someone he wanted to bed to a world of caring he'd only hoped existed and grew for finding it did. *And I'm losing it.*

Desperation saturated Jean's plea. "If you really love me, listen with your heart, please." Her grip was now desperate, but it brought her a wave of strength that held back her tears.

Bill's eyes moistened, but too much a part of a generation where a man shouldn't cry, he didn't. Disheartened and immobile, he listened to the next ax stroke.

"I mustn't marry anyone, not anyone." Fatigue was depleting her, but knowing Bill was listening, she continued.

Bill's blue eyes changed to a shade of question, and knowing her honesty, he understood. Something else was terribly wrong.

"Bill, you're very dear to me, but if I loved you enough to marry you, I still couldn't marry you. Oh, Jesus."

Bill's predicament brought her pause, and she noticed her fingers. *He'll be black and blue tomorrow.* Then words tumbled. "There's something wrong with me. I'm not sure what it is, but it's real." The little she could tell, she did; beyond that, there was nothing.

Bill listened, the ax went deep, and it was over.

Oh, damn, how nothing can hurt.

Downstairs, Marian, seeing Joe was still bothered asked, "Joe, are you thinking about Jean's conversation with Bill?"

"Somewhat. But with all our remembering, I'm really thinking about the things we carry around inside us that we can't set aside and how they can destroy what we value most because we don't."

Marian remembered well, but the mother in her kept reaching for Jean until he said, "In spite of them, I've been very lucky and very human. I hoped the kids wouldn't have to deal with such problems. They're five years apart in age, and yet they both have something bothering them, and I don't know how to help them. Guess it's simply their turns."

Marian's smile and thoughts came back from Jean to say, "I wonder about that too. What corners life will take Joey and Jean through is a complete mystery, but, hon, we've never been spectators, so if we can help, we will, but it is theirs to do."

A warm smile eased Joe's expression, as he took Marian's hand to say, "I'm glad to have all of us together and home. God only knows what mischief our adults or to use Jean's word *adventures* they'll get into and considering our own corners, life is going to get very interesting again."

Marian laughed squeezed his hand, saying, "That's my guy," while wishfully thinking, *She'll tell us something when she's ready.* A little bit of a sad "grrrr" snuck into her mind, knowing she probably wouldn't. *Because I taught her independence.*

Joe almost absentmindedly said, "Mar, I'm glad you taught her to be independent her generation needs it."

Upstairs, torn and exhausted, Jean continued her destructive analyzing allowing her intellect to recognize why men offered marriage but understanding they wanted a Jean who didn't exist, one who could exist but maybe never would.

The one who told them to keep their hands off for obvious reasons was ready for marriage and motherhood. That was the Jean full of competence who enjoyed switching from hometown girl to sophisticated lady in a blink. None of which mattered, all she knew was she had no right to any man's love until she had her answer.

As she changed to pajamas, she lingered over a drawer where she fingered a pretty negligee her parents bought her, still unworn. Lovely, ultra-feminine items filled the drawer.

"Oh, God, please help me. I'm going crazy. Why don't I enjoy lovemaking with someone I care about?"

The stuttering began. "It doesn't excite, it t-t-terrifies me. Oh, Blessed Mother, wha-what am I, a le-lesbian? Wha-what di—why a-am I b-being punished?"

Jean's muted prayers scurried along a busy byway. The spirits were having a hectic night.

She slipped into bed to weary to cope and took refuge in a familiar fantasy, a companion since her thirteenth year. It took her into the blue sky, with her hand on the stick of a P-38 plane while she practiced aerial acrobatics freeing a troubled soul to enjoy the Marine corp lieutenant winging into the room to shade his eyes watching the prop job land.

Her wave changed thoughts to feelings for them both. The Marine corp husband Robert warmed her just being there. It was meant to be real. Suddenly home, the lover's caressing breath sought to send infinite needles to heighten wanting and pronounced changes of arousal to delight the viewing. Fingering the firm shapes of his muscles, she softened and curved into a caressing bundle.

Her fingers find his flight zipper and tempts her glow by unbuttoning her, he strokes to induce its wave to her being, to flush an scatter private urges he knows are for him alone. But half dressed and teasing, they bare each other and laughing dive for the bed.

But its fantasy, her mind said the passionate words, but she felt nothing but loss and returns to the darkened room, still the virgin, without an orgasm and not knowing why. The diversion ended in dreamless sleep. If there were real dreams, she never remembered any of them. For years, the fantasy kept hope and believing alive only to turn into a devastating horror when with a man she cared for.

The fantasy begun in youth, grew as she did. Her hunk called Bob remained the same until the crink in her neck dropped his height from six-two to five-ten. The flying never changed, but a troubled mind created measurements of herself as a woman that deluged her with self-contempt deep within. It was real world and shared with no one.

Her watcher turned from Jean to the archer's command to observe another watcher and found himself in a huge gymnasium for the selections of the U.S. Olympic Wrestling team. The other watcher, an ancient, a man of Native American heritage waited to claim his charge, an Annapolis Midshipman, class of '62 vying for a place on the team. His opponent, a Marine corps non-com stood ready on the gym floor.

The ancient quickly changed his direction, and they were now in a locker room, as a young man hurriedly rushed to dress.

A loud speaker explained, and the middie cheering section left to comfort a mate; a father was dead.

The archer explained, "He may be important if Jean's decisions find him. You may see him soon."

"He can help her?"

"Only her decisions will decide that, as will his."

"May I help her now?"

"Not in this time, for she is one who can help not only herself, but others. She has yet to choose."

The watcher was returned to Jean and asked, "Can she hear us?"

"Not as a voice, but all have a capacity to hear us and the evil one, if they chose to hear us."

"You must pull from your being a sensing and share it to ease a floundering mind and threatened soul without doing it for them. Only when the evil one interferes unfairly can we help openly, as we did for her as a child."

Pausing in departure, the student, remembering the "Candy Man," questioned, "Just a little help?"

In this place of no time, the archer eyed the ancient's effort, nodded, felt that wonderous moment of Joy only "The Father" could give and withdrew a shaft from his quiver and pulled the bow of hope to offer Jean's spirit a knowing. What she would do with it good or bad, only her choices will tell.

In the human world, a hidden door imploded, and the dreamless world of one human crossed the threshold of a sleeping mind bathed in a blinding flash of light to stand in a world of perpetual notion where twisting, molding secrets of the person you are rule and manipulate.

Suddenly, the colors and shapes meshed into Jean seeing herself eleven years old. A lanky, skinny frame set on long legs beneath an elongated neck that made much below look clumsy. Bright chestnut hair in a perm doing a Watusi proud bordered a long, freckled face. The adult felt odd watching herself huddled with her friend Dora.

The girls epitomized that age of wonder and finding out about life and a mystery called sex. Dora, now twelve, stood joyous in pubescent growth already at home with a heating body's new shape and growing beautiful who longed to test its merits. Both had yet to leave the realm of a mind's innocence.

They were laughing at the comparison of their figures while the adult Jean remembered it was at the height of her sexual curiosity both experimental and excessive while still awaiting the mysterious body change called puberty.

The scene becomes a handsome young man's smile. The girls' experiment in flirting had worked.

The young veteran, a maintenance man, shined with the sensitive good looks that draw women of all ages. He was working in the laundry room connecting federal project building 28 to 27 where the girls lived.

The long room had self-locking steel doors in each structure. On both sides of the steel doors were steel-mesh walls, floor to ceiling, designated as storage rooms that narrowed these entry points to four feet with an open area for about ten feet before the room opened from window to window on either side of the building. The children liked to run sticks through the steel fences as they approached the doors.

The room held four washtubs back to back with ringer washing machines on both sides of the room. Lines for indoor drying were attached to both sides of the storage areas to stretch across the room for maximum use.

Looking through the laundry room windows, Dora said, "Isn't he cute?"

"Like a movie star." Jean giggled.

As they sensed his catching their interest, they circled the outside area, strutting their stuff, not sure what their stuff was, but "it" responded to his handsome smile and drawing them into the laundry room from the entrance in building number 28.

Awareness became fuzzy as the door slammed behind them. The fascinating young man loomed right before them isolating them between the shadowed storage rooms and the closed door.

His smile, different, frightened them, yet neither knew they should scream.

The man grabbed Dora with one hand, tripping her to the ground. The other hand reached for Jean. She ducked. His hand touched her skin, but her shoulder blade crashed into the storage room allowing her to instinctively bend her knees and slide under his grab to run.

Dora could not escape. A vicious strength held her below a hot breath. A handsome face, red with urges the girls knew little about, frenzied her while Jean had panicked and run.

At the opposite door, Jean saw a two by four holding the door closed, kicked it free, grabbed the knob, and heard Dora's, "Oh no, please, no." The sobs of a friend forced Jean's looking back. The man, straddling Dora's legs, clawed at her panties.

Jean's hand left the knob to run back. In desperation, she brought clenched fists down on the man's head and neck again and again.

Suddenly, he came off the ground his penis erect. Violent eyes grabbed at Jean, as his hands could not because she ran.

Fearing his nearness, she abruptly changed direction to dodge around the washtubs, yelling, "Dora, run."

Dora jumped up and pulled at the door while Jean's nightmare included ring around the tubs as she kept them between her and that.

Dora's slamming door distracted the beast, and Jean beat him to the number 27 exit. Fear and need drove her upstairs running for home until hearing Dora's frantic, "Jean, wait, please."

Dora caught up and whispered, "Don't tell anyone."

Jean blinked with surprise and snapped. "I have to."

The imploring friend grabbed an arm. Jean backed away. A sense of self-preservation and training commanded her response to Dora's, "Jean, if you tell, I swear on the Blessed Mother I'll never speak to you again."

Jean glared at Dora, her nostrils flared in anger as she whirled, shot upstairs, and tore through the door to home.

Joe, seeing terror on his daughter's face, came out of his seat like a rocket suddenly free of atmosphere. Jean stuttered and stammered through the tale.

Joe encountered the unthinkable. "Honey, slow down." The safety of his hands on her arms slowed the stuttering, as a squatting dad looked deeply into frightened eyes while his gut full of rage tried to dismantle the father. Still he asked, "Are you all right?"

Jean felt protected, but Joe's expression bewildered her as she answered a rasping, "Yes." The sound hindered the father.

"And Dora?"

"Yes."

Joe's struggle continued between hatred and love in rushing thought, *Oh, Christ, thank you.*

What must be done doused Joe's urge for violence, so he held his shaking sparrow close and said, "Come on, honey, we have to see Dora's parents."

Later, the police arrived, and Marian came home. The girls did not see the man again except from the protection of their windows.

The handcuffed prisoner entered the police car, and the father looked up at his daughter safe with her mother and mulled, *Honey, are you really all right?*

Jean, the twenty-five-year-old, sat up in the darkened room with sudden clarity racing through a startled mind to realize a child controlled her with misread values on sexual wanting and handsome. One a true measure, the other twisted into an uncontrollable fear.

The adult became furious with the child for the warping and demanded perfection like an unthinking parent. The normal acts of a child in a time full of enticements did not need forgiving, but the struggling adult made a mistake worse than the child's.

Softening, she stared at Fred's picture and said, "Fred, did you have something to do with this? Who was it that said and the enemy is me?"

In the land of the spirits, her watcher was saddened by her decision and the conflict of her chosen direction. He realized, as the archer predicted, she could find a world of problems in spite of believing. She'd left him with no way to help for the child was not the enemy. Elsewhere, her dark watcher pleasurably anticipated her direction.

Jean knew reality was something she could deal with, but she shackled the child, saying, "You're not doing this to me anymore. Whatever I have to do to keep you in your place, I will."

In other ways, wise ways she was thinking clearly. "Our father who art in heaven, thank you." She realized how little humans knew about the mysteries of their minds. Her subconscious seemed a drain clogged by enormous clutter, and she felt as though some force had kicked a hole in her cognitive plumbing.

Oh, Lord, I have to tell Bill about this, but it doesn't change anything. At least he'll understand why I can't marry him or anyone. And please, he deserves someone who loves him completely. Please. She reached for a pen. Caring for him deeply in the sense of a comrade, she wanted him to find someone loving him for himself, and he needed the truth to realize his childhood fears had nothing to do with their parting.

As she mailed the letter, she remembered another reason he'd been so special to her. Some among the many men she dated had been troubled when she beat them at a sport. One night, she and Bill went bowling, and her scores left him far behind. Reluctant to deal with a guy's ego, she deliberately threw a bad ball, and before she turned around, she felt him standing next to her and heard these words both humorously and firmly, "Don't you ever throw a game with me. You're too fine an athlete to play down, and believe me, I'm not a kid who needs to feel good about beating a woman."

When she met his eyes, she realized how seriously he meant all he said and in now said, "Oh, Bill, I only wish I had been ready for you. Can a girl be that lucky again?"

Downstairs, her parents, Marian and Joe hoped the pondering of their families living their lives would help whenever they reached to ease a daughter's sadness or a son's indecision.

Living has brought the family to <u>now</u> and only the future will answer Jean's question, can she be that lucky again?

"I close hoping you will join us again, for that telling to see how this very human family takes their new corners."

A note to you, my reader, follows.

Dear Reader,

Thank you for sharing volume I (Children Within) of this family's journey with me. I hope the history was interesting and that the antics within the family were enjoyable.

Jean's growing and seeking will continue in *Family Corners Volume II (Children Within)*, where decisions open doors to both good and bad.

Joey's search also moves on while he continues to strongly believe in the ways of the world he has chosen and his luck.

Their searches introduce living events I hope you'll enjoy.

As for Marian and Joe, their love continues right to the last page of volume II. There was no fiction in their story.

In volume II, I found fiction irresistible, so I tuck Joe and Marian safely within a family nook and take Jean with Bob (oh yes, he's real) along with other family and friends on a dark adventure. Then I return you to Joe and Marian and the family in a time more dangerously human than any fiction.

If you have questions about what you read in volume 1, feel free to join me on my website.

I will be happy to exchange thoughts with you, and thank you personally for sharing your time with us.

Sadly, I am not a writer but rather a storyteller more at home in social narration.

Website: _____

About the Author

Joan T. Petrosine—born in 1934, blessed with loving parents—is living a long life full of changes, family, laughter, and heartache. She started hoping for a gym teacher's career but the timing didn't fit the plan. She shifted gears, found a spot in the business world, and fed a thirst for adventure whenever making a living would allow. Remaining single, she traveled, loved people, and worked her way through life within family and friends, loving and finding both good and bad, both in her world and theirs. Joan loved, lost, and knew failures but found the wonders of happenings within that framework to be worth passing on. Unskilled in writing, she decided to put it on paper fictionally hopeful that someone might take something from her stories that will help them in their search for self and faith. She's lucky enough to have found both.